Peter Collar holds a PhD in German Histo
London, and has had a distinguished career as a scientist.

THE PROPAGANDA WAR IN THE RHINELAND

Weimar Germany, Race and Occupation after World War I

PETER COLLAR

I.B. TAURIS
LONDON · NEW YORK

New paperback edition published in 2017 by
I.B.Tauris & Co. Ltd
London • New York
www.ibtauris.com

First published in hardback in 2013 by I.B.Tauris & Co. Ltd

ISBN: 978 1 78453 669 5
epdf ISBN: 978 1 78673 214 9
eISBN: 978 1 78672 214 0

A full CIP record for this book is available from the British Library
A full CIP record is available from the Library of Congress

Library of Congress Catalog Card Number: available

Printed and bound by CPI Group (UK) Ltd, Croydon, CR0 4YY

CONTENTS

LIST OF ILLUSTRATIONS

ABBREVIATIONS

AA	Auswärtiges Amt (Reich Foreign Ministry)
ADAP	*Akten zur deutschen auswärtigen Politik* (Documents on German Foreign Policy)
ADV	Arbeitsausschuß Deutscher Verbände (Working Committee of German Associations)
BArch	Bundesarchiv
BASF	Badische Anilin- und Soda-Fabrik
BDC	Berlin Document Centre
BDF	Bund Deutscher Frauenvereine (Association of German Women's Organisations)
BG	Besetzte Gebiete (Occupied Regions)
BHStA	Bayerisches Hauptstaatsarchiv (Munich)
BMP	Bayerische Mittelpartei (Bavarian Middle Party)
BVP	Bayerische Volkspartei (Bavarian People's Party)
BVR	Bayerischer Vertreter beim Reichskommissar (Bavarian Representative in the Office of the Reich Commissioner)
CDU	Christlich Demokratische Union
DBFP	*Documents on British Foreign Policy*
DDP	Deutsche Demokratische Partei (German Democratic Party)
DDR	Deutsche Demokratische Republik
DEF	Deutsch-Evangelischer Frauenbund (German Protestant Women's Association)
DNVP	Deutschnationale Volkspartei (German National People's Party)

DVP	Deutsche Volkspartei (German People's Party)
FO	Foreign Office
Gestapo	Geheime Staatspolizei
GmbH	Gesellschaft mit beschränkter Haftung (limited company – Ltd)
HHSPf	Haupthilfsstelle für die Pfalz (Central Office for Welfare in the Pfalz)
IRHC	Inter-Allied Rhineland High Commission
KFD	Katholischer Frauenbund Deutschlands (Catholic Women's Association of Germany)
KPD	Kommunistische Partei Deutschlands (German Communist Party)
M	Marks
NSDAP	Nationalsozialistische Deutsche Arbeiterpartei (National Socialist German Workers' Party)
OHL	Oberste Heeresleitung (High Command)
PA AA	Politisches Archiv des Auswärtigen Amts (Political Archive of the Foreign Ministry, Berlin)
Polwona	Politische West-Ost Nachrichtenagentur (East-West Political News Agency)
RDS	Reichsverband Deutscher Schriftsteller (Reich Association of German Authors)
RfH	Reichszentrale für Heimatdienst (Reich Centre for Homeland Service)
Rkei	Reichskanzlei (Reich Chancellery)
RK	Reichskulturkammer
RM	Reichsmarks
SPD	Sozialdemokratische Partei Deutschlands (Social Democratic Party – Majority Socialists)
SWDV	Südwestdeutscher Verlag (South-West German Publishing Company)
TNA:PRO	The National Archives: Public Record Office (Kew)
USPD	Unabhängige Sozialdemokratische Partei Deutschlands (Independent Social Democratic Party – Independent Socialists)
WPG	Wirtschaftspolitische Gesellschaft (Society for Political Economics)

GLOSSARY

Abwehr	defensive struggle to retain the Rhineland for Germany
Aufklärungsarbeit	civic enlightenment
Auswärtiges Amt	Reich Foreign Ministry
Bahnhofsmission	charitable organisation for helping railway travellers in difficulty
Bayerisches Hauptstaatsarchiv	Bavarian Central State Archive
Besetzte-Gebiete-Stelle (BG-Stelle)	Office for the Occupied Regions
Bund der Asienkämpfer	Association of Asian Campaign Veterans
Bund Deutscher Frauenvereine	Association of German Women's Organisations
Deutsche Evangelische Bahnhofsmission	German Protestant mission for railway travellers in difficulty
Deutsch-Evangelischer Frauenbund	German Protestant Women's Association
Deutsche Kolonialgesellschaft	German Colonial Society
Deutsche Liga für den Völkerbund	German Association for the League of Nations

Deutsches Nationalkomitee zur Bekämpfung des Mädchenhandels	German National Committee to Combat the Trafficking of Girls
Deutscher Notbund gegen die Schwarze Schmach	German Emergency League against the Black Humiliation
Deutscher Verband zur Förderung der Sittlichkeit	German Association for the Encouragement of Morality
Deutschvölkische Freiheitspartei	German Völkisch Freedom Party
Deutschtum	German values and culture
Einwohnerwehr	citizens' militia
Gauleiter	Regional Leader (Nazi)
Geheime Staatspolizei (Gestapo)	secret police (Nazi)
Gleichschaltung	enforced coordination
Kabinettsitzung	Cabinet meeting
Katholischer Frauenbund Deutschlands	Catholic Women's Association of Germany
Lebenslauf	curriculum vitae
Napoleonsfeier	event held in celebration of Napoleonic rule
pénétration pacifique	penetration by peaceful means
Politisches Archiv des Auswärtigen Amts	Political Archive of the Foreign Ministry
Politische West-Ost Nachrichtenagentur	East-West Political News Agency
Regierungspräsident	chairman of the regional council
Reichsgericht	Reich Supreme Court
Reichskanzlei	Reich Chancellery
Reichskommissar für die besetzten Gebiete	Reich Commissioner for the Occupied Regions
Reichsministerium des Innern	Reich Ministry of the Interior
Reichsministerium für die besetzten Gebiete	Reich Ministry for the Occupied Regions
Reichsschrifttumskammer	Reich Writers' Association

Reichszentrale für Heimatdienst	Reich Centre for Homeland Service
Rheinische Frauenliga	Rhineland Women's League
Rheinische Volkspflege	Social Welfare in the Rhineland
Schwarze Schmach	Black Humiliation
Vaterländischer Frauenverein	National Women's Association
völkisch	pertaining to extreme ethnic nationalism
Volksbund 'Rettet die Ehre'	People's Alliance 'Save Our Honour'
Zentralfürsorgestelle für die besetzten Gebiete	Welfare Centre for the Occupied Regions
Zentralstelle für Auslandsdienst	Central Office for Services Abroad
Zentrum	(Catholic) Centre Party

ACKNOWLEDGEMENTS

I should like to express my gratitude to Dr Eckard Michels at Birkbeck, University of London, for his ever helpful and friendly advice and encouragement. I have benefited greatly from his knowledge of the turbulent and fascinating early Weimar years. His enthusiasm for the subject and his unobtrusive support have helped me complete what at the beginning of my research seemed a daunting task.

I am grateful to the Bayerisches Hauptstaatsarchiv in Munich, the Bundesarchiv (Lichterfelde and Dahlwitz-Hoppegarten) and the Politisches Archiv des Auswärtigen Amts in Berlin for access to the extensive archival material available there. This includes a number of illustrations reproduced by kind permission of the Bundesarchiv at Coblenz. The help I have received from each of these organisations greatly eased my task and has been much appreciated. Acknowledgement is also made to the National Archives at Kew.

The library at the German Historical Institute in Bloomsbury and the British Library have provided invaluable reference material and I would like to record my thanks for access to these facilities and for the assistance that I have received. I am grateful, also, to the Landesarchiv and Landesbibliothek Rheinland-Pfalz in Speyer for help on several occasions.

On a more personal note I should like to thank my good friends Heinz Schnaubelt and Carola Genzel in Munich for their interest and for their kind and memorable hospitality whenever I visited the city.

My family has been a constant source of support and encouragement and this has been much appreciated.

Above all, I am deeply grateful to my wife, Sandra, for her understanding and unflagging interest throughout as well as her practical help in so many ways.

INTRODUCTION

Under the terms of the Armistice Agreement that ended World War I, those regions of Germany that lay to the west of the Rhine were immediately occupied by Allied troops. At the subsequent Peace Treaty negotiations presupposition of German responsibility for the war led to the imposition of extensive penalties on the nation. Included in these was the continuing occupation of the Rhineland for a number of years in order to guarantee German fulfilment of Peace Treaty clauses relating to reparations and disarmament.

Within Germany the terms of the Versailles Peace Treaty were widely regarded as being unduly harsh and were greeted by the majority with anger and dismay. However, the use of force to overturn the situation was out of the question: the only way forward was to use persuasion. Following the reluctant signing of the Treaty, therefore, strenuous efforts were made using propaganda to influence international opinion against the allegation of German war guilt and against the Treaty provisions. It was hoped that the Allies would agree to revision of the Treaty. The Rhineland occupation was one of the main targets of the stream of propaganda of all kinds that came out of post-war Germany and it is with this aspect that this book is concerned.

However, German propaganda against the occupation was aimed not only at an international readership. At home, there was the necessity of maintaining morale in the occupied regions, which at first were virtually isolated from the remainder of Germany. It was equally important to keep the public in unoccupied Germany well informed and to maintain its interest in, and support for, the occupied regions. Propaganda came from a wide range of sources. Some were official or semi-official bodies, though at the time efforts were made by the governments of the Reich and those of the constituent states to conceal this fact. Private individuals and organisations, some set up specifically for the purpose, also took part.

The Allied armies occupied individual zones in the Rhineland territory of four German states: Prussia, Bavaria, Hessen and Oldenburg. Much German propaganda embraced the Rhineland as a whole, making no particular distinction between the territory of individual states. This was generally the case where private organisations and individuals were involved. Naturally, the Reich government had a national perspective. But propaganda was also organised at the level of the individual states, though even then the themes often included national issues. The picture overall was thus a very complex one. The roles of the different agencies actively engaged in this propaganda, often with conflicting interests and motivation, have so far not been comprehensively addressed by historians.

I have concentrated on one particular region, the Bavarian Palatinate, or Pfalz. There are several reasons for this. By virtue of its position and the nature of its terrain the Pfalz in the southern Rhineland held a unique strategic and military importance for both France and Germany. For France, deeply concerned about her future security, the future of the region at the end of World War I presented both opportunity and frustration. Ideally, the Rhine, which formed the eastern border of the Pfalz, would also have made a natural eastern frontier for France, for it provided a natural line of defence against attack from the east. Direct annexation of the Pfalz, however, was out of the question in the face of hostility from other Allies. Instead, the policy adopted by the French government was to encourage the local German population to form a Rhineland state, independent of the German Reich and friendly to France, which could act as a buffer zone.[1]

On several occasions since the seventeenth century the Pfalz had seen violent struggles between French- and German-speaking peoples. For Germany, France represented the traditional enemy and to have a French presence once more in the southern Rhineland was far more humiliating than to experience Belgian, British and American occupation in the northern part. Furthermore, even from the German point of view it could be predicted with some confidence that within a few years British, American and Belgian troops would withdraw. Given the history of the region, the same confidence could not be expressed concerning a French withdrawal. Propaganda, and what came to be called the *Abwehr* – the defensive struggle to retain the Rhineland for Germany – thus tended to be directed rather more against the French occupation, and rather less against the presence of the other Allies in their respective zones.

Added to the strategic significance of the Pfalz was the fact that it was a province of Bavaria, though in terms of distance, culture and even religion it was well removed from the mother state. How close, then, was the relationship between the two? And what was the influence of Bavarian propaganda, which urged the people of the occupied Pfalz to remain true to the German cause at a time when they were being wooed by French-supported separatists? Furthermore, the early Weimar years were punctuated by frequent periods of tension between Reich and states. These were largely associated with the question of whether Germany should be a unitary state, with power and authority vested fundamentally in the Berlin government, or whether the model should be a federal one, with individual states enjoying a considerable degree of autonomy. Relations between Bavaria and the Reich were particularly troubled, to the point at which the secession of Bavaria from the Reich was at times seriously contemplated between 1918 and 1924.[2] This raises the further question of the effect this may have had on the development of a coordinated approach to propaganda.

Of the four German states with Rhineland interests, Bavaria, after some initial apparent indifference, was to prove the most active in generating propaganda. When cooperation with other states developed it was Bavarian officials who took the lead. Without doubt this resulted partly from their recognition of the particular strategic importance of the Pfalz. Partly also it reflected Bavarian determination to assert its own authority and independence of the Reich.

This study concentrates on the early Weimar years 1919–24. These were the years of greatest crisis for the new Reich, which were brought to an end in 1924 when the way ahead out of the impasse of the reparations crisis was foreshadowed by the Dawes report.[3] In that year, also, the violent end of the French-supported separatist movement in the Pfalz marked the effective end to French ambitions to detach the Pfalz from unoccupied Germany. And although German propaganda continued virtually to the end of the occupation in 1930, both of these events contributed to the cessation in 1924 of a major Bavarian propaganda activity related to the Pfalz.

Of all the many propaganda themes of the early Weimar years none aroused as much passion and caused as much uproar as the campaign against the use of non-European colonial troops in the French army of occupation, the propaganda against the so-called Schwarze Schmach (the Black Humiliation).[4] It was intended to bring events in the Rhineland to the attention of the outside world, to influence foreign public opinion and so bring pressure to bear on foreign governments, especially that of the USA, where race had long been an issue. The underlying aim was to pressure the Allies into revising the terms of the Peace Treaty. At the same time the campaign was intended to mobilise support in unoccupied Germany. The origin, organisation, main themes and national and international impact of this campaign are therefore a subsidiary focus of this study.

Schwarze Schmach propaganda has already received considerable attention from other historians. Among the early studies, that by Keith Nelson[5] drew mainly, though not exclusively, on archives in Washington to assess the international impact of the campaign and particularly its effect on the North American public. Gisela Lebzelter[6] analysed the character and symbolism of the campaign in terms of the national mood prevailing in Germany following defeat in 1918, bringing in attitudes concerning racial superiority and drawing parallels with the development of anti-Semitism. The official sources cited by Lebzelter are almost exclusively drawn from the files of the Auswärtiges Amt (Reich Foreign Ministry) in Berlin, to which organisation she attributed major influence on the campaign.

The work by Reiner Pommerin[7] had as its main theme the fate suffered by the few hundred children of mixed race who were born as a result of relationships between colonial troops and local German women. Such children offended against National Socialist concepts of racial purity and in 1937 a programme of enforced mass sterilisation was carried out on them. Pommerin outlined the development of the Schwarze Schmach campaign, and noted the main organisations taking part, before exploring concerns about racial purity – evidently already beginning to surface in the Weimar period – through to the National Socialist era. The role of neither the Pfalzzentrale nor the Rheinische Frauenliga (Rhineland Women's League), organisations that feature prominently in this study, received much mention. This may have resulted from a reliance mainly on the records of the Foreign Ministry, for relatively little reference was made to the extensive records that are available in the Bavarian State Archives in Munich. In passing it may also be noted that at the time these two studies were made records held in the Potsdam archives of the former DDR were not available.

Sally Marks,[8] on the other hand, has approached the topic mainly using records available in British and French state archives, relying on conclusions drawn by Pommerin and Nelson to provide a German perspective. Marks examines a number of aspects of the Schwarze Schmach campaign, including the numbers and details of the coloured[9] troops involved in the occupation, their racial origins, how they were received by the local German population and the nature of the campaign against them. Her conclusions are broadly in line with those reached at the time by the French authorities, namely that the campaign, emanating largely from Berlin, Hamburg and Munich, was orchestrated by the German government. This is also one of the points made by Christian Koller[10] in the course of a wider and very informative study of the use of colonial troops by European powers from the latter part of the nineteenth century through until 1945. In his view the Schwarze Schmach campaign could be divided into two more or less distinct components, official and unofficial. The official campaign was directed by the Reichsministerium des Innern (Ministry of the Interior) and the Reich Foreign Ministry, while the unofficial campaign was simultaneously being conducted by a variety of private individuals. However, while original sources for Koller's work included material from a number of German and Swiss archives, little or no use was made of the substantial archive in Munich relating to a major Bavarian contribution to the campaign.

Amongst the penalties imposed upon Germany at Versailles was the loss of her colonies. Jared Poley[11] argues that this loss helped to shape post-war German attitudes. No longer imperialist masters, Germans were now colonial subjects. Poley has undoubtedly touched on a significant element in the post-war discourse but, as this book shows, German propagandists approached their tasks from a variety of standpoints. Poley's analysis seems to imply a greater degree of coherence than actually existed.

The most recent studies are those of Sandra Maß[12] and Iris Wigger,[13] who have approached the subject from completely different standpoints. Maß has analysed contrasting images of the colonial soldier in relation to the white European in two different spheres. In the first he is the loyal Askari, serving and reinforcing the aura of his heroic master, the German officer fighting an honourable war in the best knightly tradition in German East Africa. In contrast, in the Rhineland army of occupation he represents an insidious danger to civilisation, threatening the white woman and reducing her erstwhile protector – the white man – to a humiliating state of impotence. Wigger examines the wide variety of sources from which emerged the appallingly racist caricatures of the colonial soldier. She then analyses some general constructs relating to gender, race and social class which help in the understanding of why and how the campaign against the Schwarze Schmach came into being.

Almost alone amongst the principal publications on the Schwarze Schmach, the work by Le Naour[14] makes substantial use of French archive material. In outlining the background to the employment of colonial troops, later consequences for the troops themselves and attitudes on both French and German sides, the work provides a valuable French perspective on the campaign. Moreover it materially improves the balance of the several studies made of the topic.

In contrast to previous work this study considers the Schwarze Schmach campaign in the wider context of propaganda against the Rhineland occupation and it therefore brings in, to a greater extent, organisational issues. On the whole, existing scholarship paints a picture of a well-coordinated, centrally organised campaign, which purported to reflect the attitude of most Germans. I have challenged this view. This work explores the way in which the organisations that played a significant part in Rhineland propaganda were set up, the extent to which they interacted with each other and the extent to which rivalry and conflict over resources affected the conduct of the campaigns. I also examine in greater depth than has been done hitherto the role of the individual in organising and creating propaganda. Did Rhineland propaganda – and especially the Schwarze Schmach campaign – in fact owe everything to the energy and convictions of a few leading people or did it really reflect the attitudes of large segments of the German population in the occupied and unoccupied territories? In the knowledge that propaganda came both from Bavarian and Reich government sources it is also pertinent to ask what, if any, the consequences were for the campaigns resulting from the often difficult relations between the two governments. Was there a specific Bavarian approach in contrast to the initiatives from Berlin? Finally, taking an overall perspective, I discuss the nature of the propaganda itself, assessing its effectiveness in support of the German cause and how it related to the progressive ideals of the new Republic, an aspect that has not been addressed hitherto.

The first chapter establishes the historical background of the Pfalz and its people and outlines the course of events, national and international, against which German propaganda developed between 1918 and 1924. In the early months of 1919 there had been little or no propaganda activity directed against the Rhineland occupation by either the Reich or the state governments. In the case of Bavaria this was a consequence of a preoccupation with the turbulent internal situation and, perhaps, a lack of interest from its left-wing revolutionary administration. The Reich government, too, faced civil unrest and political turbulence but, more likely, its policy was shaped by reluctance to disturb the status quo because in the forthcoming peace negotiations it would press for the removal of all French troops. The first action was in fact taken on behalf of the Bavarian government when its most senior official in the Pfalz, Dr Theodor von Winterstein, was expelled across the Rhine for failing to side with the French-supported separatist movement.[15] Winterstein's first action following his expulsion was to set up a centre in Mannheim, subsequently known as the Pfalzzentrale.

Its first and most urgent task was to organise protests and to generate and disseminate propaganda against the threat presented to the Pfalz by separatism. When the Peace Treaty was signed a month later the Pfalzzentrale was ideally placed to begin the propaganda battle.

Such was to be the importance of this organisation and its leader – Dr August Ritter von Eberlein – during the occupation of the Pfalz that it has seemed logical to begin the discussion with the development of the Pfalzzentrale. I have also laid emphasis on the way in which the Pfalzzentrale interacted with other organisations and individuals engaged in propaganda.

By far the most critical relationships in the existence of the Pfalzzentrale were those with the Reich. The Reich government itself had actively engaged in propaganda throughout World War I and from these activities evolved in peacetime the Reichszentrale für Heimatdienst (Reich Centre for Homeland Service). Hereafter this will be referred to as the Heimatdienst. In 1920 an offshoot emerged from the Heimatdienst, the Rheinische Volkspflege (Social Welfare in the Rhineland). This will be referred to as the Volkspflege. Its task was to support the Rhineland population, encouraging it to resist French cultural penetration and to remain true to the German nation. The press offices of the Foreign Ministry and the Reichskanzlei (Reich Chancellery) were also to play a part in the propaganda battle.

Chapter 2 follows the expansion of the Pfalzzentrale and its collaboration with Prussia and Hessen up to mid-1921. The relationship between the Pfalzzentrale and the Volkspflege, however, was at times acrimonious. Permanently short of funds and dependent on the Volkspflege for financial support, the Pfalzzentrale regarded the Volkspflege with a mixture of envy and resentment as a well-funded but interfering and incompetent rival. This not only reflected the schism that existed between Bavaria and the Reich, it related also to two different concepts of propaganda – an aspect that is taken further in the final chapter.

Following discussion of the origins of the Schwarze Schmach campaign in Chapter 3, attention is turned in Chapter 4 to the specific part played in this campaign by women. Women were alleged to be the main victims of the stationing of colonial troops in the Rhineland

and this was to provide the main thrust of the campaign. The most influential organisation was the Rheinische Frauenliga (Rhineland Women's League) set up under the aegis of the Volkspflege, which in turn was responsible to the Ministry of the Interior. The Frauenliga consisted of a group of women's organisations, wide-ranging and disparate but essentially middle-class. Trading on the alleged vulnerability of women and children to the misdeeds of coloured troops, its protests and propaganda were orchestrated from Berlin by the civil servant Margarete Gärtner. Contributions were also made to the campaign by individuals, amongst whom a female American journalist, Ray Beveridge, was without doubt the most prominent. Two important questions that have hardly been addressed so far are first, at a time when middle-class women were beginning to play a more assertive role in national life, could a distinctive female perspective be said to exist? Second, the contribution of women's groups to the campaign largely took the form of widespread organised protests. Did this really represent the expression of widespread and spontaneous support from the grass roots in unoccupied Germany and abroad – or was it simply clever exploitation by the nationalist Right?

Neither the Pfalzzentrale nor the Frauenliga was alone in campaigning against the Schwarze Schmach and other aspects of the occupation. Chapter 5 explores the contributions from other sources, both official and private. While considerable research has been done previously on the themes of the Schwarze Schmach propaganda, the contributing organisations, and in particular the individuals behind them, have received very much less attention. In the course of my research I have become convinced that, while propaganda against the occupation was sanctioned or encouraged from above by Reich and state governments, to speak simply of centrally coordinated or directed campaigns is to misread the situation. It is my belief that much in fact rested on the energy and drive of relatively few individuals. Highly motivated, on the whole they ran their organisations and activities as personal fiefdoms. While they undoubtedly cooperated with one another at a certain level, the relationships between them could not generally be described as close. Close coordination of activities was not an absolute priority. Also, the nature of the contributions was remarkably wide, ranging from crude and inflammatory racist outpourings from some individuals to scholarly argument from respected academics.

Chapter 6 explores the later development of the Pfalzzentrale until its dissolution in 1924. Internal German politics had until 1921 been the major influence on the development of official Bavarian propaganda but henceforth international factors would become increasingly important. The Pfalzzentrale had won plaudits from many in the Reich and Bavarian governments but, amid fears that German economic and financial interests could be damaged by adverse reactions from the Allies to its propaganda, the Pfalzzentrale was obliged to operate clandestinely after 1921.

Increasing Bavarian frustration at the inability of an under-resourced propaganda campaign to bring about change in the status of the Rhineland was heightened by three major events in 1923. These were the French occupation of the Ruhr following German default on the payment of reparations, the subsequent failure of the campaign of passive resistance and, finally, the seizure of power in the Pfalz by a resurgent separatist movement. The increasing tendency of the Pfalzzentrale to indulge in extremist violence came to a head with its assassination of the separatist leadership, which effectively ended the threat of separatism in the Pfalz. Extremist violence had succeeded where propaganda alone had not. But it provoked Allied – especially British – fears that the stability of the entire region was being compromised just when progress to overcome the international stalemate over the vital reparations issue at last seemed possible. Under Allied pressure Bavaria was obliged to close down its Pfalzzentrale.

Analysis of the propaganda of the Pfalzzentrale has been left to the penultimate Chapter 7 because, to an extent greater than for any other organisation, its propaganda was for much of the time shaped by a need to react quickly to events in the Pfalz. In particular it reflected the need to make a counter-response to separatism, which, though it came and went, could never be ignored. It was shaped, also, by the history of the organisation itself. Leaving the Pfalzzentrale propaganda to the last also enables a better comparison to be made with that from its contemporaries.

Pfalzzentrale propaganda bore all the hallmarks of its leader, Dr August Ritter von Eberlein. Less lurid than some of the material written and spoken by some extreme right-wing contemporaries, it was nevertheless wide-ranging and it carried the imprint of aggressive and vengeful nationalism. Eberlein, an alleged war criminal, continued his war in peacetime, conducting his fight at the level of a personal vendetta. Many of the themes were shared with other propagandists. The opportunist Eberlein participated in the Schwarze Schmach campaign, but for him this was only part of a much wider picture: this particular campaign simply presented him with another stick with which to beat the French occupiers.

Finally, Chapter 8 considers German propaganda against the Rhineland occupation in its totality. In the early years of the Weimar Republic the very concept of propaganda was controversial in Germany, for it was identified with the excesses, failures and falsehoods of the old Wilhelmine regime. Several leading political theorists argued for a new approach to presenting Germany's case abroad, in keeping with the progressive ideals of the new Republic. The view of the reformed Heimatdienst was that its task was to provide a sufficient and valid basis to enable the citizen to draw his or her own conclusions. This *Aufklärungsarbeit* was to be contrasted with propaganda, which pressed preformed conclusions on the individual.[16] Such a view might be considered to match more closely the ideals of the new Republic than did much of the propaganda discussed here, most of which was undeniably fragmented, to a large extent unsubtle and wholly negative. Although it embraced many themes it had but one focus: the expression of outrage against the provisions of the Versailles Treaty in general and against the occupation of the Rhineland in particular. Above all it reflected the personal styles and obsessions of those producing it. The concluding discussion puts forward the argument that this really reflects the fractured nature of the Weimar Republic. Rather than represent an effective way to present Germany's case abroad, its propaganda merely served to provide catharsis for an embittered political Right.

Primary source material used in the study, much of it previously unused by scholars working on German Rhineland propaganda, includes a wide range of material archived in Munich, Berlin and London. Most of that relating to the history of the Pfalzzentrale and Bavarian propaganda is to be found in the Bayerisches Hauptstaatsarchiv (Bavarian Central State Archive) in Munich. Further material relating to the Pfalzzentrale has been accessed in the Bundesarchiv (German State Archive) in Lichterfelde in Berlin, where the records of the former Berlin Document Centre are also kept. In several cases these records have enabled the later involvement of individuals with the NSDAP to be verified and have added valuable biographical information concerning their activities before 1933. The branch of the German State Archive in Dahlwitz-Hoppegarten in Berlin contains material formerly held in the DDR State Archive in Potsdam. That relating to the Frauenliga, the Volkspflege, the Reichskommissar für die besetzten Gebiete (Reich Commissioner for the Occupied Regions) and the Reichsministerium für die besetzten Gebiete (Reich Ministry for the Occupied Regions) has been found to be particularly useful. Recourse has also been made to the Politisches Archiv des Auswärtigen Amts (Political Archive of the Foreign Ministry) in Berlin. The Foreign Ministry, probably of lesser importance in the early days of the Pfalzzentrale, became increasingly involved as German propaganda (not always correctly attributed to the Pfalzzentrale) began to irritate the French authorities.

Britain was not directly involved in the administration of the Pfalz and on the whole relations between occupier and occupied were considerably better in the British zone than in the French zone. Nevertheless Britain was, if somewhat unwillingly, drawn into the Schwarze Schmach affair. Later, concerns that events in the Pfalz would imperil a possible settlement of the reparations issue led to direct British diplomatic intervention. For these reasons recourse has also been made to the National Archives at Kew in order to provide a British perspective in assessing the international impact of German Rhineland propaganda.

Other primary sources have included, in particular, Cabinet minutes of the early Weimar governments; also propaganda material and books written during, or soon after, the period under study. Since emphasis throughout the book has been laid on the role of the individual, recourse to autobiographical texts has in several cases provided much useful insight into leading personalities and their actions.

1

THE PFALZ: FOCUS OF FRENCH AMBITIONS IN THE WEIMAR CRISIS YEARS

With the signing of the Armistice Agreement, which brought World War I to an end, came also the occupation by Allied forces of those margins of Germany that lay to the west of the Rhine. On 1 December 1918 Allied troops crossed the German frontier and within a few days the occupation of the Rhineland was complete. Initial reactions to the arrival of enemy troops were muted. While there were peace negotiations in the offing there was always hope that the Allies would withdraw following a settlement. Such hopes were dashed, however, when the Allied terms for the peace settlement were made known on 7 May 1919. These were punitive. Underlying them was the insistent claim that Germany bore full responsibility for the war. The reaction in Germany was one of both dismay and fury and there was initial agreement across the political spectrum that the terms should be rejected. This position could not be sustained, however. In the face of Allied demands for unconditional acceptance, with the threat of renewed hostilities, the terms were accepted by the Reich government with only minor modification from the original draft.

The act of signing the Peace Treaty at Versailles on 28 June 1919 following a majority vote in the National Assembly was to lay bare the schism that existed in post-war German society. Reluctantly agreed to by the left-of-centre SPD-Centre coalition government led by Gustav Bauer, following the resignation of the Scheidemann Cabinet over the issue, the signing was bitterly opposed by the political Right. It was seen as a shameful act of betrayal. Together with the accusation that the civilian home front had metaphorically stabbed the army in the back and thereby lost the war for Germany, the acceptance of the Versailles terms was to provide the mainstay of the ideological hostility shown by the Right towards the revolution of November 1918 and the Weimar Republic that emerged from it. The extent to which this hostility influenced the propaganda campaign that was conducted against the provisions of the Peace Treaty will emerge in the following chapters.

The final settlement at Versailles was very much to the detriment of the German Reich. Amongst the measures imposed upon Germany were the payment of reparations, the confiscation of German colonies and the loss of substantial German territory to adjacent nations. In the east, parts of Silesia, West Prussia and Posen were ceded directly to Poland, while in the west an area around Eupen became part of Belgium. Plebiscites to determine future statehood were to be arranged in certain other areas. Alsace, taken by Germany in the Franco-Prussian War in 1870, was returned to France and the future of the Saarland was to be the subject of a plebiscite following a period of administration by the fledgling League of Nations. The occupation of the Rhineland would continue as a guarantee of payment of reparations, the amount of which would be determined by a Reparations Commission established for the purpose.[1]

Those regions of Germany that lay to the west of the Rhine, together with bridgeheads at Cologne, Coblenz, Mainz and Kehl (Strasbourg), were occupied by the forces of four Allied nations, France, Great Britain, Belgium and the USA. A complicating factor in the administration of the zones was the fact that the territory belonged to different German states: Prussia, Hessen, Bavaria, Oldenburg and Baden. The partitioning arrangements are shown in fig. 1. The French zone was the largest of the four and included part of the Prussian Rhine Province, territory belonging to Hessen and the Bavarian Pfalz. It extended from Bonn in

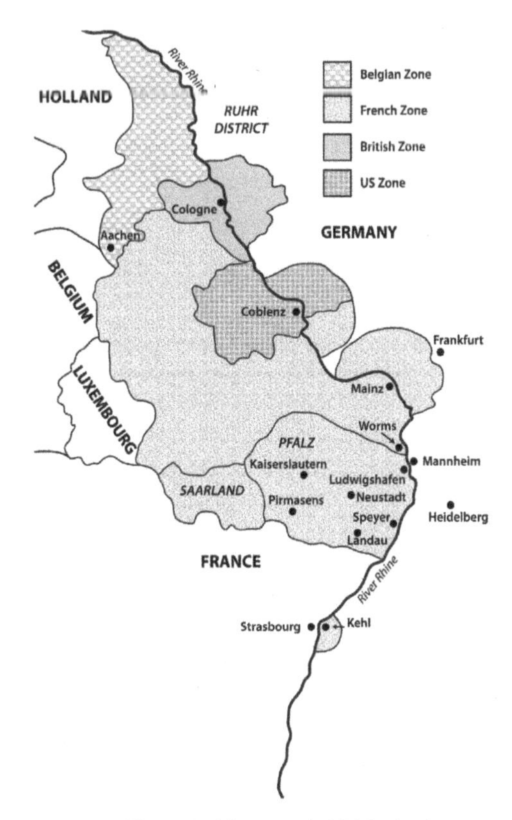

Figure 1. The occupied Rhineland

the north to the border with Alsace in the south, with the addition of the bridgehead at Kehl.

Zones of occupation were to be progressively vacated by the Allies after periods of five, ten and fifteen years, beginning with the northernmost areas. Amongst the last areas to be evacuated was to be the French-occupied Bavarian Pfalz. This was no accident. The Pfalz had always held considerable geopolitical significance for both France and the German-speaking peoples east of the Rhine. The reason lay in the topography either side of the Rhine valley. The river itself, together with the hilly terrain on either bank, provided a natural defensive frontier for both countries. Only where the Rhine bordered the Pfalz – and perhaps a smaller area around Cologne – would an invading army from either side have found relatively easy access to the territory of the other side.[2]

As a consequence the region had endured a violent history. Now, in 1918, the strategic importance of the Pfalz was perceived by France to be as great as it had been in earlier times and this was a principal factor in determining French post-war policy towards Germany. It comes as no surprise that the turbulent history of the region was exploited in the propaganda of both sides during the Rhineland occupation. It is therefore worth examining briefly the history of the Pfalz before returning to the events of 1918.

Arguably the most notorious episode associated with the region took place between 1688 and 1697 when a French army under the command of the Compte de Mélac rampaged through the countryside at the behest of Louis XIV. Louis had laid claim to the Pfalz[3] on the death of its ruler, the childless brother of his sister-in-law. When he failed to achieve his aims by diplomacy he resorted to force. This war of succession was conducted with extreme brutality and it resulted in the systematic sacking and pillaging of major towns and numerous villages on both sides of the Rhine. While Mélac himself was not solely responsible for the atrocities committed in the southern Rhineland, he applied himself so ruthlessly to his task that it is with his name in particular that the events of the time are still associated.[4]

There was a renewed French presence in the Pfalz a century later when in 1792 the revolutionary government in Paris sought, in missionary style, to free the peoples of the Rhineland from what was regarded by France as the tyranny of the German princes. It could be said that it was simply a case of the expansionist ambitions of the old regime in France re-emerging in the foreign policy of the new regime, though now clothed in a new moral ideology.[5] The occupation of Mainz, Speyer and Frankfurt by revolutionary troops met relatively little resistance but soon the French intentions were meeting with difficulties inasmuch that the Rhinelanders' concept of freedom differed from that of the liberators. Over the next few months a campaign that had begun as an act of liberation was transformed into an occupation in the face of an increasingly hostile population. Also, with changes in perceived political priorities French national defence interests then took precedence. A particular goal was the occupation of the west bank of the Rhine, in this way to establish the Rhine as the eastern frontier. In the winter of 1793–4 French troops plundered the Pfalz in a manner reminiscent of the action of a century earlier[6] – an act that was exploited by propagandists for the old feudal regime.

By 1798 French policy had changed again and the emphasis was now on the incorporation of the Rhineland rather than mere occupation. The subsequent years under Napoleon brought far-reaching administrative, political, economic and social reforms. By and large the population came to accept the new regime, for the benefits of reform offset accompanying disadvantages such as increased taxation and conscription into the imperial armies. The Rhineland could even be said to have shown, to a certain degree, political loyalty to France while, however, retaining its German identity and culture at its core.[7] The liberation of the Rhineland by the combined armies of Prussia, Russia and Austria in 1814 brought yet another upheaval. The territory on the west bank of the river that corresponded to the Pfalz of the early twentieth century was administered jointly by Austria and Bavaria from 1814 to 1816.

Before 1792 the original region, the Kurpfalz, had also included areas east of the Rhine. It had long been linked with Bavaria through various branches of the royal Wittelsbach dynasty. The connection had become particularly close when in 1777 the ruler of the Kurpfalz, Karl Theodor, Duke of Sulzbach, also inherited the Electorate of Bavaria. His title and authority were subsumed into that of Elector of Bavaria and he moved his seat from Mannheim to Munich. In 1802, in addition to the annexation by France of Kurpfalz territory on the west bank, areas east of the Rhine, including Mannheim and Heidelberg, were ceded to Baden. Following the collapse of the Napoleonic regime Bavaria was able to make justifiable demands at the time of the Congress of Vienna for the restoration of her Rhineland territories. With the signing of the Treaty of Munich in 1816 territory on the west bank – with some additions – once again became a Bavarian province under Wittelsbach rule. The reacquisition of territory east of the Rhine which would have provided a direct connection with Bavaria was never realised, however, in spite of Bavarian efforts to achieve this.[8] Thus the Bavarian province on the west bank – given the name Die Pfalz in 1838 – was left physically isolated from the mother state. It was a failure that was to have serious consequences a century later.

The change in governance in 1816 was greeted in the province with rather less enthusiasm than had been anticipated in Bavaria. It could be said that the years spent under French authority, and the fact that the Rhineland had effectively been isolated from developments in mainstream German society, had led to the beginnings of a Rhenish identity, distinct from its German parentage. There was now considerable uncertainty throughout the Rhineland as to what the future might hold. There were worries that the reforms that had been gained during the Napoleonic era would be overturned in a return to the old feudal systems still in place elsewhere in the German states,[9] though in fact this did not happen in any of the Rhineland provinces. An additional reason lay in the fact that the Pfalz had little in common with strongly Catholic Bavaria. Not only did it have a slight Protestant majority,[10] but its customs and its dialect differed markedly from those of Bavaria. This fact was well illustrated a century later when recruits to the Bavarian army from the Pfalz at the outbreak of World War I were said to have experienced great difficulties because they could not understand what was being said to them.[11] Underlying all of this was the undeniable fact that the Pfalz was far distant from Munich, the centre of Bavarian power (see fig. 2).

Whether as a result of enlightened administration or through practical expediency, Bavaria made only limited changes in the Pfalz and left the civil constitution essentially unchanged. The reforms brought about during the Napoleonic era were reduced but not lost. In this respect the Pfalz enjoyed a special status within Bavaria. Yet in another sense it was substantially disadvantaged. It was under-represented in government and so lacked influence. Furthermore the Bavarian government proved to be consistently neglectful of the economic well-being of its province. Under such pressures the sense of local identity in the Pfalz was reinforced, and this was accompanied by a growing degree of liberal radicalism. There emerged also a growing desire for German national unity, a feeling encapsulated in the first mass rally in

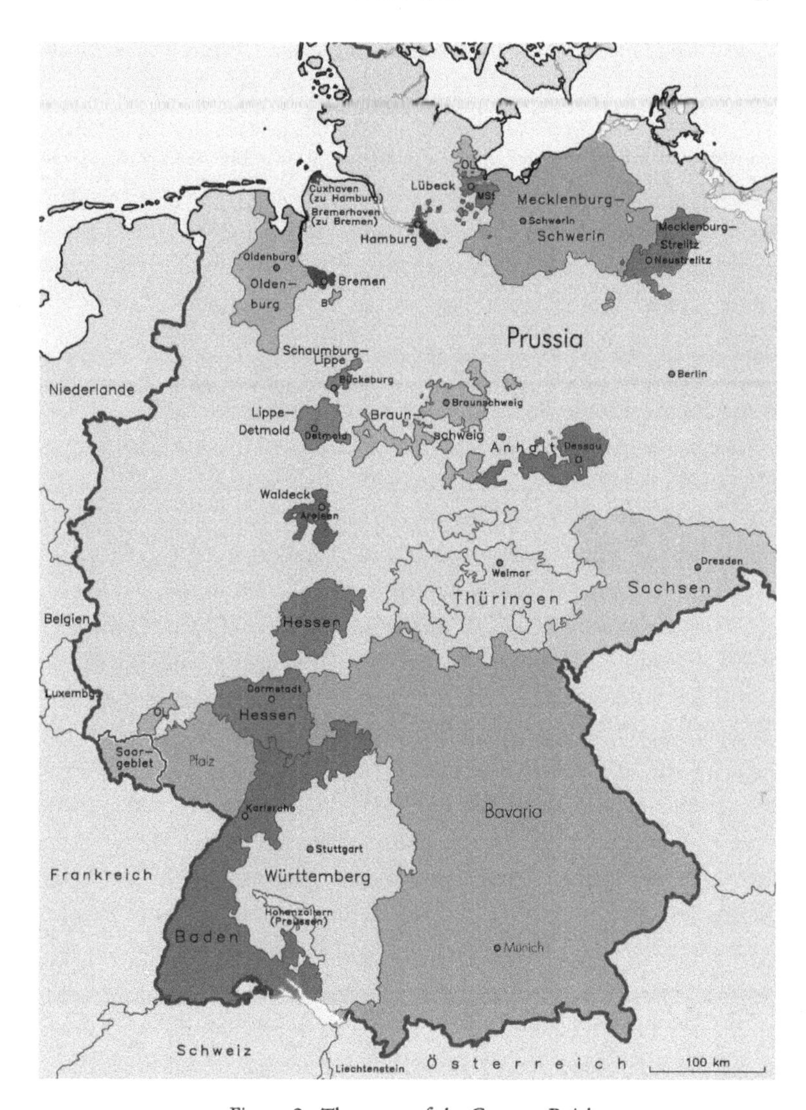

Figure 2. The states of the German Reich

support of this ideal that took place in May 1832 at Hambach in the Pfalz.[12] These feelings culminated in the revolutionary uprisings of 1848–9. Revolution was, however, effectively suppressed in the Pfalz and the following decade was marked by economic depression and passive acceptance of the political status quo.

With a gradual revival of political and economic life in the 1860s emerged a new elite in the Pfalz which was to form the backbone of the National Liberal political party. This comprised wealthy bourgeois landowners, winegrowers, senior government officials and, as industrialisation gathered pace, the new captains of industry. Rapprochement with Bavaria was accompanied by continuing support within the Pfalz for the unification of Germany although the sense of local identity was preserved and indeed encouraged by the new elite. In 1870 the Pfalz formed the springboard for the Franco-Prussian War and this served simply to reinforce the support for the creation of the German Reich that took place under Bismarck in the following year.[13]

The sense of regional identity in the Pfalz was further nurtured in the latter part of the nineteenth century by the concept of Heimat. This was a new consciousness which was awakened quite widely in Germany and which took particularly strong root in the Pfalz. It embodied the sense of belonging, the sense of community and a feeling of empathy with the local culture, local surroundings and the way of life. It came to represent the very quintessence of being German. The so-called Heimat movement organised a wide range of events in the community, which included not only cultural activities based on local history, nature, archaeology, literature and art, but also recreational pastimes in the local countryside. It was largely, though not entirely, a middle-class phenomenon. At the same time – fostered by the recent unification – the strong identification of self with local traditions and culture encapsulated the feeling of being a part of a wider German nation. As Celia Applegate has observed:

> The Heimat associations promoted a German nationalism of which the most important determinants were domestic: a nationalism defined by its constituent parts, not its opposing counterparts, by the regions within Germany, not the nations outside it.[14]

Yet, in the four decades before the outbreak of war in 1914, the link between the Pfalz and Bavaria was undisputed. Many from the Pfalz sought positions in Bavaria, especially in the administration, while Bavarian government officials in the Pfalz were well regarded.[15] In the latter half of this period the Wittelsbach royal family was an important influence. In contrast to his predecessor, Prinzregent Luitpold was an active and popular figure and this was reflected in the warmth of the relationship of the Pfalz with Bavaria.[16] Yet at the same time, the Pfalz could still not be said to be wholly integrated within the Bavarian state. It had its own regional identity, it had more in common with Baden and Hessen than with Bavaria. Moreover, Berlin rather than Munich was regarded as the centre of political power.[17]

In late July 1914 the realisation that war might be imminent came as a bolt from the blue to the average person in the Pfalz and created widespread uncertainty and anxiety. The announcement of general mobilisation some days later came almost as a relief. The depressed mood gradually gave way to a degree of patriotic fervour in which it was widely held that Germany had been forced into an unwanted war.[18] This view of the situation in the Pfalz is in general agreement with the picture in rural Germany as a whole. It contrasts to some degree with the situation in the large cities where a sense of war enthusiasm found rather greater expression, though David Welch cautions against overgeneralisation of the unanimity of enthusiasm that existed, pointing to the protest meetings against the war that also took place.[19] Jeffrey Verhey makes the point that the essence of the August experience was not so much pure enthusiasm as a range and depth of emotions that encompassed everything from pride and enthusiasm to fear and despondency – sometimes all combined in the same individual.[20] It is dangerous to generalise, but it seems that social class also played some part. The working class was generally despondent at the prospect of war. Only among the more nationalistic elements of the middle class was there much real enthusiasm for it.[21] A similar picture emerges from a study of the public reaction in Freiburg to the outbreak of hostilities.[22]

People in the Pfalz were acutely aware that they lived in a frontier region. Barely a few months after the beginning of World War I worries began to surface that the Pfalz would become a war zone. Although these were dispelled for the time being by the early successes in the German military campaign the feeling grew steadily that the sooner an honourable peace could be achieved, the better.[23] The sense of being in a relatively exposed position compared to their compatriots elsewhere in Germany was heightened by the presence of large numbers of troops, for this was a staging area and the Front was not far distant. For this reason, also, military hospitals were located in the Pfalz to serve the wounded evacuated from the Front. Not the least of reminders of the proximity of war was the fact that bombing raids were made on the Badische Anilin- und Soda-Fabrik (BASF), a major industrial complex at Ludwigshafen.[24] Increasing hardship was endured, in common with other regions of the Reich. By 1915 shortages of some basic foodstuffs were already being experienced in a few local areas. By the following year, with the Allied naval blockade of Germany well under way, shortages of all kinds became an increasingly serious problem.[25]

There is little doubt that a gradual loosening of the relationship between Bavaria and the Pfalz took place during the wartime years. As early as 1916 complaints were being heard that the Pfalz was being treated unfavourably compared with other regions of Bavaria. Among the general population the effect of shortages of basic necessities, and war-weariness generally, had become so severe that by 1917 people in the Pfalz were said to be completely indifferent as to their future nationality – Bavarian and German or French – just as long as the war would come to an end.[26] Such yearning for peace and normality was further conditioned by renewed awareness of the vulnerability of the Pfalz to military occupation by the enemy. Towards the end of 1917 rumours began to circulate that a victorious France would seek to create an independent neutral state on the west bank of the Rhine and that this would be occupied by French troops until all the conditions of a peace treaty were met. While such fears receded somewhat during the subsequent temporary improvement in the German military situation during the spring offensive of 1918, they returned with a vengeance as matters worsened during that summer. By October of that year the possibility of French occupation of the Pfalz as a precondition for an armistice was being openly discussed.[27]

In passing it may be noted that there is some difference in how the fears of the Rhineland population at this time have been interpreted. Heinrich Thalmann mentions that the German authorities directed propaganda at the home population with the intention of maintaining the spirit to see things through. It deliberately recalled the destructive events of the French occupation in the Napoleonic era – but in the autumn of 1918 this simply aroused fear in the wider population.[28] On the other hand a recent French study[29] claims that the predominant worry was that revenge would be exacted on the Rhineland population for atrocities committed by German troops in the early months of the war.[30] The first notion presupposes that people would be significantly swayed by events well beyond living memory. The second seems a slightly tenuous argument, for it is unlikely that the civilian population would have had knowledge of such acts. Nevertheless, that apprehension at the prospect of occupation by a foreign power was widespread can surely not be denied.

The Revolution, when it came in November 1918, did little to alleviate the situation, though the imminence of occupation accompanied by dread of its unknown consequences could be said to have increased the desire in the Pfalz to remain within the German nation. At the same time, while the people of the Rhineland identified themselves with the German nation they, like many across Germany, nevertheless regarded the administration in Berlin with bitterness and distrust for its mismanagement of the war, in particular for the failure of earlier peace initiatives, and for its deception.[31] In the Pfalz the authorities in Munich were little better regarded. Not a voice was raised in defence of the Bavarian monarchy, though the royal household was not subjected to any personal vilification.[32]

With the signing of the Armistice Agreement and the subsequent occupation of German territory to the west of the Rhine, France had, in a purely military sense, achieved her war aim of making the Rhine effectively the western frontier of Germany. Now, in order to provide for her future security on her eastern frontier it was necessary to consolidate this in the political sphere. The return of Alsace, lost in the 1870–1 Franco-Prussian conflict, had always been a cornerstone of French policy. However, formally stated aims concerning the Rhineland emerged only slowly in the face of differences within the French government and with the Allies. In the end the aims were less ambitious than originally intended. With the underlying desire to achieve neutralisation of the Rhineland, the strategy eventually adopted was not one of direct annexation but of pressure for a lengthy military occupation by the Allies – and the quiet encouragement of those elements in the Rhineland who had ambitions for autonomy.[33]

In fact three distinct phases can be identified in French policy in the Pfalz between 1918 and 1924.[34] From 1 December 1918 until the provisions of the Peace Treaty took effect the occupied Rhineland was under direct military rule. The Pfalz was occupied by the French 8th Army under General Augustin Gérard, with headquarters at Landau. To the north the remainder of the French zone was controlled from Mainz by General Charles Mangin and the 10th Army. During this first period the imperative for the French government was to isolate, as far as possible, the French-occupied territories from unoccupied Germany, to exercise close control of the local administration and the economy and to encourage the creation of a buffer state on the west bank of the Rhine.[35] Gérard made no attempt to conceal this ambition, lending support to a separatist movement in the Pfalz, whose origins are discussed below. At the same time he put heavy pressure on the Bavarian administration in the Pfalz to concur in this. To the north, Gérard's colleague and rival Mangin followed a broadly similar path, although there existed differences of opinion between them over the form that the buffer state should take. Mangin wanted to create a Rhineland republic that would include the Pfalz and eventually was prepared to accept that this should lie within the ambit of the federal Reich. Gérard, however, favoured a fully independent and neutral Pfalz republic.[36] The hope of both Gérard and Mangin was that the fait accompli of a Rhineland buffer state could be presented to the Allies by the time that the Treaty negotiations took place. Gérard's tactics led to several months of strained relationships between the newly installed French authorities and the Bavarian provincial government and culminated in the expulsion of its leader. But these early attempts to create a buffer state were ultimately unsuccessful. The project was abandoned for the time being. Its champions were recalled from their posts in the autumn of 1919, ostensibly on purely operational grounds,[37] although there was some suggestion that the French Prime Minister Georges Clemenceau had been put under pressure by the British and US governments to remove them.[38] Meanwhile, attempts by France to achieve her Rhineland ambitions through the peace negotiations had been no more successful in the face of opposition from her Allies.

With the signing of the Treaty began a second phase in French policy – that of *pénétration pacifique* (penetration by peaceful means). This sought to convince the people of the Pfalz that they had essentially Celtic characteristics and that they had much more in common with the French people than with those of the Germanic races. Moreover, they had been the victims of exploitation by Prussian influences.[39] The local population now became the target of a large-scale cultural propaganda campaign, in which a range of media and methods was employed, including film production, theatre, art exhibitions, the setting up of French bookshops and French language classes. This phase was destined to last until the Ruhr crisis in 1923, when a much more direct approach was once again adopted.

Before making any assessment of the impact that French policy had in the small province of the Pfalz we should, however, first consider what was happening to the nation as a whole. Collectively, the German people were in a state of trauma, having – against expectations fuelled by government propaganda – found themselves on the losing side in World War I. In spite of the fears and mood of depression that had existed alongside euphoria at the beginning of the war, an outcome to the hostilities that would be anything other than a victorious peace had been inconceivable. The reality of life in wartime had soon set in, however, and as war dragged on and casualties mounted the necessity that the war economy should take precedence over all else had led to increasing shortages at home. The situation in the Pfalz, depicted earlier, also prevailed throughout Germany. Matters had been worsened by the Allied blockade and the entry of the USA into the war had then decisively altered the balance against Germany. Morale both at home and at the Front had slumped and by the time the Armistice had been signed in November 1918 the country was in a state of economic crisis and political turmoil. The army was disintegrating, desertion was rife and there existed a state of near-revolt.[40]

In the wake of defeat the national mood was shaped by many factors. Profound social changes had taken place in wartime, which affected every sector of society. Aside from the emotional and economic impact of the huge number of war casualties, the old structures of authority that had existed before the war had been weakened at all levels. This was felt not least within the family unit, where the absence of the breadwinner at the Front had often led to the housewife being obliged to take on this role, thereby achieving a new-found, if temporary, measure of independence.[41] Materially, people were generally worse off than had been the case in 1914, but the middle classes, including public employees and those on fixed incomes, had been more adversely affected. Amongst the working classes substantial and divisive differentials had opened up between those employed in industries related to the war effort and those catering for civilian needs. Recourse to the black market was rife.[42]

The distortion of the national economy that had taken place during wartime – in which imposition of state controls and inept management by government had played a part – had also further impoverished agriculture and thereby generated tensions between town and countryside. Within an increasingly divided society there was, however, some commonality of feeling, particularly bitterness and anger arising from a sense of betrayal by the Reich government, which in spite of all the sacrifice had not only failed to fulfil its promise of victory but had also been deliberately misleading the public.[43] At the same time this was accompanied by a universal yearning for a return to normality and the re-establishment of social and moral order. It has been suggested[44] that before 1914 such a state of normality and stability in fact hardly existed for most people, but amid the deprivations of 1918 such idealisation of pre-war everyday life was surely a natural reaction. Deep underlying feelings of grief and trauma at having lost the war were most prominent among the political and military classes, for the decisive nature of the military defeat was at first concealed from the population at large. In the Armistice period people looked forward to future Peace Treaty negotiations from which, it was expected, a just peace would emerge which would not be unfavourable for Germany.[45]

Thus Germany in late 1918 could justifiably be described as politically and economically unstable and deeply fractured socially. The Revolution had swept away both the old Wilhelmine order and, in Bavaria, the Wittelsbach dynasty. In their place Soldiers' and Workers' Councils temporarily held the reins of power. Within weeks the first National Assembly convened, from which emerged the first Cabinet of a new republican Reich government under the leadership of the socialist Philipp Scheidemann. Within a few months the new Weimar Constitution would be adopted for the Reich, bringing with it fundamental changes including suffrage for women. In Bavaria, too, there emerged a left-wing government. Power at the beginning of 1919 lay in the hands of a coalition of the Independent Socialists (USPD) and the Majority Socialists (SPD) with Kurt Eisner at its head. Yet this was far from being a peaceful and orderly transition from the old regime to the new. Civil unrest was widespread. At the risk of some oversimplification it could be said that this resulted from the struggle for power of three very different groupings. Pent-up dissatisfaction with the old order and overwhelming desire for change, especially among the working classes, was driving the creation of the new, democratic order. Against this were arranged those on the extreme Left, who, mindful of the successful 1917 revolution in Russia, were pressing for a Soviet-style system of government for Germany and were hostile to the form that the new republic was taking.[46] The prospect of the new political force of Bolshevism now taking root in Western Europe was creating a fear bordering on paranoia among sections of the middle classes. Neither was this fear confined to Germany: it was prevalent among the Allies.[47] Fear that a hungry Germany would otherwise turn Bolshevist helped to bring about a gradual easing of the food blockade before the peace negotiations were concluded,[48] although it was not until after the signing of the Treaty that the blockade was fully lifted.

The third, and arguably most dangerous, grouping included those on the political Right, who were embittered by having lost the war, and to whom the new political and social order in prospect for Germany was anathema. Many were former monarchists, some of whom had not given up hopes of a restoration. Others simply sought mental solace in extreme right-wing nationalism. Both of these strands of opinion were united in denying their own culpability for Germany's situation and in doing their utmost to undermine the new republic from the very beginning. This was manifest in the attempt to blame the civilian Left and the Jews for the military collapse in the previous autumn (the so-called *Dolchstoß*, or stab-in-the-back, legend).[49] The same grouping would subsequently bitterly oppose the signing of the Peace Treaty and would attempt to lay the blame for Germany's situation squarely on the new republican Reich government. At the same time France remained the arch-enemy and much of the more virulent anti-French propaganda that came out of Germany in the early Weimar years originated from this part of the political spectrum.

In the midst of the upheaval and uncertainty prevailing at the end of 1918, how did the people of the Pfalz react when their worst fears regarding occupation by the enemy were realised? In fact French troops seem initially to have had a reception that augured reasonably well for future relations between occupier and occupied. Any initial apprehension in the local population was soon dispelled by the realisation that the west bank of the Rhine was being spared the upheaval and uncertainties arising from the Revolution in unoccupied Germany. Furthermore, since the occupied areas were being provisioned by France, food was more plentiful than in the remainder of Germany, which was continuing to suffer the effects of the Allied blockade. This generally favourable initial attitude towards the occupying forces was not to last, however, in the light of the slowness of the French authorities to repatriate German prisoners of war, even before the major issues of war guilt and the terms of the Treaty took centre stage in May 1919.[50]

The struggle for everyday existence under the occupation was not the only issue for the people of the Pfalz to face at the beginning of 1919. The very future of the political and social relationship of the Pfalz to Bavaria had now been put in question. The cohesive influence of the long-established Wittelsbach royal family had been swept away in the revolution, leaving behind it a power vacuum. At the same time, it was not clear to what extent the Pfalz in its present difficulties – and especially in what lay ahead – could count on any economic support from the Bavarian government, which itself faced an uncertain future. For many on the political Right, including disaffected monarchists, the new left-wing republican government was associated with the feared Bolshevism. Eisner himself was Jewish and came from Berlin – a fact that in itself gave cause for Bavarian suspicion. He was a committed pacifist and as a result had been imprisoned during the war. He had very decided views on the attitude to adopt towards the Allied Powers, believing that reconciliation could be achieved only by a frank admission of German war guilt, qualifying this only by attributing responsibility to the previous Wilhelmine regime. In promoting such a view he was at odds both with the political Right and with Berlin, where the feeling was that any such admission would be counterproductive in the forthcoming peace negotiations. From this difference of opinion developed the first of a series of crises that were to bedevil relationships between Bavaria and the Reich in the next few years.[51] The significance of this for German propaganda is considered in later chapters.

Following the Armistice, in the period before the occupation was fully established, there were relatively few voices actively raised in the Pfalz in favour of cutting the ties with Bavaria, even though the press contained some lively discussion concerning the future of the province.[52] This contrasted with the situation in the Prussian Rhine Province, where a popular movement with the slogan 'Free from Berlin – Free from Prussia'[53] quickly got under way. This has been attributed to the long-standing antipathy of a strongly Catholic population towards Prussia, made much worse in mid-November 1918 by certain measures proposed by the new socialist Prussian government in Berlin. These measures included the separation of Church and state, the secularisation of schools and the end of state subsidy of the Churches.[54] It has been suggested, also, that the Pfalz differed from the remainder of the Rhineland in that it was dependent on Bavaria for certain elements of its food supply.

The situation was critical and the need for pragmatism outweighed any political ambitions.[55]

Thus, the loosening of the ties with Bavaria that had taken place during the war did not manifest itself in direct ill will towards the mother state. Rather, the public attitude towards Bavaria and its monarchy, the constitutional linchpin of the Wilhelmine era, was one of indifference.[56] With the monarchy gone, this general indifference persisted during the early years of the occupation. It was reported to the Reich government that the Pfalz was only loosely linked to Bavaria and that the people of the Pfalz felt somewhat neglected by the mother state. In spite of this there was no significant support for a merger with either Baden or Hessen.[57] A further report noted that although traces of Napoleonic influence could still be found in the Pfalz and that cross-border relations with France had always been good, its people had since 1870 strongly supported the fundamental concept of the Reich. In the first instance they considered themselves to be German, in the second, Bavarian.[58]

Nevertheless, within this general indifference towards the future relationship with Bavaria existed at the same time some sharply polarised opinions. These tended to be along party political lines, with religious persuasion also playing a part. Among the political parties in the Pfalz those of the Left were certainly loyal to Bavaria and to the Reich.[59] But among the recently formed bourgeois parties, the German People's Party (DVP) and the German Democratic Party (DDP), there existed elements – including former monarchists – who, not liking the developments in Munich and fearing the rise of Bolshevism, wanted to sever the ties between the Pfalz and Bavaria. Such attitudes concerning Bavaria would virtually reverse after March 1920 following the displacement of the socialist government in Munich by the right-wing administration of Gustav Ritter von Kahr.[60] Also linked to the DVP was a small but wealthy and influential group of landowners within the Pfalz wine trade who had for some time been pressing for a reorientation of the Pfalz away from Bavaria, regarding this as advantageous to their business interests.[61] Also, in February 1919 the Association of Pfalz Industrialists was formed. At the inaugural meeting unanimous support was declared for Pfalz membership of the German Reich. Members called on the National Assembly to agree a Constitution and to establish a strong legislature as quickly as possible. Interestingly, there seems to have been no similar declaration of loyalty to Bavaria, and clearly with an eye on the political complexion of the Berlin government it was demanded that private enterprise should remain the basis for the national economy and that the government should refrain from experiments with nationalisation.[62] The industrialists were clearly looking to Berlin, rather than to Munich, as the centre of political power.

Bourgeois concerns in the Pfalz over the momentous change in the political landscape in Bavaria were reflected also in the policy of the newly founded Bavarian People's Party (BVP), into which the Bavarian wing of the Catholic Centre Party had been subsumed at the end of November. Initially supportive of the link with Bavaria, the BVP in the Pfalz became increasingly unhappy with the manner in which the Eisner government was seeking to change the relationship between state and Church in Bavaria to the disadvantage of the Catholic Church. By the middle of March 1919 there was no longer support within the party for a pro-Bavarian policy. There was, however, disagreement between leading party figures as to the future direction for the Pfalz: whether it should amalgamate with the state of Baden, or become a totally independent state within the Reich. One proposal that went even further was for the entire west bank of the Rhine to declare independence of the German Reich. The policies being followed in Berlin and Munich were regarded as nothing less than the manifestations of the relentless progress of Bolshevism towards the Christian West.[63]

Thus in the first few weeks of 1919 there existed a growing groundswell of separatist feeling in the Pfalz, if not throughout the Rhineland, even if the direction it should take was not yet clear. While the impetus for severing ties with Bavaria came from within the Pfalz, ideas for redefining the boundaries of some of the existing states were also being considered elsewhere in connection with the creation of a new Reich Constitution. Thus was envisaged the merging of the Pfalz, the Prussian Rhine Province and the Oldenburg enclave of Birkenfeld to form a new Rhineland state, the motivation being the redressing of the imbalance between the enormous political weight of Prussia and that of the smaller states.[64] This, however, came to nothing.

Probably the most effective catalyst for the growth of separatism in the Pfalz was unwittingly supplied by Eisner himself. On 18 November 1918 a delegation from Neustadt Soldiers' and Workers' Council had been sent to Munich to seek urgent help from the Bavarian government in the provisioning of food and fuel, which was running short, presumably as a result of demand increasing as soldiers returned home from the Front. According to the subsequent report of the group they received an unsympathetic reception from Eisner and his Minister of the Interior, who felt that the overall picture in the Pfalz was not as bad as was being portrayed. Eisner was said to have remarked that help could be expected from the French occupying authorities, with whom his government had good relations,[65] though there is some suspicion that Eisner was deliberately misrepresented by the group.[66] It has to be remembered that the composition of Soldiers' and Workers' Councils varied considerably and in the Pfalz in particular there existed a substantial bourgeois influence. Of the three-man Neustadt delegation one was an SPD member, one was the secretary of the former National Liberal Party (subsequently DVP) and one was closely linked to the sectional interests of the wine trade. Overall it is safe to conclude that the delegation had a national liberal outlook, and was hostile to the socialist government in Munich.[67] Equally, however, it could be said that it was a lack of political acumen on Eisner's part[68] which resulted in him underestimating the scale of the looming problem in the Pfalz and led to clumsy handling of the delegation. Eisner subsequently declared that the Pfalz was an integral part of Bavaria and should remain so, a key element of policy that would be stated again and again by every Bavarian government until the National Socialists came to power in 1933.[69] But it was too late. Eisner's response was taken up by the press and the impression was created that he and his left-wing government in Munich were indifferent to the fate of the Pfalz – and indeed had already written it off. A rift that occurred between Bavaria and the Reich at the end of November – created by Eisner's animosity towards the Foreign Ministry over the issue of war guilt – only served to heighten this impression. It thereby helped to reinforce the growing campaign for an independent Pfalz,[70] while also fuelling a virulent and vicious anti-Semitic campaign against Eisner himself. It was to culminate in his assassination in February 1919.

Meanwhile, in pursuit of her aim to create an independent buffer state on the west bank of the Rhine, France had introduced from the start a number of measures aimed at isolating the Pfalz from unoccupied Germany, though some of these were later to be eased. Actions included the blocking of all traffic and telephone communications across the Rhine, surveillance of the post and censorship of the press and publications. Restrictions were placed on personal freedoms, including freedom of assembly. It became obligatory for adults to carry an identification card and for German officials in uniform to salute French officers and their flag. In Speyer, the Bavarian administration of the Pfalz, led by Dr Theodor von Winterstein, was forbidden to make contact with the authorities in Munich. Any new Reich or Bavarian laws or indeed local ordinances had first to be authorised by the French Controller of Civil Administration, Colonel Adalbert de Metz, newly appointed to oversee the Bavarian administration.[71] De Metz was to be a pivotal figure in the events in the Pfalz over the next four years. He had been born to Alsatian parents in Beauvais in October 1867 and had attended military college before following a career in the cavalry and on the General Staff. During World War I he had served with distinction. Promoted to the rank of general in July 1920, he served in the Pfalz until the autumn of 1924.[72] Winterstein, his uncompromising adversary, was an archetypal Bavarian civil servant. Born in Limbach in Lower Franconia in December 1861 and educated in Würzburg, he had held posts in Upper Bavaria, Speyer and then in the Ministry of Education and the Arts in Munich before being appointed chairman of the regional council in Speyer a few months before the end of the war. His relationship with the French authorities was to prove difficult,

Figure 3. Dr Theodor von Winterstein

resulting in his early expulsion from the Pfalz. In 1921 he was also removed from a subsequent post, that of State Commissioner for the Pfalz, at the behest of the Allies. He retired from his final post as chairman of the regional council of Regensburg and the Upper Pfalz in 1927.[73]

As Helmut Gembries has remarked,[74] the draconian measures introduced by the French authorities in the early period of the occupation seem contradictory to a policy of encouraging the Celtic spirit of the people of the Pfalz. This was not to remain the sole example of inconsistency in French policy towards the Rhineland, as will be seen later. However, worse than the measures taken to isolate the Pfalz from Germany and humiliate its population was to follow, for the French authorities then actively encouraged the development of the separatist movement.[75]

In the Pfalz, the first movement to make any attempt to gain power was Freie Pfalz (Free Pfalz), led by Dr Eberhard Haas, a chemist from Landau. A similar group was established in the Prussian Rhine Province at about the same time, led by Dr Hans Adam Dorten, a lawyer from Wiesbaden. Dorten was supported at first by Konrad Adenauer, Mayor of Cologne, and others prominent in the Centre Party, though internal disagreements soon led to Adenauer withdrawing from the movement. The motivations and objectives of the two groups differed appreciably, reflecting rival concepts that the French military authorities in the two regions, General Gérard in the Pfalz and General Mangin in the Rhine Province, would have liked to have seen implemented.[76] Religious persuasion played a part in Dorten's movement, for the Prussian Rhine Province was predominantly Catholic and there was incentive to break free from Protestant Prussia. Dorten sought to create an independent Rhineland republic – which would also embrace the Pfalz – within a federal German Reich. Haas's ideas on the other hand envisaged the creation of a fully independent and neutral Pfalz state.[77] It was hoped that such an act, in meeting French desires for a neutral buffer zone on her eastern frontier, would result in the concession by France of reduced reparations payments by the Pfalz and thereby provide considerable economic benefit.[78]

Attempts by the French authorities to exploit these feelings and to encourage the nascent separatist movements not unnaturally brought them into conflict with the local German administration. In the Pfalz matters came to a head in May 1919, when an attempt was made by de Metz to persuade Winterstein to lead a formal separation from the Reich. This proposal Winterstein rejected out of hand.[79] Haas had misjudged Winterstein, expecting him as a former representative of the old, royal Bavarian government to view with extreme disfavour the newly established Bavarian republican government of Johannes Hoffmann. Hoffmann, formerly Minister for Education and the Arts in Eisner's administration, and a Majority Socialist, had assumed the leadership of a coalition following a period of chaos after Eisner's assassination. Soon afterwards he had had to contend with the outbreak of civil war when, on 7 April 1919, having twice unsuccessfully attempted to seize power in Berlin, the extreme Left had decided to take Bavaria, and had proclaimed the Bavarian Soviet Republic. Although the uprising was eventually suppressed with the help of the Reich government, Hoffmann and his Cabinet were obliged to seek refuge for several weeks in Bamberg. Contrary to Haas's expectations Winterstein remained committed to the Reich and to Bavaria, in spite of the chaotic political situation. Winterstein emerges as the loyal government official, politically impartial in his official duties, arguably cautious and with a strong sense of duty. His personal views, however, were closely aligned with those of the dominant conservative BVP. He was sufficiently well regarded by that party to be invited to accept nomination as Bavarian Prime Minister in 1924, following the resignation of the Cabinet of Eugen Knilling. This invitation, however, he was to decline. His grounds for refusal were said to have been the tendency of the BVP to elect a Prime Minister and then fail to support him in his decisions.[80] Heinrich Held took the position instead.

De Metz was determined to press ahead with plans for an independent Pfalz but Winterstein was clearly an obstacle in his path. On 23 May 1919 de Metz invited Winterstein to leave the Pfalz voluntarily but this Winterstein refused to do. On 31 May he was expelled on the pretext that he had incited rebellion amongst his staff against the occupying power. The very next day, with Winterstein now out of the way, a putsch was attempted by Haas and the Free Pfalz movement with the encouragement of de Metz.[81] This was incompetently carried out and proved unsuccessful but the whole episode served to make French intentions perfectly clear. At the same time, notwithstanding the chaotic scenes that had often prevailed in unoccupied Germany during the previous months, it pointed to an absence of popular support in the Pfalz for a decisive break with the Reich.

It is these events, less than a month before the signing of the Peace Treaty, that can be said to have marked the beginning of the German propaganda campaign, in which Bavarian influence was to be prominent. The manner in which this came about and then subsequently developed in an organisational sense is explored in the following chapter. Before turning to this, however, we should remind ourselves of the wider political climate prevailing in Germany in the early Weimar years. It is important to keep this in mind, for the way in which German propaganda developed arguably owed as much to internal political divisions as it did to the specific actions of the occupying powers.

It would be a mistake to imagine that the Allies were united in their outlook concerning the future of Germany. National interests and policies at times proved hard to reconcile. France, heavily in debt and with industrial production barely two-thirds of the 1913 level, wanted to extract the maximum possible reparation in order to make good the devastation suffered in the German invasion, in particular to finance the reconstruction of her industrial base in the north.[82] As already noted, she also had ambitions to create a buffer state in the Rhineland, born of fears over her future security. For some in France even this would not suffice: a permanently weakened Germany was seen to be essential to French interests.[83] The British government, however, did not particularly favour an independent Rhineland, and it certainly did not like the idea of a lengthy military occupation, not least on financial grounds.[84] The British economy had suffered damage as a result of World War I, and Britain was a debtor to the USA, though a creditor to the European Allies. For Britain it was a priority to get industry and trade back to normal as quickly as possible, though the penalisation of German trade for a period was desired and it was intended to seek reparations.[85] Alone among the Allies the USA had emerged from the war considerably wealthier than at the beginning – and was now the major creditor. This gave her substantial influence in post-war negotiations, even if this was diminished somewhat by growing isolationism at home and her subsequent failure to ratify the Peace Treaty. The USA had been sympathetic to French concerns about security to the extent of persuading Britain to accept the Rhineland occupation but was subsequently critical of French policy there. Matters were to come to a head in 1923 when Germany defaulted on reparations and France occupied the Ruhr basin. In response, the USA withdrew completely from Germany.[86]

From 1919 to 1924 war reparations were in fact a dominant theme not only in relations between the Allies and Germany but also among the Allies themselves. War debts of the individual Allied countries were inextricably linked to the reparations question and led to profound disagreements between them before agreement was finally reached on the amount that Germany should pay. Thereafter German claims of inability to pay and subsequent default were to lead to a state of crisis that endured until the proposals of the Dawes committee presented the opportunity to find a solution in 1924.[87] National differences were to be reflected, also, in the workings of the Inter-Allied Rhineland High Commission (IRHC), which was charged with supervision of the civilian administration of the Rhineland from the date of the implementation of the Peace Treaty and the Rhineland Agreement, on 10 January 1920.[88]

The French chairman of the IRHC, Paul Tirard, born in 1879, was an exceptionally able civil servant, who had been educated at the École Libre des Sciences Politiques. He had gained experience in colonial administration in Morocco before being entrusted with the administration of recently retaken areas of Alsace in 1914. His personal style was to have a profound influence on French policy in the Rhineland and on the manner in which the IRHC operated. It has been said of him that 'Tirard was the man to carry out a policy of administrative infiltration and usurpation – he was not the man to foster goodwill and reconciliation between France and the Rhineland.'[89]

It has been said that the history of the Weimar Republic consisted of three phases. The first phase, which coincides with the period under study, was essentially one of continual crisis. It was followed by a period of relative economic and political stability before a final, self-destructive phase began in the late 1920s. Among the enormous problems facing the Reich government during that first phase was that of transforming the domestic economy from a wartime to a peacetime footing amid massive social and political upheaval. It was accompanied by hardship for many, made worse by a steady rise in inflation, which was to reach catastrophic proportions in 1923. Externally, the compensation to be paid by Germany to the Allies, foreshadowed in the Peace Treaty, was valued in April 1921 by the Reparations Commission at a nominal level of 132 billion Gold Marks.[90] These issues alone would have been daunting enough but matters were made far worse by the fact that the country was fundamentally divided in its attitude towards the new Republic and its system of parliamentary democracy. This, it will be argued, was to be a key factor in shaping German Rhineland propaganda. From the beginning the new Republic was under attack both from the extreme Right and the extreme Left. The extreme Left, represented by the USPD and the German Communist Party (KPD), took an ideological stance based on a dictatorship of the proletariat and wanted a system of government based on soviets. Its weapons were strikes, the fomentation of industrial unrest and armed uprising. The extreme Right included members of the German National People's Party (DNVP) as well as disaffected monarchists and some former military personnel. Nurtured by the myth that the defeat in 1918 was attributable not to mismanagement by the Wilhelmine regime but to the machinations of the civilian Left, the extreme Right did its aggressive best to undermine the Republic. The new Republic was held to be culpable for the severe terms of the Peace Treaty. Publications and rallies directed the fury of the Right against the government. In March 1920 this resentment was to lead to the unsuccessful attempt by a group of extremists, led by Wolfgang Kapp and Generals Erich Ludendorff and Walter von Lüttwitz, to overthrow the Reich government.[91]

In the face of all this the Reich government struggled to assert its authority. Broadly supported by the Prussian government, which favoured the creation of a unitary state, it sought a greater centralisation of power with Berlin as its focus.[92] Fundamentally, it was this aim that was to underlie a prolonged period of friction with Bavaria throughout the years under study. The situation worsened when the SPD government of Johannes Hoffmann was ousted by the right-wing BVP led by Gustav Ritter von Kahr. Henceforth, extreme right-wing elements – extremely hostile to the Republic, which they regarded as akin to Bolshevist – would feel encouraged to make their presence felt.[93] The extent to which the ideological rift between Berlin and Munich permeated officialdom on both sides and thereby influenced the propaganda campaign against the occupation of the Rhineland will be examined in the following chapters. Theodor von Winterstein, chairman of the regional council in the Pfalz, has already been identified as a key figure in that campaign. It is to his actions immediately following his expulsion from the Pfalz that we now turn.

2

THE BAVARIAN PFALZZENTRALE AND THE RHEINISCHE VOLKSPFLEGE: A DISCORDANT EVOLUTION

Following his expulsion from the Pfalz, Winterstein lost little time in setting up an organisation on the east bank of the Rhine amongst whose main functions would be to counter separatist activities in the Pfalz. This organisation, the Central Office for Affairs in the Pfalz, was to undergo several transformations during the next few years, accompanied by changes of name, though its underlying purpose and its leadership remained essentially unchanged. Often informally referred to as the Pfalzzentrale – a term which will be used throughout this book – its leadership was entrusted to Dr August Ritter von Eberlein. Through his drive and uncompromising hostility towards the French occupiers, and with the backing of the Bavarian government, Eberlein would ensure a prominent place for the Pfalzzentrale in the propaganda battle against the occupation. Crucial to this was the manner in which the organisation was set up and its relationship to those Reich organisations that were concerned with propaganda. In discussing the early development of the Pfalzzentrale I shall in particular examine the extent to which it embodied the determination of the Bavarian government to maintain full control of what it considered to be its own affairs.

Eberlein was the central figure in the Bavarian propaganda effort. The son of a primary school teacher, he was born in Kitzingen am Main on 7 January 1877. Following attendance at a grammar school he studied German, history and geography to qualify as a teacher in 1899. He held teaching posts in Munich, Gunzenhausen in Central Franconia and Pirmasens in the Pfalz before becoming the headmaster of a girls' school in Pirmasens in 1905.[1] Eberlein was awarded a doctorate in philology at Erlangen in 1911.[2] During World War I he saw service as a reserve officer, initially commanding a company of infantry on the Western Front, later rising to deputy regimental commander, with the rank of captain. Within weeks of the commencement of hostilities he had already distinguished himself through acts of bravery. On 26 August 1914 he was awarded Bavaria's highest decoration, the Max-Joseph military medal, which carried personal ennoblement, adding the title *Ritter von* to his name.[3] There were, however, other traits in Eberlein's character – such as his readiness to disregard

Figure 4. Dr August Ritter von Eberlein

rules and instructions in order to achieve his aims[4] – which were later to have a decisive influence on the affairs of the Pfalzzentrale. Disregard for what Eberlein regarded as niceties may account for an incident that occurred on 27 August 1914 at St Dié in Alsace, where he was alleged to have made hostages of civilians and to have shot prisoners of war. The French military authorities accused him of war crimes and included his name on the list of those whose extradition to face charges was demanded at the end of hostilities, known in Germany as *die Auslieferungsliste*.[5] Eberlein vehemently disputed the allegations and later went so far as to publish his own version of events as an addendum to a novel that he had written.[6] Whatever the truth of the accusations, the matter was to haunt him for years afterwards. He was unable to return to the Pfalz when hostilities ceased and he had the threat of war criminal proceedings hanging over him. As a consequence of German refusal to hand over alleged war criminals Eberlein never appeared in person before a war crimes court. The compromise eventually reached with the Allies was that alleged cases of war crimes should be tried before the Reichsgericht (Reich Supreme Court) at Leipzig.[7] In 1924, the case against Eberlein was put before this court but it was then dropped on the grounds that his unit had been mistaken for another.[8] French dissatisfaction with this verdict – as in many other cases[9] – subsequently led to a retrial before a French court, which sentenced Eberlein *in absentia* to five years' imprisonment.[10]

What led to the recruitment of Eberlein to lead the Pfalzzentrale cannot be determined with complete certainty, but it is likely that he himself approached the Bavarian Prime Minister Johannes Hoffmann. At the time Hoffmann and his government were temporarily resident in Bamberg for safety in the face of the Communist insurgency in Munich. Eberlein was his security chief.[11] Hoffmann, determined to maintain the link between the Pfalz and Bavaria, referred him to Winterstein for assessment of his potential usefulness, and on receiving a positive response from Winterstein, then appointed him. However, the records that exist are much later recollections of the events, and Winterstein may have found some difficulty in admitting his part in appointing Eberlein in view of his later record.[12] Whatever the facts of the case, French accusations against Eberlein clearly did not present any obstacle to his appointment.

The business of setting up the Pfalzzentrale began on 4 June 1919, just three days after the expulsion of Winterstein from the Pfalz. This was to be an office that would function at least until a peace agreement was finalised. It would act to some extent as an official organisation but not in any bureaucratic manner. It would provide a vital link between the Pfalz, agencies of the Bavarian government and the press. Little wonder that Winterstein acted swiftly. In the aftermath of the attempted separatist coup the situation in the Pfalz was critical. Complaints were coming in from across the political spectrum in the Pfalz that too little was being done by either the Bavarian or Reich government to safeguard the future of the region.[13] In fact the Bavarian government, preoccupied by its own immediate fight for survival, had probably been unable to do much anyway. This is borne out by a claim by the secretary of the SPD in the Pfalz, Friedrich Profit, that he had tried to set up a Pfalzzentrale in Mannheim in December 1918. However, his attempt had failed as a result of the chaos associated with the short-lived Soviet Republic in Munich.[14] Whatever the reason for Bavarian inactivity, the situation in the Pfalz had not gone unnoticed elsewhere: the Prussian Finance Minister, Albert Südekum, noted that the French were enjoying great success because the Bavarians had been unconcerned about the Pfalz. In his view part of the population now wanted a merger with Baden, another section supported France.[15]

The Reich government was arguably no better positioned than the Bavarian government to exert influence on local events within the Pfalz in a manner that would encourage loyalty in the local population. In response to the crisis and criticisms levelled at the Reich it gave Hugo von Schmidthals,[16] a diplomat then serving as Prussian envoy in Karlsruhe, the task of maintaining the links between the Reich and the Pfalz. In fact the record rather implies that it was the Reich government that had taken the lead in trying to meet the charge of neglect and that this was followed by the Bavarian response in setting up the Pfalzzentrale. What is not in doubt is that there existed considerable uncertainty, if not confusion, at the beginning of June

1919. Nobody was looking further ahead in time than the signing of the Peace Treaty. It was a matter of real concern that the French army would immediately occupy the east bank of the Rhine if agreement on the terms of the Treaty were not reached and the signing did not take place. The Pfalz would then be even more isolated. Winterstein, however, had already worked out ways of maintaining contact across the Rhine. He hoped to persuade the Reich government to bear the additional costs of doing so.[17]

By 7 June Winterstein and Eberlein together had already met representatives of the main political parties and had allocated funds for the Pfalz that had been made available by the Bavarian government. The allocations included a grant of M 10,000 to the SPD and M 5,000 to the DDP. Further contributions were anticipated from the Association of Pfalz Industrialists. The funds were to be used in support of agitators, in the compensation of those who had suffered in the failed putsch of 1–2 June and for printing pamphlets, leaflets and placards. Winterstein had also taken steps to set up an action committee which would work in an advisory capacity in conjunction with the Pfalzzentrale. Amongst those invited to serve on this were members of the political parties, Pfalz business leaders and Hugo von Schmidthals, acting on behalf of the Reich government. Also invited was Hermann Oncken, an eminent historian from the University of Heidelberg, who would himself make a personal contribution to Rhineland propaganda. As well as providing assistance to expellees, overseeing agitation activities in the Pfalz by students and organising protest meetings in Mannheim and Heidelberg directed against alleged French brutality, the committee was to establish a channel through which news of the conditions in the Pfalz could be conveyed to the press in neutral countries. Even at this early stage the imperative of appealing to neutral international public opinion was uppermost in Winterstein's mind.[18]

The formal founding of the Pfalzzentrale as a semi-official department of the Bavarian government took place a few days later, at a meeting of the action committee.[19] With the agreement of the government of Baden it was located in Mannheim, just across the Rhine from Ludwigshafen, for it was important to have close contact with the occupied Pfalz. Propaganda was to be the main weapon in the political struggle to preserve German unity in the face of the French occupation. The Pfalzzentrale was to be led, however, by a person who seemingly lacked any experience in this field. This contrasts with the situation in the Reich government, which had amassed a wealth of experience in propaganda within several departments during the course of World War I. Throughout its existence the Pfalzzentrale was to have a substantial degree of interaction with those departments and agencies of the Reich government likewise engaged in propaganda. These included the press offices of the Foreign Ministry and the Reich Chancellery as well as the Heimatdienst. For reasons outlined later the Heimatdienst created a cover organisation, the Rheinische Volkspflege, specifically to counter French influence in the occupied Rhineland. The Volkspflege is of particular significance because it not only encouraged the formation of a campaigning network of women's organisations, the Rheinische Frauenliga, but it also provided financial support for Eberlein's organisation in Mannheim.

The relationship between the Pfalzzentrale and both the Heimatdienst and Volkspflege was far from harmonious. The reasons for this were partly political and were associated with wider relationships between the Reich and its constituent states. But disharmony also arose because certain individual propagandists had fundamentally different perspectives on the form that propaganda should take. These aspects are discussed in later chapters. First, however, the relationship of the Reich government to Rhineland propaganda should be established before the influence it had on the fledgling Pfalzzentrale is considered. To do this a brief outline is required of the way in which the Reich propaganda effort had developed.

The need for a dedicated Reich propaganda organisation to explain German war aims to neutral countries had become clear in 1914. The Zentralstelle für Auslandsdienst (Central Office for Services Abroad) had been set up for this purpose under the aegis of the Reich Foreign Ministry. This was joined by a number of other semi-official and private press agencies and organisations such as the German National Committee, supported by the Reich Chancellery, whose purpose was to influence the civilian population. The military High Command (OHL) had its own press and propaganda organisations. From 1916 onwards it had placed increasing emphasis on military propaganda and had even set up a military department within the Foreign Ministry. If the overall aim of both political and military authorities was to stiffen the resolve of the nation, one of the principal concerns of the military authorities, perhaps with an eye to the post-war period, was to maintain the system of rigid hierarchical discipline against the pressure for increasing democratisation coming from the working-class movement in Germany. This aim applied not just in the military sphere, but also in areas such as government, trade and industry as well as administration.[20]

By 1917, at a time when the public mood at home, no less than that at the Front, required careful nurturing in the face of both the entry of the USA into the war and increasing shortages, there still existed relatively little coordination of the various propaganda organisations.[21] The situation began to improve in September 1917 with the creation by Reich Chancellor Michaelis of an official press service, subsequently followed by a merger with the news department of the Foreign Ministry. In March 1918 the head of the press service, Erhard Deutelmoser, was appointed to lead the newly created Heimatdienst, which came under the aegis of the Reich Chancellery. Deutelmoser had a clear vision of what was required and proceeded independently of the military authorities, who were hostile and did their best to be obstructive. Initially he set out to convince the population that Germany would ultimately be victorious, adopting a see-it-through-at-all-costs approach. By September 1918, however, in the light of a deteriorating military position, and in spite of a major propaganda drive, he was obliged to issue new guidelines for the enlightenment of the civil population. These guidelines emphasised the responsibility of the individual and his duty on the one hand and on the other put forward cautiously liberal ideas to help adjustment to the post-war world.

Thus began the transformation of the Heimatdienst into an organisation that within weeks was working in support of a new republican government under Friedrich Ebert. During this period of tremendous social and political upheaval, its work included the production of material calling for the population to support the government in upholding law and order and the preparation of publicity material for elections to the National Assembly early in 1919.

The organisational history of Reich wartime propaganda activities alone, however, provides an incomplete background against which to assess post-war developments. It is necessary to consider what the propaganda itself, and the manner in which it was employed, left behind by way of a legacy. It was earlier noted that the OHL, with General Erich Ludendorff at its head, had championed the use of propaganda during World War I. Indeed it was Ludendorff who had done his best, though unsuccessfully, to persuade the government to establish a fully fledged propaganda ministry. Ludendorff and others in the OHL, however, had a very blinkered view of propaganda. In their eyes it was there to be used much as one would use any other weapon of war, admittedly a powerful one, and it could be used regardless either of any adverse circumstances prevailing at the time, or of the mood of the target population. Propaganda in their view could be used quite simply to transform reality. Within the ruling military elites there existed no understanding of mass psychology and certainly no empathy whatever with the civilian population,[22] which, it might be argued, was regarded simply as another resource to be exploited in the furtherance of war.

This attitude towards the German public was manifest in two ways as the military outlook and the economic condition of the country both deteriorated in the final months of the war. First, the propaganda emanating from Berlin continued to stress the certainty of ultimate victory, and second, censorship was applied in order to disguise the true nature of the situation facing the country. Beyond that, the government relied on the traditional obedience of a largely subservient public to accept authority from above.[23] When the final collapse came this strategy heightened in the public consciousness the sense of betrayal, the realisation that the government had been peddling lies and the sacrifices of the past four years had been in vain.

In the aftermath of World War I there existed differing views of the concept of propaganda and its role and, in the public at large, a distrust of official propaganda. Leading figures in the former Wilhelmine regime, like Ludendorff, promulgated their view that the army, victorious on the battlefield, had been undermined by a combination of Bolshevism and its propaganda, Jewish intrigue, failings in German propaganda and the superiority of enemy propaganda. This was all part of a portrayal of events that included the so-called stab-in-the-back legend and it represented an attempt to shift the blame for the mishandling of the war from the military to the civilian government and so discredit the new republican government.[24]

In contrast to this, the Heimatdienst quickly distanced itself completely from the jingoistic nature of wartime propaganda. Its concept of propaganda was quite different from what had gone before and emphasis was now placed on cultural rather than political matters. The Foreign Ministry, also, redefined its task in projecting the image of Germany abroad as *Aufklärungsarbeit* (civic enlightenment). Even the use of the word propaganda was strictly forbidden from the start.[25]

By the time the Rhineland was occupied the Heimatdienst had already established a substantial background in publicity and propaganda activities. In addition, an important part of its task was to maintain a network of trusted agents throughout the Reich, in order to keep the government informed on the current local political situation. Based in Berlin, the Heimatdienst had branch offices in each of the states within the Reich. Offices in Gummersbach, Frankfurt am Main, Darmstadt and Heidelberg had responsibilities for the Rhineland, while the so-called Volksaufklärungsstelle (Office for Civic Enlightenment) in Munich had particular interest in the Pfalz.

The Heimatdienst was organised in four departments. Three of these, including the branch offices, were concerned with internal and external economic and political issues, as well as social and educational matters relating especially to the young and to women. The fourth was a technical department, concerned with the production and dissemination of the publicity and propaganda material and with exploitation of film and slide material.[26] It was not until the autumn of 1919, however, that a section was set up devoted exclusively to the occupation and its consequences. The main purposes of this new section were to support the German cultural structure within the Rhineland and so counter the blandishments being offered by the French authorities in pursuing their policy of *pénétration pacifique*; also to stiffen resistance to the separatist movement and to maintain the link between the occupied Rhineland and the rest of Germany.[27]

The Heimatdienst saw its task as one of supplying the information needed to enable an informed electorate to form its own judgement and exercise its democratic right to choose. There was no intention to mould public opinion from above.[28] It intended to 'embed the new type of state securely in the hearts of the German people through quiet, purposeful and factual information and civic education'.[29]

This, then, was the background against which the Pfalzzentrale would undertake its propaganda work. Its ethos, and that of some other organisations heavily involved in Rhineland propaganda, was to contrast strongly with the characteristics of the Heimatdienst and the Volkspflege. This was arguably one cause of the antipathy with which – as will be seen – these organisations were regarded by Eberlein and others. It was also to result in the Pfalzzentrale eventually falling into disfavour with the Reich Foreign Ministry.

The Heimatdienst was not the only Reich government organisation concerned with countering the Rhineland occupation. The situation in the Rhineland had first been raised at a Cabinet meeting of the Reich government on 12 March 1919, when action against both separatist and French activities and their propaganda was discussed. This followed a press report of a public meeting in Cologne, at which the establishment of an independent Rhineland state within the Reich – including the Pfalz – had been called for. The Cabinet decided that the separatist movement should be opposed vigorously. It envisaged MPs of the occupied territories playing a part in developing counter-propaganda against enemy machinations. At the same time Ulrich Rauscher, chief Reich press officer, was to make the press aware of the gravity of the situation and he was put in charge of countermeasures.[30]

These measures were, however, deemed insufficient to deal with the increasing amount of French propaganda being directed at the Rhineland population. Just two months later a proposal was made for the creation of a special propaganda office for the occupied regions.

The intention was to locate the head office in Berlin, with branch offices in Karlsruhe, Frankfurt, Essen or Elberfeld and Marburg.[31] In fact the proposal was never implemented, even though it received Cabinet approval, because it was overtaken by a decision to form a central propaganda office within the Reich Chancellery. This would serve the Reich and Prussian governments, and would achieve better coordination of government press and propaganda activities, together with rationalisation of technical facilities such as film and photographic studios. The decision was not universally popular. A dispute broke out between the Reich Chancellery and the Foreign Ministry press office over the division of responsibilities for press propaganda and the distinction between internal and external propaganda. The Foreign Ministry was determined to maintain control of what it regarded as its own preserve, as is shown in a letter from its news department to Ulrich Rauscher:

> Propaganda against the enemy's plans for dismemberment [of the Rhineland] should remain within the jurisdiction of the news department of the Foreign Ministry, as it is linked with foreign policy and should act in support of this. It must of course also broadly conform to internal policy requirements, of which there is adequate knowledge within the Foreign Ministry. Naturally, in such cases where there is a degree of overlap between internal and foreign policy I shall gladly take into account Your Excellency's wishes concerning the propaganda. All propaganda relating purely to internal policy I shall leave to the press office concerned. On the other hand I attach great importance to the adherence to proper areas of jurisdiction. In particular all matters pertaining to the press and propaganda that relate to foreign policy should be left to the news department of the Foreign Ministry.[32]

Evidence of attempts to achieve coordination between the Reich and Bavarian governments is provided by the attendance of the Reich representative Hugo von Schmidthals at an early meeting at the Pfalzzentrale.[33] Both Schmidthals and Eberlein welcomed the prospect of collaboration but shortly after this Schmidthals was withdrawn from his post and the representation of Reich interests in the Pfalz was handed over to the Heimatdienst.[34] This action may have been linked with a critical review of the propaganda activities of the Foreign Ministry ordered some weeks previously by the Reich Cabinet. Simultaneously an instruction had been given by the Reich Chancellor that the Foreign Ministry should cease any internal propaganda activity.[35] At the time that Winterstein was establishing his Pfalzzentrale with the support of the Bavarian government, Reich propaganda activities were therefore still fragmented, though the urgent need for coordination had been recognised. While some action was being taken to try to achieve this, departmental rivalries were not helping the situation.

In the meantime Eberlein had been encouraged to put forward his ideas for the development of the Pfalzzentrale, at that time occupying just three rooms in a hotel in Mannheim. Written just before the signing of the Peace Treaty at Versailles, his memorandum argued the case for the continued existence of the Pfalzzentrale and for its further expansion. It pointed out what had been achieved in its first three weeks in providing a channel for official information, in discussions with political parties and industrial leaders, in the publication of articles and in the organisation of public protests against separatism in the Pfalz. It further recommended that an independent office should also be set up in order to provide a reliable news and intelligence service to and from the Pfalz.

The grounds for continuation were based on political, economic and social factors. First and foremost was the need to counter the threats posed by separatist activity, supported by French money. To this end Eberlein proposed an immediate large-scale propaganda campaign. Notably, he also favoured a close working relationship with Schmidthals in Karlsruhe, who had similar objectives on behalf of the Reich government. In the economic sphere, industrial companies were concerned that French capital might be used to buy out large sections of German industry and their Association was prepared not only to second advisers, but also to provide M 30,000 to support the work of the Pfalzzentrale. In social matters, it was anticipated that the signing of the Peace Treaty would provide the signal for the disciplining of the Pfalz population by the French authorities. Inevitably deportations would ensue, with a consequent need for social welfare. Finally, Eberlein invoked patriotic grounds, with distinctly nationalistic overtones, recalling that the spiritual bonds that had once made the Netherlands and Switzerland part of the nucleus of the German race had become weakened over time. Neglect of the situation by Germany, he believed, had led to estrangement and hence ultimately to political detachment. This must never happen to the Pfalz. Thus a major task for the Pfalzzentrale was to organise mass meetings in Bavaria and in the wider Reich in order to protest to the world against every infringement or excess that was allowed by the League of Nations to take place in the Pfalz. In this way the people of the Pfalz would be shown that the German Fatherland was standing with them. Eberlein was confident that they would be appreciative of his propaganda and that it would provide them with the necessary encouragement to mount successful resistance.[36]

There is therefore no doubt that Winterstein and Eberlein intended to fight with the utmost vigour any attempt to detach the Pfalz from the Reich. The Pfalz was to be the focus of their efforts. Even though the main threat for the moment was that of separatism, a mental state of war with France would continue.

On being given the task of representing Reich interests in the Pfalz, the Heimatdienst, through its office in Munich, developed proposals for collaboration with the Bavarian government against the separatist threat. It was to establish its representative, Captain Oberhofer, in Heidelberg, where he would be able to draw on the technical resources of the Baden government. The Heimatdienst was ready to contribute M 50,000 to counter separatism in the Pfalz, but on condition that the Bavarian government should put up a similar sum. It should also accept that the funding would be controlled through the Heimatdienst, which had already concluded such an agreement with Prussia for the occupied territories in the east and with Hessen-Darmstadt for Rheinhessen.[37]

On meeting Oberhofer and learning the content of the proposal, the Bavarian Prime Minister Johannes Hoffmann referred the matter to Winterstein, but not before making it clear that the existence of two propaganda organisations side by side was completely unacceptable, and that before reaching overall agreement the aims of the propaganda would have to be decided jointly. Moreover, the propaganda activities of the Heimatdienst would have to be subordinate to those of the Bavarian Pfalzzentrale.[38]

At this time the controversy over the future structure of the Reich – whether it should be a unitary state or have a federal structure – was beginning to surface although it had yet to develop fully. Already, sharp disagreement had arisen between Reich and Bavarian governments over a plan for control of the railway systems to pass from the states to the Reich[39] – and there were to be more serious disputes ahead. Yet we should not read into Hoffmann's insistence on putting Bavarian interests first any inherent animosity towards the Reich. He was, together with his party, a strong supporter of the Reich and was basically in favour of the unitary state, though with one vital caveat: it should not be dominated by Prussia.[40]

In spite of the negative reception that its initial proposal had received, the Heimatdienst maintained its position. It made it clear that the Reich was involving itself in the matter because Bavaria lacked resources and because there was currently a lack of any united response from the German side to what was an active, well-coordinated and potentially successful French propaganda campaign. A long-term view was being taken here, for, restating the intention to set up a branch office in Heidelberg under Oberhofer, the Heimatdienst undertook, on behalf of the Reich, to meet the costs of producing propaganda for the fifteen-year duration of the occupation. Where special Bavarian needs were concerned, the Reich would, as an exception, not object to meeting the costs involved.[41] No decision had been taken at that point as to whether the Reich would continue its own propaganda campaign in the event of a rejection of the proposal by Bavaria. But the Heimatdienst was quick to point out that any subsequent propaganda would be designed to serve only Reich interests.

From a Bavarian perspective, effectively ceding control of the propaganda effort to the Heimatdienst in Berlin – or worse, to an outpost of the Heimatdienst in Munich – was out of the question. It was vital for Winterstein that propaganda should be controlled by the

Bavarian authorities, though he did acknowledge that the Reich had a legitimate interest in the matter and he undertook not to do anything against its interests. In his view the interests of the Reich were coincident with those of Bavaria, and Bavaria would work for both. However, the Reich had responsibilities as well: 'It is therefore only right and proper that the Reich, with the considerable means available to it for civic enlightenment, should stand in support at the side of the Bavarian state.'[42] Winterstein also considered that the competence of the Heimatdienst had not been sufficiently demonstrated to take on the difficult task of generating propaganda for the Pfalz.

In short, Winterstein, like Hoffmann, was agreeable to collaborating with the Heimatdienst provided that it subordinated itself to the Bavarian effort, while at the same time providing financial support.[43] Within a few weeks it was agreed that an official would be seconded from the Heimatdienst to work under Winterstein, thereby to provide the necessary liaison between the two organisations. Financing of propaganda activities would be shared between the Reich and Bavarian governments. As Helmut Gembries has remarked, the question of who should lead the propaganda campaign for the Pfalz was finally decided in favour of the Bavarian government.[44]

Winterstein's personal position was strengthened when, on 2 August 1919, he was appointed to a newly created post, State Commissioner for the Pfalz, within the Bavarian Foreign Ministry.[45] At the same time he continued his duties as chairman of the regional council, thereby meeting wishes unanimously expressed by the Bavarian Parliament on 4 July.[46] Furthermore, an expert on Pfalz affairs was appointed to each ministry in the Bavarian government that had responsibilities for the Pfalz.[47] If the Bavarian government had earlier been criticised for passivity in the face of the threat to the Pfalz, it was at least now trying to organise itself to meet that threat.

Winterstein now proceeded to build up the capability of the Pfalzzentrale to generate propaganda, with the creation of a press office in Mannheim. Its function would be to liaise with the press in unoccupied Germany and to secure the publication of propaganda articles and reports, as well as to develop contacts with the foreign press and to supply suitable material to it. An agency to serve the press was also established in Ludwigshafen under the leadership of the editor of the newspaper *Pfälzische Rundschau*, Dr Hans Englram. The task here was a particularly difficult one, namely to attempt to correct anything considered to be a falsehood or distortion in a press that was under constant surveillance by the French authorities. In addition, attempts were to be made to get the Bavarian and Reich viewpoints reflected without falling foul of the rigid censorship that was being imposed.[48]

During the late summer and autumn of 1919 there seems to have been relatively little activity directed towards the building up of a united propaganda front. This was in spite of deep anxiety over the future of the Rhineland, both in the Reich Cabinet and in the states concerned with their own particular regions. The anxiety was not without good reason. In this period, before the setting up of the IRHC in Coblenz, which was intended to oversee the implementation of those Peace Treaty provisions pertinent to the Rhineland, there was an overwhelming sense of political vacuum. It was barely a month since a proposal to form a new Greater Hessen Republic from Hessen, the Prussian province Hessen-Nassau, Birkenfeld and the Bavarian Pfalz had been put forward as a means of sustaining the viability of the now-emasculated state of Hessen.[49] This had been strongly opposed by Bavaria and Prussia and had come to nothing. Furthermore, pressure was again building from separatist movements. Besides an anticipated attempt in Rheinhessen to declare the founding of a Rhineland republic by Dr Adam Dorten, a further and rival attempt at a putsch by the Haas separatists in the Pfalz was thought to be imminent.[50] There were worries about the measure of support that Dorten was receiving from elements within the Centre Party and the priesthood and certain financiers. The loyalty of the local officials in the event of a successful coup was also in question. Added to this, there were concerns not only about the political indifference of an undoubtedly weary population and the way in which this might be exploited by the French authorities, but also about the lack of an effective German voice abroad:

> Dorten's movement is gaining ground amongst civil servants and public opinion is being swayed. This is having an effect on the English and the Americans, who don't hear any German voices

> speaking out. Furthermore the neutral press is getting the impression that most Rhinelanders support the plans for separation.[51]

Unsurprisingly there existed a groundswell of feeling that the Reich government was too passive and lacked understanding of the problems facing the occupied regions, when what was needed, in the opinion of the states, was strong leadership. The Reich government, however, found itself frustrated and in a relatively weak position, unable to intervene directly against the separatist movements. Playing the role of honest broker, it freely admitted its inability to find a way forward for the Rhineland that could be agreed by all the parties involved:

> The Reich government is unable to offer a definite programme for the future of the Rhineland. If we find one that does not suit an individual party then that party is up in arms against it and that does more harm than good. There simply is no programme that pleases all political parties.[52]

Amidst the turmoil Winterstein saw clear differences between the situation of the Pfalz and the other occupied areas of the Rhineland. In his view Foch and Mangin were being relatively circumspect in the occupied territory to the north of the Pfalz. Gérard and Clemenceau, however, were working hard to deliver the Pfalz to France. He could foresee a hard struggle ahead and there was urgent need for much stronger protest from the Reich government.[53] It has been suggested that on being appointed State Commissioner Winterstein might have lost interest in collaborating with the Reich on joint propaganda activities.[54] However, it seems unlikely that he would have gone out of his way to avoid collaboration, given that he wanted support from the Reich government in making a protest at international level. Also he was presumably by now receiving financial support from the Reich. Nevertheless, much as he wanted to maintain the integrity of the German Reich, Winterstein strongly believed in Bavarian sovereignty in the Pfalz, and had been insistent, with Hoffmann's backing, on the Bavarian government taking the lead in developing propaganda for the

Pfalz. The uncertain internal political situation, which, as remarked, had led to the proposal for the Pfalz to be ceded to a new middle-Rhine state, or even merged with Baden, may well have increased Winterstein's resolve to maintain a grip on all matters relating to the Pfalz. Then again, a further factor was the low regard in which the propaganda activities of the Reich government, conducted through its press office and through the Heimatdienst, were held. Even Dr Theodor Lewald, State Secretary in the Reich Interior Ministry, meeting with representatives from the occupied Rhineland, accepted criticism that the Reich was not doing enough to support the region but pointed out that it was extremely difficult to influence the press. He admitted that the Reich press office and the Heimatdienst would just have to work harder and be more effective. Part of the solution, he thought, lay in the expansion of Reich propaganda activities. Others present did not share this view.[55] Three months later in a similar forum, it was clear that little had changed, even though in the intervening period measures to coordinate Reich government press and propaganda policy had already been taken and the merger of the press offices of the Reich Chancellery and Foreign Ministry under Ulrich Rauscher had been agreed.[56] The Heimatdienst was considered by those present to be completely ineffective:

> MP Dr Meerfeld criticised the activities of the Heimatdienst in the occupied territories, which he described as clumsy. It was desirable that it should stop its work and let the political parties take over.[57]

Dissatisfaction with the Reich government itself was undiminished in the Rhineland. The feeling was reportedly widespread that both the government and the rest of Germany were insufficiently aware of the suffering in the occupied regions. This did not mean that the Reich should abnegate its responsibilities – far from it. The pressure from the Rhineland representatives present was, rather, that the Reich should act decisively and create an effective *Abwehr* organisation in place of the Heimatdienst. The Pfalzzentrale of Winterstein and Eberlein was held up as the model to follow.[58]

Winterstein viewed the situation in the Pfalz as being even more serious than that faced elsewhere in the Rhineland, thus adding to the need for urgency. But whatever his attitude towards a collaborative propaganda campaign involving the Heimatdienst, it would have been quite obvious to him that the situation of the Pfalz could not be addressed in isolation from other occupied areas west of the Rhine. Early in 1920 an anxious Reich Interior Ministry likewise stressed the pressing need for measures to support and maintain German culture and tradition in the occupied regions. It enquired about progress with such activity and the degree to which this was being coordinated with other states according to agreed guidelines.[59] The concern was shared in Bavaria, where on 16 August 1919 the state Parliament had voted M 10 million as relief aid for the Pfalz. Of this, M 2 million was to be spent sustaining theatre and the arts, while M 1,750,000 would be reserved for political purposes and in particular for the Pfalzzentrale.[60] In his reply Winterstein referred to the foundation in Würzburg of a relief agency for the Pfalz. He had hopes that the work of the agency would develop to form the basis for a western borderland alliance. Winterstein also noted that he had contacted representatives of Hessen and Baden in order to further collaborative effort.[61] There can be no doubt about his willingness to undertake joint activity with other states at this time, though from the fact that he wanted this to be based in Mannheim it can be inferred that he envisaged Bavaria taking the lead in the matter.

Winterstein was also hopeful that Prussia would join a collaborative venture at some point in the future. It should be remembered that these events were taking place against a background of cool, if not difficult, relationships not only between Bavarian and Prussian state governments but also between Prussia and the Reich.[62] Barely two months previously the representative of the Prussian government in Munich had reported on the hostility towards Prussia that was prevalent in some circles in Bavaria. Equally lamentable in the eyes of the Prussian authorities was the tendency in Bavaria to blame Prussia for actions taken by the Reich government that were adjudged to be against Bavarian interests. This was happening regardless of whether or not Prussia had any influence in the Reich government.[63] Thus was a traditional rivalry and antipathy between Bavaria and Prussia being deliberately rekindled in Bavaria, especially by the Right. From a Bavarian perspective the fact that Prussia, like the Reich, had a Social Democratic government and had its seat of government in Berlin made it easy to equate – whether falsely or not – the interests of Prussia directly with those of the Reich. Such attitudes, accompanied by agitation in some circles for Bavarian independence of the Reich, were to intensify following the resignation of Hoffmann's government in Bavaria and its replacement on 16 March 1920 by the right-wing government of Gustav Ritter von Kahr.[64]

Nevertheless, discussions on collaboration continued throughout the spring of 1920, doubtless spurred on by the fear of the effects that the occupation was having in the Rhineland. A feeling of isolation from the remainder of the Reich had intensified among the local population, and with the prospect of fifteen years of occupation the situation did not augur well for future cohesion. In such circumstances the hand of the separatist movements would surely have been strengthened enormously. In the view of the Reich Cabinet this sense of isolation was a greater threat than French propaganda and the Reich had to do more than it had done hitherto to counteract it. Skilful though French propaganda was, it had not yet really influenced people, though in the longer term its potential to do so was not to be disregarded.[65] As far as Bavaria and Hessen were concerned, fears about the separatist threat clearly transcended any disagreements between the Reich and the states in other matters. In April 1920 – almost a year after an earlier proposal to establish a Reich Centre for the Occupied Regions in Berlin had been abandoned[66] – a proposal to set up a Reich Centre in Mannheim was once again under serious discussion. This, however, differed greatly from the earlier model. It was not to be a centralised organisation staffed by Reich officials, but would be based on the existing organisations set up by Bavaria and Hessen. These would retain their independence. An outstanding political figure would be sought to take on the leadership.[67] Eberlein was evidently the driving force behind these proposals, although he undoubtedly had the tacit support of Winterstein.

At first sight it seems curious that Winterstein should apparently change his position with regard to collaboration with the Reich on propaganda and on other matters relating to the Pfalz. It can be argued, however, that Winterstein was a realist. Quite apart from the continuing fragmentation of effort with regard to propaganda, it would be both financially and politically disadvantageous in the longer term if the Reich were not involved. Costs that would then have to be met by Bavaria alone included not only those associated with propaganda and intelligence services but also the costs of welfare and support associated with any future mass expulsions. Neither could an individual state bring as much political weight to bear as a united Reich, weakened though this had been by the recent Kapp putsch. At the same time the French authorities would be quite capable of exploiting differences between the states in their policies relating to their individual Rhineland districts.

Winterstein could also feel reassured that the new Centre would be no monolith organised and run from Berlin. Eberlein had been assiduous in canvassing support for the proposals in Berlin and had received assurances that the Heimatdienst would in no way be involved. The favoured approach, so he had learnt from Theodor Lewald at the Reich Interior Ministry, would be an organisation modelled on that already in existence for the Pfalz. An approach had been made to Friedrich Profit to head the organisation. Profit had expressed, with some reservations, his willingness to do so, though not before the forthcoming Reichstag elections. In view of the perceived need for urgency, Eberlein had therefore been asked to take on the task in the interim.[68] Thus Winterstein would even have a substantial degree of control of the organisation if the proposals were agreed by the Reich government.

By June 1920 Eberlein had finalised his proposals. He was confident of enough support in Berlin to tell Winterstein that the Reich government would agree to a Centre for the occupied territories being set up in Mannheim. It would be organised along the lines favoured by him and Winterstein.[69] It would operate independently of government but would embrace all political parties and economic, cultural and sports organisations. It was to be responsible to the Reich Interior Ministry and its budget would be drawn from the relief funds of that department. Eberlein was particularly careful to draw a distinction between the duties of the Centre and those of the Reich Commissioner in Coblenz, a post that had been created in December 1919 with the agreement of the Allies, in order to provide the interface between Reich and state governments and the IRHC.[70] In Eberlein's view the agency would complement the work of the Reich Commissioner and so close a serious gap in the political work relating to the occupied regions.

A widening of the remit of the proposed Centre in comparison with the original concept of the Pfalzzentrale was now evident, for the organisation of strikes in the occupied Rhineland was now a new specific duty. At the same time Eberlein proposed to create a press department within the agency. This would operate in a manner unlike that of existing press offices in Berlin and Frankfurt. It would maintain a watch on the Allied – and especially the French – press, also on the press in both occupied and unoccupied Germany, which it would also supply with news items. It would create an archive and, based on this, would issue a fortnightly digest to German officials and politicians of news concerning implementation of Allied policy in the occupied areas and the effects of this.[71]

A perceived lack of interest among the wider population of unoccupied Germany in events in the occupied Rhineland was a permanent cause for concern for Eberlein. This he attributed largely to a lack of suitable news coverage in the German press. Eberlein believed that the situation could be rectified by his press department. Through its regular digest or newsletter relating to events in the occupied territories this department could provide a news service to small regional newspapers which could not afford to set up their own monitoring service. However, Eberlein's intentions were not confined to improving the flow of information to the public. He wanted to provide a propaganda tool which could, in a more active sense, mould public opinion.[72] His ambitions were to meet with some opposition. To understand the situation that now developed it is first necessary to outline developments that had been taking place in the Heimatdienst in the preceding months.

As noted earlier, a major part of the work of the Heimatdienst involved the maintenance of a network of trusted agents through which the Reich government was supplied with intelligence. For the occupied Rhineland this network took on particular significance because information on the activities of the French authorities and, equally, the reactions, inclinations and loyalties of the German population were of vital importance. A courier service had been developed to transfer news and information across the Rhine and to convey secret correspondence to and from local government officials, for post and telegraph services were under continuous surveillance. It was perhaps inevitable that one such courier, a trade union official and Centre Party representative in the Prussian Parliament, was eventually intercepted. In his possession was found material that the French authorities interpreted as instructions for declaring a general strike in the Saar. The French government immediately demanded the dissolution of the Heimatdienst. This demand the Reich government rejected but gave an undertaking that the Heimatdienst would henceforth cease its activities in the occupied territories. Since August 1919 these had been coordinated through its Besetzte-Gebiete-Stelle, or BG-Stelle (Office for the Occupied Regions), in Berlin. Naturally, it was both impractical and totally unacceptable to the government in Berlin to close down its links with the west bank of the Rhine. The solution adopted was therefore to withdraw the BG-Stelle from the Heimatdienst and to reconstitute it as an apparently independent private agency, giving it the name Rheinische Volkspflege.

This subterfuge was a matter of some concern to the Foreign Ministry because it felt that certain of the activities of the Volkspflege constituted a breach of the conditions of the Peace Treaty. Its fears were allayed on assurance that a seemingly private agency could readily be sacrificed should the need arise and any official connection to the Reich government vigorously denied. The operation of the Volkspflege was therefore conducted under conditions of strict secrecy. Considerable care was taken to restrict the number of channels of communication between the Volkspflege and the Heimatdienst. Thus contact with the branch offices in individual states had to be expressly agreed and authorised by the leadership of the Heimatdienst.[73]

The Volkspflege had but a small staff, led by Alfred von Wrochem. Wrochem, son of an army officer, was born on 6 June 1883 in

Neustrelitz. A grammar school education was followed by attendance at military college and subsequent commission. In 1914 he participated in the military mission to Turkey then saw active service at the Front as a major in a Berlin guards regiment.[74] Wrochem remained in charge of the Volkspflege until fundamental disagreements with his superiors over the basis on which the work should be carried out led to his replacement in June 1921.[75] Soon afterwards he published his ideas concerning the Rhineland situation,[76] a decision that led to a sharp exchange with his former superiors over the use of official material.[77] The content of the book, discussed later, provides valuable insight into the thinking within the Volkspflege up to this time and highlights the difference between Berlin and Mannheim in the approach to Rhineland propaganda.

One of the first acts of the newly constituted Volkspflege, which had inherited responsibilities not only for the Rhineland but also for occupied Silesia in the east, was to create a press agency, the East-West Political News Agency (Polwona). Each day Polwona gathered news published in the press in the occupied regions and made these press reports available to the authorities and the press in unoccupied Germany.[78] Polwona was in fact already in existence at the time that Eberlein made his proposal for a press department within the Pfalzzentrale. But whereas Polwona presented Rhineland press reports in the style of dispatches without added comment, Eberlein intended that his department should operate otherwise and so saw his proposed activity as complementing those of Polwona rather than representing a duplication.[79]

It must have been hoped within the Reich government that the transformation of the BG-Stelle into the Volkspflege would help to end the widespread criticism, already remarked on, that had been levelled at the Heimatdienst. Even Margarete Gärtner, an employee of the Heimatdienst who had been transferred to the Volkspflege, felt that it was still following a now wholly inappropriate policy that had been adopted during the last year of World War I.[80]

Neither had the cause of the Heimatdienst been helped by the widely held view among the state representatives that any organisation directed centrally from Berlin would be out of touch with the local situation in the Rhineland and must therefore inevitably fail.[81] In fact the Volkspflege was to attract as much criticism as its parent. In part this stemmed from a perceived sense of its remoteness, and partly also from intense mistrust of the Reich government by the local population.[82] Fierce criticism would come, also, from Winterstein and Eberlein. It should not be forgotten that in a wider context this was a time of increasing tension between Bavaria and the Reich. While Hoffmann, in spite of disagreements, was fundamentally supportive of the Reich, his replacement by Gustav Ritter von Kahr had led to a much more antagonistic Bavarian stance towards it.[83] This is not to suggest that worsening relations exerted a direct influence on the affairs of the Pfalzzentrale, rather that it all helped to create a climate of intolerance and mistrust. Moreover, a gulf lay between the philosophy underpinning the Volkspflege propaganda and the ideas of the Pfalzzentrale.

At the time that Eberlein was submitting his proposals for an expanded Centre in Mannheim, the Volkspflege had been in existence for a relatively short time. Eberlein could surely not have doubted that his proposed Centre might be regarded as a rival and hence would attract opposition, but this was not going to get in the way of his ambitions. At a meeting organised to canvass support among members of the Reichstag for his concept and for the creation of a parliamentary advisory group which would oversee it, he stated:

> If we are to succeed in setting up the Centre we must overcome opposition from within the Reich and Prussian governments as well as from the Reich Commissioner in Coblenz and from the political parties. The issues include the question of personnel. Basically the head person in Berlin must be somebody prominent who is trusted in the occupied regions – like, for example, Dr von Winterstein.[84]

Clearly the working relationship with Winterstein was to Eberlein's satisfaction, and if Winterstein were to take charge of an expanded organisation funded directly by the Reich, it would benefit Eberlein considerably.

In fact Eberlein received substantial support from the Reichstag parliamentarians, who endorsed his proposals for a unified Centre at Mannheim under the umbrella of the Reich Interior Ministry. Several present commented favourably on what the Mannheim Pfalzzentrale had achieved and unfavourably on the Heimatdienst.[85] However, the relationship of the new organisation to the Reich government was not to be realised quite in the form that Eberlein had perhaps envisaged. At a subsequent meeting held to discuss the new organisation, State Secretary Lewald paid tribute to the outstanding contribution that the Pfalzzentrale had made. He confirmed his support for expansion of the work and promised better coordination with the Interior Ministry. At the same time, however, he pointedly referred to the Volkspflege – now independent of the Heimatdienst – and the good progress it was making.[86] What emerged from the meeting was a proposal that the Volkspflege, acting as headquarters and located in Berlin, should effectively form the link with the Interior Ministry. The Mannheim Centre, substantially independent, should be formed from the Pfalzzentrale and the Hessen and Hessen-Nassau Centres. Presumably in anticipation of Prussian collaboration in the future, an existing Centre in Düsseldorf should also be included in the reorganisation. As was remarked years later, Lewald had always been a champion of the Volkspflege.[87]

The representatives of the states, among whom Eberlein played a prominent role, did however insist that each individual Centre should have full independence in carrying out its work. Also, there was clearly some suspicion that if the population of the occupied Rhineland became aware that the Mannheim Centre was now part of an organisation with headquarters in Berlin its operation might be adversely affected. Consequently a caveat was entered:

> Should it not be possible for the organisation of the Rheinische Volkspflege to conform to the above principles and should it not be possible to convince the authorities in the occupied regions of the importance of this work and of the need to collaborate in this, as already happens in the Pfalz and in Hessen, then the Pfalz and Hessen will refuse to collaborate within the framework of a Reich organisation.[88]

Much can be learned of Winterstein's views and intentions from a memorandum submitted by him to the Reich Interior Ministry. This made extensive use of a recent report by Lieutenant Gärtner, Eberlein's deputy, on the Rhineland situation. It painted a sombre picture of renewed French actions aimed at undermining German authority. Alleged activities included attempts to establish links to the USPD and the KPD in order to drive a wedge between the political parties of the Left, and thereby weaken the working-class movement. This would substantially reduce the chance that calls for general strikes in the Pfalz would be heeded. Other actions by the French authorities included attempts to stifle the press through penetration of the German press bureaux, censorship and the intimidation of editors. Economic espionage was widespread. And while there was increased surveillance by the French authorities and draconian punishments were being handed out for any infringement of regulations, at the same time a renewed cultural offensive was being waged on a population that had become demoralised and indifferent.[89]

Winterstein acknowledged that no differences of opinion existed between the Reich and the states over the need for a unified *Abwehr* organisation that would serve the entire Rhineland. Equally, he was in no doubt why no united and ambitious counter-propaganda programme had yet been realised. It was because the Prussian government, with wholly understandable reservations, had deliberately kept itself away from the current and planned activities of the Heimatdienst and the Volkspflege.[90]

For his part, Wrochem had been no less forthright in complaining about the lack of cooperation that he had experienced. His work had been made much more difficult because individual states worked solely for themselves and strongly resisted joint action or any sharing of funds.[91] Wrochem was hardly less critical of Reich government officials in Berlin for their failure to appreciate the importance of the cultural propaganda effort and also of the press for its indifference to the Rhineland issue.

In contrast to Eberlein, Winterstein himself appears to have been somewhat detached from the bid to create a unified Reich Centre. Helmut Gembries has commented that as a southern Catholic,

Winterstein was much less in favour of a centralised German Reich than the Protestant Eberlein.[92] Certainly Winterstein had always insisted that responsibility for, and control of, propaganda and related activities should remain with individual states. Given the apparent differences in the two approaches to achieving a unified front, the implication is that Eberlein now enjoyed considerable freedom of action in developing his ideas, even to the point of pressing for a course of action that Winterstein did not particularly favour. An alternative explanation is that Winterstein encouraged Eberlein to press for a formal incorporation within the Reich government framework, knowing that it was unlikely to be granted, but in the hope that this would enable additional financial concessions to be extracted from the Reich government by way of compensation. For it was arguably financial support that Winterstein needed beyond all else. He had earlier stressed the need for more support from the Reich for cultural propaganda and for funds to help those unjustly expelled from the Pfalz. Now he asked that between M 50,000 and M 60,000 per month be made available from the Reich, pointing out that Bavaria alone had so far spent M 8,500,000. Drawing directly on the budget of the Reich Interior Ministry, he asked that apportionment should be made through a standing committee of Reichstag representatives, though excluding members of the USPD. The new Centre should be modelled on the merger of the existing organisations set up by Bavaria for the Pfalz and by Hessen. Under a unified leadership each organisation should retain its own identity and territorial responsibilities, each establishing a network of agents in its zone, thus providing regular reports on the local situation and maintaining a courier service.[93]

During the summer of 1920 agreement was reached between the Reich Interior Ministry and the Bavarian and Hessen governments, and a unified organisation emerged, with the Volkspflege forming the link to the Reich government. By the autumn Prussia had decided to join Bavaria and Hessen.[94] Within a matter of weeks Eberlein was able to inform Winterstein that a Prussian department had been set up. He suggested that the new organisation be known as the Zentralfürsorgestelle für die besetzten Gebiete (Abteilung Bayern, Abteilung Hessen, Abteilung Preussen) (Welfare Centre for the Occupied Regions with independent sections for Bavaria, Hessen and Prussia). Eberlein did, however, point out that guidelines were needed for the smooth operation of the Centre, particularly insofar as the boundary between the work of the three states and that of the Reich was concerned.[95] Even though the three states with interests in the occupied Rhineland had taken a major step forward in cooperating on a joint organisation, the fragmentation of effort still remained.

For Winterstein the extent to which the Reich should have any responsibility for propaganda and related activities in the Rhineland, beyond providing financial support, remained a live issue in the following months. From a meeting of representatives of the three states it was reported that:

> Dr W. stated the view of Bavaria, namely that the activities of the Heimatdienst and Volkspflege have to cease. Cultural propaganda and *Abwehr* activity must be carried out by the state governments which have the relevant organisations at their disposal. The Reich should simply provide the money.[96]

The Volkspflege was as unwanted as the Heimatdienst when it came to propaganda. On the following day, at a meeting with Lewald, Wrochem and state representatives, the whole matter of coordination was again discussed, seemingly without agreement. Wrochem defended the Volkspflege and its work in cultural propaganda, praising the pioneering activities of its daughter organisation the Rheinische Frauenliga. Winterstein again pressed his views, though somewhat more emolliently than before, and suggested that the role of the Volkspflege should be confined to dealing with the press. Lewald, in exploring possible ways to resolve the impasse, was obliged to discount a new idea of setting up a special organisation to deal with matters in the west because of opposition from the Reich Commissioner in Coblenz. Winterstein was dismissive of the notion that coordination could be achieved through a new Reich Ministry for the Occupied Regions – another idea that was circulating within the Reich government.[97] The overall picture was clearly one of indecision and vacillation in the face of vested interests on all sides. Nobody was willing to give way. The authority of the Reich government was insufficient to allow it to take control.

The fact that in 1920 the situation in the Pfalz was markedly different from that of a year earlier and that the need for unified effort had never been greater was well recognised by Winterstein. He looked back, almost nostalgically, to the early months of the occupation:

> The situation in the Pfalz seemed so threatening then, yet the *Abwehr* was successful. At that time, under Gérard's brutally repressive regulations, the people were able to unite behind a defensive political front, encouraged by the workers and local officials. The circumstances with regard to Dr Dorten's movement further down the Rhine were similar. Unfortunately that satisfactory situation has now changed. The Reich and state governments must recognise that the people of the occupied regions will no longer summon up the basic will to resist French machinations and traitorous [separatist] efforts, as they did at that time of heightened national tension.[98]

But while the states themselves managed, albeit slowly, to achieve a degree of collaboration by the end of 1920, two years after the beginning of the occupation a coherent strategy for German Rhineland propaganda still did not exist. To be sure, active propaganda campaigns were being waged, but in a fragmented manner. As will be considered later, a major factor in this was the differing perception of Reich officials and of those working in the Mannheim Centre with regard to the nature of the propaganda needed. But also there was undoubtedly tension between the Reich and the states over the issue of leadership, with the Reich government unwilling to cede control. A further element in an already complex situation was the important role played by privately funded organisations and individuals.

An independent observer in 1920 expecting to find a coherent strategy for Rhineland propaganda would have had his sense of bewilderment heightened, also, when the Reich Minister of the Interior, Erich Koch, was reported by the Chamber of Commerce in Cologne as describing a national propaganda campaign in the Rhineland as completely unnecessary.[99] Koch foresaw no danger of the Rhineland population becoming estranged from the Reich; morale and spirit were increasing in spite of the treatment by the French. This was completely at variance with the view taken by Lt. Gärtner in his report to Winterstein. It also contrasts with the view of the Reich Minister Eduard David in the previous government, who, on a visit three months earlier, had concluded that the Rhineland population felt isolated.[100] We can only speculate on the reasons for this. Was Eberlein's intelligence service better than that of the Reich government? Was Gärtner deliberately overstating the situation to help build a case for expanding the Pfalzzentrale? Or, more likely, was Koch simply misreading the situation? Koch was also particularly critical of the activity of the Heimatdienst, describing it as an insult to the people.[101] A few days later orders came from Berlin for the Volkspflege to stop its work, for the Mannheim Centre to be disbanded and for a monthly contribution of M 10,000 from Reich funds for work in the occupied Rhineland to be suspended while the relationship between Reich and states was examined afresh.[102] This caused Winterstein to comment – not without an element of *Schadenfreude*: 'Regrettable though the winding up of the Rheinische Volkspflege may be, in view of the various dubious incidents that have occurred the decision has to be welcomed.'[103]

The way in which official Rhineland propaganda should be handled in future was the subject of much discussion during the autumn of 1920. The Volkspflege, which had seemingly avoided being closed down, pressed its case for a unified effort, led by an agency of the Reich government from Berlin. It argued that propaganda should be regarded as a national activity governed by national policy towards the Rhineland. This would provide a more effective counter to the nationally organised French onslaught. It would enable the Reich – the primary target for French attack – to defend itself more effectively and it would help to avoid the problems arising from Germany's internal divisions.[104]

This argument was thus much along the same lines as in the wider dispute over the future structure of the German Reich – should it be centrally unified or a federation of states? In this instance, however, direction from Berlin was never likely to be agreed in the face of Winterstein's antagonism and the way in which the states were now cooperating in the work of the Mannheim Centre. Furthermore, it was effectively an expanded Pfalzzentrale, which had received plaudits for the way in which it had set about its work. Pressing home his advantage, Winterstein demanded that the Volkspflege should henceforth be made directly responsible to the Reich Ministry of the Interior rather than indirectly to the Reich Chancellery, as had been the case hitherto.[105] This was agreed to by the Reich government and it was hoped that, together with firmer leadership of the Volkspflege, improved coordination would result.[106] The changes were effective from 1 January 1921. At the same time some thought was devoted to replacing Wrochem by Dr Sigmund Knoch, hitherto Bavarian representative at the Reich Commissioner's office in Coblenz, but Knoch was not available.[107]

The changes at the Volkspflege brought little immediate improvement in the relationship between Mannheim and Berlin, however. Winterstein continued his relentless criticism. In February 1921 his feelings about the overlap of the work of the Volkspflege with that of the Mannheim Centre surfaced again. He accused the Volkspflege of trying to force its way in, collecting intelligence from political and union organisations and issuing directives on ways to influence public opinion. In his view the Volkspflege was in danger of repeating the mistakes of its parent Heimatdienst.[108]

The record of a meeting in February 1921 shows apparent agreement in principle on the guidelines for collaboration between Reich and states, with the states taking a leading role. The details of how this should work – in the form of a properly constituted business plan – had clearly not been settled.[109] The funding of the Mannheim Centre remained a problem. In Winterstein's eyes the Volkspflege was extremely well resourced – something that did not endear it to him. Yet attempts to get the earlier financial contribution from the Volkspflege reinstated were met with a blank refusal, though the Volkspflege declared itself ready to contribute in special circumstances. Eberlein and Schneider, leader of the Hessen section, were furious. Winterstein, strongly supporting Eberlein, complained to Berlin about the manner in which the Volkspflege had behaved. He demanded reinstatement of the monthly payments – and an increase to M 15,000 – noting that the Volkspflege was content to make payments of up to M 20,000 to organisations such as trade unions, which, unlike the Mannheim Centre, were free from official responsibilities.[110]

The points at issue had still not been agreed in May 1921, for Wrochem was still making proposals for the way in which collaboration should be organised.[111] Terse exchanges between the Volkspflege and the Centre and a subsequent appeal to the Reich Ministry of the Interior to deal with the situation suggest that Eberlein and his counterpart in the Prussian section were not going out of their way to be cooperative.[112]

People in the occupied Rhineland had other things to worry about. Relations between Germany and the Allies in the early months of the year had deteriorated sharply as a result of German non-acceptance of a proposed reparations schedule. Following the breaking up of the London Conference in early March, French and Belgian troops occupied bridgeheads at Düsseldorf, Duisburg and Ruhrort, and an Allied customs barrier was introduced between the occupied Rhineland and unoccupied Germany. The impact of these measures on the economic well-being of the Pfalz was serious.[113] Mounting concern within the Rhineland over the situation reached the point at which the Reich government was obliged to grant demands from the business community for closer government attention to its problems.[114] A new section was set up within the Reich Ministry of the Interior with the State Secretary for the Occupied Regions, Dr Philipp Brugger, at its head. Brugger, born on 25 May 1864 in Wiesloch, Baden, had held posts in Leipzig and Berlin before being appointed chairman of the regional council in Cologne in 1919.[115] His task was, as he saw it, to clear up differences of opinion with the Centre, not only in operational matters but also with regard to competencies relating to work on Rhineland issues.[116] In agreeing to the appointment the states, Bavaria in particular ever suspicious of Reich intentions, took care to ensure that Brugger would not be inclined to expand Reich interests at their expense. Winterstein considered that the root of the problems that had arisen in the past lay in the centralist tendencies of the previous Reich Minister of the Interior, Dr Koch, State Secretary Theodor Lewald and the Volkspflege.[117]

The Volkspflege now lay within the jurisdiction of the new State Secretary, who proved less tolerant and accommodating than his predecessor, Theodor Lewald. Margarete Gärtner, leading the Rheinische Frauenliga, viewed him without much favour: 'A retired State Secretary, Dr B, was allocated to us. He wasn't exactly well disposed towards our work, which of necessity had to disregard official regulations of the conventional sort.'[118] It comes as no surprise that Wrochem, who had been in charge of the Volkspflege until now, did not remain in post for long. He resigned at this point because he felt that he was no longer being allowed to lead the Volkspflege in accordance with his personal ideas and principles.[119]

Mid-1921 can be said to have marked the end of the initial phase in the existence of the Pfalzzentrale. During this time it had expanded from a hastily formed Bavarian outpost into the Mannheim Centre, a fully fledged cooperative venture with Prussia and Hessen in which Bavaria was *primus inter pares*. A schematic (fig. 5) shows its relationship to Reich and state governments. As Winterstein and Eberlein viewed the situation, it would be the states rather than the Reich that would henceforth lead government propaganda efforts in the Rhineland. This had, however, been a period marked by considerable enmity between the Pfalzzentrale and the principal propaganda arm of the Reich government, mirroring the wider split between Bavaria and the Reich – this at a time of intense propaganda activity when the need for unity was paramount.

The problem that existed in 1921 was highlighted at the time by the influential political journalist Edgar Stern-Rubarth,[120] who will

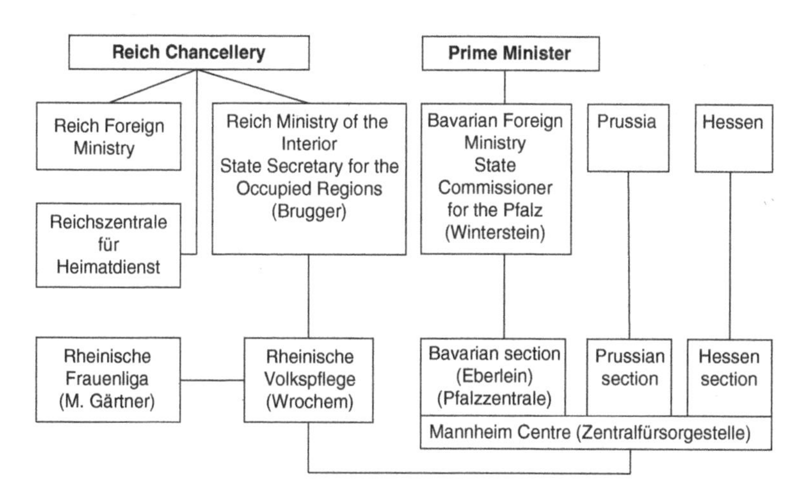

Figure 5. Relationship of the Mannheim Centre (incorporating the Pfalzzentrale) to Reich and state governments in August 1921

be introduced later as one of a group of progressive contributors to the shaping of post-war Reich propaganda. According to Stern-Rubarth:

> The thing that helped enemy propaganda to succeed in the war is totally lacking in our propaganda today: unified leadership... Today all those different hearts and minds are propagating their own ideas in so far as they have the financial means available. It is clear to anybody who has seen the street placards and walls of houses in German cities during the last two and a half years that not only does this lead to unwanted consequences, it frequently provokes reactions that set the desired goal still further back and it wastes uncounted millions. We are not waging a strategic war: it is a gang war over public opinion.

For Stern-Rubarth the solution was quite evident:

> Our weapons should be forged along the following lines:
>
> The complete standardisation of all propaganda efforts under a single directorate.
>
> Closure of all official and semi-official branches and any supported private undertakings.
>
> The establishment of a close and lasting accord with the political goals of the Reich leadership. The focus should be on foreign countries but not forgetting that it is at home where it is determined whether or not the organisation of propaganda has complete independence from the official channels of middle and lower authorities.
>
> Understanding of the importance of bringing enough resources to bear in a war that requires only a fraction of the cost of the weapons of the past. When all is said and done, this promotes thoughts of reconciliation and finally repays the cost a hundredfold in terms of peaceful endeavour.[121]

In mid-1921 the omens for Stern-Rubarth's vision of a unified propaganda effort led by the Reich were not propitious, however. While some improvements in coordination between the Reich and the states were to result from the changes described above, other factors were already beginning to assume importance that would have considerable influence on the future activities of the Pfalzzentrale. Not the least of these was the impact that the vilification of France in German propaganda – coming partly from the Pfalzzentrale and partly from private organisations – was having on Reich interests in the international sphere. Both this and an independent and aggressive Bavarian government policy were to determine the future course of the Pfalzzentrale. Before following these developments in Chapter 6, however, the nature of the most prominent and notorious propaganda theme – that of the Schwarze Schmach – is examined. The major contributors to propaganda are then identified. In this way an overall picture is built up against which the work of the Pfalzzentrale can be compared.

3

THE ORIGINS OF THE SCHWARZE SCHMACH CAMPAIGN

Of all the propaganda that was generated in the years following the end of World War I none aroused more widespread passion than that directed against the so-called Schwarze Schmach. This was the name given to the French policy of including non-white units in her armies occupying the Rhineland. The troops were drawn from a number of ethnic groups in the French colonies. Colonial troops had been used freely by the Allied armies during the conflict in Europe and black Americans had participated in the fighting at the Front, but these had been withdrawn soon after the end of hostilities.

The presence of non-white French colonial troops in the Rhineland generated fiercely expressed resentment in Germany. Initially this was an issue that was largely confined to the press, but by the spring of 1920 several organisations and individuals dedicated to this purpose were at the forefront in whipping up support at protest meetings across Germany. Propaganda was produced in a variety of leaflets, booklets, newspaper articles and even novels. The campaign very quickly spread abroad, targeting not only Allied countries but also neutral countries like Sweden and Norway and countries where an expatriate German population existed, such as former colonies and Argentina. The chairman of the IRHC, Paul Tirard, was convinced that this was a coordinated activity directed from Berlin and this is the impression left by

Figure 6. 'Black troops in a Rhineland town'

several studies made in recent years. In this chapter it is intended to outline the origins and background to the Schwarze Schmach campaign before examining in the following two chapters the contributions made by various organisations and individuals.

The use by France of non-European troops in her armies in World War I was not a new policy. Complaints had been made about the use of Algerian troops in a European theatre of war by the German Chancellor Otto von Bismarck at the time of the Franco-Prussian War of 1870–1.[1] But it was not until the first decade of the twentieth century that renewed international tension, coupled with unfavourable demography in comparison with Germany, led France to consider the creation of a major African force that would contribute to the defence of the nation. The champion of this proposal was Charles Mangin, who was later to command the French army of occupation in the Prussian Rhine Province. The proposal was politically controversial both at home and in the colonies and was met with outrage from some sections of the German press.[2] The strength of the opposition effectively killed off the idea until the outbreak of war in 1914, when necessity prevailed and the first colonial units were introduced to the Front. The number of colonial troops participating in the fighting never exceeded 1.6 per cent of the French army[3] but their use provided Germany with a good source of propaganda.

Non-white troops also formed a relatively small proportion of the French armies of occupation, which initially numbered about 250,000 men. It is not possible to ascertain the exact number of non-white troops, which in any case fluctuated over short periods of time. Senegalese troops, for example, were withdrawn from the Rhineland during the winter months and stationed in southern France because they had difficulty in coping with the northern winter climate. Christian Koller[4] has listed differing estimates of numbers of colonial troops made in recent years by various authors, and has noted that estimates vary regardless of whether French or German sources have been used. The highest estimate based on official German sources put numbers at 42,000 in spring 1920 and at 45,000 a year later.[5] Another estimate lay between 30,000 and 40,000,[6] while estimates based on French sources were generally a few thousand lower. The official German estimate of total colonial troop strength in the Pfalz in 1923 was 27,126. By 1925 this had been halved.[7]

General Henry T. Allen, commander of US forces in Germany, and later US observer on the IRHC, reported that between January 1919 and June 1920 the number of black troops was 5,200 and the number of coloured troops was 20,000.[8] Black troops were generally of Senegalese origin, coloured troop units originated from Morocco, Tunisia, Algeria, Madagascar or Indo-China. On the whole German propaganda made little distinction between the various ethnic backgrounds, and tended to portray all colonial troops as black-skinned and of negroid origin, though in fact the last of the troops who were truly black were withdrawn in June 1921. The number of coloured troops stationed in the Rhineland thereafter generally declined. North African regiments were withdrawn in 1925 and by 1928, two years before the final withdrawal of the French army, barely more than 1,000 coloured troops remained.

In the Pfalz there were major French garrisons in Landau, Kaiserslautern, Germersheim, Ludwigshafen, Speyer, Neustadt

Figure 7. 'Soldiers of the 1st Moroccan-Madagascan Infantry Regiment outside their quarters in Ludwigshafen in 1921'

and Zweibrücken in addition to smaller troop numbers elsewhere.[9] Both black and coloured troops were present in the Pfalz. Senegalese were employed for a time in Ludwigshafen, for example, while some Malagasies were garrisoned in Speyer and Moroccans were garrisoned in Zweibrücken and Kaiserslautern. The concentration of large troop numbers – regardless of colour – in relatively small towns brought severe accommodation problems and led to extensive requisitioning of private property, thus intensifying the pre-existing housing shortage. In Landau, which had a population of 15,000, accommodation had to be found for 8,000 troops. The proportions were similar in Neustadt, where 300 private houses were taken over.[10] This imposition was only one of the problems faced by the local population as a consequence of the occupation. It was exploited in German propaganda but the message was rather obscured by the furore over the presence of non-white troops.

The deployment of coloured troops in the French armies of occupation was perceived by Germany as a deliberate act carried out in order to humiliate the vanquished nation. If indeed this were the case, it would seem to have been a risky strategy to pursue in view of the efforts that were being made simultaneously to woo the Rhineland population away from the Reich. Other possible reasons have been put forward. These have included practical necessity,[11] the need for early demobilisation of white troops in order to rebuild the shattered economic infrastructure in northern France,[12] and the need to reward the colonial troops for their endeavours during the fighting at the Front.[13] New light has been shed on the matter, however, by the more recent study by Le Naour, based on French archive material.[14] A deliberate decision to employ coloured troops was made at the time of the Armistice by a French government committee comprising the President of the Council, the Minister for the Colonies, General Mangin and Blaise Diagne. Diagne was the first black parliamentary deputy in the history of France and had been elected to the Chamber of Deputies in 1914 to represent Senegal. He had been a strong supporter of the Mangin concept of the black African army and had personally encouraged recruitment during World War I, seeing in it a means of advancing the cause of political and social equality for black people. At the time of the Armistice he pressed for the sending of two Senegalese regiments to the Rhineland. In his view this would establish the principle of using black soldiers – and the right of France to employ them whenever and wherever she pleased. Moreover, it would popularise the victory of France in the eyes of the Senegalese public. But in contrast to Mangin, who apparently wished to see a more substantial black and coloured presence on the Rhine, Diagne called for a limited presence, arguing that sending a greater number of black troops would be a political error of judgement. It might therefore be said that the decision to employ black and coloured troops in the Rhineland was based as much on France's colonial policy as on her policy towards Germany.[15] However, it has also been argued that even after armed hostilities ended there existed on the French side – and no less on the German side, as we shall see – a collective state of mind in which the war did not end with the signing of the Armistice.[16] At the very least there must have been a subconscious desire on the part of the French authorities to make it plain to the Germans that France was the victorious nation and they the vanquished – even if this was not the primary reason for using colonial troops in the occupation.

Whatever the underlying reasons, they gave rise to a German propaganda campaign that, though undoubtedly reaching its peak in 1920–1, was to endure with varying intensity almost until the end of the occupation in 1930. An analysis of articles published in five major newspapers in Germany[17] has shown that while the main peak occurred in June 1920, press activity was also heightened in January, April and July 1921; the topic was then largely quiescent until February 1923. Almost certainly this activity was stimulated by the Reich press office. The propaganda discussed in this book is not easily analysed because it took a variety of forms and came from a number of widely different

Figure 8. 'Die schwarze Schmach'

sources. By looking at the manner in which these operated, however, it should be possible to assess the extent to which the campaign as a whole could be considered to be coordinated.

The precise origins of the Schwarze Schmach campaign are uncertain. Otto Hartwich, founder of the Volksbund 'Rettet die Ehre' (People's Alliance – 'Save Our Honour'), claimed to have coined the phrase Schwarze Schmach.[18] Certainly Hartwich was amongst the earliest participants in the campaign and the term was in common use by the end of April 1920.[19] Hartwich's contribution is discussed later.

That colonial troops might be stationed on German soil had not been entirely unexpected. Concerns about this possibility had been raised within the Reich government as the war drew to a close, and representations had been made to the Allies during November 1918 requesting that the use of colonial troops should be avoided.[20] German wartime propaganda had depicted black and coloured colonial troops as wild animals capable of committing the most appalling atrocities.[21] It is therefore unsurprising that close attention was paid to the behaviour of coloured troops from the very beginning of the occupation. The first reference to excesses concerned a rape allegedly committed on 26 November 1918 by a black Malagasy soldier in Niedergailbach.[22] On 3 December a sharp protest was made by the German government, conveyed through the Swiss government, against the stationing of coloured troops in the Rhineland:

> The transfer of coloured troops onto German soil shows contempt for the feelings of the white community; feelings that ought to be shared by our adversaries also, especially since they have declared their intention to set up a League of Nations after the end of the war.[23]

During this initial period of occupation there were allegedly many instances of acts of violence committed by Allied troops on the local population in all zones and these were the subject of German protest. The ethnic origin of the offending troops – who included coloured soldiers – was apparently not an issue, however.[24] Neither was the ethnic origin of occupation troops mentioned at Reich Cabinet meetings, though the rough behaviour of enemy troops was noted.[25] The occupation was discussed in Cabinet in March 1919, shortly before the peace negotiations took place. Reich Minister Matthias Erzberger stressed that the total evacuation of the occupied regions by the Allies ought to be a prerequisite for negotiating the Peace Treaty.[26] The Cabinet, however, was far from sure that this strategy would be successful, for at the suggestion of the Prussian War Minister, Walther Reinhardt, it was decided that the German negotiators should at least try to secure the withdrawal of coloured troops. Accordingly, the guidelines for the negotiators stated:

> Immediate evacuation of the occupied territories on the signing of the Peace Agreement to be demanded, if need be with the offer of alternative guarantees for our payment obligations. Should the occupation continue, the strength of the army of occupation and the limits of its authority to be laid down exactly... Exclusion of coloured troops from the army of occupation.[27]

At the earlier Cabinet meeting on 21 March Reinhardt had commented: 'Rejection of coloured occupation troops valuable. Black too limited, because according to French terminology Moroccans and Turks not black. Implementation of practical importance because coloureds are immune to Bolshevism.' However, he was pessimistic about achieving a withdrawal, later remarking: 'Unfortunately very doubtful whether withdrawal of coloured troops can be achieved because the Americans have acted similarly to the others.'[28]

At this time the Reich government obviously wanted the colonial troops withdrawn, but to say that this was solely from a sense of outrage or that it was due to excesses by the troops is not the full story. Reinhardt's remarks point to an early but unsuccessful attempt to undermine the occupation by spreading subversive propaganda among Allied troops – the fact of which the Reich Cabinet was aware. That an attempt did take place is evident both in the concerns of the British Foreign Office – 'Plans are being made for active propaganda (Bolshevik) in the British Army on the Rhine'[29] – and in the fact that German agents were caught doing this.[30] It is likely that this was part of a wider attempt to spread Bolshevism throughout Allied countries, this in spite of German fears of Bolshevism spreading within Germany. There was some doubt on the British side about who was responsible. Considerable mutual suspicion was thought to exist between the Reich Ministry of the Interior and the Foreign Ministry over the matter: 'I gather that the Berlin Home Office is seriously alarmed at the Bolshevik propaganda in Germany and elsewhere, but that it does not cooperate with the Berlin Foreign Office whom it suspects of coquetting with Bolshevism abroad.'[31] The conclusion in London was that the attempt was '...difficult to link to the German Government (Elements of the old regime trying to foment trouble and continuing work that they were doing prior to the Armistice)'.[32] The Allies were clearly dealing with a weak and divided government.

Le Naour, also, has pointed to attempts by the Heimatdienst to distribute among the occupying troops a brochure based on the writings of the French socialist and pacifist Jean Jaurès. The attempt had failed because the colonial troops were largely illiterate, and would not in any case have been able to relate to the political culture and philosophy of the industrialised countries of Europe.[33] Two aspects of this merit further comment. If the facts are correct, then this appears to have been a fairly clumsy effort on the part of the Heimatdienst and may help to account for the low esteem in which it was held by some in the Reich government. More particularly it may help to explain why Winterstein and Eberlein were adamantly opposed to the Heimatdienst undertaking propaganda activities in the Pfalz.

It might be reflected that the deliberate spreading of Bolshevist propaganda, even amongst occupation troops, must surely have carried considerable risk at a time when Bolshevism was widely regarded in Europe as a great threat.[34] At stake in Germany were not only economic and social stability but also German unity.[35] The medical metaphor that came into vogue at the time was one of infection or contagion by the disease of Bolshevism.[36] It was obviously necessary to devise suitable countermeasures or immunisation to fight the infection. Thus discussions had begun in Germany with a view to creating a citizens' militia (*Einwohnerwehr*), ostensibly for the purpose of maintaining civil order and stability.[37] This did not, however, preclude the use of Bolshevism as a weapon. With the Rhineland occupation a major source of concern and anger to the German government, what could be more natural than to use Bolshevism to destabilise France? Again, this is consistent with a mental attitude in which a state of war between the two countries continued to exist.

After the signing of the Peace Treaty, which confirmed the long-term occupation of the Rhineland, discussion of conditions in the occupied territories appeared from time to time on the agenda of Reich Cabinet meetings. In October 1919 the situation was described as unbearable in terms of the excesses that were taking place, but the main source of concern, rather than the presence of coloured troops, was the allegedly ruthless manner in which the billeting of occupation troops was being foisted on the local population.[38] When it came to firm evidence of acts of violence committed against people or their property, however, the Reich Ministry of the Interior had to admit that this was difficult to collect, and that the evidence available was meagre.[39] In fact it was another two years before an official memorandum, *Ausschreitungen der Besatzungstruppen im besetzten rheinischen Gebiete*, was laid before the Reichstag detailing 300 cases of acts of violence, including 65 murders, 65 cases of maltreatment and 170 sexual offences.[40] Thereafter relatively little can be found in Cabinet papers about coloured troops or their behaviour, and when the Reich Minister reported on his fact-finding tour of the occupied Rhineland in August 1920 the issue was not even mentioned.[41]

Sally Marks has indicated that the presence of colonial troops was not a major issue in the Rhineland itself. The attitude and behaviour of the troops were reportedly very good, better indeed than in the case of white French troops.[42] While some caution is needed in accepting local reports, in view of the way in which the French authorities exercised control of the press, there is no doubt that the case against the colonial troops was trumped up. Indeed in some instances they became remarkably popular with the local people, a fact that German propagandists studiously ignored.[43] One point needs to be borne in mind, however. Good relationships between occupiers and occupied developed only after a period of time. It is made clear in the following

Figure 9. 'The Horror on the Rhine'

chapter that at first there existed considerable female apprehension over the presence of coloured troops. Although there were other causes of the vicious propaganda campaign, fear played its part in fixing the ideas of some female propagandists at the outset.

The fact that no serious and concerted campaign was mounted directly against the use of coloured troops until late 1919 or early 1920 should not be a matter for surprise. In the first half of 1919 – quite aside from preoccupations with the forthcoming Peace Treaty negotiations and with the stability of the Reich itself – the main threat to the Pfalz lay in the perceived intentions of France to annex territory west of the Rhine if at all possible, or at least to encourage the separatist movement to achieve its goal of forming an independent state. As noted in the previous chapter, this was the primary reason for setting up the Pfalzzentrale. At that time the use by the French of coloured troops was a matter of complete insignificance by comparison with the separatist threat. It seems reasonable to assume, therefore, that it was only later, when the immediate threat of direct annexation, or secession, had receded somewhat and the terms of the Peace Treaty had mapped out the conditions under which national life would have to be carried on, that attention turned to the nature of the occupation itself and in particular to the behaviour of occupation troops.

Paul Tirard, chairman of the IRHC, made the observation that the campaign against coloured troops began in November 1919. Until that point there had been only a few isolated protests which were quickly shown to be without foundation.[44] This accords fairly closely, though not exactly, with an official Bavarian chronicle of events, in which several offences committed by coloured troops were reported during the first three months of 1919, but none thereafter until the late summer. It was recorded that the French authorities in the Pfalz introduced a ban on the use of the words 'negro' and 'black' on 15 October 1919, while on 8 November newspapers in the Pfalz were forced to print an article about the harmlessness of black troops.[45] Coloured troops had clearly become an issue in the press at that time. In the beginning, however, it seems to have arisen as much because the troops were at times given a supervisory role over the white population as through any sexual misdemeanours. The *Frankfurter Zeitung* reported that:

> It is known that the use of coloured troops by the French for the purposes of occupation, first in the Saarland and the Pfalz and then in occupied Hessen, has given rise to angry complaints. These resulted mainly from the feeling that the white race was being placed under the supervision of the blacks. Racial instincts that are otherwise foreign to us Germans then began to develop. On top of this came numerous acts of violence, which were often

the subject of reports in newspapers on the right bank of the Rhine.[46]

The press campaign had almost certainly received some stimulus from the press office in the Reich Chancellery, for it was recorded that:

> The petition was submitted to the Reich President, who on 21 October asked the Reich Chancellery to verify the details concerning the unpredictable actions of the occupation troops so that they could be published in more detail in the press. Public criticism of that sort could have an improving influence and, 'if it is made abroad, will be effective against the occupation itself'.[47]

Protests in the Reichstag followed in January 1920, but it was not until April 1920 that a widespread campaign began throughout the German press. It was believed by the French authorities that this was deliberately orchestrated. Although protest subsequently diminished after the Spa Conference, it resumed with renewed vigour immediately before important international conferences with a view to creating discord among the Allies. Tirard acknowledged the extent and purpose of the campaign:

> The scenario, set up with great care and with the luxury of extensive publicity, rapidly extended beyond national boundaries, playing simultaneously on all the principal stages where world opinion is formed. Propaganda tracts were published, illustrated with scandalous images. These have been translated into every language and spread worldwide.[48]

Tirard did, however, fail to mention that the first upsurge of protest was almost certainly triggered by the French army marching into Frankfurt on 6 April. This had followed German intervention in the demilitarised Ruhr in order to suppress the Communist uprising that had itself been triggered by the Kapp putsch. In the course of the occupation of Frankfurt nervous colonial soldiers fired into a crowd, killing and wounding a number of civilians, and thereby provoking uproar in the German press. Almost simultaneously a press campaign began in Sweden and the USA.

It was a measure of the effectiveness of these initial campaigns that Tirard felt that he could not remain silent, because silence might be misinterpreted in neutral countries. Accordingly, he proposed to the IRHC that an inquiry be set up to investigate the allegations that had been made against non-white troops.[49] Chaired by General Allen, the US observer on the IRHC, the inquiry found that many gross exaggerations had been spread concerning their behaviour. Moreover, many allegations were so imprecise in terms of date, location and exact circumstances that they could be neither verified nor refuted. In the few proven cases severe punishment had followed.[50] Tirard believed that he had been vindicated. However, extracts from a further report by Allen to the US government were released to the US press and inevitably found their way into European newspapers. These were disparaged by the press in unoccupied Germany, which cast doubt on the accuracy of Allen's information and accused him of being 'unduly influenced by French propaganda and by his own Francophile feelings'.[51]

The British Foreign Office did not doubt that German allegations of excesses had been made quite deliberately. The purpose was to create antipathy towards France in other countries, especially in the USA, where 'the black question' was always capable of arousing passions.[52] Indeed, the campaign struck a sympathetic chord in some circles in the USA, where the government was bombarded with protest letters and congressional resolutions were made asking the President to make representations to France. The campaign reached its peak in February 1921, when a mass rally took place in New York.[53] In the end, however, all the heat was of little avail in spite of a resurgence of protest the following year. The US government was unmoved.[54] In Britain there had always been disapproval in some quarters of the use of colonial troops in the fighting in Europe.[55] There were now serious reservations – shared even by some in France[56] – about the wisdom of using non-white troops in an occupation force.[57] The British government, while having a degree of sympathy for the Germans over their situation, took the view that this was solely a matter for the French government. Reconciliation between France and Germany over the Rhineland would never occur, however, while coloured troops remained.[58]

On the German side the initial impact of the foreign press campaign was noted with some satisfaction. A report from the Pfalzzentrale concluded that the French government was finding Pfalzzentrale propaganda extremely uncomfortable, especially that in the Swedish and US press. The French occupation authorities intended to try to coerce newspapers into admission that they had not verified the allegations made of excesses committed by black troops. In this way they would be able to dismiss the subsequent reports of these in the foreign press as a pack of lies.[59]

In the early summer of 1920 the nascent campaign against the Schwarze Schmach had two aims. First, as Knoch and Eberlein on the German side – and Tirard on the French side – had quickly realised, considerable damage could be done to the French position by skilful propaganda in Allied countries, especially the USA, and in neutral countries. In this way a wedge might be driven between France and her partners. Second, the intention was to raise public awareness and support in unoccupied Germany. By whipping up public anger, pressure could also be exerted on the Reich government. It will be recalled that in the previous year the feeling had been widespread that the Reich government, lacking understanding, was supine in the face of the problems of the occupied Rhineland. To what extent, therefore, was it now being pressured by Bavaria to take a more active stance against France?

The situation in Bavaria differed significantly from that prevailing the previous summer. In place of Hoffmann's steadily weakening government led by the SPD, the right-wing government of Gustav Ritter von Kahr – which was to move steadily further right – had gained power in March 1920. Almost simultaneously demands were received from the Allies that the citizens militia should be disbanded on the grounds that it contravened the provisions of the Peace Treaty. Kahr effectively took upon himself the role of champion of the movement in the face of repeated requests from the Reich government for its disbandment in Bavaria. Relations between Bavaria and the

Reich deteriorated rapidly during the second half of 1920, being completely dominated by the dispute.[60] It is hardly surprising, then, that there seems to be little evidence of matters relating to the occupation receiving much priority. Yet this was the time at which the unified Mannheim Centre, incorporating the Pfalzzentrale, was set up under the aegis of the Rheinische Volkspflege. Collaboration with the Reich was therefore taking place regardless of the impasse over the citizens militia. It was being driven forward by officials at the level of Winterstein and activists like Eberlein, even though both were generally dissatisfied with the way in which Reich agencies such as the Volkspflege and Heimatdienst operated. In fact their dissatisfaction extended well beyond this. Winterstein commented: 'I hope that from now on the Reich Ministry of the Interior will act rather more quickly and effectively.'[61]

In expanding the Mannheim Centre Winterstein, Eberlein and representatives from the other states were therefore trying to develop an authoritative organisation able to stand up to the Reich Ministry of the Interior and able to compel Reich officials to participate more energetically in the general campaign against the occupation. The Reich Commissioner, responsible for representing German interests to the IRHC but seemingly indifferent to some on the German side, was not exempt from this.[62] The frustration felt by Winterstein and Eberlein may well have provided part of the motivation for the Pfalzzentrale to participate actively in the campaign against the Schwarze Schmach.

Based on the absence from the archives of the Allied Powers of any evidence of official German requests for the withdrawal of coloured troops, it has been suggested that the Reich government in the early years actually preferred that these troops should remain. The Reich could thereby retain a propaganda advantage.[63] Whether such a conclusion is justified is doubtful. Concerns were raised about the possibility of France using colonial troops before the occupation began and German records show that at least one protest was lodged with the French government by the German ambassador in Paris in August 1921.[64] Protests were also made repeatedly to the IRHC by the Reich Commissioner[65] and at local level by the new chairman of the regional council in the Pfalz, Friedrich von Chlingensperg.[66] Furthermore, the feeling against coloured troops amongst many members of the political classes in Germany was so strong that the Reich government could not afford to refrain from protest. In May 1920 anger was expressed over the matter in the National Assembly by all political parties with the exception of the USPD. Reich Minister Adolf Köster, while refusing to associate the Reich government with any campaign of racial hatred, nevertheless denounced the stationing of coloured troops in the Rhineland: 'The stationing of Africans in the Rhineland is "nothing less than a crime". One would rather accept the allegedly worse discipline of white French troops if only Germany were freed from the "black plague".'[67] Even the Reich President, Friedrich Ebert, felt the many letters of protest he had received to be completely justified.[68]

Admittedly, following the reluctant signing of the Peace Treaty there was every intention, in the Reich Ministry of the Interior in particular, to use the presence of coloured troops as an effective propaganda tool against the occupation itself. This was hardly realistic, however. The occupation had been instituted under the terms of the Peace Treaty to guarantee the payment of reparations and was an issue of strategic economic importance. It should have been clear that the French position was hardly likely to be undermined by what was essentially a side issue.

It is argued that the situation was essentially one of sullen resignation by the Reich government to the presence of coloured troops, albeit one in which no opportunity would be lost to exploit the potential for propaganda. At the same time, the problem with making official protests at the highest governmental level was the lack of verifiable evidence of misbehaviour by coloured troops.[69] The French government would not be swayed by objections based solely on racial grounds. Indeed it always maintained that its colonial troops were well behaved,[70] and on the whole this was confirmed by its British and US allies.[71] For protest to be effective verifiable evidence of excesses on a large scale would be demanded, rather than simply isolated occurrences. The difficulties of finding such evidence have already been noted, and even when officially approved evidence was submitted by the Reich Commissioner it was met by severe criticism from the IRHC on the grounds of its lack of veracity.[72] Lack of evidence in fact persisted until mid-1920, when the first brochures claiming to be based on authentic official data were published.[73] At this time, after eighteen months of occupation, 61 cases of alleged sexual assault or attempted assault had been identified. That assaults took place was nowhere in doubt but as far as the Allies were concerned the numbers were quite unexceptional.[74] In the face of Allied scepticism it was probably felt by Reich and state governments that propaganda represented the only way forward. At the start of the campaign it would have seemed that there was, after all, little to be lost by supporting the use of propaganda. The sympathetic response initially evoked in some quarters in the USA would have provided encouragement. The Reich press office had stimulated the short-lived press campaign in autumn 1919. Propaganda activity quickly mushroomed again in April 1920, feeding on the flurry of press agitation over the incident in Frankfurt. Apart from the Reich press office it has not been conclusively established which organisations were involved at this point, but the campaign as a whole quickly assumed the form of an uncontrolled bandwagon. It attracted a number of organisations and individuals, the nature of whose contributions and motivation are examined in the following chapters.

The campaign against the Schwarze Schmach embraced a number of propaganda themes, including the alleged sexual misbehaviour of coloured troops and consequent dangers to health, racial purity and the dominant position of white European civilisation in relation to other races. Underlying all of these themes in the propaganda was the image of the white woman cast as the helpless victim. The female perspective thus became a dominant force in the campaign and it now merits discussion in its own right.

4

WOMEN IN RHINELAND PROPAGANDA: EXPLOITERS OR THE EXPLOITED?

The creation of the Weimar Republic in 1919 was accompanied by profound change in the status of women in society. Newly enfranchised, women were now in a more favourable position than ever before to make a contribution in public life. It is not surprising that they – no less than their male counterparts – were to play their part in the widespread protests that accompanied the signing of the Peace Treaty. It was to the campaign against the Schwarze Schmach, however, that they were to make a particularly noteworthy contribution. At this time of female emancipation, every effort would be made to portray Rhineland women as defenceless victims of French rapacity. But was this really the case – or were women simply the subject of exploitation by women for the wider political purpose? In examining this notion in this chapter I lay emphasis on the contributions that were made by leading activists and on their motivation.

It was noted earlier that the Volkspflege, set up largely in order to sustain the German cultural roots of the Rhineland, suffered from similar criticism to that levelled at its parent organisation, the Heimatdienst. It, too, was seen to be bureaucratic, remote and detached from the reality of everyday life under occupation.[1] From this much criticised organisation, however, was to emerge the Rheinische Frauenliga, essentially just a small coordinating secretariat, but one that would mobilise female public opinion through a wide-ranging network of independent women's organisations in Germany and affiliated groups in other countries. The Frauenliga had its origins in the protests and propaganda campaign against the Schwarze Schmach, but the intention was also to use the network to campaign on other issues of concern to women.[2]

Like the Pfalzzentrale, the Frauenliga was led by somebody with ambition, self-confidence and a forceful personality. Margarete Gärtner, a junior colleague of Alfred von Wrochem, was to prove the more significant figure of the two. Born into a middle-class family in Schweidnitz, Silesia on 22 January 1888, Gärtner had spent her childhood in Berlin. Obliged to leave school early following the death of her father, she had spent a year in a commercial college before taking a succession of secretarial posts assisting Reich government officials.[3] It was at this time that she worked for a number of influential people, for example Dr Ernst Jäckh, who after World War I became an adviser to Reich President Ebert and who in 1920 founded the Deutsche Liga für den Völkerbund (German Association for the League of Nations).[4] Gärtner was also acquainted with Professor Paul Rühlmann. Rühlmann, born in Dehnitz-bei-Wurzen in Saxony on 4 November 1875, studied at the University of Leipzig and later achieved prominence as an educationalist and political scientist. During the war he saw service on the Western Front. He was also employed by the Central Office for Services Abroad, which was attached to the Foreign Ministry, to assist in making Germany's case abroad.[5] Later, he was an adviser to the Volkspflege. Rühlmann was among the first to argue for the rehabilitation of the concept of propaganda after the war, stressing the vital importance for Germany to represent itself abroad through appropriate modern cultural propaganda.[6]

At the outbreak of World War I Gärtner had moved to the Reich Naval Office where she was closely involved with the collection of press reports and the production and dissemination of propaganda leaflets. Eventually these activities were taken over by the Foreign Ministry, and the section became the Central Office for Services Abroad. At the time of the Armistice, Gärtner – as she later recollected[7] – recognised the need in the civil population for enlightenment rather than indoctrination. Having suggested the creation of a special department dedicated to this, she was encouraged to outline her ideas in a memorandum to the Centre Party politician Matthias Erzberger, who had some influence in the Reich press office. Nothing came of this proposal, however, and instead Gärtner found herself providing logistic support for the German delegation at the Spa Conference. Once this was over, tiring of routine work in the Central Office, she began to look elsewhere. In November 1919 she was invited to join the Heimatdienst in its newly founded Office for the Occupied Regions, soon to be given a more independent existence as the Rheinische Volkspflege.

Gärtner had only been working there for a few months when the office was visited by a member of the Neven du Mont family, which owned the *Kölnische Zeitung*. Neven du Mont suggested that a variety of women's organisations in the occupied regions might be enlisted in a propaganda campaign against the use of coloured troops in the Rhineland. In Gärtner's words: 'We thought this to be an excellent idea.'[8] The Reich Ministry of the Interior quickly agreed to the creation of the Rheinische Frauenliga though it was made clear that it was not to become an organisation in its own right, but was simply to be a mouthpiece for the women's movement. It should have an existence limited to the duration of the campaign.[9] There is no evidence to suggest that up to that point the Volkspflege had been in any way active in the Schwarze Schmach campaign, or indeed in any propaganda intended to influence opinion outside Germany, and so this marked a change in policy.

Gärtner immediately set about enlisting support. The response from a wide variety of women's groups was excellent and she even received the blessing of the Archbishop of Cologne.[10] Only Der Vaterländische Frauenverein (National Women's Association), forerunner of the women's section within the German Red Cross, declined to participate on the grounds that the Association was apolitical.[11] Within a few months the Frauenliga comprised forty groups. Strong support was given by Catholic, Protestant and Jewish associations, as well as those representing housewives, academics, politically active employees and professionals (see Appendix I).[12]

An initial conference, attended by leading members of the women's organisations, was held in Frankfurt on 23–24 June 1920.[13] On the agenda were the Schwarze Schmach campaign and the housing and food situation in the occupied regions. At this meeting Gärtner was chosen to lead the Frauenliga. A second conference was held in Düsseldorf on 10 August which, in addition to the Schwarze Schmach and the housing situation, highlighted the protection of German culture in the occupied areas as being a major task for the Frauenliga. The Pfalz and the Saarland were considered to be particularly vulnerable to French influence. A further concern was to improve the supply of accurate news to the press in unoccupied Germany, notwithstanding the difficulties involved in doing so. Complaints could be heard from the press that the material passed on frequently contained exaggerations. However, the press itself, especially the Berlin-based newspapers, also came in for heavy criticism for taking insufficient interest in events in the occupied Rhineland.[14]

It seems, however, that the question of the leadership and organisation of the Frauenliga had been far from settled at the first conference, for the matter was again raised at the second meeting. A small subcommittee of five, comprising members of the Katholischer Frauenbund Deutschlands (Catholic Women's Association of Germany, or the KFD),[15] Deutsche Evangelische Bahnhofsmission (German Protestant Railway Mission), two members of the Bund Deutscher Frauenvereine (Association of German Women's Organisations, or the BDF) and Gärtner herself, was appointed to consider the issue. After lengthy discussion Gärtner was finally confirmed as *Geschäftsführerin*, or leader. There was to be no formal board of management because individual associations would not be directly involved in the actual work of the Frauenliga. Broad guidelines for the work would be determined at a series of informal conferences, the total costs of which would be met by the Volkspflege. A proposal by Gärtner to appoint a small advisory group comprising female members of the Reichstag was rejected, however. It was determined that decisions on particular issues should require the agreement not only of the subcommittee but also of representatives of all other groups affiliated to the Frauenliga. In the event this arrangement must have been found to be unworkable, for later on an advisory committee of six women was decided upon. This comprised members of the KFD, the Deutsch-Evangelischer Frauenbund (German Protestant Women's Association, or DEF), the BDF, the Centre Party, the DNVP and the DDP. Having received complaints that the Frauenliga was dominated by the middle classes,[16] Gärtner was fully aware of the need for SPD representation on the advisory committee if the working classes were to take an active part in the campaign. Her attempts to arrange this were not agreed,[17] however: the Frauenliga remained essentially a middle-class movement. The whole question of leadership, and the authority to take decisions on behalf of the affiliated groups, provoked considerable controversy. Gärtner made it clear that while she would consult the advisory group on matters such as Frauenliga publications it was not always possible for it to be immediately and directly involved, and in such circumstances she insisted on having sole responsibility and complete freedom to represent the Frauenliga.[18]

In fact relationships between some sections of the Frauenliga and its leader were never completely harmonious. An aspect of this was the campaign against Gärtner, which began during the winter of 1920, on the grounds that she should not be representing the Frauenliga because she was not a Rhinelander and moreover she was a Protestant.[19] The degree to which this campaign arose from personal animosity towards Gärtner or reflected prevailing feelings of isolation among the Rhineland population and general lack of trust in the Reich government in Berlin is unclear.[20] It did, however, force Wrochem to accede to a request from the KFD and pressure from the Foreign Ministry to appoint a Rhinelander as assistant to Gärtner.[21] Dr Cilly Klein – a Catholic from Bonn – was later to succeed her.

The objectives of the Frauenliga included informing the public in unoccupied Germany about conditions prevailing in the Rhineland, as well as directing propaganda abroad. Gärtner persuaded female representatives in both the Reichstag and the Prussian Parliament, for whom travel was both free and relatively easy, to make presentations in towns and cities across Germany in support of an international petition against the Schwarze Schmach. As a result of this activity many articles appeared in the provincial press throughout Germany in the autumn of 1920 and in the early months of 1921, covering a series of protest meetings that had taken place in cities and towns across the country (see Appendix II). Gärtner intended to exercise tight control over what was said in public. She provided a standard outline for such presentations in a form that could be updated as the situation in the Rhineland developed.[22]

Gärtner was well aware that Germany needed friends in the international community. She solicited protest from women's groups worldwide, finding some support in Britain, North and South America, Scandinavia and especially in former German African colonies.[23] She was also well acquainted with the left-wing English journalist and MP Edmund Dene Morel[24] and provided much material[25] for a campaign conducted by him in the British press.[26] However, her previous experience had convinced her that the best way to develop international links was to identify small groups of influential people from selected countries of significance to the German cause. By inviting them to Germany they could study the economic, political and social conditions at first hand and so develop an understanding of the worsening problems caused by the Peace Treaty. The visitors might then convince their fellow countrymen about the situation in the Rhineland. Understanding for the German cause would grow and, hopefully, a readiness to help might develop. Her strategy was summed up by: 'These foreigners are much more likely to be believed than we Germans. That goal can never be achieved with printed propaganda.'[27]

Among the early visitors escorted by Gärtner in this way was a British journalist, Victor Blackwell, who subsequently published a series of articles in the mainstream British press.[28] In March 1921 a Swedish delegation including a pastor, Gunnar Vall, and the novelist Elin Wägner toured the occupied Rhineland, visiting Eberlein at Mannheim en route. The delegation studied all available documents and was able to interview victims of alleged assaults. This was felt by Winterstein to be something of a coup: 'Conversations of this sort between rape victims and a sensitive and sympathetic lady like Mrs W. have far greater impact than any other propaganda.'[29]

Gärtner's priorities in propaganda lay in making the maximum possible capital out of alleged evils associated with coloured troops, giving particular prominence to any sexual misbehaviour. A campaign based on the damage that the occupation was doing to the general welfare of Rhinelanders was a less attractive proposition in her eyes. When it was established that the worst living conditions were to be found in the zone occupied by all-white American troops Gärtner refused to publicise this on the grounds that it would undermine the campaign in the USA against the Schwarze Schmach.[30]

Gärtner also saw it as an important task for the Frauenliga to monitor propaganda originating on the German side in order to ensure its compatibility with the overall aims of her campaign, or at least to ensure that it did not compromise these. In the following chapter it will be seen how she led extensive and prolonged lobbying against the wild exaggerations of the Deutscher Notbund gegen die Schwarze Schmach (German Emergency League against the Black Humiliation – to be referred to as the Notbund), led at the time by the Munich businessman Heinrich Distler. But although ultimately successful in stopping Distler, Gärtner was not always able to control the output of a number of private authors and publishing houses. A novel, *Die Schwarze Schmach*,[31] by Guido Kreutzer is one example. Gärtner requested information about the book ahead of publication, offering the publishers some approved propaganda material and warning of the dangers of exaggeration.[32] Initially Gärtner was well satisfied by what she received,[33] for she agreed to the inclusion in publicity leaflets of an acknowledgement to the Frauenliga for making material available.[34] In fact she went much further, securing the permission of the artist Walter Riemer to use one of his propaganda illustrations.[35] She also approached the Pfalzzentrale,[36] though without success, for details of any recent court case relating to the Schwarze Schmach which could be made available to Kreutzer. However, such help from the Frauenliga came at a price: conformity to Gärtner's ideas and conditions. Shortly before publication of the book she complained about an acknowledgement in it of the support of the Frauenliga.[37] This in her eyes was a rather different proposition from making material available. She objected also to the design of the cover, which illustrated a rapacious black man dragging off a white woman.[38] The objection was, however, not acted upon, for the book appeared in its original form (fig. 10).

Figure 10. The cover of a novel by Guido Kreutzer – the subject of dispute with Margarete Gärtner

Subsequent requests for the Frauenliga to help in publicising the book met with refusal,[39] doubtless because Kreutzer had recently had obscene material confiscated by the authorities. Having gone to some lengths to help Kreutzer, Gärtner must have been mortified by the reaction of her own publisher:

> That publishers have to take on such an author in order to fight the Schwarze Schmach will, I hope, provoke the same reaction in

your committee as it has with me. Factual portrayal of events is the best and most effective form of propaganda......... it does our cause no good whatever if we rely on a dubious author to portray the situation in a cheap novel.[40]

The principal publication of the Frauenliga was the booklet *Farbige Franzosen am Rhein* (fig. 11).[41] Its distribution was arranged and supported by the People's Alliance 'Save Our Honour' amongst other

Farbige Franzosen am Rhein

Ein Notschrei deutscher Frauen

Zweite Ausgabe

Den Freunden unserer Bestrebungen überreicht vom Volksbunde „Rettet die Ehre" Gartenstraße 8.

Berlin 1920

Verlag Hans Robert Engelmann

Zur Verbreitung im Auslande werden diese Bücher auf Wunsch kostenfrei von uns ausgehändigt.
Volksbund „Rettet die Ehre".

Figure 11. *Farbige Franzosen am Rhein* – produced by Margarete Gärtner on behalf of the Rheinische Frauenliga

organisations. The booklet provided details of offences allegedly committed by coloured occupation troops against women, girls and young boys, together with statements by witnesses or by the authorities. It was in a form that could readily be updated by issuing successive editions. The second edition, for example, listed details of 15 cases of rape, 19 attempted rapes, 20 cases of physical assault or harassment and 7 cases of sexual molestation. The content was claimed to be based on officially verified information. It is, however, Gärtner's foreword that provides the best insight into the way in which she approached her task.

Pathos was the chief weapon in her armoury. The image presented to the world was that of the innocent and totally helpless white woman facing a dreadful and shocking fate – that of being violated by black savages. Naturally modest and shy, she had to overcome her deep feelings of shame before she could even bring herself to speak out.[42] This image of natural feminine shyness and the need to protect women from all things unpleasant or dangerous were not confined to German society. They are well illustrated by the reaction of the British Consul-General in Frankfurt to *Farbige Franzosen*: 'Owing to the insufficiency of my staff and to the fact that that work, from its nature, could not be given to a lady clerk to type, I have merely translated a few of the cases at random, as examples.'[43]

Underlying Gärtner's pathos was the association with womanhood of the virtues of purity, and moral rectitude and behaviour. For Gärtner – and many others – this concept lay at the very heart of white civilisation and should be inviolate, providing an example that all should try to emulate. Indeed, the women's movement had since the Wilhelmine era regarded itself as a guardian of public morality. It had long campaigned on issues like prostitution.[44] The perception of increasing post-war immorality was now a principal concern. A French claim that some German women had sought out and consorted with French colonial troops was therefore all the more inflammatory: 'The negro from Madagascar has to be protected from the immoral influence of white Rhineland women!'[45] The image presented by Gärtner of defenceless Rhineland womanhood was a powerful one. It fitted neatly with the idea that German men had effectively been emasculated by the terms of the Peace Treaty and were now incapable of protecting German womanhood. Amongst activists this resounded like a clarion call for women to mobilise in support of the Fatherland. They should do so using their moral and spiritual superiority, untainted by fighting in the war.[46] Gärtner was tapping into precisely this mood. Against a background of increased participation of women in the political sphere and with their developing potential to become a force in public life, it was a promising avenue to exploit. Coupled with traditional attributes of female modesty and reserve, Gärtner knew that the image of helplessness would also be well received abroad.

There are several places in the text where the hand of the professional government propagandist can be identified. Gärtner was careful to make the point, for example, that the German press and the German government had interceded on behalf of the women of the Rhineland.[47] This was notwithstanding the fact that the press had been criticised by members of the Frauenliga, including Hedwig Dransfeld, leader of the KFD, for not doing enough in this respect.[48] As noted in the previous chapter, the Reich government, also, had been accused by Dransfeld of making insufficient protest against the use of coloured troops.

The text of a speech delivered by Gärtner to the Deutsche Kolonialgesellschaft (German Colonial Society)[49] shows that for her the issues at stake were far wider than just the Schwarze Schmach. While this was her principal target, she first addressed the issue of French intentions in the western areas of the Reich. Making the point that Germanic culture was long established here, she focused on the current situation in the Saar where, she alleged, intensive efforts were being made to detach the region and its 600,000 inhabitants from the Reich. Measures being taken by the French authorities included the introduction of French currency and postage stamps, the creation of an independent customs system, the buying up of German businesses and newspapers and the suppression of the remaining German press. The situation was less advanced in the rest of the Rhineland, which had German governance. However, Gärtner considered the current French policy of *pénétration pacifique* in these areas to be even more dangerous than the more direct tactics being adopted in the Saar. The Rhineland was being flooded with French cultural propaganda of all kinds: theatre plays, films, art exhibitions, concerts, books and lecture courses. Parallels were to be drawn with the French occupation of the early nineteenth century in that a Napoleonsfeier (a festival in celebration of Napoleonic rule) had been organised recently.

Having thus outlined the situation in the occupied Rhineland, she turned to the French occupation army. At 130,000 men it was, she alleged, nearly twice the strength agreed under the terms of the Peace Treaty. Coloured troops numbered up to 45,000 and their presence was of great concern to women. In the face of French insistence that their troops were generally well behaved, Gärtner's argument was based quite simply on the premise that the coloured races rightly occupied a lower level of civilisation and culture than the white race. In the interests of all a proper distance had to be maintained between the races. She claimed that there was no question of racial hatred in this and indeed acknowledged the bravery – and good discipline – of these troops on active service. But she accused the French army of setting its coloured troops in authority above German citizens – one of her main grievances. At the same time the troops were treated by the French as second-class citizens. Even the graves of black troops in French military cemeteries were segregated from those of white troops.

Gärtner made much of the 130 sexual attacks on women and children that had allegedly occurred up till then. She went to some lengths to appear to be reasonable, conceding that it was an exaggeration to claim that in a town occupied by coloured troops no white woman dared go out alone. Furthermore, she admitted that the number of attacks on women and children was not particularly large and that where culprits were identified severe punishment by the French authorities followed. She nonetheless insisted that talk of a Schwarze Schmach was entirely justified, maintaining that many victims were too traumatised to be able to identify their attackers and pointing out the dangers of billeting coloured troops in private houses when such troops were prone to sudden outbursts of uncontrollable temperament. The result, according to Gärtner, had been the birth of a number of children of mixed race.

The final charge laid against the French authorities concerned the provision of brothels and the requisitioning of private houses for this purpose. The location of such places was often where comings and goings could be observed by children. When describing the location of a brothel on the first floor of a working-class apartment block in Ludwigshafen, Gärtner knew the effect that her words would have on her audience when she said: 'To me the dull despair of a mother who hears her children using expressions that they have heard coloureds and prostitutes using on the staircase is unforgettable.'[50] Gärtner's speech was considered and her delivery unemotional. While it was intended to rally support for the campaign against the Schwarze Schmach, it was not particularly inflammatory or exaggerated. In essence it was the speech of a civil servant.

Gärtner was an assiduous and skilful propagandist and she left no stone unturned in promoting her cause. To a suggestion that a boycott of foreign goods might be organised she responded that rather than put over a negative message it would be better to put up placards outside shops with a less direct but positive message: 'We sell only good German products here.'[51] That approach, she felt, would have a greater influence on the buying public, who would then regard the buying of German goods as a matter of honour. On another occasion she was asked to recommend a worthy recipient for a sum of M 1,564 that had been donated by an American. Gärtner chose a seventy-one-year-old woman who had recently been assaulted by a Moroccan soldier at Griesheim. Having checked on the woman's financial circumstances, she arranged for the money to be paid to her, but stressed the importance of the donor receiving a letter of thanks. If this could then be published in the US press together with the circumstances in which it was written it would make excellent propaganda.[52] Gärtner's determination to use such material is shown in the fact that she sent two reminders when the letter was slow to appear.[53] She was equally determined to counter an assertion by the French-supported *Neue Saarkurier* newspaper that portrayed Moroccan and Algerian troops as being like big, well-mannered children, not in the least outspoken, pure in soul and with a sensitive disposition and naive good-naturedness. It was claimed that these 'angels in human form' had very quickly gained the sympathies of the Saarlanders.[54] Gärtner went to considerable lengths in trying to find evidence of wartime atrocities committed by troops of Arab origin. The Bund der Asienkämpfer (Association of Asian Campaign Veterans) was one organisation approached with this in mind. The Association, however, while sympathising with her efforts, firmly declined to be involved, especially since this would reinvigorate the debate over wartime atrocities.[55]

Gärtner knew well how powerful photographic images of life in the occupied regions could be and she purchased or commissioned propaganda photographs for supply to individuals with contacts abroad,[56] and to organisations such as the German Association for the League of Nations, which had contacts with the Hearst Press in the USA. These included scenes depicting French colonial troops examining passes at the Rhine bridges. It did not prove easy to obtain photographs under the eyes of the French authorities.[57] On such occasions, an appeal was made to Eberlein at the Pfalzzentrale for assistance through his agents.[58]

Two issues above all others appear to have aroused Gärtner. The occurrence of sexual assaults was one matter, the other was the use of coloured troops in a supervisory capacity:

> You said in your article 'the propaganda has been carried on so quickly and intensively that it is obvious that a power is behind it. Who or what sort of power is it?' I can answer your question: The power is the suffering and indignation of all German not only the rhenish women, over the outrage done to the rhenish people, to see brown and black people set over them, as watchmen, and officials of the customs and pass-offices and the indignation, that in more than 100 cases authentically proved these coloured troops mistreated and forced women and children of all ages.[59]

Such sentiments argue that this setting of 'culturally inferior races' above 'culturally superior' Germans was in Gärtner's eyes so utterly wrong that it almost outweighed the issue of sexual assaults and was no less to be regarded as a moral issue.

A further topic of some concern to Gärtner was that of maintaining racial purity in the face of the imagined threat presented by liaisons between white German women and the occupation troops. In seeking to warn people of the dangers of interracial mixing she found that photographs of children of mixed race were not convincing enough. She contacted Professor Heinrich Poll, a geneticist at Hamburg, for information on inherited racial characteristics:[60]

> You showed slides indicating that in plants, animals and humans characteristics of the species on the whole miss a generation, only to reappear in the next. This fact is of particular interest to me in my work against the coloured occupation of the Rhineland. I believe that such knowledge can be used, especially abroad, to draw attention to the dangers of racial mixing. I can easily get pictures of children of mixed race from the occupied regions, which as far as I know show negroid or mongoloid characteristics, yet in which the children are white and often even have blond hair. That is why such pictures are unconvincing.[61]

Thus was Gärtner expressing concerns that were not only to be shared by the Nazi Party, but were also later to be acted on by the Nazi government with devastating consequences for those concerned.[62]

Gärtner had in fact already commissioned a film on the subject, *Die Schwarze Pest*, intended for distribution in the USA as well as for viewing in Germany. It contained Rhineland scenes and fictional scenes of sexual assault committed on a German girl by grinning black soldiers. Quite unrelated to this, the film told the story of a child of mixed race who had a wholly white European appearance. As an adult he emigrated to the USA but, the victim of inherited characteristics, he committed a sexual assault. He was made to pay for his crime, but in the meantime his white American wife bore him a son with all the physical characteristics of a negro. At this time the medium of film, alone among the arts, was subject to approval procedures by either one of two centres, located in Munich and Berlin.[63] Gärtner's film was banned by the censorship board in Berlin. Its judgement referred to the likelihood that a public showing would damage relations with France and carried an attendant risk of further repression in the Rhineland. It questioned the implication that racial mixing would ultimately lead to domination by the black race.[64] An appeal to higher authority was rejected in terms that were no less damning. Photography and content were described as amateurish. Rejecting the entire portrayal of inherited racial characteristics, the judgement continued: 'This superficial attempt, which incorrectly portrays the consequences of racial theory, would not simply damage American opinion of German thoroughness in research, it would lead to disparagement to the point of ridicule.'[65] Gärtner's attempt at commissioning a propaganda film had been thwarted by expert testimony from a geneticist[66] and by a submission from the Foreign Ministry. Its intervention in this and other aspects of Rhineland propaganda is explored in the following chapters.

It is difficult when dealing with a skilled propagandist to establish where the boundary lies between deeply felt personal views and ideas expressly put forward for public consumption. In the light of the above discussion it is easy to brand Gärtner as a racist: by the standards of today she undoubtedly was. Her views on the fundamental inferiority of non-European races and on the dangers of placing them in positions of authority over Europeans never left her. She was to remark three decades later:

> When I now read of continual unrest in Tunisia and Morocco, which French governments have done so much to create, I ask myself if this is not the result of the seedcorn that was sown in 1919–30.[67]

Nevertheless, while Gärtner's publicly expressed viewpoint on the relationship between races would be considered unacceptable today, such attitudes were commonplace at that time, and not only in Germany. Gärtner and her contemporaries had been raised when the age of white colonial expansion and domination had barely passed its peak. Aside from direct economic exploitation, the overriding European mission had been to bring what was considered to represent civilisation to peoples regarded as little better than uncivilised savages. The extensive missionary activity in Africa in particular underscores the fact that

European intervention was considered to have a moral basis. Little wonder, then, that those of Gärtner's generation unquestioningly accepted fundamental white supremacy. When the roles of Europeans and non-Europeans were reversed in the Rhineland occupation, what was considered to be the natural and moral order was effectively replaced by disorder and immorality.

How, then, should Gärtner's contribution to propaganda be judged? In view of the change in perception of racial attitudes over the years, perhaps the most appropriate yardstick would be whether or not, in making her claims concerning the nature and behaviour of coloured and black troops, Gärtner distorted or exaggerated the facts of the situation. She always maintained that the details of the cases described were based on officially authenticated data. That she went to some lengths to try to suppress propaganda that she considered to be exaggerated has been amply demonstrated. But almost certainly this had as much to do with the fact that exaggerated propaganda would quickly be seen to be implausible as with being truthful for its own sake. On the whole Gärtner, unlike some other propagandists, avoided wild claims such as the alleged harbouring and spread of disease by coloured troops. Apart from descriptions of the alleged acts of sexual violence she largely confined herself to comments on the temperament and behaviour of the non-Europeans. It was all intended to reinforce the belief in the reader that these people occupied an essentially semi-civilised state and it was therefore immoral to set them in authority over civilised white people. There seems little doubt that in her own eyes she was championing the cause of morality against immorality. When challenged, she utterly denied the suggestion that she was stirring up racial hatred.[68] The observer of today might find it difficult to agree.

By March 1922, driven by ambition and disillusioned by the campaign against her within the Frauenliga and by changes in the management of the Volkspflege, Gärtner had decided that the time had come to leave the organisation. She must have been aware, also, of the criticism that the campaign against the Schwarze Schmach had already attracted from the Foreign Ministry and from foreign sources sympathetic to the German cause. For a while now she had been discussing with Dr Bruno Bruhn, Commercial Director at Krupp AG, ideas on ways to win for Germany friends and influence abroad. They had agreed on the need to establish a private foundation, apolitical and independent of government, which could make contacts abroad with people of influence and then arrange for personally accompanied study visits to the occupied areas of Germany. Bruhn now canvassed for support amongst prominent industrialists and was successful in securing sufficient financial backing for the launch of the new organisation, Die Wirtschaftspolitische Gesellschaft or WPG (Society for Political Economics). This took place formally in February 1922, and Gärtner resigned from the Volkspflege.[69]

Gärtner and Wrochem were jointly appointed to lead the new organisation, although Wrochem was later made redundant when financial support was reduced. The WPG was nevertheless to continue its work throughout the period of occupation and for the duration of the Third Reich. In this it cooperated closely with the Arbeitsausschuß Deutscher Verbände or ADV (Working Committee of German Associations). This had been set up by the Foreign Ministry in April 1921 as an umbrella organisation to combat the allegation of German responsibility for the war, the so-called *Kriegsschuldlüge*, or war guilt lie.[70]

That Gärtner's diplomatic skills in dealing with people of influence were of the highest order is not in doubt. A study by Donald Cameron Watt of the way in which Germany was able to influence the British government's pre-World War II policy towards the Nazi regime concluded that:

> The most important and significant work in predisposing opinion within the British foreign-policy-making elite towards accepting the foreign policy of Nazi Germany had, in fact, been done before Hitler came to power and by agencies which were far from Nazi in character.[71]

Watt attributed this remarkable success largely to the way in which Margarete Gärtner had 'laid a groundwork of British contacts and understanding for the German revisionist case against Versailles which only a few public figures would have challenged'.[72] Gärtner was later attached to the Foreign Ministry and spent time in German embassies abroad. A further tribute was paid to her outstanding ability as a propagandist in a recollection from another source that 'She was sent by way of Russia and Japan to America, where she remained until September 1940, entrusted with the thankless task of endeavouring to keep the USA out of the war.'[73] After World War II she worked at CDU headquarters before becoming General Secretary of the German branch of International Christian Leadership. She retired from this post in 1951.[74]

Margarete Gärtner is an enigmatic figure. On the one hand she was apparently neither a Nazi nor an extreme nationalist, and at one time had even been invited by the relatively liberal DDP[75] to stand for election to the Reichstag. Following World War II, however, she was summoned before the War Criminal Investigation Board although she always denied having any connection with the Nazi regime. She was found to be free of any guilt. She later claimed to have worked with Adam von Trott zu Solz, a diplomat in the Foreign Ministry. Trott was also a leading member of the so-called Kreisauer Circle,[76] which, even if it did not plot actively against the Hitler regime, did make the fatal mistake of discussing the options for Germany in a post-Hitler world. Thus, when the leaders of the group were arrested Gärtner's links to it had been sufficiently close – so she said – that she went in fear of her life.[77] Yet Gärtner seemingly had little difficulty in living with her conscience in the National Socialist environment while she pursued a highly successful career, holding posts of considerable responsibility associated with Reich foreign policy. One assessment of her has branded her as a Nazi fellow-traveller.[78]

It is argued here that a combination of personal ambition and her deeply felt conviction that Germany had been wronged provided Gärtner's principal motivation. She was, without doubt, morally outraged by what seemed to her the dominating presence of coloured and black troops in the Rhineland. Approaching the situation as a dedicated civil servant and skilled propagandist, however, her overriding intention was to work towards the revision of the Peace Treaty. What better than to portray abroad the plight of the most vulnerable section of the community and thereby secure a propaganda coup? This single-mindedness with regard to the task in hand perhaps also goes some way towards accounting for her willingness, after 1933, to work with the new National Socialist regime. After all, this too had the revision of the Treaty as one of its goals.

Gärtner was one of the leading protagonists in the Schwarze Schmach campaign. Ambitious and energetic, she led the Frauenliga in an autocratic style. Her successor, Dr Cilly Klein, was employed by what had then become the women's section in the Volkspflege. Gärtner later remarked that Klein was conscientious and hard-working, but she was extremely critical of Klein's successor, Dr Philippine Freiin von Hertling,[79] who allegedly failed to make any visits at all to the occupied territories. Furthermore, after the occupation had ended Hertling had the temerity to write a book extolling the successes of the Frauenliga while neglecting to mention the first two years of its central campaign, or Gärtner's role in setting it up.[80]

With Klein newly appointed it was time to review the aims and activities of the women's section and its associated Frauenliga. At this point its work was felt to be far from finished. In fact it was to continue until the French withdrawal in 1930. But there was to be a reorientation of ideas and responsibilities in the light of the criticisms that had been made of the Schwarze Schmach campaign. The presence of coloured troops remained an important issue but other matters where the occupation was considered to be having a damaging effect were to be given greater prominence in civic enlightenment within both occupied and unoccupied Germany. Overarching concerns were the general health and welfare of the family and the upholding of German culture and values, or *Deutschtum*, in the face of the French cultural onslaught.[81] This much can also be deduced from the nature of a questionnaire (see Appendix III) circulated at this time among Frauenliga member organisations in the occupied Rhineland. Topics included the housing situation, where problems had been created by the occupation authorities through the requisitioning of property and the billeting of troops. Billeting was a particular problem in the case of married officers, who were likely to demand accommodation for their families, and the questions aimed at establishing the proportion of single and married officers should be viewed in this light. Problems were not just those of overcrowding and housing shortage, however: moral issues were also well to the fore. Thus questions were put concerning the prevalence of prostitution and the provision of brothels (and not only for coloured troops, though these were singled out).[82] There was considerable interest also in health generally, especially among children. The footnotes in the Appendix imply an attempt to relate illness to individual occupation zones. This would have enabled, for example, the testing of the notion that sexually transmitted disease and tuberculosis were strongly associated with coloured troops. A reduction in milk supply as a consequence of Allied actions was a separate issue that featured in other German propaganda. It was alleged to have caused widespread malnutrition.[83] Certain questions related solely to coloured troops. Their payment, for example, had become a matter for anger when it was reported that coloured troops were paid more than working German women.[84] There was also suspicion that when children of mixed race were being born to coloured fathers outside marriage they were receiving support from the German state – a fact that if true would intensify moral outrage and make effective propaganda. The questions relating to French language classes point to deep concern about French cultural penetration and the reaction of the local population. Longer-term effects on the upbringing of children who would grow to adulthood during the expected fifteen-year occupation, and moral issues related to this, were not to be neglected either. The mother was clearly identified as the moral guardian in matters of family welfare.

Many of the points raised in the questionnaire are predictable. But from the nature of some questions it appears that these were now being asked for the first time, even though the Frauenliga had by now nearly completed its second year. It points to a lack of contact hitherto between the leadership of the Frauenliga and its grass-roots membership in the occupied Rhineland – a view reinforced by what Klein reported following her initial visits to the Rhineland and to the Pfalz in particular.[85]

Klein placed very different emphasis on the manner in which she led the Frauenliga. Whereas Gärtner had spent much time organising and accompanying visits by foreign notables to the Rhineland,

Klein tried to develop better personal contacts with the individual women's groups and to improve coordination with Eberlein's Pfalzzentrale. Having visited Eberlein for the first time, she reported that he attached great importance to collaboration since contact with women's groups in the Pfalz seemed to him to have been lacking until now. He had offered again to make his couriers available for handling their news and correspondence. She had accepted his offer.[86] Gärtner, while collaborating with the Pfalzzentrale, had evidently not maintained the all-important channels of communication to local women's groups and had tended to keep Eberlein's organisation at arm's length. It can in fact be argued that Gärtner – based in Berlin and relatively aloof in spite of her visits to the Rhineland – saw the situation of Rhineland women largely in terms of an exploitable resource in the propaganda battle. Her priority lay in making maximum impact with propaganda concerning misdemeanours of coloured troops to the exclusion of much else – and therein probably lay a primary cause of the friction between her and the constituent women's groups. This is not to deny, however, the point made by Sandra Maß that religious differences between Gärtner, a Lutheran, and the leader of the large Catholic women's group, Hedwig Dransfeld, played their part in this.[87]

The change in the work of the Frauenliga when Klein assumed leadership has been associated by Sandra Maß with a loosening of links between the women's groups and the Berlin-based women's section of the Volkspflege and greater involvement of the latter with parliamentary women's committees.[88] I would put forward a slightly different interpretation of events, arguing that although the three largest women's groups in particular wanted adjustments to the way in which the Frauenliga operated,[89] Klein in Berlin was no less determined to maintain a grip on the protest and propaganda activities. Certainly concessions were made in terms of the change in emphasis of the work, and changes were made to the fourth edition of *Farbige Franzosen* to reflect a less harshly nationalistic tone. As before, the Frauenliga would be used as a cover organisation for contacts abroad and in the production of propaganda. But in contrast to what had apparently happened under Gärtner's leadership, this would now be more of a joint activity. Nevertheless, the determination that the parent Volkspflege should play a central role was also made very clear. Furthermore, the monitoring of the output from private propaganda sources, checking on the acceptability of their aims and on factual accuracy, was now to be a formal task, leading to intervention if deemed necessary.[90]

Discussion in this book has so far centred on the dominant personal role of the Berlin secretariat of the Frauenliga. It remains to examine the wider motivation for the women's organisations to band together within the Frauenliga. Women's movements had begun to develop among the middle classes well before World War I. Organisations like the BDF, pressing for an enhanced public role for women, had achieved some successes, for example the opening of universities to women and their entry into professions like teaching and medicine. Such development accelerated with the outbreak of war, which was to provide opportunities to break away from a closed domestic environment and to contribute to public life, particularly in the provision of a wide range of community services.[91] It was therefore no coincidence that prominent in the leadership of each of the organisations comprising the core of the Frauenliga was a group of well-educated and strongly motivated middle-class women. Following the enfranchisement of women in the new Republic and their admission to party candidate lists, several now played an active part in the National Assembly. Some, like Hedwig Dransfeld of the KFD, later sat in the Reichstag.

The Frauenliga was associated with a fairly wide political spectrum, although its centre undoubtedly lay to the right. Of its three most prominent groups the BDF was affiliated to the DDP, while the KFD had links to the Catholic Centre Party and the BVP. The DEF had ties to both DVP and DNVP. However, women's groups associated with the SPD, though sharing concerns with their colleagues, were to some degree ambivalent towards protest. This was reflected by events in the National Assembly. In the vote on the Peace Treaty female SPD members voted in favour of its acceptance but then joined in protests organised outside afterwards.[92] The women of the USPD did not protest. The extreme Left accepted German war guilt. Its concern was that those responsible in the former Wilhelmine regime should be brought to justice.[93]

This political divergence was later to be reflected, also, in women's attitudes to the Schwarze Schmach campaign. A resolution directed at the Reich government, supported by all parties represented in the National Assembly with the exception of the USPD, alleged that coloured troops posed a threat to women and children, referring to them as savages. It described their use as a permanent insult to the German people. Subsequently two prominent members of the SPD, Reich Foreign Minister Adolf Köster and Elisabeth Röhl, qualified this, emphasising that public anger was directed not at the coloured troops but at the Allies, especially France.[94] In contrast, a USPD member provoked uproar from all sides in a parliamentary debate when she asserted that sexual offences were not confined to coloured troops and were a consequence of military occupation. She warned against indulging in a hate campaign.[95]

Leaving aside the attitude of the Left, the initial concerns of mainstream women's groups had mirrored those of all German protest groups that had been set up following the Armistice. Early subjects for campaign had, for example, included the Allied blockade and delays in returning German prisoners of war. But then, when the Peace Treaty terms became known, came a storm of protest – especially over the war guilt clause – that showed that politically conscious women were just as incensed as their male counterparts. Protest came from across the political spectrum, though above all from the Right, where the women of the DVP were particularly vociferous.[96] Among those who would later be associated with the Frauenliga, Helene Lange, doyenne of the BDF, was far from alone in believing that Germany should refuse to sign the Treaty regardless of the consequences.[97] Even Alice Salomon, one of the most politically moderate of leading female activists, campaigned vigorously against the provisions of the Treaty when travelling abroad.[98]

Were women therefore simply echoing the general protest against the Peace Treaty and did they regard the Schwarze Schmach as just another aspect of the national humiliation? In the wartime years women had regarded their role first and foremost as being the guardians of the home front. Following the traumatic end of the war and the subsequent imposition of harsh peace terms it naturally became their duty to continue this role of guardianship. Circumstances had now altered dramatically, however. Germany was perceived to be militarily and politically defenceless. What had been the home front was now the front on which the battle for Germany's survival was being waged. In this way a mental attitude persisted in which a state of war continued for politically conscious women, much as it did for their male counterparts, albeit a rather different kind of war from that obtaining hitherto.[99] But specific to female protest, it could be said, was also the sense of national duty to use newly gained political rights and to build on the involvement of women in the community during the war years in order to improve post-war society. Untainted by direct contact with war, women would be uniquely placed to make a major contribution to this. In so doing they would henceforth operate on an equal basis to men. Thus the leaders of women's groups did not regard themselves simply as subordinate agents in a male-dominated political environment. In tackling issues from a female perspective they would essentially provide a complementary approach.[100] This is to be seen, for example, in the protests by women's groups over the transfer of a large number of dairy cows to France in October 1920 under reparations arrangements. From the perspective of motherhood the issue was seen as threatening mass infanticide.[101] Little wonder, then, that the perceived plight of women in the occupied Rhineland provided a stimulus for women to unite under the banner of the Frauenliga. Indeed, the BDF had itself set up a centre to address matters affecting the Rhineland and had then incorporated it in the Frauenliga when this was created.[102] Margarete Gärtner was thus able to tap immediately into a seam of middle-class feeling that not only led back to outrage over the provisions of the Peace Treaty but also embodied attitudes of idealism and, closely associated with this, moralism.

Women tended to view events through what might be described as a moral lens. The activists felt that the complementary role of women in society should be to contribute a moral dimension, which might readily be associated with the innate purity of womanhood. They saw women essentially as the guardians of morality in society. This much was made clear by Helene Lange:

> If one is going to concede that man alone is responsible for the development of a cultured civilisation...... then not only is he responsible for the great and beautiful aspects that the concept embraces but also for all the hatred, envy and strife, materialism, destruction of life, welfare, spiritual and moral values which once again are evident today. ...... It is the universal mission of woman to overcome these aspects of civilisation and to replace them with her values, thereby creating a synthesis of masculine mental creativity and female spiritual productivity, intellectual powers and motherly feelings of humanitarianism.[103]

Likewise another leading activist, Dr Marie-Elisabeth Lüders, spoke of the moral concept of responsibility and commitment as being the driving force behind the women's movement.[104]

This perception of moral duty that lay at the heart of the women's movement had led to campaigns against several of the social evils of the day, including the official regulation, and therefore acceptance, of prostitution and alcohol abuse. Although these campaigns pre-dated the war, a widely perceived general decline in moral standards post-war meant that they had now assumed even greater importance and were taken up with renewed vigour.[105]

This strict, conservative view of sexual morality juxtaposed with moral conviction of white supremacy led the outraged Dorothee von Velsen of the BDF and Margarete Gärtner of the Frauenliga to seek a ban on a play being performed at the Apollo theatre in Berlin in October 1920. The play depicted a raid made on the harem of a sultan as an act of revenge by a black prince and his followers following the abduction of his favourite wife. The performers included black men and scantily clad white women, allegedly dancing in an obscene and provocative fashion. The Weimar Republic had ushered in – in Berlin in particular – a new era of avant-garde theatrical expression. Pre-emptive censorship had been abolished and scenes were depicted on stage that would not have been permitted in pre-war days.[106] The women's groups were having none of this. Gärtner objected strongly to three events in particular:

> As the black men stormed the harem they shook at the sight of the naked white women and fell on them with wild shrieks. At the end of this scene they carried the white women out of the harem in their arms. At the end of the play in the final cameo the black prince appeared on a raised podium and several dozen white women knelt in homage before him.[107]

Naturally, a primary concern was that the play would undermine the propaganda campaign against the Schwarze Schmach. But in almost equal measure the sexual innuendo and the symbolic setting of the black man above submissive white women were both regarded as plumbing the depths of moral depravity. The viewing of the Schwarze Schmach as an issue of morality is evident, also, in the way in which Margarete Gärtner attempted to get it discussed in an international forum through organisations such as the Deutsches Nationalkomitee zur Bekämpfung des Mädchenhandels (German National Committee to Combat the Trafficking of Girls).[108]

Raffael Scheck has linked the campaigning of German women against the Schwarze Schmach on moral grounds with the wider protest against Versailles.[109] Such a view is illustrated also by the call made to its members by the Deutscher Verband zur Förderung der Sittlichkeit (German Association for the Encouragement of Morality). Housewives were urged to protest against the unnecessary import of luxury goods, against the Schwarze Schmach and against the war guilt lie.[110] For non-German women's groups the link to Versailles was not particularly significant: the Schwarze Schmach was regarded as a moral issue in its own right. Two such cases in which appeals were made to the British government and to the League of Nations to bring pressure to bear on the French government must surely have been representative of a rather larger number. These were not requests to end the occupation, or to modify the Peace Treaty, but simply to replace coloured troops with white European troops. While the emphasis placed on the consequences of using coloured troops differed, moral grounds were in both cases cited as a major reason for the appeal.[111]

Andrea Süchting-Hänger has suggested that for right-wing women it was moral objection to the presumption of German war guilt which lay at the heart of the protests against the Peace Treaty.[112] In the eyes of those on the political Right women had the responsibility of fighting the lie for the sake of the fallen, for those returning from the Front physically and mentally broken and for the children. But apart from the impact that protest would have on foreign public opinion, Süchting-Hänger argues that for the women at least it acted almost like a form of catharsis.[113] Certainly, individual activists like Klara Mende of the DVP and Käthe Schirmacher of the DNVP campaigned through newspaper articles and speeches as vigorously against the Schwarze Schmach as they did against all the provisions of the Peace Treaty. Their campaigning was marked by the expression of extreme racist views. There is little doubt that there existed on the Right a deep-rooted female racism which required no stimulation by propaganda.

One factor has received little attention in previous studies. In the early days of the occupation it is likely that fear of coloured and black troops also played a part in shaping the attitude of some women. A considerable proportion of the women's groups later involved in the Frauenliga were within the occupied zone (see Appendix I). Evidence that fear was a significant factor initially can be found in the experiences of Marie-Elisabeth Lüders. Lüders was among the most prominent of the leaders of the women's movement in the Weimar Republic and assisted in the setting up of the Frauenliga.[114] One of the first women to be university-educated in Germany, she had been active in the BDF before World War I. During the war she, like many other educated middle-class women, had undertaken social work. She was one of the new wave of women representatives elected to the Reichstag in 1919 and she campaigned tirelessly for the rights of women and young people, taking a particular interest in education. Her outspokenness later got her into trouble with the National Socialist regime and in 1937 she was imprisoned for a while by the Gestapo before an international outcry led to her release. Politically she was a liberal, sitting as a DDP member in the Reichstag until 1933 and, following

World War II, the FDP in the Bundestag. It is clear from her writings that she, like so many others, deplored the terms of the Peace Treaty and the circumstances in which it was concluded: 'All the "victors" were simply full of thoughts of revenge and the intent to combine moral humiliation with the complete economic ruin of an exhausted people.'[115] But Lüders was certainly not an extreme nationalist. What, then, was her attitude towards the presence of coloured troops in the occupied Rhineland and what motivated her support of the Frauenliga? She was well placed to form a view because in the early months of the occupation she had spent considerable time in the Rhineland campaigning for the Reichstag elections.

The overriding emotion portrayed by Lüders was one of unbearable fear and dread among the female population, especially in the period leading to the signing of the Peace Treaty. The body searches that were conducted by coloured troops stationed at the Rhine bridges seem to have provoked the greatest fear but there was worse to come immediately prior to the signing of the Treaty, when Lüders was in Düsseldorf:

> Women lived in increasing dread after it was rumoured that the coloured troops had been promised a free hand with women. (For this eventuality a Russian doctor had promised to give me some poison.)[116]

Perhaps subconscious fear also lay behind emotions expressed by Dorothee von Velsen, another leading member of the BDF and the DDP, at the sight of coloured and black occupation troops:

> It was the time of the coloured occupation, the Schwarze Schmach, which gave rise to innumerable protest meetings...... The sight of Moroccans and Senegalese filled us with bitterness. The Gurkhas, also, standing guard in front of the English headquarters in Cologne, I regarded with intense disgust.[117]

Velsen did concede, however, that the lurid rumours of their sexual misconduct that were circulating at that time could rarely be proved.

It is as well to remember that this was all taking place in the early months of the occupation, before any significant campaign against the Schwarze Schmach had begun. In the febrile atmosphere of the time, however, the slightest rumour could be guaranteed to create panic. And although the tension may have lessened during the following months it is unlikely that such deep-rooted emotion disappeared altogether. As to the origin of rumours and allegations, it should be remembered that German wartime propaganda had deliberately depicted French colonial troops as behaving with the utmost brutality and depravity on the battlefield and there seems little doubt that such a portrayal found its way into the consciousness of the civilian population by one route or another.[118]

The feelings of anger and genuine fear of coloured troops among women in the Rhineland are confirmed also by an English woman who lived for some time in the British sector but who sometimes visited the French occupation zone. Writing about a German friend she noted:

> The one thing about which she was very angry – and I found English and German women and Englishmen as well at one with her in this – was the use of coloured troops in the French Occupation. This is a matter which makes many people see red in Germany, though I have been told that their discipline is of the strictest, and up to then I had heard no tales of them running amok. But the Germans regarded their presence as something intolerable and unforgivable, and no wonder.[119]

She described her fear of coloured troops on seeing them in Coblenz. While on a visit to the Eifel she wrote: 'We had anticipated the quiet of the country nights. Alas, the first night one of us remembered the black troops and the easiness of ascending our balcony and kept remembering it through the week.'[120]

The conclusion that fear played a part in the initial response of some women to the Schwarze Schmach is not, however, to discount a recent analysis by Julia Roos. She concludes that sexual immorality associated with the Schwarze Schmach was used deliberately as a weapon by feminists of all political shades to advance their long moralistic campaign against state regulation of prostitution. Their hope was to exploit nationalistic emotion to create an upsurge of anger over the introduction of brothels for coloured troops. This would help to undermine the long-established position of the German authorities on regulation.[121]

It is clear that there was no single source of motivation for the women's campaign against the Schwarze Schmach, but several. Nor was this an activity taken up purely for tactical purposes: the campaign was rather more loosely linked to the general protest against the Peace Treaty than has sometimes been assumed. Aside from those of the activists, reactions among women in general to the presence of colonial troops varied widely. For many this was a matter for concern only if the troops were perceived as an immediate threat to a secure everyday existence. It was reported on at least one occasion that the coloured troops were so well regarded by the local population that their departure was regarded with great regret – a fact that the activists chose to ignore.[122] This fact accords, also, with the view later expressed by Alice Salomon that 'women are more interested in human aspects than in politics'.[123]

Returning to the relationship between Berlin and the Frauenliga, the motivation of its leader was clear enough. Gärtner was a conscientious civil servant, but she was remote from everyday life in the Rhineland, working for a government whose overriding aim was to achieve revision of the Treaty.[124] The manner in which the Frauenliga was set up – which, it can be argued, amounted to nothing less than exploitation of women's emotions – points strongly in this direction, as does Gärtner's subsequent career. Perhaps another remark of Alice Salomon, made in describing the struggle to achieve social welfare reform in the face of bureaucratic intransigence, is relevant here also: 'A German civil servant was educated to think in terms of functions, not in terms of life as a whole, of human beings as entities, or of dealing with human affairs.'[125]

Difference in motivation and outlook between Gärtner and the leaders of some of the individual women's groups within the Frauenliga almost certainly contributed towards the rift that occurred between them and was a factor in Gärtner's departure. Sandra Maß has attributed the rift to religious differences and the time-honoured struggle between Berlin and the Rhineland. Religious differences there certainly were but there is also evidence to show that there was disquiet over the propaganda emanating from Berlin.[126] This again points to differences between Gärtner and the Frauenliga in their perception of the Rhineland situation.

Whatever the influence of the extreme Right on the Frauenliga and its propaganda, it was undoubtedly eclipsed in its excessiveness by some of the hysterical outpourings of one particular female propagandist. This was an American journalist, Ray Beveridge,[127] who had links with the Pfalzzentrale. Although claims were later made that she was of German extraction,[128] Beveridge came from a wealthy American family with some German ancestry and had spent much time in Germany. As early as September 1919, the Bavarian representative in the Reichskommissariat für die besetzten Gebiete (Office of the Reich Commissioner for the Occupied Regions) in Coblenz, Dr Sigmund Knoch, had introduced Beveridge to Eberlein. She had been a personal friend of Knoch for some years. Knoch had encouraged her to campaign in the USA during the early part of the war on behalf of Germany and she had become a controversial figure there, especially so once the USA had entered the conflict. By this time, however, she had left her country of birth and had spent the latter part of the war in Berlin and Stockholm.[129]

The introduction was made in order to enlist the help of Beveridge in developing links with the German-American press. Eberlein's main concern at this time was to counter French-supported separatism in the Pfalz. He was certain that the influential American press would be sympathetic to the German cause, and even the smallest amount of support would be invaluable.[130] Correspondence between Eberlein and Beveridge[131] at this point makes no mention of coloured troops but within a few months Beveridge had become a major propagandist in the campaign. Sharing a stage on occasion with Eberlein, she inflamed audiences at public meetings in towns and cities in Germany during the latter part of 1920 and in 1921. Beveridge has been reported as having spoken out against the use of black troops as early as 6 March

1920 at a public meeting in Munich,[132] though by her own account she was first inspired to speak out against the Schwarze Schmach when addressing students in Berlin on 19 June. In late 1921 she visited Finland, addressing public meetings in Helsingfors and Lakties, though amid protests from the Allies her planned lecture tour was then curtailed.

Dramatic and emotional language was the stock in trade of Beveridge, together with a capacity for outrageous, illogical and unsubstantiated statement and a distorted view of history. She introduced herself thus:

> Why do I come here, an American, to speak to you about the Schwarze Schmach? Because I come from a nation that ever since it came into being has been threatened by black and yellow problems and black and yellow peril.[133]

This contrasted with Gärtner's sober style: 'It is my task to speak to you about the coloured occupation of the Rhineland.'[134] Beveridge invariably set out to make an emotional impact:

> I appeal to every woman in the world! I appeal to all men worthy of the name! Help! White women, white boys are in danger every day, every hour of the day as long as a black is allowed to have power over white women![135]

Structure in her speeches was largely absent. Much of the content consisted of a series of inflammatory statements which were not always well connected, or logical, but were designed for dramatic effect. She depicted black men as wild and brutal savages and attributed to them a massive sexual appetite and lack of self-control:

> Victims of the promiscuous passions of the blacks are found half dead in meadows and ditches, their clothes in tatters, their delicate young bodies torn by the brutality of the attacks. Many have bite wounds which show clearly how wildly the black beast has fallen on his victim. I could quote innumerable examples

> with names and dates; and it must not be forgotten that almost all these men are infected with venereal disease.[136]

Beveridge, like Gärtner, raised the issue of brothels in residential districts, but further embellished the matter: 'In these houses every girl has to satisfy ten black men every three hours.' She alleged that 60 per cent of the children of mixed race were born with syphilis. The whipping up of racial antagonism was the main tactic employed by Beveridge, helped all the more by her enthusiastic endorsement of mob lynching of suspected black rapists in the USA. But underlying everything was agitation against the humiliation suffered by Germany:

> When a young man in Berlin pulled down the French flag out of sheer high spirits, the entire German nation had to sink to its knees and apologise. But German women, girls and boys are violated every day and nobody lifts a finger![137]

Such rhetoric paid handsomely, for her meetings were reportedly packed and her speeches greeted with huge applause.[138]

While she devoted much of her time between 1920 and 1922 in speaking out against the Schwarze Schmach, Beveridge also took up as a campaigning theme the plight of undernourished German children.[139] Even here, however, she introduced a racial dimension, comparing allegedly well-nourished children of mixed race with undernourished German children (fig. 12). She claimed to have close connections with the Red Cross, with the Salvation Army and with American Quakers, all of whom were actively engaged at the time in relief work amongst the poor in Germany. The Quakers, however, strongly denied any association and stated that her public pronouncements and persistent efforts to join their organisation had caused them great embarrassment.[140] She was also declared *persona non grata* by the British government and refused an entry visa.[141]

Beveridge seems at first sight an unlikely participant in the Schwarze Schmach campaign, but through her childhood experiences in Germany she had developed an obsessive attachment to the country, its institutions and its people. Then, having moved to Germany during

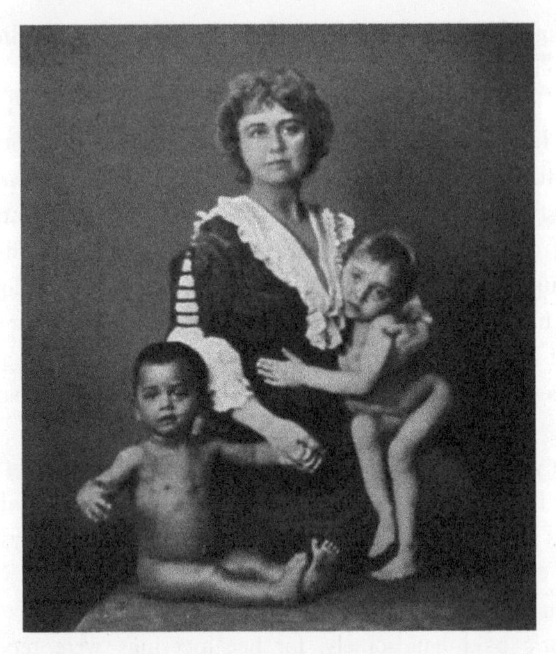

Figure 12. Ray Beveridge. The original caption made a comparison between an illegitimate negro child (left) and an undernourished German child (right).

World War I, she made the transition seamlessly from monarchist to fervent nationalist, later taking out German citizenship. She was in no way personally affected by the presence of coloured troops and her contribution to the campaign can only be explained in terms of extreme right-wing attitudes towards the supposed loss of national honour, accompanied by racial prejudice. Beveridge became an admirer of Hitler. On being honoured by the German Red Cross in 1935 for her work with children she wrote a personal letter of thanks to Hitler that is noteworthy for its sycophancy.[142] She applied for NSDAP membership shortly thereafter.[143]

Margarete Gärtner was critical of Beveridge:

> Some, in the first flush of excitement, perhaps with the best of intentions, have been led astray, accepting unproven reports at face value and then spreading them. The American Ray Beveridge, also, has fallen into this trap. As a result of a few

> exaggerations on her part the French are able to call her a liar, even though from my experience the information she had available to her was on the whole correct.[144]

As in other cases she intervened to try to reduce exaggerated claims.[145]

The contribution of Beveridge to Rhineland propaganda encapsulated the reaction of the extreme Right to the occupation and was nothing less than an incitement to racial hatred. The Schwarze Schmach was a symbol of the denigration of Germany. While the campaign of the Frauenliga – the main source of female propaganda – did not in general register such extremism it was underpinned by a complex mix of nationalism, innate racism and fear in which even politically liberal women were involved. The personality of key individuals played a significant part in driving the women's campaign forward. It is no coincidence, either, that among the leading female participants were those who had led the growing women's movement before the war. The campaign was, above all, driven on by experienced middle-class activists who considered it their duty to shoulder their part of the national burden.

The fact that in the initial years at least the Schwarze Schmach dominated female protest against the occupation was, I suggest, partly due to the influence of the more right-wing elements within the women's groups. But to a large extent it came also from the determination of Margarete Gärtner to exploit the theme as part of the wider campaign against the Peace Treaty. With some justification women of the Right can therefore be regarded as exploiters of the situation in the Rhineland. The corollary of this, of course, is that the women in the occupied zone can be regarded to some extent as having been exploited.

How far the women's campaign can be regarded as a special case, distinct from the mainstream propaganda effort, will become clear in examining other propaganda sources in later chapters. The Frauenliga was the main source of female protest. It apparently carried on its work with the tacit approval of its parent the Volkspflege. This invites discussion of the ethos of the Volkspflege, which is therefore addressed in the following chapter.

5

PUBLICLY FUNDED PROPAGANDA AND PRIVATE INITIATIVES: CONTRASTING STYLES AND MOTIVATION

It was earlier remarked that there were fundamental differences in the manner in which the Volkspflege in Berlin and the Pfalzzentrale in Mannheim each sought to counter the French presence in the Rhineland. Differences in emphasis were evident also in propaganda from other sources. Some attacked all provisions of the Peace Treaty. Others were directed more specifically at aspects of the Rhineland occupation, particularly the Schwarze Schmach, which was also the focus for the Frauenliga during the first two years of the occupation. In this chapter other major sources of Rhineland propaganda are examined, bearing in mind two aspects in particular: what can be deduced of the thinking and motivation that lay behind each contribution, and to what extent could these propaganda activities be said to be coordinated?

As the Reich government agency entrusted with the upholding of German culture and values in the occupied Rhineland, the Volkspflege provides an obvious starting point. It will be recalled that its parent Heimatdienst was undergoing a post-war reorientation to embrace liberal ideas – an important aspect that we return to in the concluding chapter. The German citizen was in future to be presented with factually correct information and encouraged to form his or her own opinion. Indeed the Heimatdienst set its face firmly against any propaganda that had any element of agitation:

> In a democratic state it can and must no longer be acceptable to whip up the emotions of the masses in an inflammatory manner. What matters is to awaken the understanding in our people of the important issues of our time through quiet, purposeful and factual enlightenment.[1]

In fact only one article of any consequence on the subject of the occupied Rhineland ever appeared in Heimatdienst publications, and that was a compilation of Reichstag speeches without added political comment.[2]

The question to be answered is whether or not these ideas also moulded the propaganda activities of the Volkspflege. The key figure in these, introduced in a previous chapter, was Alfred von Wrochem, who led the Volkspflege until June 1921. Much can be deduced about his view of the situation of Germany from the book that he published shortly after leaving the organisation. Like Paul Rühlmann, who also was associated with the Volkspflege, Wrochem was in no doubt that France had expansionist ambitions. To make the Rhine her eastern frontier had been a major French war aim. This would not only have created a defensive line but would also have provided bridgeheads across the Rhine. The intention, in Wrochem's view, was that subsequent military action by France could then lead to the separation of Prussia from Bavaria, to the destruction of Germany as an entity and ultimately to the Balkanisation of central Europe under French domination. Like some other propagandists, he drew parallels with the French campaigns of the Napoleonic era. On the other hand Wrochem considered that France could never achieve her desire to be pre-eminent in Europe. She was too small, fundamentally weaker than either Germany or – in certain respects – Russia. She had achieved her present status only through assistance from major powers. To further her long-term ambitions France intended to develop and exploit her colonial empire. Its peoples would provide the necessary military resources. Such a strategy posed grave danger for Europe.[3] Wrochem was warning of the dangers of elevating a non-European race to a position from which it could challenge the supremacy of white European civilisation – a theme that pervaded virtually all propaganda directed against the Schwarze Schmach, regardless of its source.

What then was the role of the Volkspflege in the campaign against the Schwarze Schmach? Jared Poley, in linking attitudes towards the occupation with the loss of German colonies and French colonisation of the Rhineland, sees the Volkspflege as having orchestrated much of the campaign.[4] This was certainly true of the Frauenliga, although Poley's further assertion that 'the Frauenliga... was responsible for publishing what is perhaps the most interesting and inflammatory material to come out of the occupied zone in the early 1920s'[5] might be challenged. Gärtner always tried to be factual and her presentation was relatively staid compared with that of Beveridge among others. I argue, also, that the link between the Frauenliga and its parent Volkspflege was in fact quite tenuous. Led, respectively, by Gärtner and by Wrochem, each followed its own direction more or less independently of the other. The entire Rhineland propaganda campaign was shaped by individuals and Gärtner made sure that she enjoyed considerable freedom of action in running the Frauenliga.

It can be argued, also, that the ethos of the Heimatdienst – and of the Volkspflege – would not generally have been supportive of extreme propaganda against the Schwarze Schmach.[6] Certainly the writings of principal figures like Wrochem and Rühlmann accord with this view. While France was undoubtedly the enemy and represented, in Wrochem's eyes, an enormous threat to the survival of Germany he took a dispassionate strategic view of the situation. He indulged in no diatribe of hatred, least of all against black and coloured colonial people. Indeed he spoke out emphatically against hatred, considering it to be counterproductive:

> Hatred is raging in Germany and in the entire world and a vast amount of falsehood and prejudice is building up in religious fanaticism. They are not easily distinguished from the truth

> and one cannot build on such ground. The hatred must first be eliminated.[7]

Wrochem was in fact an idealist, arguing that a united Germany should direct her future efforts towards spiritual leadership. He adopted a conciliatory tone towards France, arguing that it was only by taking account of the wishes and needs of both countries that a mutually acceptable relationship could eventually be achieved between them:

> What is needed is not unconscious hatred towards a spiritually weaker France but long-term goals for the prosperity of both peoples; also positive leadership will encourage those French politicians who are full of hatred to come over one day to our way of thinking. We must at the same time prove our spiritual superiority over France and our sense of responsibility for Europe.[8]

With such sentiments it is hardly surprising that Wrochem attracted fierce criticism from proponents of a more direct and aggressive propaganda regime. Arguably the most prominent amongst them were Winterstein and Eberlein.

Although for Wrochem the Schwarze Schmach was the early manifestation of a longer-term danger for Europe, there is relatively little mention in his writing of the presence of French colonial troops in the Rhineland. Perhaps his view of its standing in relation to other issues concerning the occupation can be judged from the literature recommended to his readership (fig. 13). The thirty-five publications listed included the terms of the Versailles Peace Treaty, analyses of both past and present French intentions in the Rhineland and of the economic, financial and cultural consequences of the Versailles settlement. The authorship included respected economists, historians and academics such as John Maynard Keynes, Hermann Oncken and Paul Rühlmann. Of these publications only two related to the Schwarze Schmach, one written by Margarete Gärtner. The other was written by Edmund Dene Morel, British Labour MP and journalist. Although Morel's text was extreme, and it earned the disapproval of the British Foreign Office,[9] it undoubtedly enjoyed heightened importance

Literatur.

Die Tagespresse.
Westdeutsche Nachrichten.
Der Saarfreund.
Der Friedensvertrag.
Keynes, „Die wirtschaftlichen Folgen des Friedensvertrages". München und Berlin, Dunker & Humblot.
Vanderlip, Frank A., „Was Europa geschehen ist". München, Drei-Masken-Verlag.
Brüggemann, Dr. Fritz, „Die rheinische Republik". Bonn, Friedrich Cohen.
Stegemann, Dr. Herbert, „Die rheinische Frage". Berlin, Puttkammer & Mühlbrecht.
Kühn, „Die Kriegsziele der französischen Bourgeoisie in Mitteleuropa". Berlin, Hans Robert Engelmann.
— „Historische und polemische Aufsätze zur französischen Politik". Berlin, Deutsche Verlagsgesellschaft für Politik und Geschichte.
— „Der Nationalismus im Leben der III. Republik". Berlin, Gebr. Paetel.
Schulte, Aloys, „Frankreich und das linke Rheinufer". Stuttgart und Berlin, Deutsche Verlagsanstalt.
Jaquot, „General Gérard und die Pfalz". Berlin, Julius Springer.
Onken, „Die Franzosen in der Pfalz". Berlin, Georg Stilke.
Noyes, „Gerechtigkeit". Mannheim, Pfalzzentrale.
Kühn, „Die Rheinpolitik der französischen Militärpartei". Berlin, Deutsche Verlagsgesellschaft für Politik und Geschichte.
„Gegen Frankreichs Anspruch auf Pfalz und Saarbecken". Protestkundgebung von Lehrkörper und Studentenschaft der Universität Heidelberg, am 1. März 1919. Heidelberg, Carl Winters Universitätsbuchhandlung.
Hauser, Henri, „Frankreichs Handel und Industrie und die Konkurrenz des Auslandes". Jena, Gustav Fischer.
Eckert, „Wirtschaftliche und finanzielle Folgen des Friedens von Versailles". Bonn, Marcus & Weber.
Curth, Hermann und Wehberg, Hans, „Der Wirtschaftskrieg. Die Maßnahmen und Bestrebungen des feindlichen Auslandes zur Bekämpfung des deutschen Handels und zur Förderung des eigenen Wirtschaftslebens". 4. Abteilung „Frankreich". Herausgegeben vom Institut für Seeverkehr und Weltwirtschaft, Kiel. Jena, Gustav Fischer.
Henning, „Die Rheinschiffahrt und der Versailler Frieden". Berlin, Deutsche Verlagsgesellschaft für Politik und Geschichte.
Rühlmann, „Kulturpropaganda". Berlin, Deutsche Verlagsgesellschaft für Politik und Geschichte.
Hartmann, „Französische Kulturarbeit am Rhein". Leipzig, K. F. Koehler.
Lien, „Das Märchen von der französischen Kultur". Berlin, Curtius.
Rühlmann, „Die französische Schule und der Weltkrieg". Leipzig, Quelle & Meyer.
„Material zur französischen Rheinpolitik" (5 Vorträge). Berlin, Druckerei Büxenstein.
Karll, „Französische Regierung und Rheinländer vor 100 Jahren". Leipzig, K. F. Koehler.
„Farbige Franzosen am Rhein", 3. Ausgabe. Berlin, Hans Robert Engelmann. (Übersetzungen in franz., italienisch., holländ. und span. Sprache.)
Morel, E. D., „The Horror on the Rhine". London, Union of Democratic Control.
„Die Fremdenlegion, eine Gefahr für das besetzte Gebiet".
Papen, Dr. F. von, „Die französische Fremdenlegion, eine Warnung für Deutschlands Söhne". Berlin, Zentralverlag.
Stegemann, „Rettet das Saarland". Berlin, Puttkammer & Mühlbrecht.
Maurice Barrès, „Der Genius des Rheins". Selbstverlag des Verfassers.
Tardieu, La Paix.
Malaurie, Tagebuch und
Ein großer Teil der französischen Werbeschriften, die P. Hartmann in seinem Buch „Französische Kulturarbeit am Rhein", Seite 51, aufzählt.

Figure 13. Propaganda literature recommended by Alfred von Wrochem

among all German propagandists. It was believed that coming from an English source it would have enormous impact.

It is noteworthy that none of Eberlein's publications received mention by Wrochem, although the booklet *Schwarze am Rhein*,[10] for example, had already been widely circulated and hailed as a substantial attack against the Schwarze Schmach. Whether this omission resulted from a lack of regard for Eberlein's work or is further evidence of a strained relationship between Berlin and Mannheim is uncertain. Whatever the reason may be, from the lack of prominence of Schwarze Schmach literature in Wrochem's list of recommended publications, it can be concluded that although the presence of coloured troops in the Rhineland was deplored by him, this was not of overriding concern. Other issues were of greater importance and it seems safe to conclude that the Schwarze Schmach campaign was not driven forward actively by him.

A few months after Wrochem had left the Volkspflege it began publishing a weekly broadsheet, *Rheinischer Beobachter* (fig. 14), containing political articles, news and comment relating mainly to events in the Rhineland. Its nature and tone revealed no significant change in Volkspflege policy following Wrochem's departure. Accusatory and strongly anti-French in content and tone, it nevertheless largely avoided inflammatory language. A variety of themes relating to the French occupation were evident, including denial of German responsibility for World War I, condemnation of French actions and intentions in the Rhineland and the threat of separatism. A favourite tactic was to publish details of speeches or articles written by prominent politicians or journalists of other nations where these were favourable to the German cause, especially when they came from an Allied country and ran counter to French interests. Thus it was noted in one issue that a member of the British Cabinet, Austen Chamberlain, had declared in Parliament that the British government was not prepared to make common cause with the French government in any future occupation of the Ruhr.[11] In another issue it published an open letter from the journalist E. D. Morel to the Archbishop of Canterbury appealing for his intervention against the injustice done to the German people by the post-war settlement.[12]

Nummer 21 21. Mai 1922

RHEINISCHER BEOBACHTER

Die Sorgen des Rheinlandes sind die Angelegenheit eines jeden Deutschen.

Inhalt:

Friedrich Hölderlin: An das besiegte Deutschland.

Gustav Reptau: Das französische Propagandasystem zur Einkreisung Deutschlands.

H. N. Brailsford: Poincarés gegen Deutschland geschwungene Peitsche — eine Bedrohung Europas.

Dr. Philipp Rott: Die Lage der pfälzischen Industrie.

Hanns Gisbert: Rheinreisen vor hundert Jahren.

Karl May: Die Kriegskasse. Eine rheinische Erzählung aus der napoleonischen Zeit.

Rheinlandchronik. — Politische Nachrichten und Glossen: Deutsche Selbstachtung und Weltgeltung. — Die vorsichtigen Besatzungstruppen. — Neue Ausschreitungen französischer Soldaten. — Ausweisungen und Unterdrückung der Geistesfreiheit. — Die Franzosen bereichern sich — die deutschen Städte verarmen. — Die Lebensfähigkeit der rheinischen Separatistenbewegung. — „Hier kann Schmutz abgeladen werden!" — **Rheinischer Fremdenverkehr:** Reist an den Rhein! — Ein Mahnwort an Reisende nach dem besetzten Gebiet. — Der Personenverkehr auf dem Rhein. — Amerika am Rhein. — Die unersättliche französische Besatzung. — Wiesbadens fünfzigtausendster Kurgast. — Ausländische Adlige als Kurgäste. — Ausländische Aerzte in Wiesbaden. — Wiesbaden als Kongreßstadt. — Bad Schlangenbad. — Beginn der Kursaison in Bad Neuenahr. — Bad Kreuznach. — Duisburg als Fremdenstadt. — **Wissenschaft, Literatur und Kunst:** Ein Roswitha-Fund in Köln. — **Kirchliches:** Die Bibliothek des erzbischöflichen Priesterseminars in Köln als Diözesanbibliothek. — **Echo des Auslandes:** Französische Pressestimmen zur „Neutralisierung" des Rheinlandes. — Englische Kritik an Frankreichs Militarismus. — Chamberlain gegen eine Ruhrbesetzung. — Die italienischen Katholiken gegen die Verwendung schwarzer Besatzungstruppen. — Eine neue italienische Kundgebung gegen die „schwarze Schande". — Die erpreßten farbigen Söldner. — **Aus dem Vereinsleben:** Die zweite Tagung des Bundes „Saar-Verein".

Einzelnummer M. 2.50. In den Bahnhofs-Buchhandlungen und Zeitungskiosken zu haben.

Figure 14. *Rheinischer Beobachter* – a monthly publication of the Rheinische Volkspflege

But the *Rheinischer Beobachter* did not limit its mischief-making to the campaign against the occupation. It highlighted other potential sources of friction between France and Britain, for example, recent direct trade negotiations between Britain and Russia which would thwart French ambitions in this area.[13] The Schwarze Schmach campaign also featured in the broadsheet but – admittedly based on a small sample – was restricted to the updating of officially recorded excesses committed by coloured troops and to republishing sympathetic articles and reports appearing in the foreign press. An example was the strong criticism that was made of the French government in the Italian press for its policy of forging ever closer ties with its colonies. With the continually declining birth rate in France this policy, it was asserted, made the future colonisation of Europe by coloured races inevitable.

The same issue quoted from an article written by the British MP Ben Spoor condemning the use of coloured troops and the requisitioning of housing for use as brothels. This was 'a tragedy, cruelly inflicted on a defeated country, cruelly imposed on our coloured fellow men, who have been misused as tools of the French hate-policy'.[14] By comparison with some other publications discussed later the language and style of the *Rheinischer Beobachter* were measured and restrained. Arguably aimed largely at an educated middle class, it was certainly no rabble-rousing publication. One might be tempted to conclude that in the spirit of the new post-war approach to propaganda the intention behind its publication was indeed to inform and to allow the readership to draw its own conclusions. But for such a conclusion to be valid, even-handedness in the presentation of the arguments is required. In the case of the *Rheinischer Beobachter* this was manifestly not so.

Of a completely different order to the propaganda of the Volkspflege was that of the Munich-based Notbund, a relative latecomer in the campaign. The Notbund was founded by Heinrich Distler in September 1920. It was much more vociferous in its campaigning than the Frauenliga, rapidly achieving notoriety on both sides of the Rhine for its extremism. The constitution of the Notbund[15] makes it clear that this was a private, apolitical association with no official connections. Its declared aims were to defend German and European culture against the criminal activities of France, to protect the legitimate interests of the white race and to reawaken the spirit of German consciousness. It would protest at home and abroad, through written and spoken word, against those measures and acts of violence that contravened the Peace Treaty and the subsequent Agreement with the enemy powers. As examples of these contraventions were cited the occupation of the Rhineland by coloured troops, the expulsion from the Rhineland of politically irreproachable citizens and the punishment of German newspaper editors simply on the grounds of their published views. The Notbund would give lectures and publish these and other material such as brochures. It would organise protest meetings and propaganda events. The intentions were to bring the plight of the occupied regions to the notice of the German people as a whole and to generate a powerful protest against the violation of the white race by coloured tribes.

Its founder had a colourful background. Born on 30 May 1885 in Burghausen, Altötting, in south-eastern Bavaria, Heinrich Distler had had a variety of occupations after spending seventeen years working as a journalist in America.[16] His second of three marriages had been nullified because he had concealed the fact that he had had syphilis. His name appeared in police records for minor offences and a number of further charges had been laid against him but had been dropped for lack of proof.[17]

In addition to inflammatory speeches made by Distler himself, which were widely reported in the provincial press, output from the Notbund consisted of a variety of posters, leaflets and booklets. One of its earliest booklets consisted of a diatribe against French policy towards Germany, alleging that the black man, likened to a sex-crazed half-animal, was deliberately being let loose on white women.[18] The underlying theme, however, repeated in various broadsheets and pamphlets, was that French policy constituted a dangerous humiliation of the white race by elevating the black man to a position of dominance.[19] This, it was maintained, would have unforeseeable consequences for the physical, spiritual and cultural life of white nations. As already remarked, it was a theme evident also in the propaganda of the Frauenliga, even if the language of the latter was generally less extreme.

This was not the only theme that the Notbund propaganda shared with that of the Frauenliga. Other topics included the construction and requisitioning of houses for use as brothels and the corruption of youth through exposure to the sights and sounds of the occupation, especially when brothels were sited in residential districts. The Notbund propaganda, however, was by far the more wide-ranging and the more extreme. Distler, like Beveridge, did not hesitate to sensationalise in lurid terms in order to whip up a response in his audience. This was evident, also, in his publications. Even the cover of his booklet *Das deutsche Leid am Rhein*[20] was far more imaginatively presented (fig. 15) than the official publications from the Frauenliga or the Pfalzzentrale. The business instinct to sensationalise in order to sell more copies must surely have accounted for much of his motivation.

Figure 15. *Das Deutsche Leid am Rhein* – published by Heinrich Distler shortly after he had been excluded from the Deutscher Notbund gegen die Schwarze Schmach

Topics covered by the Notbund ranged from an alleged denial of basic foods to starving German children while black troops ate and drank to excess, to a claim that the French army had announced plans for compulsory military service in all French African colonies, implying that a further 200,000 black troops would be garrisoned in the Rhineland.[21] Other examples included a discourse on the threat to children from the enforced billeting of coloured troops with German families and the dangers of creating a population of mixed race. However, embedded in all the hyperbole, which was not easily countered, were specific allegations that could be disproved. Examples included the naming of a village in which it was alleged that every woman had been raped,[22] and a statement that 100 rapes were being committed each day in the occupied Rhineland.[23] Such assertions, easily shown to be false, represented the Achilles heel of the Notbund as led by Distler and eventually led to action against him by the Bavarian authorities.

A particular theme of Notbund propaganda was the danger presented by a variety of fearsome tropical diseases allegedly introduced and spread by coloured troops.[24] To a population largely ignorant of such matters this must have seemed an alarming prospect indeed, especially when the documents were written in a lurid pseudo-medical style. Here again emphasis was laid on the superiority of white nations in that several of these diseases, once endemic in Europe also, had declined with the increasing refinement of European civilisation. Diseases that would supposedly be introduced, and which were claimed to be widespread in French colonies and protectorates, especially Madagascar, included leprosy, tuberculosis, dysentery, syphilis, malaria, Malta fever, Phagedänismus (noma)[25] and parasitic worms. It was alleged that those German colonists unfortunate enough to contract leprosy had become infected solely through association with negroes. A particularly terrible fate was said to await those infected by Phagedänismus, of which increasing numbers of cases were now being seen by doctors, and which was being spread through France, Germany and the Balkans by the presence of coloured troops.

At the outset Distler sought to collaborate with the Pfalzzentrale. However, the appearance of the Notbund was a matter of concern to Eberlein, for he immediately contacted Winterstein, expressing the need to be watchful of this organisation and to ask for clarification of its purpose.[26] The Notbund was a private organisation. It had nobody of any international standing behind it, and above all it did not have access to trustworthy, verifiable material from official sources. Eberlein discounted material from private sources as potentially unreliable, citing a notorious case involving the alleged discovery of four bodies of female victims in a manure heap in Saarbrücken, which had been shown to be completely groundless.[27] He was concerned, also, that the creation of the Notbund might not be an isolated instance. His overriding concern was that such activities would bring the entire campaign into disrepute abroad.[28] An organised campaign with the aim of influencing opinion outside Germany was evidently well established before Distler appeared on the scene in September 1920. It may not have been centrally directed but it is clear that those involved were following broadly agreed guidelines and furthermore that Eberlein and his organisation had been involved for some time. To Winterstein, however, there appeared to be no grounds for taking out proceedings against Distler. The Bavarian government considered the aims of the Notbund to be completely laudable even if Distler might not be the most suitable leader.

During the next few months Distler pursued his extremist campaign energetically, producing pamphlets and brochures and holding meetings at which he himself was generally the main speaker. In November 1920 an essay published in the *Bayerische Staatszeitung*, thought to have been the work of Distler, led to a three-month ban on the publication. It prompted a pointed enquiry from the Prussian Minister of the Interior[29] and a terse reply from Winterstein,[30] to the effect that the Bavarian government had no editorial influence over the newspaper. It had not taken long, either, for Notbund propaganda to provoke the French authorities. As early as 25 October the newspaper *Echo du Rhin*, published by the French authorities in Mainz, complained about Distler's allegations and accused the Reich government of having done nothing to establish the facts – indeed of being an active accomplice.[31]

The Reich government felt obliged to act. Not only was it under pressure from the French authorities, but it was also being pilloried by Notbund propaganda for being supine. The Reich Minister of the Interior accordingly complained to Winterstein about Distler and his organisation.[32] Press reports of a recent meeting in Munich[33] had contained extraordinary exaggerations, which brought discredit to the well-founded campaign to get rid of coloured troops. Distler had also alleged lack of support from officials, particularly with regard to the freeing of German girls from brothels set up for occupation troops. From this complaint it may be inferred that the Schwarze Schmach campaign had tacit approval at the highest level in the Reich Ministry of the Interior, where there was no wish to see mainstream propaganda efforts undermined by excesses. Yet Distler was not without his supporters within the Reich government. He was regarded as an exceptional speaker by some.[34] And later, when he published the booklet *Das deutsche Leid am Rhein*, one official testified to the many good points that were made in it and regretted the need to suppress it on grounds of exaggeration.[35]

The activities of the Notbund were attacked from another quarter also: the Frauenliga worked with Eberlein in seeking to silence Distler.[36] Throughout the autumn and winter Gärtner placed notices in regional newspapers distancing the Frauenliga from him.[37] For his part Distler complained of systematic undermining of his work by the Frauenliga.[38] He was not easily thwarted. Shortly after this he arranged for his wife to create uproar at a women-only protest meeting addressed by Helene Weber, Ministerial Adviser in the Prussian Social Welfare Ministry, member of the National Assembly and a prominent member of the Frauenliga. This she did by asserting that within fifteen years only mulatto children would be seen in the Rhineland. The mood of the meeting was reported by Weber as immediately becoming unpleasantly nationalistic.[39] Amongst women, just as amongst their male counterparts, there existed right-wing extremism.

The hostility between the Notbund and the semi-official Frauenliga and Pfalzzentrale continued throughout the winter of 1920–1. Eberlein became increasingly worried about the situation and he attempted to have a passport application by Distler blocked in order to thwart a planned lecture tour of the USA.[40] Eberlein's concerns lay not just in the potentially damaging nature of Notbund propaganda, but also in the fact that its meetings and propaganda were attracting considerable support[41] and as a result like-minded individuals were being attracted to the organisation.[42] Account has also to be taken of personality. Eberlein would have regarded Distler as a rival and a threat rather than somebody with whom he could collaborate. Distler was, after all, based in Munich, and was therefore much closer to the centre of power in Bavaria.

Pressure grew from Reich and Prussian governments for the Bavarian government to take action against Distler, who, though he had by now appointed a board of trustees, retained considerable powers himself. There were suspicions that Distler had created the organisation purely to use it as a source of income,[43] but no certain grounds could be found for taking action against him. In view of all the attendant publicity, the Bavarian government was reluctant to intervene for fear of damaging a cause which it regarded as fundamentally sound. Neither would it have wanted to be seen to bow to pressure from Reich or Prussian governments. Winterstein had already robustly demonstrated his determination to assert Bavarian independence of the Reich in matters concerning propaganda. Finally, however, action was taken on the grounds that the Notbund had contravened its conditions of registration through the unauthorised collection of money. The manner in which this was done, using informants, cannot fail to arouse suspicion that the situation was deliberately engineered.[44]

While the Bavarian government had no intention of allowing the Notbund to disappear, it effected changes in the board of trustees, from which Distler was removed. The new board was warned to keep to the facts when generating propaganda, to avoid exaggeration and to exert tight control over income and expenditure.[45] Distler disappeared from public view,[46] though his booklet *Das deutsche Leid am Rhein* provoked official displeasure.[47] What might be termed the Distler affair had lasted for approximately eight months. Its significance lies not only in the fact that it added considerable notoriety to the campaign against the Schwarze Schmach but also in what it revealed about the attitudes and reactions of the other major protagonists in the campaign, not least the governments of the Reich, Bavaria and Prussia.

The Notbund continued to campaign but it was now in effect controlled by the Bavarian government through short-term licensing[48] and by the requirement for all new propaganda to be officially approved prior to publication.[49] When occasion demanded it, even closer control was exercised. In May 1922 a public meeting organised by the Notbund and a number of other organisations was cancelled at short notice by the Bavarian Ministry of the Interior, evoking furious protest.[50] The justification given was that the negotiations on reparations at the Paris conference were at a delicate stage and furthermore the Prime Minister was visiting the Pfalz on that day.[51]

The Managing Director of the Notbund, Erich Klarner, who had survived the purge of the trustees, set about establishing good relationships with Eberlein, realising that this was essential if the Notbund were to achieve anything at all in the future. It needed a steady stream of news from the occupied Rhineland. Klarner made sycophantic overtures to Eberlein, dissociating the Notbund from Distler's arrogance and negligence.[52] A measure of collaboration between the two organisations resulted.[53] The Pfalzzentrale provided material to the Notbund on request,[54] but equally, when asked by the Bavarian government to advise on proposed Notbund propaganda, its comments were blunt and critical. These pointed out that the material contained nothing new. Moreover, 'The second part (a more medical section) has not been sufficiently well written to have a decisive and sustained effect on lay readers.'[55] Not only that, the Pfalzzentrale considered that financial support for this task should be withheld because the Notbund already had extensive resources.

Initial progress for the reformed Notbund was not altogether smooth. On the whole it kept to the conditions imposed upon it, going to some trouble to check facts[56] and seeking prior approval for its output. Serious recriminations followed any breach of the conditions,[57] for by early 1921 German propaganda against the Schwarze Schmach had become a sensitive international issue. A case in point was the angry reaction of the French government to press reports that the Notbund had been licensed to raise funds through collections. It rightly interpreted this as a sign of official Bavarian support.[58] On the wider international stage this was the time when Germany was following the tactic of *Erfüllungspolitik* (the policy of fulfilment).[59] The Reich Foreign Ministry wanted no distractions,[60] wishing to demonstrate to the Allies an apparent willingness to cooperate over the major issue of reparations. This was a period of improved relations between Britain and Germany,[61] although France and the Reich were in serious dispute over the future of Silesia. It was a matter of strategic importance for Germany and she was hoping for support from Britain in trying to retain Silesia in the face of French desires to cede territory to Poland – a German aspiration that Britain in fact supported. But while the Bavarian government undoubtedly shared the concerns of the Reich over Silesia, it was certainly not prepared to subordinate its own interests and would not close the Notbund down. Its position was that the presence of black troops represented a severe danger to public health and must be opposed, though there was also concern about loss of face if its earlier decision to license the Notbund were rescinded.[62] It would also have felt encouraged by the news that the Prussian authorities were likewise minded to grant the Notbund authorisation.[63] To a degree the priorities of the Reich and the two states were in conflict.

It was never likely that the Bavarian government would give way to French demands, or for that matter any demand coming from the Reich government, that it considered to be contrary to its interests. Throughout the leadership of Gustav Ritter von Kahr, Bavaria had constantly had a difficult relationship with the Reich. The most fractious dispute had been that arising over the citizens' militia, the paramilitary organisation created during the earlier Hoffmann administration to counter the threat from the revolutionaries of the extreme Left.[64] Demands by the Allies for its dissolution had been agreed to by the Reich and by other states, but Bavaria under Kahr remained obdurate, to the frustration of the Reich government. Eventually the Allies settled the issue by bypassing the Reich government and confronting Kahr directly with the threat of the military occupation of Bavaria. The citizens' militia was officially disbanded, though its activities continued clandestinely.[65] The disbandment led to the forcing of Kahr from office by the increasingly powerful dissident Right within his party. Already poor, relations between Berlin and Munich took a turn for the worse following the murder of Matthias Erzberger in August 1921 and the resulting declaration of a state of emergency throughout the Reich. For the Bavarian government this once again represented intolerable interference in the affairs of a free state. It was not until after Hugo Graf von Lerchenfeld-Köfering succeeded Kahr as Prime Minister in September 1921 that matters improved. Even then a few skirmishes took place between the two sides before everything quietened down for a while early in 1922.[66]

While the Prussian government was prepared to license the Notbund, it was concerned that the German propaganda effort was too fragmented. Authorisation was therefore conditional upon the Notbund collaborating with the Working Committee of German Associations (ADV), which had the task of 'coordinating all efforts to clarify the question of war guilt and fight the Peace Treaty terms'.[67] For the Prussian authorities the campaign against the Schwarze Schmach was just a part of the wider protest against the bigger issues of war guilt and conditions imposed under the Peace Treaty. The Bavarian government was broadly in agreement with this view.[68] While Bavaria sought at all times to maintain its independence within the Reich, there were some issues where the common cause transcended all else.

After the departure of Heinrich Distler from the Notbund in April 1921 the well-attended public rallies continued as before but were now addressed by leading members of the governing board. Two board members in particular are worthy of mention. Dr Franz Rosenberger was responsible for giving Notbund propaganda a medical slant, emphasising the allegedly extreme dangers to public health presented by the coloured occupation. But on at least one occasion he had to be reined in on account of a distortion of facts.[69] He later accused the State Commissioner for the Pfalz, Dr Lorenz Wappes, of dishonesty.[70] With the Ruhr crisis having just arrived on the scene, the Bavarian government wanted nothing to get in the way of the propaganda onslaught. It moved swiftly to remove the source of dissent and a new board of management was elected.[71] Thus, while it was able outwardly to maintain the fiction that the Notbund was a privately run organisation over which it had no control, there is no doubt about who was pulling the strings behind the scenes.

The second person of note was Felicitas Buchner, a prominent member of the Munich branch of the KFD. Buchner had for many years been an active campaigner against the evils of prostitution and especially against its regulation by government.[72] She was well respected internationally and was known to Margarete Gärtner.[73] The point to be made here is that the involvement of a person like Buchner in the Notbund activities provides further evidence of a distinct female moral perspective on the coloured occupation. What led to Buchner's appearance on the board is not known but it might be suspected that it represented an attempt to lend the Notbund campaign some moral legitimacy.

Although more care was now being taken over factual content there was no change in the near-hysterical tenor of Notbund propaganda. In August 1921 appeared the first of a monthly series of news-sheets, *Die Schmach am Rhein*, published by the Notbund and printed in German, English and Spanish. The first issue contrasted the benefits that European civilisation had brought the world, exemplified by the 1914 opening of the Panama Canal, with the current situation within a Europe burdened with disease-ridden coloured troops. It depicted the monstrous black sleeper in the desert, content with his simple life, looking up to the white man with his superior culture and civilisation. But thanks to one white nation in particular he had been dragged off from his homeland to fight another white nation, in the process learning everything that had rightly been kept from him in the interests of sound colonial policy. Now he had come to believe that he, too, could rule over a white nation. The clear warning to the readers was: 'Today the white race sleeps, while the black sleeper awakes!'[74] A later issue of the publication developed this theme further alongside the now familiar one of deprivation in the occupied Rhineland – caricatured by the well-nourished black soldier feeding his dog while the starving German child looked on.

On the whole the Notbund confined itself to propaganda against the Schwarze Schmach, but sometimes other issues were linked to this, even if a considerable stretching of the reader's imagination was required. Thus the recruitment of German youth into the French Foreign Legion was attributed largely to the evils of billeting coloured troops with German families. The troops allegedly told exaggerated tales of the pleasant life awaiting them in their tropical homelands, thereby stimulating the natural sense of adventure present in German boys.[75]

Another target for the Notbund was provided by the Bolshevists, who were identified as the driving force behind an attempt to harness the lust and ambition of black people in driving the whites out of Africa. Blacks would then be in a position to reduce the supply of food and raw materials to Europe to the unsustainable minimum. By these means the hungry masses would be made ready for revolution, resulting in the expansion of the Bolshevik Third International throughout Europe.[76] In a variation on this theme leaflets were produced purporting to come from a black underground movement which had as its goal world domination.[77] Invoking moral, hygienic and nationalistic grounds, the Notbund also became more strident in demanding that the Reich government take action against the continued occupation. Furthermore, it insisted that the Reich should make a stand against the demand from the Entente to hand over German men, who would then be exposed to the 'passions, capriciousness and thirst for revenge' of enemy courts in the occupied Rhineland.[78]

The Notbund also commissioned a film, *Die Schwarze Schmach*. Initially approved by the censor in Munich, this decision was subsequently overturned by the senior censorship authority in Berlin. The showing of the film in the Reich was prohibited on the grounds that it could endanger relations between Germany and in particular France, which had submitted two protest notes on the subject. Further grounds for banning the film lay in its gross exaggerations of the numbers both of black troops present in the Rhineland and of their alleged misdeeds. These, and the obviously contrived scenes would, in the opinion of the censors, damage rather than aid the German propaganda effort.[79]

Notbund propaganda has to be viewed against the background of events in Bavaria – and in Munich in particular. Raising the Red spectre could find fruitful ground throughout Western Europe but would find particular resonance in southern Germany, where memories of the chaos associated with the short-lived Munich Soviet were still fresh in the mind and where the right-wing BVP now held office. Moreover,

Munich, the centre of power in Bavaria, was at this time a hotbed of extreme nationalism. Hitler's organisation, growing in ascendancy, was only one of several such movements which viewed Bolshevism with particularly aggressive hatred. Even a major part of the hitherto relatively liberal press – excluding the Social Democratic *Münchener Post* – saw its main purpose as fighting Marxism.[80] At the same time, relations between the governments of Bavaria and the Reich were generally poor, following the series of disputes between the two. Admittedly, matters had improved with the replacement of Kahr by Lerchenfeld, but relations were to deteriorate once again in the summer of 1922 with the introduction of the Law for the Protection of the Republic, passed after the assassination of Walther Rathenau. The issue of the rights of individual states as opposed to the centralised authority of the Reich had been reignited. However, a compromise was then reached, to the fury of the extremist Right.[81] Lerchenfeld was weakened in the eyes of his own party and within three months felt obliged to resign in the face of a growing radicalisation of political life brought about by agitation from the Right.[82] In such a climate stirring up demands for action from the Reich government would have appealed to popular opinion in Bavaria. It is hardly surprising, then, that the Notbund laid emphasis on these aspects. It was in tune with the nationalistic Bavarian spirit of the time.

The activities of the Notbund developed further with the introduction of an Italian and French edition of *Die Schmach am Rhein* in mid-1923. In that autumn authorisation was sought to raise additional funds overseas. Financial support was received also from the Bavarian government in recognition of the importance with which its work was regarded.[83] Both the Reich Ministry for the Occupied Regions and the Bavarian government were prepared to promote an organisation which was now well under control and which was in their view fulfilling a useful function. A request by the Notbund to the State Commissioner for the Pfalz that news of excesses committed by occupation troops be conveyed to the Notbund before being made available to the press [84] was quickly granted.[85] Moreover, the information was accompanied by secret intelligence evaluations of its authenticity. Such reports from the Pfalz were acknowledged to be declining in incidence now. They were derived mostly from semi-official sources such as the press office at the Pfalzzentrale. But the best evidence that the Notbund now enjoyed complete official approval was provided by the contributors to two issues of *Die Schmach am Rhein* in 1924. These were the Bavarian Prime Minister, the State Commissioner for the Pfalz, the Bavarian Trade Minister and the Reich Minister for the Occupied Regions.[86]

Both the Notbund and the Pfalzzentrale, whose further progress is followed in the next chapter, were effectively controlled by the Bavarian government. The *Süddeutsche Monatshefte*, published in Munich, was an independent source of propaganda which exercised influence at an entirely different level from that of the Notbund. Behind it stood one man, Paul Nikolaus Cossmann. Born 6 April 1869 into a Jewish family, Cossmann was brought up in the liberal Jewish tradition, though he later converted to Catholicism. A passionate and sincere German nationalist, he used the *Süddeutsche Monatshefte*, which he co-founded in 1904, as a platform from which to disseminate his personal views. He also exerted considerable editorial influence over one of the major Munich newspapers, *Münchner Neueste Nachrichten*, and was the founder and leader of a circle of like-minded and influential personalities. Consistently supportive of the German cause throughout the war, he later campaigned relentlessly against the 'war guilt lie' and against the provisions of the Peace Treaty. Neither did he spare those whom he blamed for the defeat in 1918 – subversive left-wing revolutionary elements at home. In strongly promoting the so-called stab-in-the-back myth he did much to influence the educated and well-to-do middle classes against the new Republic.[87]

Surprisingly in view of his origins, Cossmann was anti-Semitic. While he did not subscribe to the crude anti-Semitism that followed the defeat in 1918, he did blame the Jewish intelligentsia for their allegedly destructive influence on national life. The right-wing nationalism of Cossmann was not that of the NSDAP, however. Rather, it was in the monarchist tradition and looked to a return to the Bismarckian era. Cossmann in fact attacked National Socialism as representing a danger for Germany and for being un-German. He paid the price for this, being held in captivity for a while immediately following Hitler's seizure of power and later being sent to Theresienstadt concentration camp, where he died in 1942.[88]

Cossmann's approach to propaganda against the occupation is exemplified by the issue of the *Süddeutsche Monatshefte* published in April 1922. He took a historical perspective, comparing the actions of the French occupiers with those of the Germans occupying France in 1871 (fig. 16). He wrote nothing other than the foreword, relying on external writers whom he had selected because their ideas were in tune with his own. Thus a description of the occupation of France, based on research in German military archives, was given by a doctor who had felt moved to do this having witnessed the suffering of German children as a result of the Allied blockade in World War I. Personal statements were also made by former German participants in the Franco-Prussian War and extracts from the papers of the deceased French President were cited, testifying to the exemplary conduct and magnanimity of the German High Command in the 1871 occupation of France.

English journalists and MPs of both Left and Right contributed articles to the *Süddeutsche Monatshefte* relating to the current French occupation of the Rhineland. These roundly condemned both the unjust terms of the Peace Treaty and the manner in which these had been implemented by France. Interference in the internal German administration, abusive treatment of the press, housing shortages aggravated by requisitioning and the display of arrogance towards the local population were all the subject of complaint. By comparison, the administration of the British zone was said to be exemplary. The Belgians, on the other hand, were accused of being lackeys of the French. General Allen in the American zone was criticised for giving tacit support to the use of coloured troops in the French sector while at the same time lynch justice was allowed to exist in the USA. Even though the campaign against the Schwarze Schmach was well past its peak, it featured prominently here. The by now familiar allegations of the propensity of coloured troops to sexual misconduct were made, though it was conceded that some degree of exaggeration might have taken place. A common concern was that racial wars could be a long-term consequence of allowing African troops on European soil. The

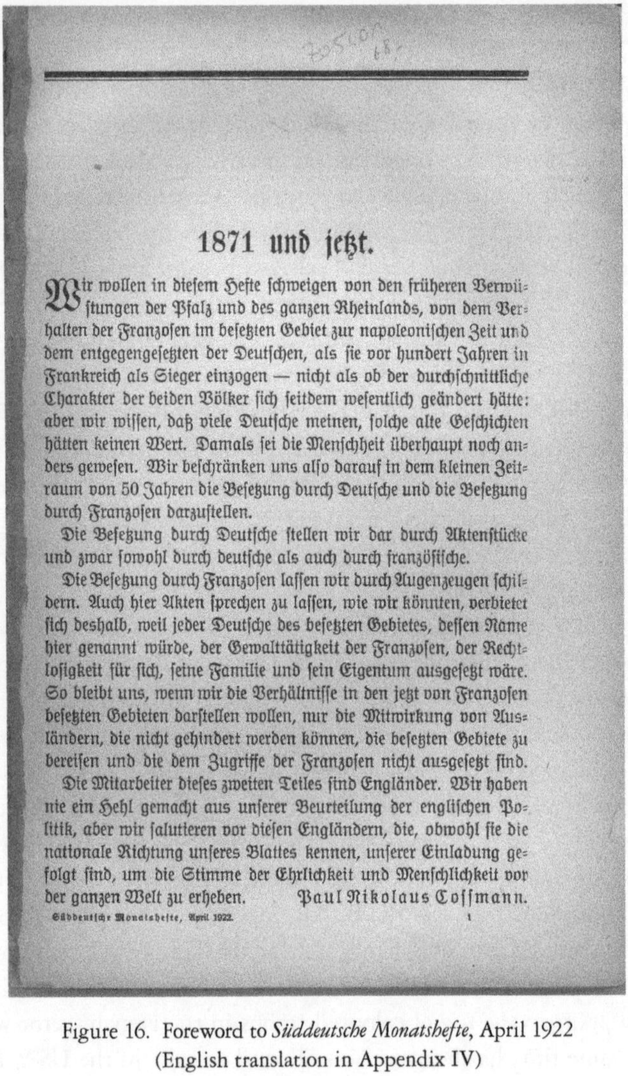

1871 und jetzt.

Wir wollen in diesem Hefte schweigen von den früheren Verwüstungen der Pfalz und des ganzen Rheinlands, von dem Verhalten der Franzosen im besetzten Gebiet zur napoleonischen Zeit und dem entgegengesetzten der Deutschen, als sie vor hundert Jahren in Frankreich als Sieger einzogen — nicht als ob der durchschnittliche Charakter der beiden Völker sich seitdem wesentlich geändert hätte: aber wir wissen, daß viele Deutsche meinen, solche alte Geschichten hätten keinen Wert. Damals sei die Menschheit überhaupt noch anders gewesen. Wir beschränken uns also darauf in dem kleinen Zeitraum von 50 Jahren die Besetzung durch Deutsche und die Besetzung durch Franzosen darzustellen.

Die Besetzung durch Deutsche stellen wir dar durch Aktenstücke und zwar sowohl durch deutsche als auch durch französische.

Die Besetzung durch Franzosen lassen wir durch Augenzeugen schildern. Auch hier Akten sprechen zu lassen, wie wir könnten, verbietet sich deshalb, weil jeder Deutsche des besetzten Gebietes, dessen Name hier genannt würde, der Gewalttätigkeit der Franzosen, der Rechtlosigkeit für sich, seine Familie und sein Eigentum ausgesetzt wäre. So bleibt uns, wenn wir die Verhältnisse in den jetzt von Franzosen besetzten Gebieten darstellen wollen, nur die Mitwirkung von Ausländern, die nicht gehindert werden können, die besetzten Gebiete zu bereisen und die dem Zugriffe der Franzosen nicht ausgesetzt sind.

Die Mitarbeiter dieses zweiten Teiles sind Engländer. Wir haben nie ein Hehl gemacht aus unserer Beurteilung der englischen Politik, aber wir salutieren vor diesen Engländern, die, obwohl sie die nationale Richtung unseres Blattes kennen, unserer Einladung gefolgt sind, um die Stimme der Ehrlichkeit und Menschlichkeit vor der ganzen Welt zu erheben. Paul Nikolaus Cossmann.

Süddeutsche Monatshefte, April 1922. 1

Figure 16. Foreword to *Süddeutsche Monatshefte*, April 1922 (English translation in Appendix IV)

mixing of the races was a further danger. One contributor clearly gave full rein to his imagination in describing the situation in German paediatric hospitals: 'Here and there amongst the rows of snow-white beds in the wards of children's hospitals dark-skinned little faces can be seen, half negro, half German, distressing little witnesses to this humiliation on the Rhine.'[89]

While the French colonial troops were clearly described by British guest authors as half-wild and uncivilised, their attitude towards them was more patronising and apparently less harsh than that evident in articles of German origin. One contributor, the Labour MP Ben Spoor, considered it to be just as much an injustice to the Africans as to the Germans, to burden primitive people with duties outside their competence. This, he believed, would hinder their development.

Even academics played a part in the propaganda battle. The history of the Pfalz was seen as a fruitful source of material with which to influence public attitudes. Organisations such as the Deutscher Schutzbund (German Protection League), whose chairman was Karl Christian von Loesch, an academic with nationalist leanings, highlighted French aggression over the centuries:

> In 500 years of German suffering, from 1370 until 1870–1, in more than twenty wars in which the Germans were never once the aggressor, the French threatened, overwhelmed and dominated the western regions of Germany. The suffering of the German people in the past must help them to bear their present suffering, to stand firm and to develop inner strength for the future![90]

The deeds of the French general Mélac, who had laid waste to the Pfalz and much of the southern Rhineland in the seventeenth century, provided a useful subject for exploitation (fig. 17).

One academic associated in particular with the Pfalz was Hermann Oncken. Born in Oldenburg on 16 November 1869, Oncken studied in Berlin and Heidelberg. He held posts in Oldenburg and Berlin before participating in an exchange with the University of Chicago. Returning to Germany, he was appointed to the Chair of Modern History at Heidelberg, where he became renowned for his teaching and scholarship. During his time at Heidelberg he was active in politics – his views were very much in the National Liberal (later DVP) tradition. Despite his right-wing tendencies he was a supporter

Figure 17. German propaganda of 1922 recalling earlier French atrocities in the Rhineland

of the Weimar Constitution. Having been greatly affected emotionally by Germany's defeat and by the terms of the subsequent Peace Treaty, Oncken devoted much time post-war to campaigning against the war guilt clause and the Rhineland occupation.[91] Initially he did not go out of his way to challenge the Nazi regime.[92] But he disliked National Socialism and he found anti-Semitic persecution abhorrent.[93] In 1935 he made a strong public attack on National

Socialist concepts of historical interpretation and as a result he was forced to retire early.

Oncken's main thesis, repeated in numerous speeches, books and pamphlets, was that continuity had existed in the foreign policy of France ever since the time of Louis XIV. It was forever driven by French desire to acquire the Rhineland.[94] Oncken pointed to what he considered to be huge inconsistencies in current French policy, which he regarded as far more dangerous than that of either Louis XIV or Napoleon I. Among these inconsistencies was the deliberate suffocation of Germany's economic capability in order to weaken her political power. This contradicted the (principally French) demand for massive reparation payments, which could only be met by a strong economy.[95] A further example of inconsistency could be found within the Rhineland where every attempt was being made, as in earlier times, to reorientate the population through the introduction of French culture. This was being done by a nation that at the same time was responsible for the Schwarze Schmach – the very antithesis of cultured behaviour.[96] Oncken condemned the Schwarze Schmach as roundly as any other propagandist.

Although he campaigned energetically against the occupation – and was deeply committed emotionally to his cause – Oncken presents a very different figure from others likewise engaged. He argued his case at a higher intellectual level. Quite apart from his interpretation of the historical and strategic significance of French intentions towards the Rhineland, he was also only too well aware of the internal tensions that bedevilled Germany at this time, and of the need for national unity. It is clear from the following quotation that he had a keen appreciation not only of the strategic importance of the western boundary territories but also of their symbolic significance for the future existence of the German nation:

> The Bavarian Pfalz is the German Pfalz. Just as the Pfalz has the certainty of remaining German only through its connection with Bavaria, so can it only remain Bavarian as part of our German Fatherland. One is dependent on the other. As in 1866, when the French tried to rob us of the Pfalz, the fate of

> all of us will be determined by the fate of this western margin of Germany.
>
> As in those days the Pfalz is like a bridge that binds North and South together, Bavaria and Prussia.[97]

Little wonder, then, that Winterstein on setting up the Pfalzzentrale should approach him with a request that he should serve on its action committee.[98]

If Oncken's carefully argued campaign against the occupation represented the moderate end of a wide spectrum of propaganda, then the output of the German Fichte-Bund was undoubtedly at the other extreme. Based in Hamburg, the Fichte-Bund became renowned for the extreme crudity of its racist outpourings. Established by Friedrich Heinrich Kessemeier[99] in 1914 to propagate German views and aims abroad, its contribution to propaganda was mainly through the distribution of Fichte-Bund pamphlets by sympathisers.[100] Chief amongst these was the monthly propaganda sheet *Ideal und Leben*, which was translated into other languages and distributed abroad. Following the defeat of Germany in 1918 topics such as the Schwarze Schmach provided the ideal source for its extreme nationalist rantings. In the example shown (fig. 18) the technique adopted by Kessemeier was to take the booklet *Farbige Franzosen am Rhein* and to exaggerate the points made by Margarete Gärtner. Despite its lurid language and sweeping allegations, Kessemeier's propaganda sheet cited exactly the same numbers of assault cases as those contained in the Frauenliga booklet. There is no evidence that Gärtner conducted any campaign against Kessemeier in the same way that she did against Distler and his Notbund. As long as propaganda contained no information that could be proved to be false, it was officially acceptable.

Of the extreme nationalist nature of the Fichte-Bund there can be no doubt. This organisation had a continued existence into the National Socialist era and had little difficulty in finding common cause with the new political masters. Funded by Goebbels's propaganda ministry and led by the son of the founder, Theodor Kessemeier, it was a source of propaganda against Britain and her Allies before and during World War II.[101]

Uebersetzung aus „Ideal und Leben"

Deutsche Monatsschrift für Fichtes Hochgedanken. Verlag H. Kessemeier, Hamburg.
Herausgegeben vom Deutschen Fichte-Bund e. V. Gegründet 1914. Sitz Hamburg.
Kanzlei: Hamburg 36, Dammtorstraße 30. Fernruf: Vulkan 7727.
Bankkonto: Reichsbank-Girokonto, Hamburg. Postscheckkonto: Nr. 8939, Hamburg.

Notruf Nr. 3 an die Engländer.
Gegen die schwarze Schmach.
Bei Bestellung anzugeben.

Wer diesen Notruf erhält, möge ihn nach England senden.

Outcry against the Black Horror! Urgent appeal to Englishmen!

An awful crime against the white race, against our German women, maidens and children is being perpetrated by the French in using black and coloured troops for the occupation of German territory in an ever increasing number without our being able to prevent it. We therefore resort to the only means at our disposal, viz: to an urgent public appeal to the conscience of all the white nations in the world.

In the Wild-West when a coloured man outrages a white woman, he is lynched without more ado. But what have our German women, girls and children to suffer from the African troops in the occupied districts? What says the world to hundred of thousands white people being enslaved by black and coloured savages? What says the world to the ever increasing assaults and crimes committed by these wild beasts on German women and children? Do the other white nations of the world know about this? It must really be doubted, for it can hardly be believed that they should have no fellow-feeling for the disgrace which is being perpetrated on us and thus on all white people. Therefore the crime committed by the French must be shouted all over the world and the other white nations must be made aware of that this disgrace hits them as well as us.

In front of us lies a pamphlet of about a hundred pages entitled: »Coloured Frenchmen on the Rhine«, a cry of distress from German women (published by H. R. Engelmann, Berlin*). These represent the police records of a large number of crimes committed by black and coloured men. Any one's blood must boil at the horrors committed on defenceless women and children reported in these pages in a cold matter-of-fact way.

In them special emphasis is laid on the fact that the cases not placed on record would be far more numerous than those officially reported which seems but natural as the feeling of shame restrains in many cases the victim from denouncement, partly from fear of retaliation, for often denunciators have been punished for libelling black troops.

Many millions are being paid by the French to suppress publication of these crimes and to stifle German appeals for help. The newspapers published in the occupied districts have been forbidden by the French to report crimes committed on white women. In some places the papers were compelled to publish declarations according to which the black troops had committed no assaults: Nevertheless

It is a fact that black soldiers push white women from the the footpaths assisting with the buttends of their rifles;

It is a fact that the French have started compulsory brothels with white girls in them for the use of coloured soldiers;

It is a fact that the number of births (coloured bastards) is steadily increasing;

It is a fact that parents, teachers, clergymen have been punished because they had forbidden to the girls in their charge any intercourse with coloured soldiers;

It is a fact that a nigger took part for months at the sittings of the Police Court and Court of Appeal at Landau and expressed his scorn and contempt for the white accused;

It is a fact that a French officer to whom an outraged young wife applied for help, bawled out to her: »These fellows have been away from home now for $2^1/_2$ years and must have it. And they are specially keen on fair hair (Police Court Sitting of 10. April 1920).

It is a fact that black soldiers are outraging boys and infect them with venereal diseases;

It is a fact that girls are seized, tied on seats or held by the black soldiers and then violated until they expire;

It is a fact that mothers who run to help their ill-used children, have been simply shot down;

It is a fact that white women have been torn from their beds and that their fettered husbands had to look on whilst their wives were being outraged:

It is a fact that up to the beginning of 1921 the following cases have been put on record by the police:

40 cases of attempted rape
70 cases of accomplished rape
20 cases of sexual misdemeanour of various other kinds
7 cases of unnatural intercourse with boys.

The French chauvinists are trying to hide these

*) To be obtained from the office of »Ideal and Life« at the price of Mk. 2.— plus increase and postage.

Figure 18. English-language version of propaganda news-sheet produced by Heinrich Kessemeier and the Deutscher Fichte-Bund

The Volksbund 'Rettet die Ehre', based in Bremen, presented a complete contrast to both the Notbund and the Fichte-Bund though it, too, was a privately supported organisation. Nationalistic and well to the fore in all propaganda themes related to the Peace Treaty provisions, its tone was, however, more moderate. Its organisation was both purposeful and systematic. Founded in 1919, it grew rapidly and by October 1920 claimed to have members in 480 towns and 375 rural districts within Germany, drawing its membership from all parties with the exception of the USPD and KPD.[102] Thereafter it grew more slowly and in 1922 only a further six towns were represented.

As much as any organisation discussed in this study, the Volksbund was the child of its creator. Otto Hartwich was born on 22 August 1861 at Swinemünde in Pomerania.[103] He studied at the universities of Tübingen, Halle, Leipzig and Greifswald. Following appointments elsewhere he became dean at the cathedral in Bremen in 1909, an important ecclesiastical post in the region. Best described as a traditionalist and right-wing conservative, Hartwich was a staunch admirer of Gustav Ritter von Kahr and especially of Erich Ludendorff[104] but was seemingly disdainful of Hitler. Before the abolition of political

Figure 19. Otto Hartwich

parties in 1933 he was a member of the DNVP. That he was a man of firm principles is demonstrated in his later dealings with the Nazi authorities. His relationship with them was uneasy. In December 1933 he applied successfully to join the Reichsverband Deutscher Schriftsteller (Reich Association of German Authors, or RDS). Shortly afterwards, however, he fell under suspicion for having been a prominent Freemason and his house was searched for evidence of subversive literature. Through appealing directly to Reich President Paul Hindenburg, he received an assurance that former members of the now disbanded German lodges would not be persecuted.[105] In 1935, however, re-examination of his 1933 application form revealed that he had actually rejected the idea of NSDAP membership: 'I have until now not become a member of the NSDAP for one reason alone – it offends my honour and self-respect to be obliged to offer surety for my patriotism and loyalty. Whosoever doubts me, insults me.'[106] This was interpreted as showing contempt for the party, and as a result he was stripped of his membership of the RDS. Undaunted, Hartwich applied to join the National Sozialistische Volkswohlfahrt (National Socialist People's Welfare) and was eventually able to convince the Gauleiter (Regional Leader) for Berlin, where he then lived in retirement, of his suitability for membership of that organisation.

During the mid-1930s Hartwich became increasingly immersed in the issue of *Gleichschaltung* of the Churches.[107] Surprisingly, in view of his difficulties with the regime, he was fundamentally supportive of the policy and intended to publish his ideas on this. In 1937 he sought the mandatory membership of the Reichsschrifttumskammer (Writers' Association),[108] only to come up against opposition from the Gestapo. The Gestapo maintained that three years previously he had made unjustified allegations to Hindenberg that the new government had introduced a system in which innocent citizens could be denounced on a whim. To such evidence of political unreliability was added a quotation from a letter that Hartwich had sent to the Zentralverein deutscher Staatsbürger jüdischen Glaubens (Association of German Citizens of Jewish Faith) in 1928 following incidents in which Jewish graves had been desecrated:

> I must tell you how angry I am over the continued anti-Semitic rabble-rousing and its consequences, and at the same time let you

> know that I know many Christians who feel that this shameless anti-Semitic slander and provocative agitation is a crime against civilisation.[109]

Such sentiments were of course completely unacceptable to the Gestapo. Nevertheless Hartwich persisted with his application. In his favour were his creation of the Volksbund to fight for German honour (fig. 20) and the authorities' belief that at seventy-eight years of age he would not pose a threat to the National Socialist state. It was also noted with approval that all five of his sons had fought in World War I, two falling in battle. His application for membership of the Kammer was approved in March 1939.[110]

The priority of the Volksbund in 1919 was to campaign against the presumption of German war guilt and the terms of the Peace Treaty under which persons adjudged to be guilty of war crimes were to be handed over to the Allies for prosecution (known in Germany as *die Auslieferungsartikel*).[111] Furthermore, it wanted to ensure that German nationals should only be brought before German courts. Protest meetings were organised throughout Germany and articles published in the press. Petitions drafted in eight languages were handed in to the governments of developed countries throughout the world. Some limited success was claimed in this campaign, in that the Allies agreed that alleged war criminals should be brought before the Reichsgericht (Reich Supreme Court) in Leipzig, although control over sentencing was retained in Allied hands. Success was mixed, however, for by the end of 1921 the Allies had decided that the Leipzig trials were inadequate and had renewed demands for the handing over of alleged war criminals.[112] Less success was achieved by the Volksbund in trying to persuade the Reich government to put forward a list of alleged Allied war criminals as a counter to the Allied allegations of German war crimes. The compilation of such a list was agreed by the Reich Foreign Ministry in February 1920, but two years later the list, though completed, had still not been handed over. It remained the subject of a continuing campaign by the Volksbund.[113]

Ehre verloren, Alles verloren!

Ein Aufruf an alle echten Deutschen im Januar 1920.

An alle, die es angeht!

In ganz Deutschland

ist eine Bewegung entfacht, dem Justizmord an Deutschlands Ehre zu begegnen, der vollzogen werden soll durch die **Aburteilung deutscher Fürsten, Beamten, Offiziere und Mannschaften vor Gerichten der Feinde.** Diese Schrift ist eingegeben von der Besorgnis, daß die Bewegung entmutigt werden, das Ziel verkennen und verlieren könnte, sofern es mißlingt, die Auslieferung der Opfer zu verhindern. Sie will Euch vor Augen stellen, daß alsdann der Schlußkampf im Laufe der Prozesse selber ausgefochten werden muß, und daß es auch dann noch an Euch ist, zu verteidigen, was noch verloren werden kann: die Ehre, die Opfer, die Lebensluft der kommenden Geschlechter. **Wir wollen zunächst die Auslieferung verhindern,** aber selbst wenn wir nur das eine erreichen, daß Willkür nicht beschönigt werden kann, Wahrheit und Recht in ihren Würden bleiben, werden wir einen entscheidenden Sieg erfochten haben.

1

Figure 20. Upholding German honour was at the heart of the propaganda campaigns of the Bremen-based Volksbund "Rettet die Ehre" (English translation in Appendix V)

By the end of June 1920 the Volksbund had established a network of sympathisers in the USA and throughout Europe, with the exception of France and Belgium, through which news and propaganda could be fed to the local press in any of seven languages. The Volksbund had also been active in whipping up support from women's organisations, especially in Germany, Austria and Holland. By October it was confidently claimed that the press agitation had already achieved some success.[114]

A year later the press information network had been extended to South America, and the Volksbund had also provided material for the mass protest meetings that had taken place in New York, Philadelphia, St Louis and Milwaukee. The same confident tone was being adopted as in 1920, but by 1922 it was acknowledged that the campaign against the Schwarze Schmach was by no means over.[115]

The main preoccupation of the Volksbund in 1921 and 1922 continued to lie in the bitter contestation of allegations of Germany's war guilt. In this matter it operated in cooperation with other like-minded associations under the umbrella of the ADV. The issue of war guilt led to a flood of pamphlets and brochures as well as more substantial literature. By April 1922 the Volksbund itself had produced three propaganda brochures, of which, for example, *Die große Lüge*[116] was printed in eight languages and 160,000 copies were produced for worldwide distribution. Hartwich considered it essential to conduct the propaganda war on a global scale. At the same time he attempted to keep the issue to the forefront on the domestic political agenda by sending copies of *Die große Lüge* to all members of the Reichstag and ministers of the German states as well as to delegates to the London Conference.[117]

The income of the Volksbund came largely from donations made by business and financial institutions. Donations were also received from abroad, though these alone did not cover the costs of overseas operations. In common with the Notbund and, as we shall see, the Pfalzzentrale, the Volksbund was unable to fulfil its ambitions through lack of funds, a situation exacerbated by currency devaluation. New donors were constantly being sought,[118] but by April 1922 the shortfall was M 1.5 million. Hartwich was, however, sensitive to any charge that the Volksbund received financial support from the government and was at pains to make clear the nature of the relationship between them:

> The widespread belief that the Volksbund gets resources from the German government is a myth. The government has used the Volksbund several times, but it gives it no financial contribution or direct support of any kind.[119]

Like the Notbund, the Volksbund found itself under attack at times, though in this case it came from the left-wing press rather than from official circles. The Volksbund was able to observe with self-satisfaction that 'The constant stream of comments on our work, some appreciative, some critical, prove that we have attracted the interest of the public to a considerable degree.'[120] To the charge that a volunteer organisation must inevitably be dilettantish in nature, Hartwich replied: 'Conscientiousness, drive and above all love for our work make for effective results, not financial reward.'[121] Although there appears to have been relatively little direct contact with the Pfalzzentrale, Hartwich was not averse to collaboration with those propagandists whom he respected. On one occasion he attempted, though unsuccessfully, to recruit Paul Rühlmann.[122] But he rejected outright any form of collaboration with Heinrich Distler and his Notbund.[123] His relationships with the Frauenliga, on the other hand, were businesslike and cordial. Information on coloured troop deployments, for example, was passed to the Volksbund by the Frauenliga,[124] while the Volksbund for its part sent it copies of its fortnightly newsletter – first published in August 1921.[125] There can be no doubt that Margarete Gärtner held Volksbund propaganda in high esteem, for she complimented Hartwich on his work.[126] While undoubtedly flattered, Otto Hartwich was, however, his own man, refusing her request for details of his sources of information.[127]

No less energetic in promoting his cause than other propagandists, Hartwich approached it from yet another perspective. Throughout his life he had adhered to a strict code in which his concept of honour was all-important to him. This was not dissimilar to the medieval concept of knightly honour and virtue, in which all actions and behaviour were based on a conventionalised set of rules and moral principles. Social standing was closely linked with honour but there existed an important prerequisite: all should adhere to the same set of rules, for not only did one bring dishonour on oneself by breaking the code, the action of others could also result in loss of honour. For Hartwich accusation of war guilt, consequent occupation of the Rhineland and the Schwarze Schmach were simply aspects of Germany's loss of honour and standing among the great (white) nations. It had been brought about solely by dishonourable acts on the part of the Allies. A particular source of grievance lay once again in the setting of the black race above the white. That France had subjected Germany to such humiliation was bad enough in Hartwich's view but the consequences of using black people to defend the French empire were already evident. From negro leaders attending All-African congresses in London and Brussels had – so he alleged – already come demands for equal rights![128]

The loss of honour in failure to observe the knightly code of chivalry was above all evident in the military sphere. In World War I total war had made its first appearance. For the first time the enemy was frequently unseen in the mass destruction that was taking place at the Front. Death was dealt out completely impersonally. There was no place for chivalry. With the end of the war came a new and changed world. To be sure, the pressures and signs of coming social change were already present at the outbreak of war in 1914 but the collapse, followed by revolution, had been catastrophic. Hartwich, mourning his personal losses and the losses of the German nation, was also reacting against the passing of what had to him been – and in his eyes still should be – the natural and proper order in German society and of Germany's place in the world.

The novel was considered by certain German propagandists to be an important medium. During the course of the war it had been used extensively to promote the Allied cause, encouraged in particular by the British government. Shortly after the outbreak of war a secret meeting of twenty-five of Britain's best-known authors had been convened to discuss ways and means by which they could contribute to the Allied war effort.[129] There followed a steady stream of short stories and novels, all intended to whip up patriotic feelings in the home population. Germany had not made use of the novel to the same extent, but now, in fighting against the Rhineland occupation, some German propagandists sought to emulate the earlier British success:

> Until now the novel has been almost completely absent in this respect and yet it could have such a lasting impact. Oddly enough, in wartime we were greatly lacking in war novels with any national feeling or intention, whereas the newspapers and

> magazines in enemy countries inundated their readers with novels and short stories, quite apart from novels published in book form. All of these had the sole purpose of whipping up national feelings and instincts.[130]

A number of novels appeared. Margarete Gärtner took it upon herself to read them. Almost all of those that she read she considered to be of a poor standard. She was, at least initially, more favourably disposed towards Guido Kreutzer's *Die Schwarze Schmach*, for which, as noted earlier, she provided some resources. With the assumption that it was nevertheless reasonably representative of its kind, the novel provides some insight into the importance that propagandists attached to the Schwarze Schmach relative to other issues.

The novel by Kreutzer was set in a small Rhineland town at the beginning of the occupation. The town was home to a national hero, a retired Prussian general who had commanded the German armies in the spring offensive of 1918 and who had subsequently distinguished himself in a determined rearguard action. Now, however, he was suspected by the French Foreign Ministry of organising a conspiracy to restore the German monarchy and renew hostilities in a war of revenge. In the absence of any evidence to support this notion, plans were laid to plant incriminating documents in his house. The agent was to be the owner of the local steelworks, a traitor who had been supplying France with steel throughout the war through a Swiss intermediary. He was now blackmailed by the French government to assure his support. A further twist was given to an improbable plot in that the French officer in charge of the Moroccan garrison in the town was the son of the owner of the steelworks, who had left the town following youthful excesses years before. He had joined the Foreign Legion, subsequently taking a commission in the French army. He, too, was a traitor but unlike his father achieved at least partial moral redemption in the eyes of the author by rediscovering his German values, and setting duty to the Fatherland above his duty as a French soldier to obey orders. All this was reinforced by his shooting of his subordinate, a half-Arab officer, who was about to violate the general's daughter. The general, his daughter, one or two victims of sexual assault and a number of local people, cut down by French machine guns during demonstrations, paid the ultimate price as a consequence of the French occupation.

Through the eyes of his characters Kreutzer reflected a distinctive view of the political situation in Germany that was closely allied to his own sympathies. Thus the Prussian war hero lamented the actions of a weak Kaiser, who had deserted the throne. He had left 70 million citizens, who had entrusted their fate to him, in the abyss.[131] And who other than a senior officer in the French War Ministry should openly admit that:

> The German Army was the moral victor. Only numerical superiority and hunger had finally forced it to its knees. France by itself would have been overrun by Germany in less than four weeks without being able to offer any serious resistance.[132]

On the German side, all of Kreutzer's characters behaved honourably, with the exception of the grasping and traitorous steelworks owner, who was harsh and pitiless towards his workforce, ingratiating towards his betters. Even his dirt-begrimed workers, though coming out on strike against his exploitation of them, denied any affinity for Communism and demonstrated publicly their support for the general, thereby showing an unrealistic degree of social cohesion: 'What we fight over politically amongst ourselves in Germany is our affair. It's nobody else's business. But against the Frenchman we all stand together.'[133] On the French side matters were quite different. Treachery, deceit and immoral behaviour abounded. The plot to implicate the general was hatched by a renegade Alsatian who had escaped to France at the outbreak of war. Blackmail was employed by the French government in order to carry it through. Scenes of debauchery were portrayed in buildings requisitioned by the French army, while German families were evicted into the streets. Army discipline was lax, allowing coloured troops considerable freedom of action, a situation of which they took full advantage. Many of the themes of Schwarze Schmach propaganda were evident in Kreutzer's work. Sexual assault, murder and massacre were woven into the plot. The ultimate insult was afforded to the general by requisitioning an annexe to his house for use as a brothel and demanding that his daughter supervise it. Moroccan troops were depicted as half-wild beasts, described as having 'a rough-hewn black-brown face; bulging yellowish eyes buried deep under the forehead beneath the steel helmet; the predatory teeth dazzlingly bright between burning red lips'.[134]

Yet while Kreutzer's book was laced with fictional excesses by coloured troops, in the work as a whole it seems as if the Schwarze Schmach was almost subsidiary in his eyes to a bigger issue – the simple fact that Germany had lost the war. The book was simply the expression of his resentment and fury.

The foreword, by Ernst Graf zu Reventlow, clearly identified the readership at which the book was aimed:

> The novel is one of the most important means of reaching the great mass of Germans, who do not understand politics and have no interest in them – those whose interests are bounded by the family, or the regulars' table in the inn or the party club or those who simply withdraw into themselves.[135]

Reventlow himself was a member of the Deutschvölkische Freiheitspartei (German Völkisch Freedom Party)[136] and he represented that party in the Reichstag until it was subsumed in the National Socialist movement. From 1927 he sat as a member of the NSDAP.[137] At one point Reventlow found some inspiration in the concept of National Bolshevism,[138] but essentially he followed mainstream Nazi ideas.

The foreword drew attention to the suffering of the German people in the occupied Rhineland, accusing France of planning to destroy Germany, not least through disease and moral decay linked to the Schwarze Schmach. Reventlow took as his theme the Christian exhortation to love thy neighbour as thyself, identifying the neighbour as the occupied Rhineland and arguing that love for the neighbour demanded hatred of their tormentors, namely France:

> It is this national hatred that we need! It must pulsate evenly throughout the German people, uniting them and driving them forward. This hatred of an entire people, despite a lack

> of weapons, will build an insuperable force and, from a certain moment in time, an irresistible one. It must act everywhere and at every moment against the French interloper. In the long term no conqueror has ever been able to withstand such hatred and at this time in Germany the conqueror is not even there by virtue of his own power.[139]

Thus in addition to an arguably distorted and perverse view of a basic tenet of Christianity we see again the resentment surfacing against a victorious France, which had only managed to win World War I by receiving help from the outside world.

Reventlow nevertheless reserved some criticism for his own side, complaining that in contrast to other peoples, where enemy actions immediately evoked a united national response, Germans were indifferent to anything that did not affect them personally. This in a sense echoed the concerns of others like Eberlein and Winterstein, who permanently strove to make unoccupied Germany aware of events in the Rhineland. Reventlow went further and elevated the task of informing the German public to a moral crusade.

The tenor of the book leaves little doubt that it reflected the views of extreme right-wing *völkisch* circles, for whom defeat had come as a crushing blow and for whom the new Republic was an abomination. For them the Schwarze Schmach was clearly but one element in the array of grievances against France. Incitement of public hatred leading to a war of revenge in the indefinite future was much in evidence.

The contribution of the Pfalzzentrale to the campaign against the Rhineland occupation has yet to be considered, but from the discussion of other major sources of propaganda several points are already emerging. In the first place campaigning against the occupation from all quarters, public and private, was dominated by the issue of the Schwarze Schmach. But was the campaign ordered at a high level in the Reich government and then orchestrated by it? As noted earlier, this was the opinion of the chairman of the IRHC, Paul Tirard – and an impression that has been conveyed by several studies.[140] Such a view seems too simplistic. Certainly the initial press campaign in the autumn of 1919 originated in the Reich press office and, having died down, was reignited by the incident at Frankfurt. But subsequently, rather than being directed from the top, the campaign quickly developed its own momentum, thanks to the energy and personal interests of relatively few middle-ranking individuals who were in a position to press home what they considered to be a propaganda advantage. In short, there was a very distinct bandwagon effect. The question then arises as to what provided the incentive to become involved.

In the Armistice period the general expectation in Germany had been of a just peace that would strike a reasonable balance between the interests of Germany and those of the Allied Powers. When the terms became known in early May 1919 fury was expressed in the Reichstag and mass protest took place across Germany. Wide sections of society – with the exception of the extreme Left – were involved in meetings attended by members of political parties, trade unions, church groups, and clubs and associations of various kinds. There was an element of orchestration in this, for it was intended to demonstrate the unity of the German nation to the outside world. But fundamentally the protests were spontaneous.[141] While individual groups had objections to specific provisions within the Peace Treaty, or would place a different emphasis on others, an overarching conviction was that the Treaty represented naked revenge on the part of the Allies and an attempt to destroy Germany. The charge that Germany alone bore responsibility for World War I, coupled with her exclusion from the League of Nations and the demand that alleged war criminals, including the Kaiser, be handed over, were for the political Right in particular associated with the loss of national honour. Payment of reparations, appropriation of colonies and occupation of border regions of Germany to guarantee payment were widely seen as humiliating punishment. In the period before the signing of the Peace Treaty the country was united from monarchists and extreme nationalists to mainstream socialists in its rejection of the terms – a degree of unity that had not been seen since the beginning of the war. As Dülffer has pointed out, in creating national unity by rejecting the provisions of the Versailles Peace Treaty the Republic had effectively founded itself on the prolongation of the experience of war.[142] In such circumstances, given the inability to take up arms again, it was perhaps only a matter of time before aggressive propaganda of one kind or another appeared on the scene, one of very few weapons that could be used against the enemy in this continuing state of war. The campaign against the Schwarze Schmach was ideally suited for this purpose because the Schwarze Schmach symbolised the humiliations of the Peace Treaty in setting the black man in authority above the white man. The use by France of non-white troops even in mundane tasks such as the checking of identity cards struck deep into the German soul and greatly magnified the sense of injustice. This is confirmed by reports from British officials in the Rhineland who on several occasions noted that there was widespread resentment against black and coloured troops being used by the French authorities to control the white population.[143] A similar conclusion was drawn by an American journalist during a fact-finding visit,[144] while a British officer observed at the time of the Ruhr occupation:

> Perhaps what I found most unpleasant was the examination of passes, which was carried out ... every time a trainload left or entered French territory, by a squad of African troops. They treated the Germans with such superior officiousness – it was so incongruous as between Africans and Europeans – that I felt ashamed, every time it happened, that they were regarded as our Allies.[145]

While anger over the assumptions and the provisions of the Peace Treaty was widespread, propaganda activity came essentially from the middle-class political Right. Yet this was not a campaign driven by a group of people sharing the same fundamental political perspectives or religious beliefs and still less were they all of *völkisch* persuasion. Many supporters of the democratic order of the new Republic campaigned as energetically as those who wanted a return to the old monarchical hierarchy or those who were extreme nationalists. Jews contributed to the campaign as well as anti-Semites and Catholics campaigned alongside Protestants. Some who contributed – especially on the extreme right – would later be closely associated with the Nazi regime, others would fall foul of it. But above all, the bulk of the propaganda came from a relatively small number of determined individuals, who used it largely to expound personal views. Between organisations there was some measure of cooperation, though little coordination of output. Each as far as possible guarded its own independence. Neither was there much attempt to tailor propaganda to reach a wider public. Thus, at one end of the spectrum Hermann Oncken addressed a highly educated audience on the political dangers arising from French foreign policy: at the other extreme the vituperative rantings of Distler and Kessemeier appealed solely to those of like mind. The Volkspflege propaganda was biased towards middle-class recipients. Relatively little propaganda was related to the actual hardships of everyday life in the occupied Rhineland or the prospects for its people. It all bore evidence of a general authorship that was detached from such matters – a fact that, as earlier suggested, led to considerable friction within the Frauenliga.

Some distinction should be made between the more vituperative hate propaganda – more often than not associated with the extreme Right – and arguably less offensive material. Hate propaganda, which appeared only after the Peace Treaty was signed, was born of both impotence and fury. Germany now lay in a humiliating economic and military stranglehold and could do little to help herself. She was ruled by a liberal republican government rejected by the extreme Right and inevitably anger was mixed with subconscious fear of what the future might hold. Coloured troops, symbol of German denigration and humiliation and at the same time of French superiority, provided a convenient scapegoat. Vilification of these troops in effect provided a form of catharsis.

To suggest that the Schwarze Schmach campaign was driven forward by a relatively small number of individuals is not to imply that the Reich and state governments played no part in the campaign. Far from it. While all was going well the mainstream campaign had powerful support at the highest level in the Reich Ministry of the Interior. This much is amply borne out by the history of the Notbund and of the Frauenliga. It is also clear that, notwithstanding Winterstein's apparent initial diffidence in the Distler affair, control of much of the Schwarze Schmach propaganda lay ultimately in the hands of a small network of officials in the Reich government and the governments of

Bavaria and Prussia. Unity of purpose in fighting the French occupation of the Rhineland ultimately transcended the chasm that existed between Bavaria and the Reich in other policy areas. Occupation was universally regarded as an imposition, while again and again in the propaganda it is made clear that the use of coloured troops constituted humiliation of the German people. This in itself was a powerful unifying force. Furthermore, the Reich Ministry of the Interior and its counterparts in the Bavarian and Prussian governments were conscious of the criticism that not enough was being done to support the population in the occupied Rhineland, and this would also have helped to fuel the campaign. On the other hand the Reich Foreign Ministry, while supportive in principle, had other priorities.

Judged against the general pattern of events and the rigours of everyday life in the occupied Rhineland, and the Pfalz in particular, the presence of coloured troops was of relatively minor importance to the population at large. There can be little doubt, either, that the propaganda campaign against the Schwarze Schmach was out of all proportion to the actual excesses of these troops. This much can be inferred from official German statistics and British records. Accounts of the occupation of the Pfalz published by local German officials immediately after the French withdrawal in 1930 also made little mention of the Schwarze Schmach. Rather, their main concerns had lain in the threat presented by French-supported separatism.[146] To counter this threat was the *raison d'être* of the Pfalzzentrale, led by Eberlein. Of all the organisations involved in Rhineland propaganda the Pfalzzentrale under his leadership was to have by far the most turbulent existence. Before discussing in Chapter 7 the themes that Eberlein addressed in his propaganda, therefore, we first consider the manner in which he undertook his task and the impact that this had on German–Allied relations and, ultimately, on the fate of his organisation.

6

THE PFALZZENTRALE: METAMORPHOSIS AND DISSOLUTION

Having earlier outlined the way in which the Pfalzzentrale was set up and how it related to other propaganda organisations, we can now turn our attention to its subsequent development and the events that ultimately resulted in its demise. While the creation of the Pfalzzentrale had been very much a Bavarian initiative, the Reich Chancellery and the Ministry of the Interior had, even if indirectly through the Volkspflege, played a part in shaping its early development. It had been caught up in the wider question of demarcation of rights and responsibilities between Reich and states. The Bavarian government had robustly – and successfully – defended the rights of individual states to organise propaganda in the occupied Rhineland. The role of the Reich had essentially been to provide support but not to interfere. Thus by the summer of 1921 the combined efforts of Bavaria, Prussia and Hessen were embodied in the Mannheim Centre, with Eberlein acting as overall leader. An accommodation – if at times uneasy – had finally been reached between Reich and states.

While the organisation of official propaganda in the Rhineland had until mid-1920 been largely influenced by the internal political and constitutional situation in Germany, external factors were henceforth to play an increasingly important role. From the standpoint of the Reich and the states the Mannheim Centre, embodying the Pfalzzentrale, was operating successfully under Eberlein's energetic leadership. As far as the Allies – more particularly the French occupation authorities – were concerned, however, it was achieving considerable notoriety. This was to rebound on the Reich government. From late 1920 onwards the Reich Foreign Ministry inevitably became more closely involved. Matters came to a head when in June 1921 the first demands were made by the Allies for the closure of the Mannheim Centre. This raises two questions. To what extent was the Foreign Ministry either willing or able to make compliance with Allied demands a priority for the Reich government? Perhaps more significantly, against a background of generally strained relations between Berlin and Munich, to what extent could the Reich government intervene and control the actions of a semi-official Bavarian agency? It is with such aspects, which forced the Mannheim Centre into a clandestine existence in the autumn of 1921 and led to its closure in May 1924, that this chapter is concerned. Furthermore, throughout this study it has been argued that German Rhineland propaganda in the early Weimar years owed much of its impact to relatively few strongly motivated and energetic individuals. Eberlein was arguably the most prominent of these. Confrontational by nature, he was able to thrive for a time in the fractured political and constitutional environment of Weimar Germany. But I seek to make clear in this chapter that the very characteristics that brought him to prominence also made the enforced closure of the Centre inevitable.

The fact that much of the diplomatic interchange concerning the occupation occurred through the IRHC was to play a decisive part in the future course of events. Its chairman, Paul Tirard, was by general agreement a shrewd, wily and skilful operator.[1] He had a forceful personality and was apt to act like a steamroller on issues over which other IRHC members had no strongly held contrary views.[2] German propaganda was an issue that early in 1921 was arousing considerable anger among the French authorities, particularly in the Pfalz, and this was therefore a matter of some importance for Tirard. But what were the attitudes of the other members of the IRHC?

For the British and American governments the Schwarze Schmach campaign was the main propaganda issue. The effect on the British public was less than in the case of America, where racial colour was already an issue of domestic importance and where a sizeable German expatriate population existed. Nevertheless Britain was a target for such propaganda and it is clear from comments in British Foreign Office files that the Schwarze Schmach campaign was causing considerable irritation in government. The issue of coloured troops was raised in Parliament on several occasions,[3] and demands were made that the British government should intervene with the French government to put a stop to their employment in the army of occupation.[4] In fact there existed within the Foreign Office some small measure of sympathy for the German position, especially when some of the coloured troops were alleged to have come from former German mandated territory,[5] although the propaganda was considered to be completely overblown.[6] The demand at home for British intervention in the matter was distinctly unwelcome in official circles. Relations between Britain and France were difficult at this time. When the USA failed to ratify the Versailles Peace Treaty, Britain had followed her US partner in withdrawing her guarantee of immediate assistance to France in the event of future German aggression. This had been a prerequisite laid down by France for abandoning her aim of annexation of the west bank of the Rhine and signing the Peace Treaty.[7] There was a feeling of bitterness in Paris that the French government had been duped by the British Prime Minister, David Lloyd George. There was, moreover, friction arising from a fundamental divergence in foreign policy between the two countries, with France invariably taking a harder line with Germany than did Britain.[8] The British priority, as later enunciated by the Prime Minister, James Ramsay MacDonald, was for Europe to regain economic stability and this – emphasised repeatedly – required a return to normality in the Rhineland.[9] It may be concluded that anything that hindered this, including both separatism and the Schwarze Schmach campaign, was an unwanted distraction, and not one in which to become embroiled.[10] The view in the Foreign Office was that the Schwarze Schmach was a matter for the French government alone.

The situation was much worse for the French government, the ultimate target for German propaganda. The campaign against the

Schwarze Schmach had been making an impact in the USA to the extent that staff advising the US observer on the IRHC, General Allen, were worried that French trade interests would be damaged.[11] Such a situation France could ill afford, for notwithstanding her position as a victorious power she was in a desperate plight economically.[12] Neither was this in the interests of the USA, the major creditor of the former adversaries. Given the standpoint of each of the Allies – and the influence of Tirard – it is not surprising that German propaganda became a matter of concern to the IRHC.

Whether as a result of diplomatic pressure, or, as discussed below, because of its own concerns about where the Schwarze Schmach campaign might be leading, the Reich Foreign Ministry shortly thereafter conducted a review of current German propaganda activities. At this time the Foreign Ministry was acting simply as a distribution centre for source material that came principally via the Reich Ministry of the Interior and the Reich Commissioner in Coblenz. It disseminated information to diplomatic missions and private individuals abroad and to organisations that had foreign links or contacts. It was not itself involved in any further processing of the information. The Foreign Ministry knew little in detail of the activities of the Volkspflege and Frauenliga,[13] which had recently become the responsibility of the Reich Ministry of the Interior.[14] It had no oversight of these agencies and its view of their propaganda was disparaging: 'There is frequently unfavourable public criticism of the Rheinische Volkspflege and the Rheinische Frauenliga. The journalistic quality of the publications is way below that, for example, of Morel's writing.'[15] It is not difficult to sense a lack of coordination, if not animosity, between the two principal ministries involved with the occupied Rhineland. It may be recalled that control of propaganda had earlier led to a dispute between the Foreign Ministry and the Reich Chancellery.[16]

The ministry's review expressed dissatisfaction at the entire state of affairs in the propaganda battle. Not only was the quality of the propaganda being produced by the agencies of the Reich Ministry of the Interior alleged to be poor, but that coming from the Notbund in Munich was considered to be harming the German cause. Worse still were the outpourings of the American Ray Beveridge, 'who outdoes the Notbund in her hysterical extremes'.[17] Although belonging to no particular group, Beveridge was, in the eyes of the Foreign Ministry, closely associated with the Pfalzzentrale, which had arranged her widely reported Munich speech and had provided the co-speaker, Eberlein.[18] Once again, the picture that emerges is one of substantial divergence of views over the nature and purpose of the propaganda.

The concerns of the Reich Foreign Ministry have to be viewed in the wider international context. In the USA a new President, Warren Harding, had recently taken over from Woodrow Wilson following the Republican landslide victory of November 1920. US policy concerning events in Europe had been in a state of stagnation while Wilson battled with Congress over issues surrounding the Peace Treaty and proposed US membership of the League of Nations. On these issues Wilson would not give way. Now, after eighteen months of stalemate, and with reparation, war debt and foreign loan policies in a state of confusion, the incoming administration was anxious to make progress. The French government viewed the change of administration with trepidation, worrying that the USA would return to its pre-war policy of isolationism as far as European affairs were concerned. It felt that the future security of France – the issue of greatest concern – would be overlooked if President Harding compromised with Congress and the USA signed a separate peace treaty with Germany.[19] In these anxious times the last thing that the French government wanted was the whipping up of anti-French sentiment in the USA.

Ironically, this view was shared by the Reich Foreign Ministry. In spite of the allegations of its lack of quality, Schwarze Schmach propaganda was creating adverse publicity for France in the USA. This could have a serious economic impact. The policy of the new US government was to secure the involvement of the private sector in raising investment capital against war debts. Accordingly, under advice from merchant bankers, it proposed to put a holding of three billion dollars' worth of French bonds on the market. The Reich Foreign Ministry feared a backlash against French interests which could lead directly to the bankruptcy of France. In turn France would then embark on desperate economic measures and these would be to the detriment of Germany.[20]

The Foreign Ministry was not against the use of propaganda per se, simply its misuse and overuse: 'The entire propaganda against the Schwarze Schmach has become so monotonous that a break from it would seem necessary if it is not to lose all its effect.'[21] There was a feeling that the sending of propaganda abroad – by rights the concern of the Reich Foreign Ministry – had got out of control. Accordingly proposals were made for the Foreign Ministry to regulate closely the activities of all organisations involved in this. The powers of the Reich Ministry of the Interior in particular should be circumscribed. The propaganda against the Schwarze Schmach should cease and alternative themes should be found.[22]

There is no evidence that these proposals were put into effect, although pressure from the Foreign Ministry may have contributed to the action taken by the Bavarian government to remove Heinrich Distler from the Notbund. Furthermore, it was the Reich Foreign Ministry that intervened on at least two occasions with the censor in Berlin to effect bans on propaganda films made about the Schwarze Schmach by the Notbund and the Frauenliga. The reasoning behind both judgements was that the film in question was liable to jeopardise relations with France.[23]

The propaganda campaign otherwise continued unabated and caused the growing irritation of the French authorities, who attempted to discredit the work of the Mannheim Centre. A personal attack on Eberlein recalled that '... this gentleman, currently leader of the espionage bureau in Mannheim, is high on the list of wanted war criminals on account of the bloodbath that took place at St Dié at the beginning of the Great War'.[24] Eberlein reacted angrily to this and pressed for the issue to be brought before the German Supreme Court in Leipzig as soon as possible in order to give him the opportunity to clear his name.[25] But the irritation was not confined to the French authorities. The US representative on the IRHC called in the Reich Commissioner, Karl von Starck, and left him in no doubt that German propaganda – which he attributed solely to the Mannheim Centre – was damaging German interests in the USA. Furthermore, the US government thoroughly disapproved of the manner in which propaganda was being orchestrated by an organisation supposedly concerned with charitable matters.[26]

At this point the propaganda activity of the Mannheim Centre was not the only issue confronting the Allies in the Rhineland. An increasing number of attacks were being made on French soldiers, the offenders taking refuge in unoccupied Germany. It was felt that the German authorities were showing some reluctance to arrest and hand over the perpetrators to the Allies.[27] There existed also fundamental differences in German and Allied interpretations of the Agreement in relation to the status, authority and obligations of German officials towards the IRHC. A key figure in this situation was the Reich Commissioner, whose function it was to provide the channel of communication to the Reich government. The Allies had previously complained about the obstructive attitude of the German officials and 'particularly of the Prussian officials of the old regime, who have forgotten nothing and have learned nothing'.[28] Starck was no exception to this. His protests against the use of coloured troops were to a large extent considered to consist of unsubstantiated, and at times frivolous, allegations.[29] He himself was variously described as being 'incapable of combatting the skill and brains of Tirard',[30] 'a rather stiff Prussian... not temperamentally nor by training a good appointment for this post'.[31] Starck also attracted criticism from German propagandists on account of the indifferent manner in which he had dealt with several issues.[32] Eventually the Allies requested his removal. The Reich government, left with little option, removed Starck from his post and proposed Prince Hatzfeldt-Wildenburg as a replacement. In fact dissatisfaction with the personal attributes of Starck had masked strong underlying French opposition to the office of Reich Commissioner. Its very existence had, in the eyes of the US observer on the IRHC, undoubtedly hindered the development of the separatist cause in the Rhineland.[33] There was, therefore, considerable debate before agreement was given to the appointment of a successor to Starck, and then only if certain conditions were met by the Reich government. Amongst these conditions was the dissolution of the Mannheim Centre.

It might be questioned why the Allies had singled out the Mannheim Centre when several organisations were active in the Schwarze Schmach campaign. Quite simply, relatively little was known about the privately funded Notbund, based in Munich. In contrast the Mannheim Centre and its leader were well known and the organisation was known to be officially supported. Action against the Frauenliga would have been impossible to implement because it was ostensibly a free association of women's groups without any official connection. Any attempt to suppress the Frauenliga would have presented Germany with a major propaganda coup. A further reason for singling out the Mannheim Centre lay in the bitterly adversarial relationship that had developed between Eberlein and the French authorities in the Pfalz.

The Allies were in a strong position in demanding the closure of the Mannheim Centre. The request that Germany should have representation on the IRHC had in the first place come from the Reich government,[34] which was now anxious to retain the ability to present its point of view directly to the commission. There was thus strong pressure to comply with Allied demands. The issue had arisen at a difficult time for the Reich government. At the London Conference at the beginning of March 1921 the Allies had presented their desired payment schedule for reparations. This the Reich government had rejected, only to have sanctions imposed against it. French and Belgian troops had occupied the bridgeheads at Düsseldorf, Duisburg and Ruhrort. Furthermore, the IRHC had confiscated customs revenues from the German border in the west and had established an internal customs border along the Rhine, subsequently applying additional tariffs to the movement of goods entering and leaving the occupied regions,[35] adding to the hardship of those living there. Meanwhile, relations between the Reich and Bavarian governments were also at a low point following the dispute over the disbanding of the citizens' militia. The Reich government had earlier agreed to this but the Bavarian government had only done so following the threat of sanctions made by the British government.[36] To add to the difficulties of the Reich government it was made clear by the French authorities, independently of the IRHC, that French opposition to any lifting of sanctions would be maintained unless Winterstein, whom they judged to be responsible for the activities of the Mannheim Centre, was also removed from his post.[37]

In spite of the friction between itself and the Reich the Bavarian government proved remarkably acquiescent in the matter. The

Reich government was able to agree to the Allied conditions and the Mannheim Centre was closed on 30 September 1921. The following day Winterstein was moved to Upper Franconia to serve as chairman of the regional council. His place as State Commissioner for the Pfalz was taken by Dr Lorenz Wappes, formerly director of the Forestry Department in Speyer, who had worked closely with Winterstein and who was considered by him to be well suited to the post.[38]

The reasons for Bavaria's compliance are easily understood. This issue differed completely from the crisis over the disbanding of the citizens' militia. The Pfalz was being hard hit by the imposed tariffs and representations were being made by trade and industrial interests to the Bavarian authorities to get the sanctions lifted as quickly as possible.[39] With much of the population in the Pfalz at best indifferent to Bavarian rule,[40] it was no time to make a stand on this particular issue. There was another reason, also. The Bavarian government fully intended that regardless of Allied demands the operation of its section of the Mannheim Centre (the former Pfalzzentrale) should continue clandestinely.

While the consequences of his propaganda activities were moving towards denouement, Eberlein had been busy planning a reorganisation.[41] Wanting to have greater freedom of action, he proposed to hive off his propaganda activities and incorporate them within a limited private company (GmbH). When closure of the Mannheim Centre became inevitable separate arrangements were envisaged for the former Hessen and Prussian departments, which would relocate to Darmstadt and Frankfurt or Hanau, respectively.[42] A rapid metamorphosis was not to take place, however. Eberlein had in the meantime fallen into disfavour with the Reich Ministry of the Interior for having allegedly supplied intelligence not through the agreed channels but to agencies of his own choosing.[43] Worse, it was alleged that through his carelessness French intelligence had been given details of the operation of the Mannheim Centre.[44] In the opinion of the State Secretary for the Occupied Regions, Philipp Brugger, Eberlein should be kept well away from any future intelligence activity and any attempt by him to set up a limited company should be opposed.[45]

What is to be made of this development? It would be unsurprising if Eberlein had disregarded agreed communication channels to follow his own inclinations, especially if, as was likely, the Volkspflege had been involved in the agreement. But it would be surprising if he had been guilty of a breach of security. The most likely explanation for the episode is that this was an attempt to discredit and silence Eberlein. It is known that he had made powerful enemies who were close to, if not within, the Reich government.[46] It is further evidence that the Reich government was far from unified in its view of the German propaganda effort – and Brugger, with new authority, was charged with providing a more coherent and centralised *Abwehr* effort for the Rhineland.

Regardless of the cause of the episode, its effect was short-lived. Eberlein received strong support from the new Bavarian State Commissioner, Lorenz Wappes, for the continuation of his work, initially in Heidelberg. But it can be concluded that the Reich government was uneasy at this prospect, because following discussions between the Foreign Ministry and the Bavarian government it was decided to delay setting up an office. In the mean time Eberlein and his staff would work at home and Eberlein in particular would keep himself out of the public eye.[47]

Thus although the activities of the Pfalzzentrale were disrupted by the Allied action they did not cease and by early 1922 it was again in full operation, structured largely along the lines proposed by Eberlein.[48] To lend credibility to Eberlein's presence in Heidelberg the proposal was made that he should take up a part-time lecturing post in journalism at Heidelberg University. Wappes approached the historian and member of the original action committee Hermann Oncken, emphasising that Eberlein had extensive literary experience and would easily gain his post-doctoral lecturing qualification. There was also a longer-term ambition behind the proposal: 'In time a national centre for political activity could be developed in Heidelberg that could be more thorough and effective than Berlin.'[49] Wappes claimed that these ideas originated with him but some doubt arises here in view of Helmut Gembries's exposure of Wappes as having an overweening ego.[50] But whoever was behind the ideas, it is clear that the rivalry between Berlin and Munich was well to the fore.

Eberlein himself had high ambitions. He had already written in November 1921 to the last Chancellor of the Kaiserreich, Prince Max of Baden, suggesting that the Pfalzzentrale be incorporated within a proposed privately funded Institute for Foreign Affairs.[51] Eberlein's letter received a cool response from Prince Max, who was critical of the work of the Pfalzzentrale.[52] However, it was not dismissed out of hand and Prince Max remained in touch with Eberlein. There were clearly feelings in influential circles – according with the views earlier expressed by Delbrueck[53] – that Germany was still not making the right impact on opinion abroad, for the proposal to create a new private institute was still under discussion in the early summer of the following year.[54] The basic idea of incorporating the Pfalzzentrale in a new institute was supported by the Reich Ministry of the Interior, although doubts were expressed over how this might be achieved and there was opposition to the creation of any large monolithic organisation.[55] Eberlein himself, however, was confident of a positive outcome. In authorising a subordinate to recruit part-time assistance, he stressed the need to make suitable preparations, because 'following the founding of a large political institute for foreign affairs it is anticipated that our organisation will be incorporated in it'.[56] In the event the proposals came to nothing, either through lack of resources or as a result of an overriding view in Berlin that existing arrangements were adequate.[57] The episode serves to further illustrate the fact that even in 1922 there existed dissent over the best way for Germany to make her case abroad.

From the beginning of 1922 Eberlein's activities were cloaked by setting up a private firm, August Müller Nachfolger, in Mannheim. This was to continue both the dissemination of propaganda on the other side of the Rhine via the existing courier network and the gathering of information on events and on individuals suspected of being disloyal. Propaganda was henceforth to be published by a newly created organisation, Südwestdeutscher Verlag GmbH (South-West German Publishing Company Ltd – hereafter referred to as SWDV). The task of looking after those expelled from the occupied Pfalz was to be undertaken by a so-called Wohlfahrtsstelle (Welfare Office) in Heidelberg, the finances and administration of which would be overseen by Otto

Betz. Betz, born in Nuremberg on 16 April 1885, had originally trained and worked as a schoolteacher before taking a post in a bank in 1908. He, like Eberlein, had served on the Western Front during World War I, soon reaching commissioned rank. Captured by the French, Betz had been exchanged via neutral Switzerland, only to volunteer for further active service.[58] Betz and Eberlein were to establish a close working relationship. In later years they built houses next to each other in Neckargemünd[59] and for a time were in business together, although this venture proved to be unsuccessful.[60] Betz joined the NSDAP in 1930[61] and in the same year took part in discussions related to an application by Eberlein for party membership.[62]

The SWDV was set up in the Munich suburb of Pasing, although the material to be published originated in Mannheim. It was run by Lieutenant Colonel von Oelhafen and F. W. Hausmann, who had had previous experience of a similar nature working for the Heimatdienst in eastern Germany. Initially the firm was to be funded by the Bavarian and Reich governments but Wappes's aim was for it ultimately to become self-sufficient. It was not long, however, before friction arose between Pasing and Mannheim. Oelhafen found the management arrangements inadequate and made proposals to Wappes for changes. He believed that a measure of local autonomy was necessary as far as the business of publication was concerned, together with some degree of insight into, and control of, finances. Eberlein, accused of obstructing everything emanating from Pasing,[63] responded angrily to Oelhafen's proposals:

> For the sake of the good reputation that the Pfalzzentrale, or the SWDV, has built up through two and a half years of painstaking work I cannot and must not take the risk of letting these two gentlemen loose on it. They mean well but certainly have no idea of the extremely delicate and intricate nature of the collaborative work that we have to undertake with the political parties of the Pfalz, unoccupied Germany and overseas.[64]

For his part Oelhafen predicted failure unless changes were made and was convinced 'that these difficulties, which arise from inadequate documentation and the elaborate and extremely costly management style practised by Mannheim, can all be traced back to the jealousy and influence of Mr Betz'.[65]

The episode reveals the manner in which Eberlein managed the Pfalzzentrale and his relationship with those around him. His reaction to the desire expressed – for good business reasons – for greater autonomy and for provision of financial information was characteristic. He looked upon it as a challenge to his authority and countered it aggressively. The same attitude can be seen also in a dispute with another of his staff, Max Treutler, when Treutler insisted on editorial anonymity for a brochure intended for foreign distribution, refusing to allow his name to be used in this connection.[66] However, because the complaints to Wappes were as much about the attitude of Betz as that of Eberlein it can be deduced that Eberlein and Betz were closely in step over matters affecting the SWDV.

Throughout 1922 Eberlein's organisation remained essentially in the form that had re-emerged after the dissolution of the Mannheim Centre. However, the following year was to be a momentous one in the history of the Pfalz and was to present Eberlein with major challenges. These resulted from the further deterioration in Franco-German relations that had begun over the issue of reparations. Germany, with some support from Britain, had in vain sought a moratorium on payments, citing the inability to pay in the face of a worsening financial crisis. Matters came to a head when at the end of 1922 Germany was declared by the Allied Reparations Commission to be in default. On 11 January 1923, to the disapproval of Britain and the USA, French and Belgian troops began an occupation of the Ruhr in an attempt to force Germany into compliance. Britain refused to take responsibility for any consequences of this action, while the USA withdrew its forces completely from the occupation. Anglo-French relations cooled further.

The move caused widespread anger in Germany, which was reflected in emotive propaganda (figs. 21 and 22). The governments of the Reich, Prussia, Bavaria, Hessen and Oldenburg issued instructions for a policy of passive resistance in any dealings with the occupation authorities. For the Rhineland population months of increasing

Figure 21. 'An der Ruhr!'

hardship were to result. Refusal to follow the orders of the occupation authorities was met by further sanctions, including the expulsion of community leaders and officials (fig. 23). The chairman of the regional council in the Pfalz and the core of his administration suffered this fate, and a Pfalz government-in-exile was set up in Heidelberg. The railways, which provided the main transport arteries, were a particular target and the operation of these was eventually taken over completely by the French authorities. A direct appeal by the former chairman, Theodor von Winterstein, to the French Controller, General de Metz,

Figure 22. 'With fixed bayonet against an old man'. This photograph, taken in the Ruhr in 1923, was used originally to demonstrate the brutality of French troops towards those who were not submissive.

to avoid hardship in the population was fruitless. By November 1923 it was estimated that 2.5 per cent of the population of the Pfalz had been expelled.[67]

For Eberlein himself the situation in the early weeks of 1923 presented a heightened challenge, which he relished, but one for which his existing organisation and the resources available were wholly inadequate. Quite apart from increased activity in areas related to propaganda and intelligence, provision had to be made for the increasing numbers of officials expelled from the Pfalz. Eberlein accordingly made proposals to Wappes for the creation of a Haupthilfsstelle für die Pfalz (Central Office for Welfare in the Pfalz) into which current activities and staff would be merged. The new organisation would be located in Heidelberg, with a branch office in Mannheim. Five departments would look after legal, political, press, economic and welfare matters.[68] This was quickly agreed to by the Bavarian government. Eberlein was appointed to head the organisation and was promoted.[69] The heightened tension between France and Germany had brought

Figure 23. 'Expulsion of German official from French-occupied territory at Limburg an der Lahn in April 1923. The troops on duty at the post are Moroccan.'

him enhanced status and financial benefit, doubtless helping to further fuel his personal ambitions.

Eberlein was undoubtedly a driving force in German counter-propaganda at this time. At a meeting held to discuss the future of the political and cultural *Abwehr* in the Rhineland he made a powerful speech to Reich and state representatives, pointing to the difficulties that lay ahead: 'We have few examples to follow from our past as we come to the central problem, the organisation of the passive resistance of a completely defenceless people against a ruthless enemy bristling with weapons.'[70] He was dissatisfied with the state of preparedness for the situation now confronting Germany. He praised Winterstein's far-sightedness in setting up the Bavarian Pfalzzentrale – 'To us he was both prophet and leader and was one of the first German officials to see that extraordinary times demand extraordinary means' – but was critical of other states for their slowness in countering French actions in the Rhineland and for their poor organisation. However, his strongest criticism was directed at the Reich government, 'whose original organisation of the *Abwehr* through the Heimatdienst had failed miserably'.[71] With the invasion of the Ruhr the struggle against the French had, for him, assumed heightened importance and now included an economic dimension. And while in his view Wappes deserved great credit for maintaining Bavarian support for the Pfalz and for fighting for funds,[72] the financial resources needed to address this increased threat far outstripped those available, thanks to the parsimony of the Reich Finance Minister. Frustration underlined Eberlein's every word.

Notwithstanding his sharp criticisms of the Reich government, Eberlein was held in high regard at this time by both the Bavarian government and the Reich Ministry of the Interior. Less than a month later he was invited by State Secretary Philipp Brugger to take over the leadership of the Volkspflege and he was promised a completely free hand to expand that organisation and ensure a well-coordinated operation.[73] This represented a complete volte-face by Brugger, who – perhaps misled – had earlier demanded Eberlein's removal. Brugger was clearly of the opinion that German propaganda was still not as effective or as unified as it should be. Only recently he had felt compelled to appeal for unity, in the context of the *Abwehr* in the Rhineland, and for a redoubling of effort relating to cultural propaganda.[74] We may infer both implicit criticism of the way in which the Volkspflege was being led and a feeling on Brugger's part that Eberlein would be better suited to the task. As is discussed later, this endorsement of Eberlein from the Reich Ministry of the Interior may be contrasted with continuing concerns of the Foreign Ministry over the way in which the Pfalzzentrale was being led and the extent of Bavarian support for it.[75]

Though attracted by Brugger's offer, Eberlein declined it. This comes as no surprise. But the reason for his refusal should not be interpreted as showing greater loyalty to Bavaria than to the Reich. In informing Wappes of his decision Eberlein referred to his current activity as 'the defensive action at the Front'.[76] This, he felt, should have priority in the current situation although if things improved he would consider a move to Berlin.[77] Eberlein, even more than most German propagandists, was in his own eyes fighting not only a real war but a war of attrition. In his own mind the office in Mannheim close by the Rhine represented the forward trenches, and the Rhine was effectively no man's land. Venturing across it was fraught with personal danger. This exposed forward position was ever vulnerable to attack in the event of a French decision to occupy Mannheim – hence he insisted upon records being kept back in Heidelberg. But in his view it was vital to maintain a presence at the Front in order to provide the closest possible point of contact with the occupied west bank. The situation suited Eberlein's confrontational nature perfectly. Compared with this, a post in Berlin directing cultural propaganda from afar – much as he would have liked to realign the Volkspflege to his own way of thinking – must have seemed to be a tame alternative. More than this though, the Ruhr occupation, coupled with his growing sense of frustration with the limitations of propaganda as a defensive weapon, was now providing a stimulus for Eberlein to expand his activities increasingly into active resistance. In this he was enthusiastically aided and abetted by Otto Betz.[78]

It might be questioned as to what extent active, as distinct from passive, resistance was sanctioned by the Bavarian government. Throughout the previous year right-wing nationalist movements in Bavaria had become increasingly powerful, providing more moderate conservatives with cause for serious concern.[79] Prime Minister Hugo von Lerchenfeld – a more moderate figure than his predecessor Gustav Ritter von Kahr – had attempted to reach an accommodation with the Reich government over a range of disputed issues, but faced increasing extreme right-wing opposition. His government had moved further to the right when in the summer of 1922 the DDP had left the coalition, to be replaced by the Bayerische Mittelpartei (the Bavarian Middle Party, or BMP).[80] Eventually Lerchenfeld's position became untenable and his place was taken by Eugen von Knilling. This rightward shift in the political climate had already manifested itself in the Bavarian government putting pressure on the Reich government to be much more aggressive in fighting the war guilt issue – a fact quickly picked up by Eberlein.[81] It comes as little surprise, then, that frustration in right-wing circles following the Ruhr invasion should lead to Wappes's sanctioning of active resistance by the Pfalzzentrale.[82] Wappes, as will be seen, had close connections to right-wing nationalists.

As the German campaign of passive resistance wore on so its impact on the local population in the Pfalz became ever more severe. Through his agents on the other side of the Rhine Eberlein would have been well aware of the depressed mood of the local population. Reports to the Reich government spoke of the exhaustion of the Rhineland population and of strong feelings against Berlin. One account referred to 'Berlin defending the Rhineland down to the last Rhinelander'.[83] Another referred to 'the widespread wish for peace and for the possibility of a quiet everyday life'.[84] An assessment made a few weeks earlier by the British authorities had concluded that the situation had for some time been critical and that

> ... the Rhinelanders – whose power of endurance has been strained to the limit – have now reached the limit of their endurance ... Kreuznach and surroundings and the Rhine Palatinate – whose people are greatly lacking in sturdiness and independence of character – are the spots where the line of defence is weakest.

The report continued prophetically:

> If the small and relatively unimportant Francophile party in the Rhineland decided under French backing to proclaim a Rhenish Republic, the majority of the population would close their eyes and accept the situation.[85]

This, as will later be seen, proved to be close to the truth.

On 27 September 1923 the Reich government, aware of the damage that was being done to the economy while not gaining any concessions from the French government, announced the abandonment of the policy of passive resistance. This, however, did not result in any immediate improvement in living conditions for those in the Pfalz. At the same time the French authorities saw an opportunity once more to encourage the formation of a buffer state on the eastern border of France. The excuse was the state of relations between the Reich and Bavaria. This was alleged by de Metz, the French Controller, to have endangered the well-being of the Pfalz to the extent that Bavarian sovereignty in the Pfalz could no longer be recognised.[86] Furthermore, conflict had arisen once again over the applicability to Bavaria of a Reich declaration of a state of emergency. The chief protagonist on the Bavarian side was the former Prime Minister, Gustav Ritter von Kahr, who had recently been appointed by the current Prime Minister, Eugen von Knilling, to the hugely influential post of General State Commissioner. Matters between Berlin and Munich were made worse by the refusal of the Bavarian government to uphold a Reich-initiated ban on the NSDAP news-sheet, *Völkischer Beobachter*.[87]

In the Pfalz Johannes Hoffmann, Social Democrat and former Bavarian Prime Minister, was alarmed at the rightward drift of Bavaria and saw this as a serious threat to both the Pfalz and the Reich. He was concerned also that the increasing tensions and social distress intensified by the passive resistance campaign would find their outlet in some form of radicalisation. He accordingly proposed the creation of a democratic Pfalz state within the Reich but independent of Bavaria. In doing so he necessarily consulted the French authorities. His motives were misunderstood by his fellow countrymen and the situation was made worse as a result of French duplicity. His proposal was rejected by the local Pfalz Kreistag (District Assembly) and his contact with the French led to his vilification as a traitor and political outcast.[88]

French interest then centred on the Freie Bauernschaft, an association of small-scale farmers, and its local leader, Franz Josef Heinz.[89] The movement had had its origins in the antagonism of the agricultural community towards the controlled war economy. After World War I these feelings had been heightened by the continuation of agrarian controls by the new Republic. Strongly anti-socialist, the Freie Bauernschaft stood for the interests of the small-scale producer rather than those of the urban consumer. It nevertheless modelled itself to some extent on the organisation and methods of the trade union movement, which was considered to be successful in promoting the interests of urban industrial workers.[90] No friend of either the Reich or Bavarian governments, Freie Bauernschaft flexed its muscles and between 1920 and 1922 organised a series of strikes against the controlled agrarian economy in order to win concessions from the authorities. It was not just the growing political power of Freie Bauernschaft that worried the

German authorities, however. The movement was recruiting amongst the unemployed and developing links to both the French occupiers and extreme right-wing groups in Bavaria. Equally disturbing, it was forming a paramilitary wing. Espousing the cause of separatism, all that Heinz needed in order to make a bid for power was French backing. In the late autumn of 1923 the catalyst was provided by the currency crisis and Heinz's willingness to collaborate with French plans for reform. In the wake of separatist uprisings in the occupied territories to the north, groups of separatists moved into the Pfalz using the French-controlled railway network on 5 November. A week later the establishment of Autonome Pfalz (Independent Pfalz) was declared in Speyer and was quickly given official recognition by the French occupation authorities.[91] The new republic was, however, destined to be short-lived.

The seizure of power by the separatist movement brought the Pfalz into prominence on the international stage. Over the next few months Britain was to play a considerable part in its affairs, essentially in the role of facilitator and mediator between France and Germany. At the heart of British concerns lay the 'acute and persistent dislocation of the markets of Europe',[92] and a return to economic stability was seen as being of the highest priority for all. Towards the end of 1923 committees of experts under the chairmanship of Charles Dawes had been set up by the Reparations Commission to advise, *inter alia*, on the best way to balance the German budget and restore the currency. Behind this lay the vexed question of reparations, where matters had reached an impasse. Reparations could not take place until economic stability existed. In turn this required political stability – and this was to provide the impetus for British intervention.

In early January 1924, however, Anglo-French relations were still at a low point, a situation brought about by British objections to the earlier Ruhr invasion and by a clash of personalities at the highest government level between Lord Curzon, the British Foreign Secretary, and Raymond Poincaré, the French Prime Minister.[93] Events in the Pfalz now gave rise to a further serious division of opinion within the IRHC, in which Britain held the minority view. To the displeasure of the British government, France was prepared to grant immediate recognition to the Heinz government by authorising its decrees through the IRHC.[94] There followed strong representations in Paris and Brussels by the British government. As a consequence this recognition was held in abeyance.[95]

Before any further diplomatic moves could be made to resolve the situation, however, events in the Pfalz took a decisive turn, with the assassination in Speyer of Heinz and two companions during the evening of 11 January. A detailed description of these events and the participants lies beyond the scope of this book but can be found elsewhere.[96] It may be noted, however, that Eberlein and Betz were fully implicated in the attack, which was organised within the Haupthilfsstelle, or Pfalzzentrale.

The French authorities were in no doubt as to who was responsible for the assassinations. De Metz publicly made reference to 'a former German officer, a war criminal, who tied a number of women and children to chairs in St Dié in order to use them as human shields as they fired on our brave soldiers'. Then he added further insult: 'Of course he didn't carry out the murder himself, he was too much of a coward to do so.'[97] This naturally drew a furious – and threatening – reply from Eberlein, who, without admitting complicity, justified the assassinations in Speyer as legitimate executions. Accusations of personal cowardice, however, were a different matter.[98] The *Abwehr* had now become a bitter personal vendetta against de Metz.

At a higher level the French government pressed the British government in vain to jointly approach Berlin and make a further attempt to suppress Eberlein's organisation. The British considered the Reich government to be completely powerless and in any case there existed a feeling within the Foreign Office that the only way forward was for the French government to cease support for separatism. While not condoning the assassinations, British officials felt that there had been a certain inevitability in the way that a patriotic nation would react to the circumstances prevailing in the Rhineland. Only if it could be proved that the safety of Allied troops and officials was threatened would Britain be prepared to act.[99]

The assassinations of Heinz and his companions in Speyer did not immediately produce the hoped-for collapse of Independent Pfalz.

Indeed, members of its Cabinet set out to re-establish its damaged authority. In the meantime, a delegation of professional and business people and church leaders made representations to the IRHC, drawing attention to the deteriorating situation in the Pfalz and protesting against the ordinances of the Heinz government.[100] Increasing British concern over the situation, which had been heightened by the Speyer assassinations, led to the dispatch of the British Consul-General in Munich, Robert Clive, to the Pfalz on a fact-finding mission, though not without some initial obstruction on the part of the French authorities.[101] Clive's report was presented to the House of Commons on 21 January 1924. It revealed a dearth of support for Independent Pfalz. Officials, church communities and the majority within the urban population rejected any idea of separation from Bavaria – a conclusion which dealt a blow to remaining French hopes of creating a separatist regime in the Rhineland. On the other hand a considerable section of the population as a whole was merely indifferent towards separation from Bavaria, though it wished to remain within the Reich. Peasants and the working classes were generally not averse to an independent Rhineland state including the Pfalz, and linked economically to the Reich. What they feared above all were militaristic policies emanating from Berlin and Munich.[102]

Civil unrest in the Pfalz increased, culminating in a violent confrontation between separatists and their opponents in Pirmasens in which there were a number of fatalities and the local separatist headquarters were destroyed. Faced with the new realities, the French authorities withdrew support from Independent Pfalz.[103] On 16 February an agreement was reached with representatives of the Pfalz for the resumption of German administration in the region. By the middle of March, however, there had been a chorus of complaints from the German side that the French were reneging on the agreement, creating difficulties and preventing officials who had earlier been expelled from the Pfalz from resuming their posts.[104]

Once again Robert Clive was brought into the matter, this time to let the Bavarian Prime Minister know, informally, the British point of view. The French position was unambiguous and uncompromising. Eberlein was the stumbling block. A known war criminal, under the guise of countering separatism he had continued to direct his activities primarily against the occupation forces. Reinstatement of Bavarian officials in the Pfalz, many of whom had been expelled as a result of refusal to take instructions from the separatist regime, would therefore not take place until Eberlein had disappeared from the scene.[105] In effect this was the latest round – which rapidly became conclusive – in the vendetta between Eberlein and de Metz.

On this occasion the British government was more sympathetic towards the French position – a fact that is not too surprising in the light of the replacement, at the end of January 1924, of Lord Curzon by James Ramsay MacDonald, Prime Minister and Foreign Secretary in the newly elected Labour government. The personal animosity that had existed between Curzon and Poincaré was replaced by friendly overtures from Ramsay MacDonald.[106] But it would be a mistake to suppose that British officials favoured France over the immediate future of the Pfalz. While not condoning the actions of Eberlein's organisation, the feeling within the Foreign Office was still that the French government had brought much of the present trouble upon itself through its support of the separatist movement. And while Ramsay MacDonald was anxious to improve relations with France, the French position on the Pfalz represented an irritating obstruction to progress. According to Lord D'Abernon, British ambassador in Berlin:

> At the Foreign Office they find their new Chief extremely firm on essentials in his discussions with Poincaré and with the French Ambassador. He has been particularly resolute regarding the Palatinate, demanding acts, not words – an attitude quite contrary to diplomatic tradition.[107]

For Eberlein the *Abwehr* struggle was over. While the Bavarian government was initially reluctant to close down the Haupthilfsstelle (Pfalzzentrale), the Allied demand, however informally presented, was uncompromising. Furthermore the Reich government was in no doubt as to where Germany's best interests lay and this was made clear to the Bavarian government. These events were taking place just a few days before the publication of the Dawes Report. It is probable that the

Reich government had some inkling of the recommendations. At the very least it entertained hopes for a favourable outcome, and an outcome favourable for Germany would attract French opposition. This indeed proved to be the case since the report implicitly recommended the economic reintegration of the Ruhr into Germany. The last thing that the Reich government wanted at this time, therefore, was friction with France over events in the Rhineland when these could be taken in hand and dealt with.

The tactic adopted by Bavaria was diplomatic. Eberlein was given a three-month leave of absence which would meet the British suggestion but on the other hand it was essential 'not to damage Herr Eberlein and his close colleagues and to avoid internal political discord'.[108] The issue was clearly thought to be capable of causing internal trouble for the Bavarian government. Perhaps Eberlein thought that the matter would soon blow over because he had asked Wappes for just a month's leave of absence. He was clearly encouraged in this by the Bavarian government, for his request for financial help for it was met with a payment of 300 Gold Marks.[109] At the same time the Bavarian government gave assurances that Eberlein would not resume his activities at a later date. The Pfalzzentrale would be moved and its activities reduced in scope and limited to welfare work.[110] Yet the coup de grace was delivered not by the Bavarian government but by the government of Baden, though it was later rumoured that the action was taken at the request of the Reich government.[111] The immediate cause was the arrest in Mannheim on 9 May of Eberlein's son on suspicion of distributing forged French currency. Linked with this was concern at the connection between the Pfalzzentrale and certain extreme nationalist groups. Eberlein was still on leave of absence at the time – and it is open to speculation whether the timing was coincidental – but the action taken by the Baden authorities was immediate and decisive. The Pfalzzentrale was closed down and its senior members were expelled from Baden.[112]

The move by Baden is unsurprising. Although initially Baden was sympathetic to the Bavarian initiative in setting up the Pfalzzentrale in 1919, tensions had developed between the two states. In 1922, following the murder of Matthias Erzberger, the traditionally liberal

Baden judicial authorities had traced the source of the assassination attempt to a group in Munich, only for their findings to be ignored by the Bavarian government. The Justice Minister of Baden had publicly accused certain secret organisations in Munich, tolerated by the police, of being behind the murder.[113] Then in April 1923 the Prime Minister of Baden, Adam Remmele, realising the extent of the economic and social damage being done to Germany by passive resistance, had urged the Reich Chancellery to negotiate with France – a position quite contrary to that of Bavaria. He was doubtless including Bavaria in noting that

> ...politically far-right groups are not yet ready to entertain thoughts of amicable negotiation. These groups intend to be victorious or 'die'... A policy of 'total victory or complete destruction' will not lead to victory, much more likely to the continuation of economic misery for the German people and national humiliation for the German nation.[114]

But there were wider grounds for Remmele's disquiet. Throughout 1923 Baden had experienced continuing recruitment activity by extreme-right paramilitary groups, allegedly linked to the Reich army, which were attempting to form a defensive front.[115] Acts of sabotage were being committed by such groups, including the blowing up of railway installations in the occupied territories across the Rhine, without any reference to the Baden authorities. Remmele had complained angrily to the Reich Chancellor, foreseeing the danger that France would exact retribution on Baden itself.[116] Although now, in May 1924, the era of passive resistance had passed, the issue of reparations remained to be settled at international level and was at a critical stage. Antagonism of the French authorities created by extreme right-wing groups operating out of Heidelberg was the last thing that Remmele wanted for Baden. It is known that there was personal animosity between Eberlein and Remmele, for whom the forged currency must have provided a welcome opportunity to take action.[117] Eberlein's aggressive and confrontational style had finally proved to be his undoing.

The Bavarian government was outraged that such a step had been taken without prior consultation, and the Reich government was asked to intervene between the two states. Indeed, the Reich Chancellor himself felt it necessary to write a conciliatory letter to the Bavarian Prime Minister. For the Reich government there was a positive side to the whole affair. Since the Pfalzzentrale was effectively to be closed anyway, the fact that Baden had taken the step on quite different grounds meant that the fiction could be preserved that this was a purely private organisation. Pressure was put on Baden to keep the details of the affair as secret as possible and encouragement was given to drop the case for lack of evidence. Bavaria was concerned to protect both the reputation of the Pfalzzentrale and the name of its leader, especially as proceedings against Eberlein on war crimes charges were soon to take place in a French court.[118] Even when the French authorities alleged that a connection existed between the Pfalzzentrale and the forged banknotes,[119] Reich and Bavarian governments decided to remain silent over the affair.[120] Through the Reich Chancellor the Bavarian government even attempted to get the Pfalzzentrale publicly absolved from blame by Baden on the basis that further investigation had shown that nationalist groups were responsible and that the Pfalzzentrale had done nothing wrong.[121] This the Baden government declined to do pending completion of enquiries since substantial incriminating evidence had already been found.[122]

At the same time that it was trying to smooth over relations between Bavaria and Baden, however, the Reich Foreign Ministry was bluntly warning the Bavarian Foreign Ministry not to attempt to resurrect the activities of the Pfalzzentrale in any guise whatever. An undertaking had already been given not to allow Eberlein to continue his work but there had then followed a suggestion that the Pfalzzentrale would be reconstituted in Hessen.[123] There is no doubt that the Reich Foreign Ministry was extremely annoyed both at the activities of the Pfalzzentrale and at the ambivalent attitude of the Bavarian government. The immediate cause of the annoyance is obvious: the British government had made it clear that any attempt by the Pfalzzentrale to resume its activities would result in the immediate cessation of British efforts to persuade France to regularise the situation in the Pfalz.[124]

The Reich Foreign Ministry therefore demanded of the Bavarian government that Eberlein be kept well away from Heidelberg.[125]

The root of the problem for the Reich lay in the presence at the heart of the Bavarian government of some on the extreme right, who were simply not prepared to compromise in asserting Bavarian independence. In support of this conclusion we need do no more than point to the testimony of Hans Schmelzle, a key figure in relations between the Bavarian government and the Reich – and, arguably, a relative moderate. Born near Illertissen in Schwaben on 1 October 1874, Schmelzle had held various posts as a Bavarian government official before being invited by Kahr to join the Bavarian Foreign Ministry as a senior adviser in the autumn of 1920. With promotion the following year he had become Kahr's right-hand man, especially since the posts of Foreign Minister and Prime Minister were combined. He went on to serve Kahr's successors, Lerchenfeld, Knilling and Held, and in the course of the next few years was himself offered ministerial appointments and even the post of Prime Minister. Eventually he accepted appointment as Finance Minister, a position from which he retired in 1930, although he presided over the Administrative Court until well into the National Socialist era. Schmelzle was a traditional conservative imbued with the values of the pre-war administration. Close to the BVP, he nevertheless acted in a politically non-partisan way. He had his disagreements with Kahr, notably over the issue of the citizens' militia,[126] and is on record as regretting the non-participation of the SPD in government.[127] He was loyal to the concept of a German Reich, though believing that it should comprise a federation of independent states rather than form a unitary authority. In many respects he was a similar figure to Theodor von Winterstein.

Schmelzle held a post of considerable influence and authority. But when the Reich government representative in Munich, Braun von Stumm, commented to Schmelzle that there was a strong feeling in Berlin that Wappes sometimes worked together with Eberlein behind his (Schmelzle's) back, Schmelzle replied, to the astonishment of his listener, that he himself sometimes had this same feeling. Stumm went on to report that 'Apparently powerful forces stand behind Wappes and Eberlein. Schmelzle himself cannot get the better of them.'[128] This single episode provides evidence that the Bavarian government was to an extent fractured, containing powerful elements of the extreme Right who were given to following their own uncompromising agenda.

Schmelzle finally succeeded in delivering an undertaking that the Bavarian government would not reconstitute the Pfalzzentrale. But it would not support any intervention made by the Reich government in the affairs of Hessen if the Reich attempted to suppress a reconstituted Pfalzzentrale.[129] Moreover, it reserved the right to pursue former separatists, contrary to the French wish to protect them.[130] The dispute was finally settled later in the year. The current chairman of the Pfalz regional council, Jakob Mathéus, was able to resume his office in Speyer on 8 September 1924.[131]

The Bavarian government held to its agreement not to reconstitute the Pfalzzentrale, although in spite of the slackening of international tension in the Dawes era it provided some support for continued propaganda by organisations such as the Notbund. With the closure of the Pfalzzentrale Eberlein's more prominent propaganda activities came to an end, although subsequently he published a novel, which is discussed in the following chapter. A suggestion from the Bavarian government that he should be given a post in the Reich press office was firmly vetoed by the Foreign Ministry. A proposal by Eberlein himself to take a post in the sports industry in Frankfurt was also discouraged on the grounds that he would be too close to former associates. The solution preferred by the Foreign Ministry was that he should resume his teaching career in a German school overseas, but this was not found to be practical.[132] Eberlein represented a considerable embarrassment for the Reich government, which was only too well aware that he was well thought of in extreme nationalist circles.[133] Furthermore, his usefulness to the Bavarian government was clearly outweighed by the international anger that his further employment would bring. The solution was to pension Eberlein off. He and Otto Betz were provided with mortgages and loans for houses and for setting up jointly in business.

Eberlein was later to claim that his departure from office resulted from the report by Robert Clive and an appeal from Wappes to his patriotic spirit of self-sacrifice. He denied direct involvement in the handling of the counterfeit money but asserted that the Bavarian government had been fully implicated in the affair. Moreover he claimed to have been present at a meeting with Wappes in Berlin at which a much more extensive attack on the French currency had been decided upon.[134] He also claimed that the Baden government and its Prime Minister Remmele had closed the Pfalzzentrale and had subsequently excluded him from Baden, fearing that the French would otherwise occupy Mannheim.[135]

Eberlein's later life was no less turbulent than hitherto. In 1925 he was sentenced by a French war crimes court *in absentia* to five years' forced labour and twenty years' exclusion from the occupied territories for his role in the events at St Dié in 1914. Within a short time his business interests had failed and he and Betz subsequently filed for bankruptcy.[136] Betz later joined the Gestapo.[137] For four years Eberlein worked for a propaganda film undertaking, Emelka, but was then made redundant. Under financial pressure, he threatened to sue the Bavarian government for the lack of the financial support that he felt had been due to him.[138]

Some mystery surrounds Eberlein's political affiliations. Knoch, in discussion with de Metz, denied an allegation that Eberlein was a Pan-Germanist by citing his membership of the SPD.[139] Later, Eberlein himself denied having any party affiliations. Yet in an application for membership of the Reich Writers' Association in 1939, he stated clearly that he had been Young Liberal before World War I.[140] Wolfgang Krabbe defines this in the following terms: 'The Young Liberal Association of the National Liberal Party was nothing other than a collection of young, reform-minded party members who politically had not yet had their chance.'[141] The suspicion must be that Eberlein was something of a political chameleon, able to adjust his apparent political allegiance to suit his prevailing needs. What is not in doubt is that he joined the SA in 1933 and the NSDAP in 1938, having been commissioned at the rank of major in the new Wehrmacht in 1937.[142] During World War II he served in the Balkans, where he again distinguished himself in the eyes of his compatriots with his bravery on active service. He died in captivity in Yugoslavia in 1949.[143]

To a greater extent than any other organisation involved in Rhineland propaganda at that time, the fortunes of the Pfalzzentrale were determined ultimately by the personality of its leader. Its rise is to be associated with his motivation and drive and its closure under international pressure is no less bound up with these personal characteristics and with his aggressive instincts. In the following chapter we turn to the nature of the Pfalzzentrale propaganda itself. The degree of coherence and effectiveness of Rhineland propaganda as a whole is then reviewed in the concluding chapter and related to the political circumstances prevailing at the time.

Two other points stand out in the later history of the Pfalzzentrale in its various guises. The first is the extreme reluctance of the Bavarian government to close down the operation of its agency. We have already pointed to the existence of extreme nationalist forces at work behind the scenes in the government. Such elements were prepared to do anything but accede to demands from the Allies, or, indeed, from a Reich government established under a Constitution that was viewed with suspicion and hatred. The second is that, although matters concerning the Pfalzzentrale finally came to a head in the spring of 1924, the Reich Foreign Ministry had had long-standing concerns about Eberlein's organisation. It had, of course, already been closed down once before under pressure from the Allies.[144] The Foreign Ministry had also disapproved of the way in which Bavaria had behaved subsequently. While Prussia had complied with Allied demands, Bavaria had simply turned its section of the Mannheim Centre into a limited company (GmbH) and continued its actions clandestinely, a move that the Foreign Ministry felt would bring little benefit and would cause serious conflict. It had little regard for the nature of the propaganda that Eberlein was producing, citing comments by a neutral Swedish observer following a visit to London: 'I can completely agree with your view that clumsy, overblown propaganda that is lacking in objectivity does more harm than no propaganda at all. I would welcome it if the Mannheim Centre took this comment to heart.'[145] A further worry was that State Commissioner Wappes not only had too close and inappropriate a relationship with Eberlein's organisation, but was also engaging in some form of conspiracy that would ultimately endanger the security of the occupation troops.[146] This would have been a matter of importance for the Foreign Ministry because it would have represented infringement of the Rhineland Treaty (Article 3)[147] – and nothing was more likely to upset the IRHC than assaults on Allied troops or officials. Yet in spite of this concern there is little evidence that efforts were made through the Bavarian government to restrain Eberlein's activities. The answer is to be found in the fact that it was through the direct intervention of the British government with the Bavarian government that closure of the Pfalzzentrale finally took place. The Reich government was divided and was fundamentally too weak to impose its will.

7

PFALZZENTRALE PROPAGANDA: ANTI-FRANCE, BUT PRO-BAVARIA OR PRO-REICH?

Two factors can be said to have dominated the course, policies and ultimate fate of the Pfalzzentrale. The first of these was the personality of its leader, August Ritter von Eberlein. The second factor is the considerable enmity that existed between Bavaria and the Reich – and which, as we have seen, spilled over into the working relationship between agencies of the two governments. A major question to be addressed in this chapter, therefore, is to what extent did such factors help to shape the style and content of Pfalzzentrale propaganda?

Bavarian propaganda against the Rhineland occupation – no less than that of the Reich – got off to a slow start for wholly understandable reasons. In the first place there existed a deep feeling of shock and trauma over the terms of the Armistice, which amounted to a capitulation. The monarchy had been swept away and there was massive political upheaval and social unrest. Attention was focused on the internal situation within the Bavarian mother state rather than on the distant Pfalz. Indeed, the republican government under Eisner was widely considered to be neglectful of the Pfalz.[1] Then there was the feeling of wait-and-see. There would have been little point in inflaming relations with the Allies ahead of the Peace Conference. The intentions of the Allies were not yet sufficiently clear and it was to be hoped that the terms of the Peace Treaty would not be too onerous.

This situation changed when the Allies made known their demands in May 1919. However, any attempt to influence neutral foreign opinion through propaganda would have taken time to organise at a time when the governance of Bavaria was in turmoil and the Hoffmann administration had fled from Munich to Bamberg in the face of a Communist uprising. In the Pfalz itself a more immediate threat had now arisen – that of a separatist coup. The chairman of the regional council, Theodor von Winterstein, would have received little help from outside at this time, but with firm support from the SPD was able to thwart French ambitions for the time being. Propaganda had not, up to then, played a significant part in events.

With the expulsion of Winterstein from the Pfalz immediately before the unsuccessful separatist coup at the end of May 1919, French intentions towards the Pfalz were unmistakable. A defensive strategy would be needed to counter these in the short term: renewed separatist attempts at a coup could not be ruled out. This was the immediate task for the newly created Pfalzzentrale. If Allied demands were deferred to at the Peace Treaty negotiations then taking place, a long-term strategy would be needed. From Winterstein's standpoint this might be considered to contain three elements: first to influence public opinion abroad so as to bring pressure to bear on the French occupiers, second to maintain morale in the Pfalz and encourage its population to remain steadfast and true. Third, it would be essential to keep unoccupied Germany aware of events in the Pfalz and supportive of its population. In the weeks following the signing of the Peace Treaty Winterstein therefore called together his action committee for the Pfalz and agreed a six-point plan for the way ahead. Particular emphasis was laid on the need for propaganda that would bring the Pfalz into closer contact with the cultural values of the east bank of the Rhine and Bavaria.[2]

There was, however, a divergence of opinion within Winterstein's action committee as to the general mood in the Pfalz in the period immediately following the signing of the Peace Treaty at Versailles. Some felt that there was no particular need for concern, others regarded the situation as potentially serious. What was not in doubt was that in spite of the abortive putsch attempt the activities of the Haas separatists were continuing. Such concerns were to resurface on a number of occasions during the summer and autumn of 1919.[3]

In spite of his earlier reservations over the future of the Pfalz,[4] Winterstein himself now believed that the population would maintain its loyalty to the Reich. Only in the area of Landau was there evidence of strong support for an independent Pfalz: this was in the farming community and among the urban middle classes.[5] Officials in the Pfalz continued to reject the efforts of the separatists and certainly the working-class population – with the exception of the USPD membership – was solidly behind the Reich government.[6] The concept of an independent Pfalz did, however, find some support within the Centre Party, which was deeply divided over the issue.[7] Overall the Reich government was assured by its envoy to the Bavarian government, von Schmidthals, that in the Pfalz the feeling of belonging to the Reich was extraordinarily strong, thanks to the short-sightedness of French policy and its unbelievably clumsy actions.[8] Yet from the chairman of the DDP in the Pfalz came a warning that there was no sign of the Reich showing any concern for the local people there or that it understood their problems and anxieties. Furthermore, he asked that the uncertainties surrounding the future administration of the Pfalz should be resolved as soon as possible, so that at long last people would know where they belonged.[9] Clearly the general political and constitutional uncertainty was beginning to affect the public mood.

When it came to the issue of loyalty to Bavaria, however, matters were wholly different. Not one of a group of leading members of the Pfalz local government with whom Schmidthals had had discussions supported the continued attachment of the Pfalz to Bavaria.[10] Apart from feelings that Bavaria had neglected it, the political unrest in that state can have done little to encourage the feeling of belonging. It should be remembered that the Bavarian government under the leadership of Johannes Hoffmann was still resident in Bamburg, away from the unstable and violent milieu of Munich. Beyond this, however, this was a time of wider political uncertainty. Discussions were in progress on the form that a new Constitution for the Reich should take. There was the fundamental question as to whether the Reich should be a unified state or consist of a federation of independent states. Other forms of constitutional reorientation were also being talked about and were provoking controversy. Bavaria and Prussia opposed a proposal by Hessen for the creation of a new middle-Rhine state in which would be incorporated Hessen, Nassau, Rheingau, the Pfalz and Birkenfeld.[11] Winterstein himself was said to favour the merger of all the southern and south-western states to form a unified free state, while Eberlein had the impression that Prime Minister Hoffmann, born in the Pfalz, was beginning to accept that the Pfalz should split from Bavaria and seek a new and more natural connection elsewhere. Although Hoffmann as a Bavarian official could not possibly condone such a move, he had, however, hinted that he personally was basically not unsympathetic towards it.[12] He finally dismissed the idea, however, because Baden would resist it. Hugo von Schmidthals, advising the Foreign Ministry, favoured the amalgamation of the Pfalz with Baden and Hessen. Such an amalgamation would be 'large enough to secure the Pfalz within the Reich but not large enough to represent a threat to northern Germany's hegemony – unlike Winterstein's Greater Southern Germany project'.[13] Such divergence of opinion and political confusion, in which the north–south divide was all too evident, did not augur well for a unified and effective propaganda effort.

It was against this background that Eberlein distributed his first propaganda leaflets in the summer of 1919. With the continuing fear of a putsch in mind these addressed the people of the Pfalz as a whole and were directed primarily against the separatist movement, Free Pfalz, rather than against the French occupiers. The leaflets were intended to counter a largely economic argument for separation (fig. 24), although they acknowledged that France would enjoy greater security through the creation of a neutral buffer state. The people of the Pfalz, it was argued, would be materially better off in a politically neutral, independent state under the protection of the League of Nations. Amongst other inducements, France would guarantee the supply of raw materials for industry and would guarantee the value of the Pfalz currency (valuta), offering near-parity with the French franc. Greatly reduced

Vorteile einer selbständigen neutralen Republik!

Die 3 Bezirke Homburg, St. Ingbert und Zweibrücken werden während der 15-jährigen Besatzung durch wirtschaftlichen Anschluß mit der Pfalz verbunden sein. Uns selbst wird die Ausbeutung der pfälzischen Bergwerke verbleiben. Für den Mehrbedarf an Kohlen, sowie für die Belieferung mit Erz werden die Westmächte Sorge tragen.

Bauern, Städter, Beamte, Arbeiter, Handeltreibende, Fabrikanten, wenn ihr eine beträchtliche Milderung der Kriegssteuer wünscht, wenn ihr Kohlen, Eisen, Kleidung, Rohmaterialien, Euer Brot nicht so teuer bezahlen wollt, so wißt, daß Frankreich sie einer freien Pfalz-Republik geben wird, andernfalls nicht.

Unsere Valuta (Geldwert) wird wohlwollend zu Gunsten der Pfalz geregelt sodaß unsere pfälzische Mark annähernd 1 Franken Wert erhält.

Mütter, Schwestern, Bräute, Frauen, alle die Ihr noch Eure Lieben in Gefangenschaft habt, ruft es laut hinaus, daß Ihr eine freie Pfalz-Republik wollt und Eure Angehörigen kehren sofort heim.

Die Franzosen wollen keine französische Pfalz-Republik! Sie wollen eine freie neutrale Republik wie die Schweiz!

Die Besatzung dauert 15 Jahre, es ist zu befürchten, daß wir wegen Deutschlands Zögern mit der Unterschrift des Friedensvertrags wieder in Kriegszustand geraten.

Wir werden einer goldenen Zukunft entgegengehen, in 15 Jahren wird im Saargebiet eine Abstimmung stattfinden. Das Saargebiet wird dann weder Frankreich noch Deutschland angeschlossen werden wollen, sondern sich unserm Pfälzer Freistaat anschließen.

Die Männer, die unsere, für eine Pfalz-Republik eintretenden Freunde festnahmen, glauben sie, richtige Pfälzer zu sein, die uns hindern wollen, einen freien, reichen, ruhigen Staat zu errichten?

Es lebe die Pfälzische Republik!

Figure 24. Separatist propaganda leaflet extolling the advantages of an independent, neutral Pfalz

reparations payments and a reduced period of occupation would also follow. The wine trade, which had been a source of separatist thinking, was not omitted: favourable export conditions would be set up for Pfalz wine producers.[14]

Eberlein could only dismiss all of this as empty promises, while quoting from articles opposing French support for an independent republic which had appeared in the French left-wing press and in the American journal *The Nation*. Bitter criticism was levelled at the allegedly traitorous leaders of the Free Pfalz movement, with whom he linked war profiteers and those engaged in black market activities – a link that he knew would find a resonance among the hard-pressed people of the Pfalz. Eberlein appealed also to their sense of honour, making comparison with the honourable behaviour of the occupied French and Belgian peoples during World War I.[15] Wisely, given the political and constitutional uncertainties prevailing, Eberlein's appeal invoked qualities that he regarded as inherent in Germans as a people, rather than categorising them as citizens of Bavaria or of the Reich. Of the need to maintain bonds linking the Pfalz to Bavaria or even to the Reich there was no mention.

In anticipation of an attempted putsch later in the summer, Eberlein requested authorisation for 10,000 pamphlets to be prepared in the name of the Bavarian or Pfalz government. These would deny recognition of any self-styled separatist government and would instruct officials and the population at large not to cooperate with it. A key factor in any attempted putsch would of course be the attitude taken by local officials. Winterstein was fairly sure that his officials would not condone separatism. Nevertheless, to be on the safe side the pamphlet was to emphasise that the rights and privileges of those officials who remained true to Bavaria would be guaranteed.[16] It betrayed a slight degree of nervousness on the part of the Bavarian government.

A major source of concern for the Pfalzzentrale was the control now being exercised over the press in the Pfalz through French censorship. This was resulting in the impression being created that the government was indifferent to the fate of the people of the Pfalz: 'The old sayings that the Pfalz is Bavaria's poor relation and that the Pfalz is Bavaria's milch cow are being bandied about by Free Pfalz in every possible way.'[17] It is a measure of Eberlein's relative helplessness that in advocating attack as the best form of defence he could only advise the submission of articles and notices that conveyed the desired message in such a way that the French censors in the Pfalz could not object.[18]

At this point in the propaganda battle it can be concluded that the Pfalzzentrale was operating very much on the back foot, being obliged to respond to events and not being able to seize the initiative. It was, however, a situation that was destined not to last.

By the autumn of 1919 the perceived danger of a separatist putsch had faded. The movement had scaled down its ambition to that of achieving autonomy rather than of creating an independent and neutral state.[19] The Pfalz was settling down to the reality of life under the occupation. French policy towards the Pfalz had changed, too. Following the failure of the policy of encouraging the independence movement, General Gérard, French military commander in the Pfalz, had been replaced by Adalbert de Metz, who now put greater emphasis on the policy of *pénétration pacifique.*

Eberlein was now able to turn his attention to the occupation itself – and to the occupiers. His priorities at this time were twofold. Abroad, he wanted to create a channel through which news and articles could be fed to the press in neutral countries such as Switzerland and Sweden. At home, Eberlein and Winterstein were concerned at the lack of awareness in unoccupied Germany of the threat that in their view faced German culture and values in the occupied Rhineland.[20] Their concern over this potential loosening of ties was well founded. This is borne out by the complaints that subsequently surfaced from time to time from the Rhineland, to the effect that people were isolated and lacking in support from unoccupied Germany. The Reich government was most frequently singled out for alleged lack of action but in the Pfalz dissatisfaction at the Bavarian government was expressed also by the indifference with which people regarded ministerial visits.[21] The charge of lack of support was also levelled more generally against their fellow citizens on the east bank of the Rhine.

There were two aspects to the problem facing Eberlein. On the one hand the population at large in unoccupied Germany had problems enough without worrying about conditions in what was at the time a relatively remote western fringe of the nation. Getting back to a semblance of stability at home in the face of shortages, increasing inflation, social upheaval and political uncertainty was undoubtedly of higher priority.[22] In Bavaria, where disruption had been particularly severe during and after the Soviet Republic, conditions in the Pfalz were unlikely to attract much attention from the man in the street. A British report on conditions in Bavaria a few months earlier had concluded:

> The nerves of the German people appear to have broken down. A people of little political understanding, they imagined when the Armistice was signed that peace was immediately at hand and that the privations of four and a half years were over. From heights of hope last November they have been plunged into the depths of despair.[23]

A second, and crucial, aspect was the role of the press, which, until radio broadcasts became universal, was the major channel through which news could be quickly disseminated. This had been recognised by Winterstein and Eberlein – naturally also by the Reich government – and the necessary mechanisms had been put in place to feed articles and news to the established press agencies and to newspapers. However, the response of the German press was often not as positive as could be desired and complaints were heard concerning its lack of interest in the Rhineland.[24] Later, while it was acknowledged that the attention of the press had improved, its output was often degraded by false reporting and inaccuracy. In the Pfalz strict censorship by the French authorities ensured that little was printed to the detriment of the occupation in general. If an editor did overstep the mark the newspaper was immediately banned and he himself was punished with a fine, imprisonment, or even expulsion from the Pfalz together with his family.[25]

All of this indicates that Eberlein was faced with a formidable task in the autumn of 1919. But, seen from his perspective, keeping unoccupied Germany aware of conditions in the Rhineland mattered enormously. It was important that he should succeed not only in keeping up the supply of news and information but in doing so in such a way that the population was moved to protest against the occupation. This would serve to raise morale in the Pfalz by showing that something was being done on its behalf and it would bring pressure to bear on the

Reich and Bavarian governments to be more active. The turning point came for Eberlein when an allegedly official French document came into his possession.[26] This had been written by an officer, Major Paul Jacquot, on the staff of General Gérard and was apparently intended as an account of Gérard's actions in the Pfalz and a justification of his policy. Published in Strasbourg, it was quickly withdrawn when its existence became known to the French authorities. Jacquot was said to have been court-martialled subsequently.[27] The proposal by Eberlein to have the document translated into German and published in full provoked disagreement within the Pfalz action committee because it made reference to several members of the Centre Party who, it alleged, were sympathetic to the creation of an independent Pfalz. Eberlein was not to be deflected from his intention. He did, however, allow those politicians who were not already known to be separatist sympathisers to make statements of denial alongside the original text. Published simply under the title *General Gérard und die Pfalz*, the document was intended for both unoccupied Germany and neutral countries abroad. For Eberlein it represented a propaganda coup.

The significance of the document was that it did not merely contain embarrassing political indiscretions: in Eberlein's eyes it was an official document and therefore it was an explicit statement of the policy of the French government. What did the document contain that made him determined to publish it? It described measures – such as the promotion of cultural and historical links between the Pfalz and France – that had been taken to encourage a Francophile attitude and to generate moral support for the separatist movement. But behind them was the openly declared intention

> to follow an economic policy which – beyond satisfying short-term needs, immediate interests and selfish inclinations – has the ultimate goal of drawing the source of wealth in the Pfalz into our national sphere of activity so that it can operate to our advantage.[28]

Nothing could have been more provocative. A recurrent theme in Jacquot's document was the malevolent influence exercised by

Prussia[29] not just in the northern Rhineland but in the Pfalz also. French policy of *pénétration pacifique* sought to awaken 'the old democratic instincts of the Pfalz' and rescue the Pfalz from 'the barren, sandy-heathland-dwelling men of the east: poor, hard, disciplined and violent Prusso-Slavs'.[30] This was held to be essential for France given the strategic importance of the Rhineland to the emergence of a resurgent Germany.[31]

The book's continual – and almost obsessive – references to the military, economic, cultural and moral dangers represented by Prussia can with some justification be interpreted in terms of a deep underlying French fear of a resurgent Germany. That this fear did exist in spite of the victory in 1918 is beyond doubt: it was commented on by several leading figures on the Allied side.[32]

Eberlein hoped that the exposure of French intentions in an official document, together with the demonising of Prussia, would resonate with unoccupied Germany, of which, after all, Prussia formed a large part. There is, however, little evidence to suggest that publication of *General Gérard und die Pfalz* had much impact in terms of stirring up protest, although it undoubtedly embarrassed and angered the French authorities.

From the standpoint of the Pfalzzentrale little changed in the propaganda battle before the summer of 1920. Although the separatist threat had not completely disappeared and indeed was showing signs of re-emergence,[33] it was not considered by Eberlein to present imminent danger. There were, however, growing concerns over many aspects concerning the Pfalz. While a contemporary report of the Reich Commissioner played down the threat presented by French economic and cultural penetration,[34] the Pfalzzentrale took the state of affairs in the Pfalz more seriously. There is no doubt that the French were very active. Their efforts were both refined and carefully targeted and economic espionage was rife. Attempts were also being made to penetrate the press, both in Germany and in neutral countries like Switzerland. The press in the Pfalz was completely intimidated and the activities of the population were being controlled through censorship and by draconian punishment for breaking regulations. To add to this, the French army was reportedly being strengthened and there was open talk of the annexation of the Pfalz. In short, the French occupiers were apparently full of confidence and in control of the situation. To make matters worse, there were now worries concerning the reliability of the local officials and also the steadfastness of the working class. Largely represented by the SPD, this section of the community had been at the very core of the resistance to separatist activity in the previous year. In unoccupied Germany the press was still not being sufficiently supportive and, owing to the fact that it was being badly informed, was sometimes publishing false and alarming reports.[35] To complete a gloomy picture, relatively little progress had been made in the first few months of 1920 in influencing the neutral foreign press, which hitherto had been largely indifferent to the occupation.[36]

In view of the fact that the Reich Commissioner played down any threat posed by French economic and cultural activities, there is the possibility that the situation in the Pfalz was being overdramatised by the Pfalzzentrale. Certainly at a time when Eberlein was trying to build up his *Abwehr* organisation it would not have been in his interests to minimise the threat. On the other hand, as noted in the previous chapter, the Reich Commissioner had met with criticism from his own side for his alleged indifference to matters others regarded as important. But even allowing for some overstatement, the position for Germany with regard to the Pfalz was certainly no better than it had been a year earlier. Notwithstanding the failure of the separatist putsch that France had actively encouraged, the grip of the occupier had tightened.

In the face of such a situation it might be asked whether the propaganda activity was achieving anything. Eberlein himself was dissatisfied with the results of the whole effort to date. He laid the blame squarely on the Reich government: 'Until now the entire effort has suffered because the Reich government has not dared to declare openly that we have the right and the duty to look after the occupied regions, which are German to the core.'[37] It was a reflection of the power struggle that had been going on between Reich and state.

In April 1920 an opportunity had presented itself for a new front in the propaganda battle. The shooting incident involving Moroccan troops during the occupation of Frankfurt had led to widespread outrage in the press and this had marked the effective beginning of the campaign against the Schwarze Schmach. As we have seen in previous chapters this was a theme enthusiastically taken up by Margarete Gärtner and Heinrich Distler, whose organisations were set up specifically for this purpose. Eberlein, however, seems to have been slightly more circumspect in tackling the issue. During the summer of 1920 his emphasis lay in countering the threat to German values presented by the French policy of cultural penetration and he gave a number of lectures to young people in Bavarian schools.[38] By the end of the year, however, he was organising mass meetings against the Schwarze Schmach in centres such as Munich and Würzburg.[39] On these occasions he appeared with Ray Beveridge as second speaker, a format carefully arranged to produce maximum impact. An introduction was usually made by a notable public figure, at Würzburg for example by the chairman of the regional council, Julius von Henle. Beveridge was the charismatic orator, speaking exclusively on the Schwarze Schmach, able to whip up her audience into a frenzy. Eberlein complemented this with a much wider-ranging attack on the occupation, dealing with the attempts of the French authorities to separate the Pfalz from Germany by economic, cultural and political means and by supporting traitorous separatist movements. Issues such as lack of press freedom, the desperate economic and social circumstances prevailing, and the humiliations that were being inflicted on the people of the Pfalz also featured prominently. The Schwarze Schmach was for Eberlein simply a part of a much wider picture.

It was not until the spring of 1921 that the first of two significant publications on the Schwarze Schmach emerged from the Pfalzzentrale. These were *Der Schrecken am Rhein*[40] and *Schwarze am Rhein: Ein Weltproblem* (fig. 25),[41] both ostensibly prepared by Eberlein himself in 1921, although in the latter case a dispute occurred between Eberlein and his journalist colleague Max Treutler over the authorship.[42] *Der Schrecken am Rhein* (fig. 9) was distributed widely in unoccupied Germany and at least 50,000 copies of an English-language version were distributed in the USA.[43]

Although he devoted significant effort to the Schwarze Schmach it was for Eberlein far from being an isolated issue on which to

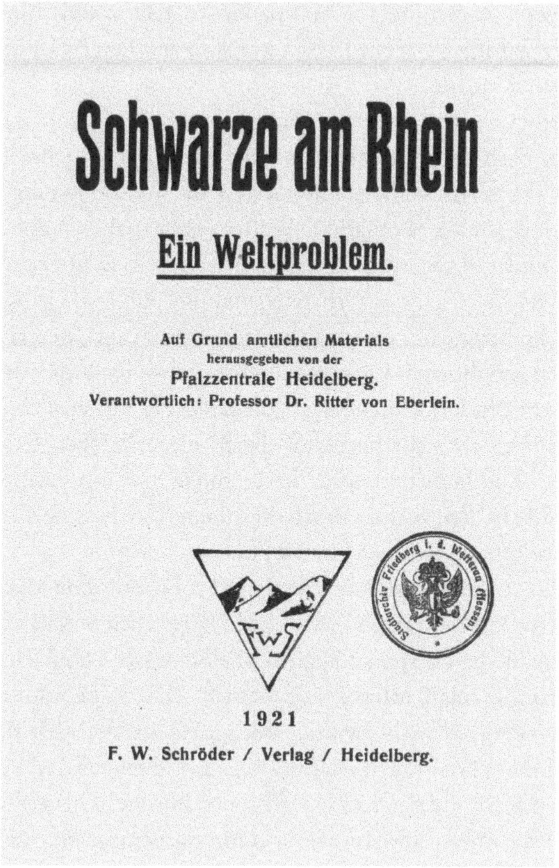

Schwarze am Rhein

Ein Weltproblem.

Auf Grund amtlichen Materials
herausgegeben von der
Pfalzzentrale Heidelberg.
Verantwortlich: Professor Dr. Ritter von Eberlein.

FWS

1921

F. W. Schröder / Verlag / Heidelberg.

Figure 25. *Schwarze am Rhein: Ein Weltproblem* (note the stamp of the Stadtarchiv Friedberg i.d. Wetterau (Hessen); Eberlein distributed copies widely amongst local authorities)

campaign. He viewed it in the wider context of the Rhineland occupation. It was just one more manifestation of the fundamental French desire to dominate and humiliate Germany. Thus, while much of *Der Schrecken am Rhein* was devoted to the Schwarze Schmach its underlying dispute was with the militaristic and annexational policies being pursued by the French government. This wider view led Eberlein to adopt a scattergun approach to propaganda in general, attacking every single aspect concerning the occupation that he could think of and frequently flailing from one line of attack to another. At times it made for disjointed reading.

In respect of the Schwarze Schmach Eberlein took up similar themes to both the Frauenliga and the Notbund, in painting a picture of a licentious soldiery, intoxicated by victory, forcing itself on a defenceless female population. Victims of sexual assault were then forced to undergo the humiliation of testifying to their experiences in front of French officers and thereby making public their shame. For Eberlein, however, this was not the most significant issue concerning the Schwarze Schmach. Of greater consequence for him was the way in which the black man of a lower cultural order was now able to exercise dominance over the people of the Rhine, with their long history of culture. The humiliation of the German race was exemplified in everyday life by the manner in which coloured soldiers now controlled the Rhine crossing point at Ludwigshafen.

Eberlein did not hesitate to pour scorn on those on the German side – including the USPD – who had expressed reservations or even opposition to the campaign against the Schwarze Schmach. Neither did he spare a small minority of women who, as he admitted, had willingly consorted with coloured troops. He asserted that the majority of children born of such relationships would be infected by syphilis and thus present a danger to the whole of Europe. This concern with sexually transmitted disease was a common, almost obsessive theme among German propagandists. We have already noted its presence in the publications of the Notbund and the Frauenliga as well as in the speeches of Beveridge. Groups like the German Protestant Women's Association maintained that all negroes suffered from sexually transmitted disease.[44]

But why should such emphasis be placed on sexually transmitted disease and syphilis in particular? There are several aspects to the answer to this question. In the first place, syphilis was a relatively well-known disease and had long existed in Europe. It had also long been associated with immorality and with retribution for committing immoral acts. With the ending of World War I and the return of the troops from the Front, the common perception was that the incidence of sexually transmitted diseases had increased dramatically, although Richard Bessel has pointed out that this had more to do with social issues than with any real increase over pre-war rates of incidence.[45] Syphilis was certainly feared, for no truly effective method of treatment yet existed. There is a parallel here with tropical diseases, for which, also, no effective treatments existed. But more than this, in the early part of the twentieth century the view had become entrenched in the minds of physicians that syphilis was endemic in the black races, probably as a result of having encountered it in the colonies along with a variety of tropical diseases. Eberlein was able to seize upon the conclusions of a Professor Gongerot from the medical faculty at the University of Paris, who asserted that infection was being introduced into France mainly by people from the colonies, including colonial soldiers.[46]

It has been pointed out by Paul Weindling that Germany at this time was obsessive about the risks presented by infectious disease.[47] In the east, where substantial post-war movements of refugees were taking place across the new frontier, often in unhygienic conditions, a great fear existed of typhus. A series of precautionary measures was introduced, which included the compulsory screening and disinfecting of those arriving in Germany, often conducted in a less than sympathetic manner. With the exception of the worldwide influenza pandemic in 1918, Germany had remained free of major infections throughout the war. It now regarded itself as a bastion of cleanliness and health and intended to maintain this state of affairs. There was, however, another aspect to the matter. Many of those entering Germany from the east were Jews. In the minds of some it did not take much to link this situation with ideas about racial hygiene, namely the infection of the pure white (and Christian) European race by people of other races whose presumed state of cleanliness and health – and indeed morality – was dubious. This was, of course, one of the many obsessions of Hitler, who, however, associated sexually transmitted disease less with colonial troops than with prostitution, immorality generally and, inevitably, the Jews.[48]

Given all of this it is not surprising that the imposition on the Rhineland of colonial troops, whose freedom from disease of all kinds was a matter for suspicion, aroused additional fear and anger. And unlike the situation in the east, Germany had no control whatsoever over Rhineland occupation forces.

The notion that the black man represented a reservoir of infection was not confined to Germany. In the USA at that time, quite apart from tropical diseases, syphilis was considered to be the quintessential black disease, an attitude that prevailed for decades. In 1930 an experiment relating to this topic was begun in the Southern USA involving black subjects. It was not terminated until 1972 and it became notorious for the damage that it caused to the participants.[49] It was not until some years after the Weimar period that black and white races were placed on an equal footing regarding their susceptibility to disease. So Eberlein, whilst grossly exaggerating the danger presented by infection, was probably doing no more than repeating a commonly held belief – something that he could expect to appeal to a wide readership. Behind the propaganda was the underlying fear of yet another threat to German security.

According to Eberlein, the Schwarze Schmach was not the only danger facing the people of the Pfalz in everyday life. He claimed that in the first year of occupation two murders had been committed by French troops, 73 people had been shot and 143 pedestrians had been fatally injured by French motor vehicles. In other acts of violence 32 Rhinelanders had been killed and 1,018 had been seriously injured. These events were illustrated graphically in a series of images, at least one of which had been reprinted from the satirical magazine *Simplicissimus*. They were intended for further use by the reader as letter seals.

The booklet *Schwarze am Rhein*, also, was aimed at an international readership, but was altogether of a different order from Eberlein's earlier publication. It was intended to counter the booklet *La campagne contre les troupes noires* which had recently been published by the French authorities in Mainz with the authorisation of the IRHC. This had itself been produced in answer to the earlier vociferous propaganda campaign in the German press. *Schwarze am Rhein* was distinguished in two main respects from what had been published previously. In this booklet, Eberlein adopted a confrontational style, challenging the

French arguments point by point by arranging the response on the page opposite a German translation of the original French document. He also drew heavily on official reports and on those reports and articles from the domestic and foreign press that could be construed as favourable to the German cause.

La campagne contre les troupes noires (hereafter *La campagne*) had outlined the chronological course of events and had complained about the hatred directed against the Allies and in particular against France. France had felt obliged to press for reparations since of all countries she had endured the most suffering. The campaign against the black troops, it was maintained, amounted to cheap propaganda. It was calculated to inflame hatred against France in neutral countries and to influence the Allies in a manner prejudicial to her interests. The Reich government stood accused of orchestrating the whole affair, which amounted to nothing more than a series of wild and inaccurate accusations. Contrary to the situation portrayed by the English journalist E. D. Morel in his press articles, by Beveridge in her speeches and by Reich Minister Adolf Köster in the Reichstag, 50,000 wild negroes had not been let loose on German women and children. Numbers of colonial troops had never exceeded 25,000, of whom only 4,000 were black Senegalese – and these had been withdrawn in June 1920, amid expressions of regret from the local German population.[50] As was only to be expected, the withdrawal of the black troops had not ended the German campaign because its aims were still unfulfilled. The Germans might not have any sympathy for the black troops in the Rhineland but they, too, had needed the help of black troops in the struggle against the Allies.

La campagne alleged that many of the complaints had been fabricated or were trivial and it made the point that all had been or were being investigated. The investigations, however, had been handicapped, even prevented, by inaccuracy in the detail presented and by intentional delays in submitting complaints.[51] Thanks to the resulting uncertainty, the German authorities had achieved their goal of preventing the exposure of dubious claims and had thus been able to continue their dishonourable campaign. The French authorities did not consider the behaviour of the coloured troops as completely above

nybody suspected of violence would be tried by military found guilty would be severely punished. The punish-ments handed out for relatively minor offences had testified to this, as for example in the case of the Moroccan soldier sentenced to three months' imprisonment for breaking a window in a house and threatening two young girls with a bayonet. On the other hand another typical complaint, when investigated, was found to have been made solely on the grounds that children had refused to cross a copse in which coloured soldiers were working.[52]

The German press was criticised by the French authorities for reporting allegedly new offences by coloured troops when they had already been dealt with by the courts. Use was also made of dissent on the German side. This was mainly to be found in left-wing socialist, pacifist or religious publications. Thus articles and editorials from publications such as *Der Christliche Pilger*, *Sozialistische Republik* and *Deutsche pazifistische Monatsschrift* were quoted, that had testified to the good conduct of the coloured troops.[53] Harsh criticism of the campaign against the Schwarze Schmach was even found in a letter published in the Social Democratic newspaper *Münchener Post*, which blamed German war profiteers rather than black troops for the incidence of undernourishment and tuberculosis among German children.[54]

Several major sources of German propaganda, including the Frauenliga, were identified in *La campagne*. Surprisingly, in view of his contribution to the upsurge in propaganda activity in autumn 1920 and the disquiet that he had created in the Reich and Bavarian governments, there was no mention of Heinrich Distler and the Notbund. Neither was the relationship of the Pfalzzentrale to the Bavarian and Reich governments fully understood, for Eberlein (Dr Ritter) was described as the leader of the Mannheim branch office of the Heimatdienst – a gaffe seized upon by Eberlein in his response. The Heimatdienst, with backing from military circles, was in fact thought to be the coordinator and the source of funding for the Schwarze Schmach campaign. French concerns over German military power were again evident here also.

It was conceded by the French that the Schwarze Schmach campaign was being more robustly and more skilfully driven than other

German propaganda campaigns and that it had been successful in making an impression on a sector of foreign public opinion. This was a surprising admission – though true – in view of the encouragement it must have given to the German propagandists. In French eyes the goal of the Schwarze Schmach propaganda, as expressed in an issue of *Medizinische Wochenschrift*, was clear enough:

> Let our compatriots write to their friends abroad, let our medical colleagues lay out brochures about the Schwarze Schmach in their waiting rooms and give them to their patients. Let teachers, the clergy, the doctors, the local authorities get to work on the farming communities, especially in America. Perhaps then foreign governments will put pressure on the French government![55]

Eberlein's response placed the matter on a different plane altogether. For him the Schwarze Schmach was not simply a matter of the humiliation of a defenceless people following the imposition of the Peace Treaty, or even an issue to be resolved between France and Germany: it would lead to the systematic awakening in the black race of a feeling of power over the white race and therefore represented a threat to white civilisation and culture worldwide.[56] It was noted earlier that the concept of morality was closely associated with the campaigning by women against the Schwarze Schmach. Eberlein, too, attributed a moral dimension to the issue. While he carefully avoided any discussion of his ideas, he made it plain that in his view morality was equated to level of civilisation. White European civilisation was fundamentally moral, and its supremacy was preordained as part of the natural and moral order. Non-white races had lower moral standing. Thus in a riposte to a quotation from the *Christliche Pilger*, which testified to the generally good behaviour of black troops in the face of sexual provocation from German women, he sarcastically remarked: 'it testifies to the success of the work of the missionaries, whose Christian moral teaching of young coloured boys has had such an impact that they fall into the arms of a whore at the very first temptation'.[57] To be sure, there were some German women who had consorted with the enemy but these had for the most part been forced into immorality by hunger, deprivation and misery.[58]

Unsurprisingly, this line of thinking was followed by several German propagandists. Strong feelings over the use of coloured troops had long existed and were a particular feature of German World War I propaganda. Germany had at that time mounted a virulent campaign against the use of coloured troops in the Allied armies. These were variously depicted as barbarians, wild animals, subhuman cannibals, guilty of all kinds of brutal atrocities committed against the armies of civilised nations.[59] But the use of coloured troops to control a white civilian population represented for the propagandists a new and sinister development.

Eberlein considered that *La campagne* was aimed principally at neutral foreign opinion. To be seen to be adopting a moral stance, while at the same time awakening concern in neutral countries where racial harmony was generally not an issue, would serve his purpose well. At the same time it would play well in the USA, where the race issue was already generating considerable internal tension.

The strategy of appearing to take the moral high ground also required Eberlein to distance his organisation from that of the now-discredited Heinrich Distler, and from any similar organisations. He not only declared *Schwarze am Rhein* free from any exaggeration of facts, but also expressed his intention to counter any further instances emanating from what he described as irresponsible organisations, however well intentioned. However, he also sought to turn the Distler affair to his advantage, accusing the French authorities of obstructing the immediate and thorough investigation of alleged offences by coloured troops. As a result, horror stories of all kinds had developed. These, Eberlein maintained, could easily take root in the febrile imagination of a tormented people.

A tactic adopted extensively in the publication was to seize on any support that could be found in the foreign press. This was usually in the form of statements made by prominent individuals of neutral or even Allied countries who, for one reason or another, were sympathetic to the German side of the argument. Examples included newspaper articles written by E. D. Morel for the *Daily Herald* in London, articles in *Stockholms-Tidningen* by the Swedish author and member of the Swedish Commission Elin Wägner and a speech by the Swedish Prime Minister Hjalmar Branting. Presented by Eberlein as impartial comment, such quotations were felt to give greater credibility to the German argument. Comment did not have to be based on facts: insinuation served the purpose well enough. A letter of protest sent by a bishop to the French ambassador in the USA, claiming that negroes had been let loose on helpless white women,[60] was reproduced in full.

In addressing a major source of contention in the propaganda battle – the number and nature of the offences committed by coloured troops – Eberlein strenuously denied inventing cases where offences had taken place. All documented cases were derived from official sources, he maintained, contrasting his claims to those of certain irresponsible elements who exaggerated acts and falsified statistics. In response to Tirard's claim that complaints laid before the IRHC had included a large number of inadequately documented, trivial or dubious cases, he responded that the Frauenliga had established 111 sexual offences as fact. Further, the report[61] by General Allen, the US observer on the IRHC, had documented no fewer than 66 cases – in contrast to a mere 21 cases authenticated by the French authorities. Eberlein disputed anything and everything coming from the French side on principle rather than on the basis of rationality. He contrasted, also, the punishments meted out to offenders by the French authorities – ranging from thirty days' to ten years' imprisonment – with the lynching that would take place in the USA for the same type of offence.[62] By making such a comparison, he was surely not only implying that lynch-mob rule was a regular part of US justice but was also investing this with some degree of acceptability. It is all consistent with the nature of a man who had few scruples. For Eberlein, the end always justified the means.

As in the case of the Frauenliga propaganda, the excesses of coloured troops were linked with the harshness of living conditions in the occupied areas, housing shortages and the enforced billeting of troops on householders. Another aspect related to the provision of brothels, allegedly provided on occasion through the requisitioning of private houses and the eviction of their occupants. Denial by the French military authorities that any town was legally obliged to provide brothels or even to contribute to the costs of running them was challenged with an excerpt from the American journal *The Nation*, which, according to Eberlein, usually adopted a pro-French stance. This stated that France, alone among the Allies, had ordered the setting up of brothels, and there followed a list of sixteen towns and cities where this had taken place, accompanied by details of costs.[63]

The image of German womanhood, associated with purity, honour and moral value, contrasted starkly with the evil and destructive effect of the Schwarze Schmach. This portrayal was a major theme behind the protests of the Frauenliga and it attracted complaint in *La campagne*. This inevitably drew a response from Eberlein, who used a fencing metaphor. Where was the much admired French chivalry in the vilification of the women of the Frauenliga? he demanded to know. They were simply fighting for the honour and safety of their sisters: 'The German woman is certainly fair game, ideal for hunting down in order to satisfy sexual urges. She is hardly regarded as a worthy opponent whom one fights with open visor and before whom one lowers the rapier in salute before the contest.'[64] In support were cited a number of press articles and letters of protest written by women's organisations in the USA, Norway, Sweden, Denmark and Hungary.

Naturally Eberlein made a point of extolling the values associated with German womanhood. His reaction to the alleged assault on it was to reproduce a cartoon (fig. 26) that had appeared in a French satirical magazine and to denounce it. Even Eberlein, however, could not deny that a small minority of German women had consorted with the enemy, as indeed had French and Belgian women during the war. Such women, he conceded, were present in every nation, but no German or German newspaper would ever think to associate the respectable French or Belgian woman with the whores and sexual perverts of their country.[65] It was the duty of every decent woman to protect her femininity, honour and purity, setting herself apart from those among her contemporaries who would drag themselves through the mire. Eberlein was again seeking to take the moral high ground, holding up the image of pure German womanhood and depicting those who failed to meet this standard as unworthy. Yet there was inconsistency

Figure 26. German reproduction of French satirical cartoon. According to Eberlein the original caption read: 'We were going to guard an eagle but were forced to defend ourselves against a sow'

here, for it was earlier noted that he excused those women who had prostituted themselves because, for the most part helpless, they had been driven to it by hunger, deprivation and misery.

Eberlein's attitude is symptomatic of two conflicting images of the role of women in the early Weimar years. On the one hand we see the pure but weak and helpless white woman at the mercy of wild colonial troops, the focus for the Frauenliga protests and for the propaganda of Eberlein amongst others. Yet on the other hand the new Republic had brought with it the concept of gender equality. Eberlein employed this idea of equality, too. Women, no less than men, were troops in the struggle against the French occupiers. If they failed to uphold the standards of behaviour expected of German women then they were no less guilty than men of a dereliction of their duty.

From the French viewpoint the campaign against the Schwarze Schmach was extreme, full of inaccuracies and exaggeration, and was motivated by hatred. This had been the basis of the complaint made in July 1920 by Tirard as chairman of the IRHC to Reich Commissioner Starck, demanding a general retraction by the German press. It is not surprising therefore that *La campagne* included a number of letters, written by German inhabitants of occupied Rhineland, that testified to irreproachable standards of behaviour and discipline of the coloured occupation troops and, in one case, even sought to justify French policy in setting up brothels. Eberlein scornfully dismissed such testimonials of good character, noting that Germans would remember that the exception merely serves to confirm the rule. To reinforce his point he noted, with ample use of sarcasm, irony and contempt, that those providing testimonials mostly hid behind a cloak of anonymity – and he included graphic statements made by alleged victims of new sexual assaults.

The IRHC was a particular target for Eberlein, who regarded it as a puppet controlled by France. He accused it of lying about the misdeeds of coloured troops, or, where these had been so obvious that they could not be ignored, of seeking to gloss over them. In contrast, he maintained, the fundamental truth of the German campaign was based not simply on German evidence, but on the evidence of French, English, Swedish and American eyewitnesses. To the charge that the Schwarze Schmach campaign had from the very beginning been drummed up and orchestrated from Berlin he responded angrily:

> ... in the face of such spontaneous condemnation of the activities of a wild band of soldiers and their leaders, arising from their sense of justice and morality, the IRHC irresponsibly dismisses

> this pitiful cry of distress from a tortured people, mentally shattered and in the depths of despair, as groundless propaganda produced and directed by the government. Such cynicism and lack of feeling for human misery, mental suffering and physical torture can hardly be exceeded![66]

The IRHC was also castigated for controlling the press in the occupied Rhineland by force of threat and punishment. *La campagne* had made no secret of the penalties imposed by military courts, which for the editors of the local newspapers concerned meant fines of up to M 20,000 and a year of imprisonment. The commission, for its part, had issued banning notices to a number of newspapers for breaches of the regulations in force. Several newspapers, including the *Kölnische Volkszeitung*, the *Rheinische Zeitung* and the *Wiesbadener Neueste Nachrichten*, had published articles attacking the use of coloured troops and had been obliged to publish statements retracting allegations that could not be proved. Eberlein made great play with the concepts of journalistic honour and the public reputation on which the German newspaper was founded. He accused Tirard of having personally played the major part in destroying press freedom and of vindictively punishing the German press simply because the press in neutral countries was not within his control.

Eberlein had little time for those on the German side who did not fully share his commitment to the struggle against the French occupiers and, as we shall see later, he was vindictive towards those who were suspected of collaboration, even in the slightest degree. His propaganda was accordingly directed at times at his own side. An example of this is to be seen in his response to an article reprinted from a German pacifist monthly which criticised the basis of the campaign against the Schwarze Schmach. Intertwining a thinly disguised attack on German pacifists with the ever recurrent themes of French militarism and imperialism, Eberlein argued that while these existed, pacifists would never achieve their ambitions. Militarism and imperialism had been destroyed by the Revolution in Germany – if indeed they had ever been present. But they were rampant in France, sustained by an inexhaustible supply of African manpower. The Schwarze Schmach was, however, just one manifestation of the terrible dangers threatening the civilised peoples of Europe. Eberlein pointed to concerns expressed by Pierrepont B. Noyes, US representative on the former International Rhineland Commission, regarding the dangers of renewed conflict in Europe. In the west, France, in spite of being ruined by war, was intent on military domination, while in the east lay the threat of Bolshevist invasion by a vengeful Russia, reinforced by countless millions of Asians. A despairing Germany was simply awaiting its opportunity.[67] Eberlein's message was unequivocal: this was no time for pacifism in Germany – and the underlying threat was barely concealed.

The very word *Pazifist* used by Eberlein reveals something of his attitude and his nature. This was the language of World War I, used to describe those who for reasons of conscience were unwilling to fight. Pacifists were invariably punished and endured some degree of social stigma. It is not made entirely clear to whom Eberlein was addressing his remarks but it can reasonably be assumed that the recipients included anybody who was not committed to the struggle against the terms of the Peace Treaty. Eberlein was both prolonging the ethos of wartime and using the word *Pazifist* as a term of abusive contempt. Like any other zealot he believed that 'if you are not for us, then you are against us'. His intolerant attitude towards pacifists, it might also be noted, was not dissimilar to that of Hitler:

> In exactly the same way our German pacifist will accept in silence the bloodiest rape of our nation at the hands of the most vicious military powers if a change in this state of affairs can only be achieved by resistance.[68]

Schwarze am Rhein was well received in some quarters on the German side, less enthusiastically in others. Eberlein himself seems to have been gratified with the outcome of his work.[69] He sent personal copies to leading officials in state and local government, and to political parties (see fig. 25). Few responses survive, but in one of these the Bavarian Minister of Justice commented that *Schwarze am Rhein* was an extremely valuable complement to Professor Gallinger's article 'Gegenrechnung' in the *Süddeutsche Monatshefte*,[70] while a letter from the DVP requested the widest possible circulation of the document and commended it for use in the DVP Youth Group.[71] A response from the local authority in Bensheim in Hessen indicated doubt about the veracity of some of the claims from the German side, but considered that there must have been some truth in the assertions if they were based on official material. Accordingly it would support distribution of the document because it would warn German men and women to exercise care in dealings with black troops.[72] The DNVP in Hessen commented that from the German standpoint the French propaganda seemed weak, but so was the German counter-propaganda, and it would have little impact on the so-called masses. Perhaps its purpose was more to influence people abroad?[73]

Eberlein was keen to publish an English version of the booklet, noting that it had aroused interest, especially in Holland and the USA.[74] An application to the Volkspflege for funds for its translation was met with refusal, however, on both political and propaganda grounds.[75] Clearly the Volkspflege was not well disposed towards Eberlein and the Pfalzzentrale. Another quarter from which *Schwarze am Rhein* met with strong disapproval was the Reich Foreign Ministry. It was noted in the previous chapter that there had already been strong internal criticism of current official propaganda and its damaging effects abroad. Now, at a time when even neutral opinion held that the campaign against the Schwarze Schmach had been overplayed – and Eberlein had earlier been warned of this[76] – he had set about producing his booklet. Opinion within the Foreign Ministry was damning:

> Dr Ritter's recent publication on the Schwarze Schmach does *not* seem likely to produce a favourable reaction in the Anglo-Saxon countries: the best propaganda there is the sort that confines itself to objective reproduction of real events.[77]

The recommendation was again made that the Pfalzzentrale should only be allowed to disseminate propaganda abroad if sanctioned by the Foreign Ministry.

By the time that *Schwarze am Rhein* appeared in mid-1921 Eberlein's propaganda had succeeded in irritating the French authorities to the

as outlined in the previous chapter, they successfully he dissolution of the Mannheim Centre. There were, of reasons also. There was the matter of the alleged war ...mes and in addition Eberlein stood accused of having sent a raiding party to forcibly break up a meeting organised by the French authorities.[78] But without a doubt the aggressive and personal style of Eberlein's propaganda had brought him notoriety in French eyes. He was considered to be a danger. Even at this stage there was some indication that he was moving towards more active resistance against the occupation.

With the dissolution of the Mannheim Centre on 1 October 1921, propaganda output virtually ceased until the SWDV, the new publishing arm of the Pfalzzentrale, began its operations in Pasing in the following year. As remarked earlier, relations between Mannheim and Pasing were initially far from perfect. What was essentially a power struggle spilled over, also, into arguments over propaganda themes. The consultant employed at Pasing, F. Hausmann, with support from the Notbund, wanted to pursue the topic of children of mixed race in the Rhineland,[79] much against the will of Eberlein, who considered it politically inexpedient to do so.[80] In effect the propaganda war had entered a new phase. From now on relatively little was to be heard of the Schwarze Schmach from the Pfalzzentrale, although it did not disappear altogether.

Some of the main propaganda publications that emerged from Pasing in the course of 1922 are shown in fig. 27, which reproduces the rear cover of the booklet *Spielen wir unser Spiel am Rhein.* The emphasis now lay on wider political aspects of the occupation rather than on expressions of outrage over the minutiae of events in the Rhineland. Particular use was also made of reports on debates in the Reichstag and Landtag, clearly aimed at a more serious readership. Gone was the inflammatory and aggressive tone of the earlier publications. *Spielen wir unser Spiel* was written by Eberlein under the pseudonym of Dr Amrhein. This was an exposé of correspondence that had taken place between the separatist leaders and French authorities two years previously and in effect aimed to associate this relationship with duplicity and corruption.

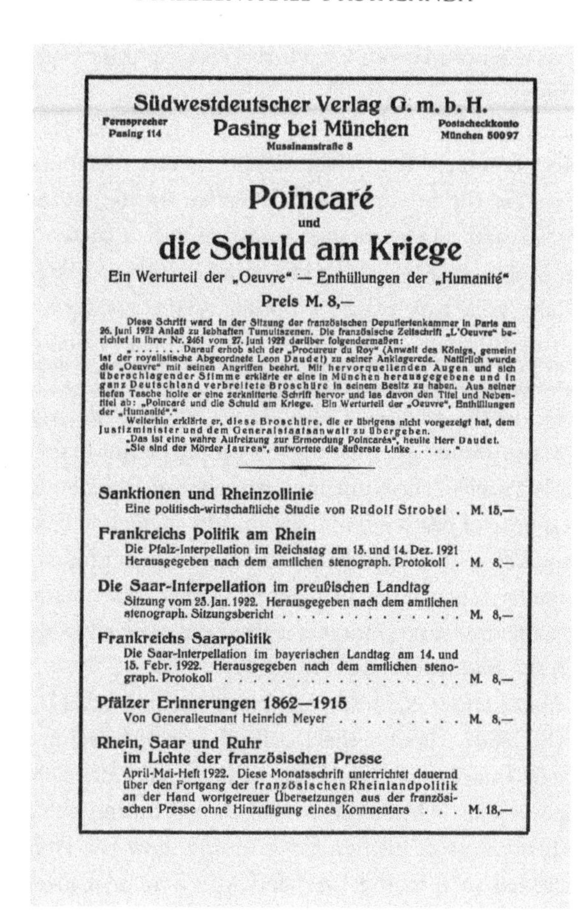

Südwestdeutscher Verlag G. m. b. H.

Fernsprecher Pasing 114 — Pasing bei München — Postscheckkonto München 50097

Mussinanstraße 8

Poincaré

und

die Schuld am Kriege

Ein Werturteil der „Oeuvre" — Enthüllungen der „Humanité"

Preis M. 8,—

Diese Schrift ward in der Sitzung der französischen Deputiertenkammer in Paris am 26. Juni 1922 Anlaß zu lebhaften Tumultszenen. Die französische Zeitschrift „L'Oeuvre" berichtet in ihrer Nr. 2461 vom 27. Juni 1922 darüber folgendermaßen:

„. . . . . Darauf erhob sich der „Procureur du Roy" (Anwalt des Königs, gemeint ist der royalistische Abgeordnete Leon Daudet) zu seiner Anklagerede. Natürlich wurde die „Oeuvre" mit seinen Angriffen beehrt. Mit hervorquellenden Augen und sich überschlagender Stimme erklärte er eine in München herausgegebene und in ganz Deutschland verbreitete Broschüre in seinem Besitz zu haben. Aus seiner tiefen Tasche holte er eine zerknitterte Schrift hervor und las davon den Titel und Nebentitel ab: „Poincaré und die Schuld am Kriege. Ein Werturteil der „Oeuvre", Enthüllungen der „Humanité"."

Weiterhin erklärte er, diese Broschüre, die er übrigens nicht vorgezeigt hat, dem Justizminister und dem Generalstaatsanwalt zu übergeben.

„Das ist eine wahre Aufreizung zur Ermordung Poincarés", heulte Herr Daudet.

„Sie sind der Mörder Jaures", antwortete die äußerste Linke . . . . . ."

Sanktionen und Rheinzollinie
Eine politisch-wirtschaftliche Studie von Rudolf Strobel . M. 15,—

Frankreichs Politik am Rhein
Die Pfalz-Interpellation im Reichstag am 13. und 14. Dez. 1921 Herausgegeben nach dem amtlichen stenograph. Protokoll . M. 8,—

Die Saar-Interpellation im preußischen Landtag
Sitzung vom 25. Jan. 1922. Herausgegeben nach dem amtlichen stenograph. Sitzungsbericht . . . . M. 8,—

Frankreichs Saarpolitik
Die Saar-Interpellation im bayerischen Landtag am 14. und 15. Febr. 1922. Herausgegeben nach dem amtlichen stenograph. Protokoll . . . . M. 8,—

Pfälzer Erinnerungen 1862—1915
Von Generalleutnant Heinrich Meyer . . . . M. 8,—

Rhein, Saar und Ruhr im Lichte der französischen Presse
April-Mai-Heft 1922. Diese Monatsschrift unterrichtet dauernd über den Fortgang der französischen Rheinlandpolitik an der Hand wortgetreuer Übersetzungen aus der französischen Presse ohne Hinzufügung eines Kommentars . . . M. 18,—

Figure 27. A range of publications from Südwestdeutscher Verlag

There are several probable reasons for the quieter tone adopted during 1922. In the first place, the political situation in the Pfalz was relatively quiet. And although the Notbund was continuing its campaign against the Schwarze Schmach, even Eberlein would have acknowledged that nothing much was to be gained for the time being by pursuing this overplayed theme. It was also better that he and his organisation should for the time being maintain a low profile, following the intervention of the Allies the previous year. Finally, he was beginning to entertain ideas of a more active resistance to the occupation, for which lack of public visibility was advantageous.

In the autumn of 1922 the French policy of *pénétration pacifique* was well established and the State Commissioner, Lorenz Wappes, became very concerned at the amount of effort that was being put into French cultural propaganda. In particular, publication had commenced of a French-inspired newspaper which was being distributed free throughout the Pfalz, at a time when inflationary pressures were driving up the cost of German publications. The German response was the monthly *Deutsche Nachrichten*, first published by Eberlein in December 1922, subsequently renamed *Südwestdeutsches Nachrichtenblatt*.[81] Its importance as a means of reaching the people of the Pfalz increased in January 1923 when the Ruhr invasion was quickly followed by the German response of passive resistance and the inevitable French countermeasures. Yet it was only partially successful in this aim: a survey of its readership in May 1923 revealed that inadequate coverage existed in some areas and, more worrying, the readership was largely confined to the middle classes.[82]

The *Südwestdeutsches Nachrichtenblatt* was well regarded by its readership in the Pfalz, though there existed a strong feeling that the authorities in unoccupied Germany had left the Pfalz to its own devices for too long. One local official in welcoming the arrival of the news-sheet wrote of his despair on seeing 'how the French news-sheets succeeded in reaching the hands of German readers in their hundreds in order to contaminate and poison their hearts'. He added: 'I felt like screaming at you, "Are you all asleep over there? Are you all Communists? Or are you all from the gilded, glorified so-called international brotherhood?"'[83]

What did the news-sheet contain that appealed to its readers? It provided a mixture of local news – usually of French misdeeds – interspersed with allegation, exhortation and scorn. To this might be added any supportive quotations gleaned from the foreign press. Increasingly, Eberlein came to regard the consequences of the campaign of passive resistance as another manifestation of economic warfare in which France was the aggressor and whose intention was to ruin Germany. An economics supplement was therefore added to the newspaper.[84] As the year wore on, exhortation to remain true to the German cause became more prominent. The July issue contained a full page testifying to the steadfastness of the people of the Pfalz in such adverse circumstances and appealing to them – with apparent confidence – to remain true to Fatherland, State and Reich. Sometimes a particular group was singled out for attention, as for example the wine producers, who were thought to be susceptible to the lure of separatism. On another occasion the workers at BASF in Ludwigshafen, who were under pressure to ignore the German ban on using the French-controlled railways, were urged to remain steadfast. For the first time, however, another tone could also be distinguished – that of threat and revenge. In each issue of the *Nachrichtenblatt* was published a roll of honour, containing the names of those who had been punished for contravening IRHC edicts or who had been expelled by the French authorities. It also included a roll of shame, making known the names of those suspected of collaboration. Included in one issue, for example, was a Speyer railway inspector by the name of Fischer, whose sole offence was that he had been seen driving in a car with French army officers.

On another occasion two hotel owners were singled out, one of whom, Josef Schäfer, the owner of the hotel Zum Engel in Speyer, was alleged to have given preferential treatment to French customers and to have allowed his premises to be used for meetings of spies and separatists. Vindictiveness and incitement to violence were evident in the comment: 'People of the Pfalz make a note of these traitors! And citizens of Heidelberg, give them the right response when they cross the Rhine!'[85] From such roots would later grow the attitudes prevalent in the Third Reich.

The problems confronting Eberlein intensified as the policy of passive resistance dragged on. He had in the previous year remarked on a tendency for those in the Pfalz to regard any propaganda coming from outside with suspicion, regardless of whether or not it was from the Reich or Bavaria.[86] This he had to overcome. With the mood in the Pfalz becoming increasingly depressed and apathetic he wanted to redouble his efforts but was frustrated by a severe shortage of funds, worsened by the deteriorating economic situation.[87] Added to this were limitations in his capability to distribute the material widely within a reasonable time frame.[88]

However well the *Südwestdeutsches Nachrichtenblatt* had been received in the Pfalz, it was not without its critics within the Bavarian government. Dr Sigmund Knoch, former Bavarian representative in the Reich Commissioner's office and now active in the State Secretariat for the Occupied Regions, was persistently critical. Knoch was respected on all sides as an industrious and extremely capable official.[89] Some weight has therefore to be attached to his complaints to Wappes that the *Nachrichtenblatt* was adopting too aggressive a tone and that this, together with personal attacks on the French administrator Adalbert de Metz, were counterproductive and damaging to the German cause.[90] These charges were angrily rejected by Max Treutler[91] and there is no evidence that he and Eberlein modified their approach. Indeed there is evidence of an attempt to hit back at Knoch, by accusing him of making a false report of another and unrelated matter.[92] Knoch's outspoken complaints betray unease within the Bavarian government over the policy being followed by the Pfalzzentrale – a moderate strand of opinion, which, however, was not listened to. The situation accords with remarks made later by Hans Schmelzle concerning the Pfalzzentrale and is further evidence of officially sanctioned recklessness. Not for the first time it demonstrates also the lack of unity that existed – even within the Bavarian government – over the content and style of German propaganda.

The increasing bitterness with which the campaign of passive resistance was conducted is reflected in the way in which exhortation directed at the people of the Pfalz at times gave way to threat. Propaganda leaflets were used extensively and were usually devoted to specific topics. The railways were one such example. Of immense strategic importance, these had been taken over by the French in retaliation for the campaign of passive resistance. Any refusal of German employees to cooperate was met with dismissal and expulsion from the Pfalz. French military staff supervised the running of the trains, but language difficulties, unfamiliarity with operating systems and sabotage led to accidents.[93] This was a gift to the propagandists. When the people of the Pfalz were urged to boycott the French-controlled trains the propaganda was crude, direct and threatening (figs. 28 and 29).

Macht Euer Testament!

Wenn Ihr mit den

Franzosen-Zügen fahrt!

Warum? Schaut Euch die Leute an, die für die Franzosen in Ludwigshafen Eisenbahndienst machen! **Arbeitsscheue, Verbrecher, Dirnen**, das sind die "zuverlässigen" Leute, denen die Franzosen den **verantwortungsvollen** Eisenbahnfahrdienst anvertrauen. Dazu kommen noch einige Eisenbahnbeamte als **Verräter**, wie die berüchtigten Eisenbahn-Inspektoren **Couturier** und **Magnier** aus Speyer. Erkundigt Euch, wie viele **Eisenbahn-Unglücksfälle** bislang im Rheinland vorgekommen sind! Wer mit einem **Franzosen-Zug** fährt, steht als Verräter mit einem Fuß im **Zucht-Haus**, mit dem andern im **Grab**!

Figure 28. The text of a leaflet urging a boycott of French-controlled railways in the Pfalz (English translation in Appendix VI)

Throughout the summer of 1923 Bavaria in particular pressed for the passive resistance campaign to continue to the bitter end. But with the Pfalz enduring ever harsher economic conditions the political will of the population was becoming weaker. French propaganda alleged that many citizens expelled over the Rhine were suffering hardship and that passive resistance was coming to an end. Eberlein took a more optimistic view[94] and directed his response at officials and workers in particular. Using morale-boosting, heroic language, he had no doubts about the success of the campaign of passive resistance and he had only contempt for the faint-hearted:

> The exploitation of the Rhineland has been thwarted. Poincaré's brutal policy has been given a resounding 'No' and from that he will learn his lesson. The attention of the world has been directed to the Rhine and the Ruhr and Poincaré's shameless intentions have been exposed. The world dissociates itself from him...

Figure 29. 'Those entrusting themselves to French trains, with no signals or track maintenance, risk life and limb.'

> A ray of power shines in the German people! The world sees this with amazement and newly awakened interest. We see it with joy and with hope. Isn't that enough for you faint-hearted?[95]

If contempt was being shown towards those losing faith in passive resistance, then it is no surprise that those who were thought to be guilty of collaborating risked being publicly branded as such. Not only were the names of such people published in the *Südwestdeutsches Nachrichtenblatt*, but posters exposing them and their alleged treachery were distributed.[96]

The seizure of power by the Independent Pfalz movement a few weeks after the campaign of passive resistance had been brought to an end by the Reich government was the final straw as far as the Bavarian government and Eberlein were concerned. Little encouragement was needed to proceed with the assassination attempt on the separatist government. In turn this provoked the Allies to move against the Pfalzzentrale for a second time, bringing its activities to an end.

Closure of the Pfalzzentrale did not quite represent the end of Eberlein's activities related to the Rhineland occupation, however. His short novel *Die Spionin vom Rhein*[97] appeared in 1930. Unlike the work of Guido Kreutzer discussed earlier, Eberlein's novel contained no glorification of the German armies, no appeals to any *völkisch* instincts, or any particular denigration of, or hatred towards the French as a people. It was couched in much more moderate tones.

Eberlein's principal character, guilty of criminal embezzlement, had betrayed his country and now exercised his criminal talents in an underhand and deceitful manner in the service of the French Sureté in Ludwigshafen. For him alone Eberlein reserved his anger and contempt. Otherwise the people of France differed in no way from the people of Germany. Each side had its war victims. The central theme was the outwitting of the French Sureté following the arrest of innocent German civilians when important documents were found to be missing from the house in which the local French commandant was billeted. The documents contained details of French plans to support the separatist cause. Naturally, the French were soon outmanoeuvred, a rescue was effected and the documents ended up in German hands. The reader is led to believe that this favourable outcome was all orchestrated by a certain Dr August Müller who occupied offices in Mannheim.

It hardly needs restating that Dr August Müller was the pseudonym under which Eberlein himself operated from the beginning of 1922, following the first enforced dissolution of the Pfalzzentrale.[98] This again points to Eberlein's egotistical personality, a man not afraid of publicity and certainly not prepared to give in quietly. From the manner in which he portrayed himself throughout the novel he clearly wanted to be seen as a man of action, successfully leading the heroic struggle against the enemy: 'This Dr Müller seemed a really energetic person for as they entered he was speaking vehemently about a newspaper article. He did not mince his words and what he said on the telephone was certainly not flattery.'[99]

By the mid-1920s the Schwarze Schmach had subsided in the public consciousness and the novel contained only peripheral reference to it. Moroccan troops were indeed present, and it was deeply shameful for a German to have to step off the pavement into the road when passing the French flag guarded by its Moroccan sentry. But coloured troops did not present any real threat. As personified by the French commandant's servant, they were basically simple-minded and harmless. Eberlein made a contemptuous analogy with a faithful dog:

> Pierre was like a faithful dog. Since Hilde's arrest he had suffered mentally and physically. He was pining . . . . . . This time he was longing for the return of his master. He crouched in the corner like a predator simply awaiting the opportunity to spring at the throat of the hated enemy.[100]

Eberlein's book also contained in a second and separate section his own self-justifying account of the events at St Dié that had led to him being arraigned as a war criminal. The book was completely self-centred. Evidently it owed as much to what Eberlein saw as his personal duel with the French authorities as it did to deep nationalistic conviction.

Herein lies the key to understanding Pfalzzentrale propaganda. It was driven by the personality of its leader, who, it might be noted, had gathered like-minded people around him. With some justification the metaphor of the wartime trenches was introduced earlier. For what distinguishes Eberlein's approach to the campaign against the Rhineland occupation from that of all others is the fact that, characteristically, he was in the front line, close to the action. The office desk in remote Berlin or Munich was not for him. He was closer than anybody in unoccupied Germany to events on the opposite side of the Rhine. Frequent intelligence reports were available to him and he had immediate access to those expelled from the Pfalz. It all suited his confrontational personality perfectly.

For some who fought in World War I the legacy was post-war trauma. For Eberlein, however, who had distinguished himself within weeks of its beginning, the war had provided an immediate stimulus. This stimulus was to be repeated in World War II. Little wonder, then, that the adrenalin of war carried across into a peace that for him was unjust. The deep anger that he felt expressed itself first in his propaganda then, when compounded with frustration, in direct action against the occupation. Initially, propaganda was the sole weapon available to him. But in spite of some limited tactical success, it was never going to provide anything more than a series of pinpricks against the occupying power. Much in the same way that Margarete Gärtner of the Frauenliga saw the futility of continuing the Schwarze Schmach campaign and became involved in the lobbying of influential British politicians, aristocrats and businessmen on behalf of Germany, Eberlein also changed his mode of attack as the screw of the occupation tightened. But in his case it was to become based on direct action. Gärtner had the backing of big business interests, Eberlein the backing of extreme right-wing elements in Bavaria.

Eberlein could not have continued in the way that he did without the support of first Theodor von Winterstein and later Lorenz Wappes. Both were traditional conservatives, staunch defenders of Bavarian independence. Winterstein had a distaste for the concept of the unitary state, particularly as led by a centrist or centre-left government. As we saw in the previous chapter, Wappes had connections with the more extreme right-wing elements in Bavaria. Under both men Eberlein enjoyed freedom of action to a significant extent. To judge from his propaganda, Eberlein largely held himself aloof from any quarrel between Bavaria and the Reich, even though, like Winterstein, he had little regard for the agencies and officials in Berlin. In his case this was not because they were Prussians but rather because they were not sufficiently active in carrying the fight to the enemy. What mattered to Eberlein above all else was the preservation of German culture and values and the unity of the German people. This transcended any dispute between Reich and state. Another motivation for him was the necessity that the German people should recover from the shameful injustice that had been done to them at the post-war settlement and that they should again take their rightful place in the world. But Eberlein's outlook was essentially authoritarian and the methods that he would employ to achieve those ends were not those enshrined in the new Republic. Rather, they were those methods that would become commonplace a decade later. Eberlein was essentially a bare-knuckle pugilist. Pacifists – or those who would in his eyes avoid their duty to their country – received very short shrift. And, as we have seen in the Pfalzzentrale propaganda, those who lent support of any form to the enemy were vilified and publicly threatened with retribution. It did not end there. When the Independent Pfalz government collapsed in February 1924 Eberlein and Betz were involved in the hunting down of collaborators. It comes as little surprise that Eberlein and Betz in due course joined the NSDAP.

The Pfalzzentrale was a major source of propaganda against the Rhineland occupation and the earlier material in particular carries the stamp of Eberlein's personality. That the thematic content was wider-ranging than that from many of the other sources was partly due to Eberlein's closer personal identification with – and enthusiasm for – the *Abwehr*. In contrast to the Notbund, which campaigned against the Schwarze Schmach as a single issue, and the Frauenliga, which based its campaign partly on the Schwarze Schmach, partly on the vulnerability of women and children, Eberlein's approach was both pragmatic and opportunistic. He picked up themes for propaganda wherever and whenever they might provide scope for harrying the French authorities. The output from the Pfalzzentrale was undoubtedly less lurid than that of some propagandists – for example the Notbund – and for the most part it avoided factual errors because they could be disproved. But it was often confrontational, crude in the sense of lacking subtlety, and aggressive. Characteristically it carried the fight to the enemy and this, probably more than the fact that it made some of the right noises, is why it found favour with the political Right.

Pfalzzentrale propaganda bore no evidence of the enmity between Bavaria and the Reich, echoed in the relationship between the Pfalzzentrale and the Volkspflege. Little reference to Bavaria was made in exhortations to remain loyal and true. This can be attributed partly to Eberlein's concern to promote *Deutschtum* beyond all else, though there were also good tactical grounds for ignoring the disputes between the Reich and Bavaria when preparing propaganda material. As we have seen, people in the Pfalz generally felt that they were citizens of the Reich in the first place and only secondly citizens of Bavaria.

Pfalzzentrale propaganda was, however, just one element in the campaign against the occupation of the Rhineland. We have seen that this embraced a wide range of themes but basically all were dedicated to the same end. The most vociferous of all – and the most extreme – was without doubt the campaign against the Schwarze Schmach. It now remains in the final chapter to examine German propaganda in its totality in the light of the values and aspirations of the new Republic, and the political circumstances prevailing at the time.

8

GERMAN RHINELAND PROPAGANDA: THE PRODUCT OF A FRACTURED SOCIETY

This study has shown that propaganda directed against the French occupation of the Rhineland was far from being the smoothly organised, centrally coordinated activity that it is sometimes assumed to have been. The most striking aspect is the extent to which German propaganda was dominated by the activities of relatively few energetic and strongly motivated individuals, notably Gärtner, Eberlein, Beveridge and Distler. Usually, though not always, they were at the head of a small organisation which, private or state-supported, they ran as their personal fiefdom. Their backgrounds and experience, though essentially middle-class, varied widely and although there were underlying themes common to all, the propaganda they produced reflected to a large degree their own personal styles, motivations and obsessions. In the particular case of the campaign against the Schwarze Schmach this diversity resulted in varying degrees of exaggeration and luridness.

It has also been shown that there existed some deep divisions between those engaged in propaganda activities. The dispute between Reich and states – more especially between the Reich and Bavaria – over the fundamental issue of sovereignty created a climate of hostility which spilled over into the relationship between the Pfalzzentrale and the Volkspflege.

Even within the Reich government itself inter-departmental rivalry played some part in shaping propaganda activity, especially between the Reich Ministry of the Interior and the Foreign Ministry. Also, there were often differences in opinion between non-governmental organisations, even within an organisation, over what constituted effective propaganda and what was unacceptable. From all of this it can justifiably be concluded that the propaganda directed against the Rhineland occupation was fragmented and largely uncoordinated. But why should such a state of affairs exist when at the same time it could be confidently said that all involved in propaganda shared the great depth of feeling that Germany was the victim of gross injustice perpetrated by the victorious Allies? In taking an overall view of the Rhineland propaganda campaigns and their impact it is this question in particular that is addressed in this concluding chapter.

Before doing so, however, it is first necessary to recall the events from which the post-war situation developed. During the war propaganda had been used extensively by both the Central Powers and the Allies, but following the cessation of hostilities it was generally accepted that on the whole German propaganda had been much less successful than that of her adversaries.[1] The far Right went one step further and attributed the German defeat to a susceptibility to superior Allied propaganda.[2] Hitler, for example, described the form of German propaganda as inadequate, its substance as psychologically wrong.[3] Non-partisan assessments of the effectiveness of German World War I propaganda have changed somewhat over the years. An early assessment considered that slowness to engage in propaganda – a quick military victory had been anticipated in 1914 – and general ineptness in developing it meant that Germany was never really able to shrug off the initial impression created by her invasion of neutral Belgium that she was the aggressor. Much international resentment and suspicion was created, for example, by highlighting a War of German Culture, at the same time that British propaganda was laying stress on the fight to protect international law against the monster of autocratic militarism.[4] Later, factors contributing to a lack of success were considered to include the predominance of unimaginative military bureaucracy, a lack of coordination of the work of several organisations engaged in propaganda and a propaganda policy that could not be readily adapted to rapid changes in the course of events.[5]

Recent assessment confirms that Germany was forced to take a defensive stance as far as external propaganda was concerned but points to a more sophisticated content than had been credited at the time. The fundamental problem for Germany lay rather in the fact that the ruling military and conservative elites were completely lacking in empathy with the civilian population. No attention was paid to the opinions of a public suffering increasing hardship and whose acceptance in 1914 of the idea of a short defensive war had been betrayed by the true war aims of the military hierarchy.[6] Furthermore, 'The support of impeccably conservative groups was held up to justify official policy, whereas complaints or open dissent were seen as a challenge to hierarchical authority and dismissed as defeatism.'[7] Little wonder, then, that in 1917 exhortations to persevere in supporting the war, appealing to national unity and patriotism, simply contributed to the final disillusionment of the public. No amount of propaganda, however good, was going to overcome this state of affairs. It undoubtedly had important consequences for the way in which post-war official pronouncements were received by many, even though a new, democratic government was now in power.

The perceived failure of German propaganda in comparison with the success enjoyed by the Allied material not only provided the old Wilhelmine regime with an excuse for defeat, it also focused post-war attention on the way in which propaganda was used. It was noted by a US commentator in the 1920s that 'There is today a more luxurious flowering of treatises upon international propaganda (its nature, limitations and processes) in Germany than anywhere else.'[8] Such rethinking in the early Weimar years of the way in which Germany should present itself to the world was stimulated by the views of liberal-thinking people like Paul Rühlmann, Edgar Stern-Rubarth and Johann Plenge.[9] Rühlmann, who as we noted earlier had been engaged in propaganda activities during World War I and was later to advise the Volkspflege, stressed the close connection between the foreign policy appropriate for a modern democracy and the concomitant need for appropriate cultural propaganda. In his view this should be based on intellectual and moral values rather than as hitherto on military might and the influence of the German industrial base. In fact the need for cultural propaganda had been recognised in Germany in the years immediately before the war, though long after it had been made an instrument of official policy in France. It had received little priority in Wilhelmine Germany, however. In 1913 the cultural historian Karl Lamprecht attempted to persuade Reich Chancellor Bethmann Hollweg of the need for Germany to be more active in this area. Hollweg's response was equivocal and his intentions have since been the subject for much discussion.[10] During the war some substantial efforts were made – for example in Scandinavian countries and Switzerland – to project a positive image of Germany through the medium of culture, but any benefits were effectively lost in the negative impression created internationally by Germany's acts of aggression and by her nationalistic and militaristic propaganda.[11] Rühlmann considered that the content of the wartime propaganda and the manner in which it had been implemented had been counterproductive:

> Too little regard was paid to the fact that propaganda is an art which needs to be learnt well and which to some extent has its own well-developed methods. The art of circumvention was hardly appreciated at the time – at any rate it was not practised. What was particularly bad was the lack of intimate knowledge of the political psyche of foreign countries. Many of those neutral countries that were well disposed towards us therefore felt more offended than won over by that kind of German cultural propaganda.[12]

At the same time Rühlmann warned that the sins and omissions of wartime propaganda should not lead to the rejection of cultural propaganda as an unnecessary luxury in view of Germany's straitened circumstances in the post-war world. This was a view prevailing in some government circles. But he pointed to the vital importance of the image that Germany presented abroad:

> The creation of really modern cultural propaganda is and will remain a fateful question for the shaping of Germany's foreign

> policy, for only in the cultural sphere do possibilities for future development lie. Germany's inferiority in external instruments of power makes the opportunity to disseminate her intellectual strengths and achievements absolutely vital.[13]

While Rühlmann was a strong proponent of a policy of liberal enlightenment, he also had very determined views on the threat to Germany presented by France. In his belief French cultural propaganda, which he considered to be far more advanced than that of any other nation, had but one skilfully cloaked purpose – that of ultimate world domination. Nevertheless the methods and organisation of the French cultural thrust were to be admired in Rühlmann's opinion.[14]

Equally convinced about the form that future propaganda should take was Dr Edgar Stern-Rubarth. Born in Frankfurt-am-Main on 15 August 1883, he was a prominent journalist. Before the war he had contributed to the satirical magazine *Simplissimus* and to newspapers such as the *Frankfurter Zeitung* and the *Kölnische Zeitung*. Following wartime service he became editor-in-chief at the Ullstein publishing house and lectured at the German College for Political Studies in Berlin. As co-founder of the European Customs Union, later secretary of the German-French Society and co-editor of the *Deutsch-französische Rundschau*, he devoted much time and energy towards achieving reconciliation with France. This did not endear him to the Nazi regime and he was later obliged to flee to Britain, where he then remained for the duration of World War II.[15] Stern-Rubarth was greatly influenced by the particular manner in which British propaganda had been organised during World War I. In proposing a system that he considered suitable for peacetime and the particular circumstances in which Germany now found herself, he therefore laid emphasis on the need for personal creativity, coordinated but unfettered by bureaucratic machinery. At the same time, however, he also strongly advocated an ethical approach to propaganda:

> Only by objective organisation on the part of all leading departments and by allowing the best of these to take the lead can lasting success really be achieved. Not only will the best always

> be the cleverest, the most psychologically aware, the most understanding, the most patriotic and the most creative but also the one that carries out its national task, in the short and possibly long term, from the strongest and noblest moral feelings and from deep ethical convictions.[16]

Stern-Rubarth made a clear distinction between positive propaganda and negative propaganda. Negative propaganda, he conceded, could be used but only as a last resort when no other material was available. It was frequently counterproductive and it diminished the moral standing of those who employed it:

> Extremely few of the techniques of negative propaganda can be regarded as harmless and suited to the purpose of retaliation. Every action that disparages one's adversaries has to be ruled out not only because it is immoral but because in the long term it inevitably makes our view of things ineffective. We need neither fabricate slogans which deride our opponents, however effective they may be, nor allow literature which preaches revenge or portrays the enemy from yesterday in a distorted and mendacious manner, because in one foreign country or another it will provide welcome sustenance for thoughts of revenge.[17]

The conviction that the new direction for propaganda should satisfy moral considerations was shared also by Dr Johann Plenge. Born in Bremen on 7 June 1874, Plenge became Professor of Economics and Political Science at the University of Münster, where he founded the Institute for Political Science in 1920.[18] A Social Democrat, he was one of a group of German intellectuals who believed that a perceived sense of national unity that prevailed at the outbreak of war in 1914 – epitomised as the Ideas of 1914 – could provide a means to overcome social conflict in the longer term. Plenge warned that

> propaganda is a dangerous thing, because it can use spurious arguments in its ruthless will to succeed. Propaganda can become deceptively seductive. Academic involvement with propaganda

> means countering propaganda with the truth. We must observe and describe all forms of propaganda objectively and in accordance with the truth. But through propaganda we must also give the truth new power and new effectiveness.[19]

Progressive ideas like those expressed by Rühlmann, Stern-Rubarth and Plenge represented an attempt to make a clean break with the past and to set Germany on a new and more ethical course. With justification they can be associated with the spirit in which the new Republic was to provide a new beginning for Germany. This immediately raises the questions of how such ideas were received and to what extent such ideals influenced the nature of government-sponsored propaganda after 1918.

From the discussion of the preceding chapters the conclusion can only be that the vast bulk of the propaganda against the Rhineland occupation was negative. Much of it was immoderate in tone. Admittedly, the form of some propaganda was constrained by the pressure of immediate circumstances. Thus the early material directed at the Pfalz was a hasty counter to the perceived threat of an imminent separatist coup. In contrast to the wartime propaganda, much of which had been aimed at Britain, the thrust was now directed with considerable antagonism against France. Although each of the western Allies was participating in the occupation, France was seen by the propagandists to be the principal enemy. The French occupation of the Pfalz was to have by far the longest duration and the French army was numerically the largest. Even more to the point, France was Germany's principal rival in continental Europe and was considered to have been influential in imposing harsher peace terms than those originally envisaged in the Fourteen-Point Plan formulated by Woodrow Wilson. Yet, other than the concern that France would subvert the local population of the Rhineland through cultural penetration and thereby achieve her alleged expansionist aims, in the propaganda there was little of the fear of the victor that is normally associated with the vanquished. This much was remarked upon by the British ambassador in Berlin:

> The war increased the German's respect for, and his dislike of, the English, but has done nothing to diminish his belief in his

> own superior sturdiness compared with the French. This will continue subconsciously and subcutaneously whatever happens – even though France possesses an overpowering army and the Germans have no organised means of resistance.[20]

Rather than betraying fear, the tone in much of the propaganda was that of contempt for a nation, France, that had been obliged to rely on others of inferior status to achieve a dubious victory and then to occupy the Rhineland. This was evident in the remark of Eberlein: 'Without her coloured troops France is not in a position in the present tense situation to maintain her militarism and imperialism.'[21] There was all the more reason, then, to campaign against the Schwarze Schmach. And in the propaganda of the Pfalzzentrale in particular the threat of a future settling of scores was evident on more than one occasion. It was hardly an acknowledgement of French superiority.

The campaign against the Schwarze Schmach was the most extreme of all the propaganda themes. At first sight it appears to represent the very antithesis of Weimar ideals. But here, care must be taken to judge not against present-day values but against the social mores of the time. This was a time at which the aggressive colonisation of much of Africa by competing European nations was still in the recent past. The manner in which each nation had set about this had done much to shape racial attitudes at home, leading to considerable variations in the degree of prejudice against other races. In Britain for example, shortly after World War I, a limited study found prejudice to be considerably greater than in France.[22] Nevertheless, throughout Europe the black or coloured man was generally considered by the white European to be his inferior. At best this was manifest in a paternalistic or patronising attitude; at worst in contempt and disdain. It goes some way towards accounting for the fact that even liberal-thinking people were moved to protest against the presence of black and coloured troops in the Rhineland.

While it achieved far greater notoriety than that resulting from other German grievances, Schwarze Schmach propaganda was likewise aimed at the occupation and at the perceived injustice of the Peace Treaty provisions. But it achieved greater prominence because, more than any other theme, the use of colonial troops in the occupation had struck a devastating blow at German self-esteem and the hitherto universally accepted notions of racial hierarchy. Not only was Germany now being denied Great Power status by being occupied by black and coloured troops, she was now being deliberately placed by France below the level not only of other European nations but also of the 'inferior' colonised races. As we have remarked, although propaganda against the Schwarze Schmach came from a variety of sources a common theme was ever present. This was the humiliation of the German people through being watched over and supervised by those of an allegedly inferior race. Little wonder that a British Foreign Office official remarked: 'What a pity they employ these troops in the occupation of a white country. It will never be forgiven or forgotten in Germany.'[23]

Underlying the propaganda was a wide groundswell of protest which covered much of the political spectrum, with the exception of the KPD and the USPD. The politics of those involved ranged from the centre left to the far right. The Majority Socialists (SPD) could be described as fellow-travellers in the propaganda war rather than a driving force, although there was no lack of feeling from this quarter. SPD members of the Reichstag and even Reich President Ebert expressed outrage over the Schwarze Schmach,[24] while the women's section of the SPD was a member organisation of the Frauenliga, though it did not play a prominent part in its activities.

While in general terms the propaganda campaign was associated predominantly with the political Right, there were, as we have seen, contributions of varying degrees of luridness and vituperation. Generally, the more extreme material came from the far Right, from individuals like Ray Beveridge and organisations like the Notbund in Munich. It reflected the greatest measure of nationalist fury and frustration. Others, like the right-wing traditionalist Otto Hartwich, who would, if they could, turn the clock back to the old pre-war order, were more measured. Contributions also came from those who, while supportive of the new Republic, nevertheless resented the perceived humiliation of Germany and the all-too-evident loss of her Great Power status. To this group belonged members of the DDP, Catholic

;y and even some whose views were further to the right, like National Liberal Hermann Oncken.

)ilisation of women's organisations at home and abroad to protest against the Schwarze Schmach was tantamount to a separate campaign. The perspective presented to the outside world was one of terrified Rhineland women and children, helpless in the face of occupation by a licentious and violent coloured soldiery. Implicit in this portrayal was the idea that this was an act of gross immorality, offending the norms of civilised and moral behaviour. The protests were largely organised by the Frauenliga, although the Volksbund also amassed early support from women's groups.

Activists in the women's campaign were almost exclusively drawn from the middle classes. Before World War I a number of them had been in the forefront of campaigns for women's emancipation and advancement. Some were now active in politics. Well educated and articulate, they regarded themselves as leaders, the voice of the female population at large. Under the new Republic, which had brought women's suffrage and promised a greater role for women in public life, they could have the confidence to put forward the female perspective. The question then arises as to the extent to which they were motivated to campaign because, as women, they identified themselves with women who were allegedly suffering in the occupied zones. To a large extent this was the case. The initial fear amongst Rhineland women that was generated by the imminent presence of black troops has been remarked on. And fear is easily communicated to others, even when it is irrational.

But there was also another underlying motivation. No less than in the case of their male counterparts, right-wing nationalism played a large part in the women's campaign. For some on the right – more especially the extreme right – the campaign against the Schwarze Schmach was essentially about the Versailles signing and the humiliating situation in which Germany found itself. The Schwarze Schmach was a symbol of this humiliation. It therefore became a good topic to exploit in the wider battle against the Peace Treaty. There is little doubt that right-wing activists, personally unaffected by the occupation, exploited fear, both genuine and alleged, quite dispassionately to further their political cause. Certainly this was so in the case of the Frauenliga when led by Margarete Gärtner, whose innate nationalism might be judged by the seamless way in which she transferred her loyalties to work comfortably with the Nazi government after 1933. It is these differences in motivation that may have been a source of the friction and dissent within the Frauenliga, leading to a change of leadership and policy in 1922.

It is unsurprising that the campaign against the Schwarze Schmach made an impact on the public in the USA. A strong reaction was also to be expected from white settlers in places like the former German South-West Africa and in German enclaves such as those in South America. Indeed, from these sources the Frauenliga received a sympathetic response to its appeal for support. But these were really transitory effects. The US government was not to be influenced, while in Britain relatively little impact was evident beyond the irritation caused in the Foreign Office. The strategic value of this extremely vociferous campaign was really quite limited. At most it may have contributed to the withdrawal of French colonial troops a little earlier than intended. On the home front, press reports of mass meetings that were organised in major towns and cities suggest that Rhineland propaganda achieved some success in whipping up strong public feeling. The question of just how widespread this feeling really was we discuss below in the context of the wider political climate in Germany.

It can justifiably be concluded that although those on the right involved in the campaign approached it from differing standpoints, their involvement betrayed a common state of mind in which basically they had yet to come to terms with Germany's defeat. Propaganda represented the only way in which they could express this resentment and outrage at the subsequent imposition of the peace terms. It may be noted that the black man was not therefore simply a symbol of French dominance, he also represented a very useful weapon for German propagandists – and one that they were able to exploit to the full.

The gathering up of the women's groups under the Frauenliga umbrella has been taken as evidence that the overall campaign against the Schwarze Schmach was at least partly coordinated. Furthermore, the resurgence of press articles directed against the use of colonial troops immediately prior to strategically important conferences has also been taken as evidence of a centrally directed campaign. But this study has shown that the part played by the individual was all-important and to think of the campaign against the Schwarze Schmach simply in terms of a closely coordinated activity is a gross oversimplification. In all likelihood a bandwagon effect was at work, in which individuals and organisations on the right felt every encouragement to join in once the initial impetus had been given by the appearance of some press reports.

The most moderate propaganda – though not lacking in nationalistic tendencies – was that of the Volkspflege. Its work, which included substantial cultural support for the occupied Rhineland, was subjected to derision by Winterstein and by Eberlein at the Pfalzzentrale. While much of this can be accounted for by the rift between the Reich and Bavarian governments, there was also clearly a clash of ideas over the content and structure of the propaganda as well as over the way in which it should be handled. Such criticism even came from some within the Reich government.

The period during which the Schwarze Schmach campaign was at its most active broadly coincided with a polarisation of political views, away from the centrist support that in 1919 had seen the new Republic founded with the backing of a coalition of the SPD, the Centre Party and the DDP. The beneficiaries of the change were the radical Left and Right. Both were fundamentally hostile to the Republic but it is the latter grouping that is significant. Its activities in seeking the overthrow of the Republic have been described as the counter-revolution.[25] Its origins can be traced back to the nationalism of the Pan-German League of the late nineteenth century,[26] and Germany's imperialist expansion. It embraced anti-Semitic, anti-Marxist and authoritarian views. Though having suffered a crushing blow with the military defeat in 1918, followed by the emergence of the detested Republic, it was now regrouping with increasing confidence. The increase in support for the conservative Right was manifest in the election of June 1920 with an increase in the number of DNVP seats in the Reichstag from 44 to 71 and in DVP seats from 19 to 65, directly at the expense of the coalition parties.[27] This was also the time of the Kapp putsch, which, though failing to overthrow the Reich government, exposed the underlying weakness of the liberal, progressive parties of the political centre. In Bavaria, however, it achieved indirectly some measure of success, for it led to the replacement of the Hoffmann government by the right-wing Kahr government. What is more, with the change in the political climate, Bavaria then became a magnet for extremists and activists of the far Right.

There is another important factor that should not be overlooked when considering the political and social environment that shaped Rhineland propaganda – and that is the influence wielded by senior state and Reich government officials. The part played by certain individuals – Winterstein and Wappes – in the Bavarian government has been discussed in preceding chapters. It is clear that in encouraging the Pfalzzentrale to promote a brand of propaganda that was both negative and aggressive they had the full support of BVP politicians such as Kahr and Knilling – themselves both former senior Bavarian government officials. This much was confirmed by the very public support shown by the Bavarian government for the Notbund after the dissolution of the Pfalzzentrale. The extreme tone of the Notbund propaganda news-sheet had changed little since its founding, yet State Commissioner Wappes was pleased to write an article for it in June 1924. Prime Minister Knilling contributed the preface to the same issue.[28]

To what extent did the situation in the Reich government differ from that in Bavaria? The civil service in 1919, though somewhat larger in size, was little different from that of the pre-war administration and was steeped in its imperial expansionist values. Now, although a new republican government was in power, the executive had not been subjected to any significant reform. Indeed this was the deliberate policy of Ebert and the SPD. The priority for the new government was to stabilise a defeated nation that was in a state of turmoil. The transition to republican democracy had to be achieved with the maximum of order and continuity, which in turn implied the minimum of open rupture with the past. The collaboration of the existing administrative hierarchy was considered by Ebert to be essential. Reform of the civil service was thus to take place only slowly over a number of years.

For their part, the upper echelons of the civil service in carrying out their appointed task naturally saw to it that any revolutionary changes proposed met with bureaucratic inertia.[29]

Unsurprisingly, the deeply conservative upper classes were heavily represented at these levels. The resulting political complexion is in little doubt, given that in the Reichstag the DNVP had a considerable number of representatives from the ranks of the civil service elite.[30] Wider discussion of the situation concerning the politicisation of the civil service and the implications for the Republic is beyond the scope of this book but there is a significant point to be made here. With executive power in the hands of a deeply conservative higher civil service, which was far from wholeheartedly supportive of the new regime, the scope for introducing and maintaining new and liberal concepts of propaganda was limited.

This is not to say that progressive ideas on how to raise the profile of Germany abroad were not embraced in the early Weimar years. In 1920 a section was set up within the Reich Foreign Ministry for the purposes of developing cultural and scientific links with other nations, of promoting the German language and of supporting German expatriate communities.[31] That this was badly needed is in no doubt. The image of Germany abroad had suffered badly as a result of World War I. A particular case is that of the so-called *Aufruf der 93* (Appeal of the 93). In this, ninety-three internationally recognised scientists, artists, poets and academics – representing many shades of political and religious opinion – had in October 1914 distributed worldwide a propaganda pamphlet. The pamphlet had forthrightly rejected accusations of German responsibility for starting the war and of violating Belgian neutrality and the human rights of Belgian civilians. It had had the reverse effect on its recipients to that intended and as a consequence cultural and scientific links with neutral countries had been severely damaged.[32]

Yet at the same time as one section of the Foreign Ministry was endeavouring to mend fences a totally different approach was being taken by another section. Through a forerunner to its Kriegsschuldreferat (War Guilt Section), set up to counter the allegations of war guilt, the Foreign Ministry embarked on a campaign of selective editing of diplomatic records relating to the period leading up to the outbreak of war in 1914.

Subsequently a report was written based on these records (the 'Professors' Memorandum') which formed the basis of a submission to the Allies at the Versailles Peace Conference. The document, which absolved the Reich from responsibility for the war, appeared in May 1919 under the names of a group of eminent historians. These persons, however, had had little to do with the writing of the report and had been given little time to authenticate it. This exemplifies the problem facing the Reich government in leaving the higher civil service unreformed.

The inability of the Reich government to exercise close control over events was demonstrated also at Versailles. The leader of the German delegation, Ulrich Graf von Brockdorff-Rantzau, chose to ignore instructions from the Reich Cabinet and pursued his own strategy of aggressive denial of war guilt.[33] There can be no doubt, therefore, that in some parts of the senior bureaucracy there existed a determination to provide continuity with the policies of the past. It all encouraged a general climate in which those of the Right not supportive of the new Republic felt free to pursue their own agendas, regardless of any official policy.

Closely linked to war guilt was the issue of Allied demands to hand over those accused of committing war crimes. Senior army officers and the Right succeeded in making extradition a test of the relationship between old elites and the Republic. Significantly, it was noted by the British that the mass of the people were indifferent to the issue, but that a campaign was under way to try to rectify this. A potentially dangerous situation was avoided by the Reich government acceding to the demands of the Right in refusing to hand over the accused.[34]

The situation concerning the Rhineland occupation can be regarded in much the same way. From the perspective of the Right, Germany had suffered humiliation and subsequent betrayal by the Republic at the Peace Conference. Now, in spite of the ultimate insult of occupation by French colonial troops the same government was doing little to protect German interests. The way ahead was surely to rouse a somewhat indifferent public to anger, which could then be directed at the culpable Reich government in order to force it to take action. Propagandists like Eberlein and Distler had to work hard in the face of public indifference. Hints that the Reich government was a target of their propaganda can be seen in their allegations of its inactivity and lack of leadership.

To what extent did the extensive Rhineland propaganda help the situation in the Pfalz? The early separatist threat had really been countered through the efforts of the workers and the SPD before any officially inspired propaganda appeared. Following the miserable failure of the first putsch attempt, separatism presented relatively little danger thereafter until the burdens associated with the failure of passive resistance led to its resurgence in 1923. At that time, in spite of Eberlein's best efforts, propaganda proved to be of little value – a fact recognised by the right-wing government in Bavaria, which felt obliged to sanction the use of assassination to remove the Independent Pfalz government. The complaints of propagandists, heard on more than one occasion, that the population of unoccupied Germany was apathetic towards the fate of the occupied Rhineland and that the press was largely indifferent in its attitude were a measure of the failure of propaganda. The apparent success of the mass meetings addressed by speakers from the Frauenliga and by propagandists like Beveridge, Eberlein and Distler can be put down to the response of a particular social group. Parallels can be drawn with the situation at the outbreak of war in 1914 when euphoria was to a large extent confined to the urban middle class and expressed in mass gatherings in the big cities. Now, in 1920 and 1921, the urban middle class was again well to the fore in the meetings held to protest against the Schwarze Schmach and the occupation. But this time the mood was one of right-wing frustration, compounded with feelings of uncertainty and of being threatened in a post-war world in which the established order had been turned upside down. Into this mood the Right was able to tap. None of this, however, materially affected the course of events in the Pfalz, or indeed in the Rhineland as a whole. The occupation of the Pfalz in particular was too important strategically as far as France was concerned for propaganda to be effective. German propaganda undoubtedly irritated France and her Allies and even gave rise to concern on occasion but it made little strategic impact. At best it provided temporary catharsis for the embittered political Right.

To conclude, there existed in Germany a fundamental disagreement over the value of propaganda and the use to which it might be put. To the idealists of the new Republic it offered a way for Germany to advance her cause abroad in the widest sense and to get away from the excesses of the Wilhelmine era. At home it was to provide the public with the facts and to encourage individuals to make their own judgements. By implication, propaganda should be forward-looking and positive.

The Right saw things quite differently. In the far Right, exemplified in party political terms by the DNVP and by some within the Bavarian BVP, there existed a deep desire to return to past authoritarian certainty, a past that was idealised in the imagination. The concepts behind the new Republic were totally alien and were to be opposed at every opportunity. Thus the propaganda of the Right was inevitably backward-looking rather than visionary, negative rather than constructive. For many, also, fury over the perceived national humiliation meant that a mental state of war with the Allies persisted – and the only weapon left in the armoury was propaganda. Such feelings combined to produce forms of propaganda that at times were vituperative and vengeful. Here, however, we should make a distinction between the democratic Right which accepted the new political order and the anti-republican Right which did not. Nevertheless, while the DDP – and even the DVP with some reluctance – supported the Republic, the sense of outrage at Germany's treatment by the Allies was strong enough to dispel liberal sentiments.

Woven into this generalised canvas was a dominant range of individual contributions to the propaganda against the Rhineland occupation. Each was motivated by a mixture of personal experience, belief and ambition, and was able to flourish in a climate in which there was no overall agreement on the way ahead. Added to this was the lack of harmony caused by a deeply divided federal system of government and a civil administration in the Reich that, while it acted in support of the government, was hardly in the vanguard of reform. Even the civil administration itself was subject to interdepartmental jealousies and rivalries. Little wonder, then, that German Rhineland propaganda was both fragmented and largely negative. Although it had some limited tactical success in inflaming some sections of public opinion at home and abroad, its overall strategic impact was negligible. It was truly the product of a fractured society.

APPENDIX I

Constituent Organisations of the Rheinische Frauenliga in May 1921[1]

Katholischer Frauenbund
Evangelischer Frauenbund
Israelitischer Frauenbund
Frauenausschuß d. Christl. Gewerkschaften
Frauenausschuß d. sozial-demokratischen Partei
Bund deutscher Frauenvereine
Rheinisch-Westf. Frauenverband
Bezirksausschuß f. Frauenarbeit
Verband Hessischer Frauenvereine
Inter.-Kath. Verband d. Frauenvereine i. Saargebiet
Stadtverband Düsseldorf
Verband Kölner Frauenvereine
Kath. Frauenbund f. d. Pfalz
Verein f. Fraueninteressen u. Neustädter Frauenvereine
Frauenvereine Mainz
Pfälzischer Verband f. Fraueninteressen
Volksverein f. d. kath. Deutschland
Verband Frankfurter Frauenvereine
Allgemeiner deutscher Frauenverein Worms

Gesamtverband d. Frauenvereine d. Kreises Ottweiler
Stadtverband f. Jugendfürsorge Wiesbaden
Verein Frauenbildung-Frauenstudium
Verein d. kath. Sozialbeamtinnen
Verein d. kath. Oberlehrerinnen
Verein d. kathkaufm. Gehilfinnen, Köln
Verein d. kathkaufm. Gehilfinnen, Wiesbaden
Verein kath. Hausangestellten
Allgemeiner dtsch. Lehrerinnen-Verein
Verband d. dtsch. Reichs-Post-und Telegrafenbeamtinnen
Verband weibl. Handels-u.-Büroangestellten-Berlin
Stadtverband für Frauenbestrebungen
Kath. Jungfrauenvereine
Kath. Bahnhofsmission
Nationalverband d. kath. Mädchenschutzverein
Kath. Fürsorgeverein Speyer
Evangel. Frauenhilfe Wiesbaden
Evangel. Frauenhilfe Speyer
Verband Evangel. dtsch. Bahnhofsmission
Rheinische Frauenhilfe
Allg. dtsch. Hausfrauenverein

APPENDIX II

Presentations Made by Leading Members of the Rheinische Frauenliga in Autumn 1920[1]

3 Oktober	Cassel	Rednerin	Dr. Marie Elisabeth Lüders M.d.R.
3	Freiburg		Frl. Gärtner/unter anderem Namen gesprochen
8	Leipzig		Frau Dorothee von Velsen. Geschäftsführerin des Bundes Deutschen Frauenvereins
11	Plauen		Aus Plauen
13	Naumburg		Frau von Rosen
18	Elberfeld		Frau Lola Bruns
19	Schweidnitz		Frl. von Groote aus Schweidnitz
21	Giessen	Redner	Univ. Prof. Dr. Schian-Giessen
22	Weimar	Rednerin	Frl. Dr. Lüders
22	Stuttgart		Frl. Reineck von der Ev. Bahnhofsmission
29	Oldenburg		Frau von Rosen

30	Wilhelmshaven	Frau von Rosen
4 November	Osnabrück	Frau Dorothee von Velsen
4	Magdeburg	Frl. Dr. Lüders
5	Mannheim	Frau Ministerialrat Helene Weber/ Pr. Wohlfahrtsministerium

In Vorbereitung sind für die nächsten Tage und Wochen Versammlungen in Breslau, Liegnitz und Steinau a.O. mit Frau von Velsen; Halle a.S., Dortmund mit Frl. Teusch, M.d.R.; München mit Frau Helene Weber; Karlsruhe, Offenbach a. M., Pforzheim, Witten a.d. Ruhr, Lahr iB, Tübingen mit Frl. Reineck; Bremen mit Frl. Dönhoff, M.d. R.; Delmenhorst mit Frl. Dr. Lüders; Hannover mit Frl. Paula Müller, M.d.R.; Jena mit Frl. Dr. Bäumer, M.d.R.; Heidelberg mit Frl. Dönhoff, M.d.R.; Rathenau und Erfurt.

APPENDIX III

Questionnaire Sent Out by the Rheinische Frauenliga, February 1922

Author's Translation

Questions concerning problems with housing in the occupied regions

1. What is the size of the civilian population?
2. Current strength of occupation troops?
3. Where are the troops accommodated (barracks, huts, schools, other public buildings etc.)?
4. How many private dwellings or single rooms have been requisitioned?
5. How many Germans are on the reserve list for housing?
6. How many of the requisitioned dwellings and other rooms are not occupied by troops but have been taken up by civilians?
7. How many rooms does an unmarried officer take up on average?
8. Ratio of married to unmarried members of the occupation forces accommodated in German dwellings?

9. Description of particularly extreme cases:
    a) of lack of housing for Germans.
    b) of edicts by the occupation authorities or by individual officials.

Questions concerning coloured troops

1. Names of places occupied by coloured troops?
2. Population of places occupied by coloured troops?
3. How many colonial troops are stationed in the places concerned?
4. Where are brothels available for coloured troops?
5. From which places have colonial troops been withdrawn in the past six months? How many?
6. Where, in the past six months, have new coloured troops been introduced and how many?
7. How much are the coloured troops paid?
8. To which tribes do the coloured troops belong (Senegalese, Malagasies, Moroccans, Algerians, Tunisians, Anamites etc.)?
9. Is the behaviour of coloured troops such that complaints should be made? What particular cases of harassment etc. have occurred recently?
10. Have any coloured troops been accommodated in private quarters?

Questions concerning French schools and language propaganda

1. Where have French language courses taken place up till now?
    a) for schoolchildren.
    b) for adults.
2. Who teaches the French language courses?
3. What rooms are used for that?
4. How often are courses held in town? Weekly or monthly?
5. What was the average number of participants?
6. Which sections of the community mainly take part?

7. What special concessions were granted to participants in French language courses? (subscription to the French news-sheet *Echo du Rhin*, *Revue Rhénane*, rewards, travel opportunities)
8. Was compulsion used to ensure participation and how?
9. Is the interest in the language courses increasing or decreasing?
10. Where are the courses being held at present, where will they start again in the autumn?
11. Which books are used for teaching?
12. Which French propaganda leaflets are distributed?

Note: Please enclose examples of printed leaflets or books.

Questions concerning the state of public health in the occupied regions

1. Comparative figures for the increase in sexually transmitted diseases, especially among minors? The position:
   a) before the war.
   b) in 1918.
   c) in 1922.
2. Increase in numbers of cases of tuberculosis, especially among minors?
3. Increase in children's diseases?

Note: It would be particularly useful if it can be made clear in the data what proportion of illnesses is attributable to the occupation. In the case of (3) possibly also a report on the risks relating to the milk supply.

Questions concerning immorality in the occupied regions

1. Increase in prostitution: where were brothels to be found before the war?
   Where have brothels been opened since the occupation?
2. Are these brothels exclusively for the use of occupation troops or are they also open to the civilian population?
3. How many registered women were there before the war?
   How many were there at the last count?

4. Has there been an increase in non-regulated prostitution?
5. To what extent has the occupation made a generally demoralising influence evident, especially on the young?
6. Details of cases in which official German social security business has been hindered by the occupation authorities?
7. How many illegitimate children can demonstrably be traced back to the occupation troops?
8. How many of them are of mixed race?
9. Are maintenance payments being made by occupation troops who are fathers of illegitimate children?
10. Details of court maintenance orders relating to illegitimate children of occupation troops.

German Text[1]

Fragen, die Wohnungslasten im besetzten Gebiet betreffend.

1. Wieviel Zivilbevölkerung?
2. Jetztige Besatzungsstärke.
3. Wo sind die Truppen untergebracht (Kasernen, Baracken, Schulen, sonstige öffentliche Gebäude usw.)?
4. Wieviel Privatwohnungen bzw. Einzelzimmer sind beschlagnahmt?
5. Wieviel deutsche Wohnungssuchende stehen auf der Liste der Vorgemerkten?
6. Wieviel von den beschlagnahmten Wohnungen und sonstigen Räumen sind nicht von Angehörigen der Truppen, sondern von Zivilisten in Anspruch genommen?
7. Wieviel Zimmer beansprucht durchschnittlich ein unverheirateter Offizier?
8. Verhältnis der verheirateten, in deutschen Wohnungen untergebrachten Besatzungsangehörigen zu den unverheirateten.
9. Schilderung besonders krasser Fälle.
   a) von deutscher Wohnungsnot,
   b) von Aussprüchen der Besatzungsbehörden oder einzelner Besatzungsangehöriger.

Fragen, betreffend farbige Truppen.

1. Namen der Orte, die durch Farbige belegt sind.
2. Wieviel Zivilbevölkerung haben die durch Farbige besetzten Orte?
3. Wieviel Kolonialtruppen liegen in den betreffenden Orten?
4. Wo sind Bordelle für farbige Truppen vorhanden?
5. Wo sind im letzten halben Jahr Kolonialtruppen zurückgezogen worden? Wieviel?
6. Wo sind im letzten halben Jahr neue farbige Truppen eingetroffen und wieviel?
7. Wieviel beträgt die Löhnung der Farbigen?
8. Welchen Stämmen gehören die Farbigen an? (Senegalesen, Madagassen, Marokkaner, Algerier, Tunesier, Anamiten usw.)
9. Ist über das Benehmen der farbigen Truppen Klage zu führen? Welcher besonderen Fälle von Belästigungen usw. sind in der letzten Zeit vorgekommen?
10. Ist es vorgekommen, dass Farbige in Privatquartier gelegen haben?

Fragen, die französische Schule und Sprachpropaganda betreffend.

1. Wo haben die bisher französische Sprachkurse stattgefunden?
   a) für Schulkinder
   b) für Erwachsene
2. Wer erteilt den französischen Sprachunterricht?
3. Welcher Räume wurden dafür benutzt?
4. Wie oft in der Stadt? Wöchentlich oder monatlich?
5. Wie hoch war die Durchschnittsanzahl der Teilnehmer?
6. Welcher Kreise der Bevölkerung beteiligten sich vorzüglich?
7. Welcher Vergünstigungen wurden den Teilnehmern der französischen Sprachkurse zugestanden? (Abonnement auf das französische Nachrichtenblatt 'Echo du Rhin', Revue Rhénane, Preisverteilungen, Reiseveranstaltungen).
8. Wurde ein Zwang zur Teilnahme auf die Bevölkerung ausgeübt und wodurch?

9. Lässt sich steigendes oder abnehmendes Interesse der Bevölkerung an der Sprachkursen feststellen?
10. Wo finden sich die Kurse heute noch statt bzw. wo werden sie im Herbst wieder eröffnet?
11. Welcher Bücher werden zum Unterricht verwandt?
12. Welcher französischen Propagandaschriften gelangen zur Verteilung?

Anm. Es wird gebeten, Druckschriften oder Bücher beizulegen.

Fragen, den Zustand der Gesundheit in den besetzten Gebieten betreffend.

1. Angabe über die Zunahme der Geschlechtskrankheiten, am besten Vergleichszahlen, besonders Zunahme unter den Minderjährigen.
   a) Stand vor dem Kriege
   b) Stand 1918
   c) Stand 1922
2. Zunahme der Tuberkulose, besonders Zunahme bei der Minderjährigen.
3. Zunahme der Kinderkrankheiten.

Anm. Besonders wertvoll sind solche Darstellungen, aus denen der Anteil der Besetzungen des Rheinlandes an der Zunahme der Krankheiten ersichtlich ist. Bei Punkt 3) evtl. auch Bericht über die Gefährdung der Milchversorgung.

Fragen, den sittlichen Zustand im besetzten Gebiet betreffend.

1. Zunahme der Prostitution, Wo waren vor dem Kriege Bordelle/ Wo sind seit der Besetzung Bordelle eingerichtet worden?
2. Sind diese Bordelle ausschliesslich für Besatzungstruppen bestimmt oder stehen sie auch für die Zivilbevölkerung offen?
3. Wieviel kontrollierte weibliche Personen gab es vor dem Kriege? Wieviel wurden bei der letzten Festellung gezählt?
4. Ist eine Zunahme der heimlichen Prostitution festzustellen?

5. In wie fern macht sich ein demoralisierender Einfluss der Besetzung im allgemein, besonders bei der Jugend bemerkbar?
6. Fälle, in denen die Fürsorgetätigkeit der deutschen Stellen durch die Besatzungsbehörde gehemmt wurde.
7. Wieviele uneheliche Kinder stammen nachweislich von Besatzungstruppen?
8. Wieviele davon sind Mischlinge?
9. Erfolgt Alimentenzahlung durch Besatzungssoldaten, die Väter unehelicher Kinder sind?
10. Inanspruchnahme des Vormundschaftsgericht und des Armenpflege durch die Fürsorge für uneheliche Kinder von Besatzungstruppen.

APPENDIX IV

1871 and Now

We do not wish to say anything in this issue concerning the devastation caused in the Pfalz and the entire Rhineland by the behaviour of the French in the occupied regions in Napoleonic times as opposed to that caused by the Germans when, a hundred years ago, they entered France as victors. It is not as if the average character of both peoples will have changed fundamentally since then: but we know that many Germans think that such old history has no value. At that time humankind was somewhat different. We therefore restrict ourselves to the short time span of fifty years in portraying occupation by the Germans and occupation by the French. The description of the German occupation we base on both German and French records. The French occupation is based on eye-witness accounts. The use of records here, however, has to be ruled out because every German in the occupied regions who would be named would himself, as well as his family and his property, be at the mercy of French brutality and lawlessness. So all that remains to us, if we wish to depict the circumstances in the regions presently occupied by the French, is the cooperation of people from abroad, who cannot be prevented from travelling around the occupied regions and who are not subject to interference by the French. The collaborators in this second part are Englishmen. We have never made a secret of our judgement of England's policy but we salute these Englishmen, who, although they know the national persuasion of our paper, have taken up our invitation in order to let the voice of honesty and humanity be heard throughout the world.

Paul Nikolaus Cossmann.

Süddeutsche Monatshefte, April 1922.

(Author's translation of fig. 16.)

APPENDIX V

Appeal by the Volksbund 'Rettet die Ehre'

If honour is lost,
all is lost!
An Appeal to all true Germans
in January 1920

To all concerned!

Throughout Germany

a movement has been started to oppose the judicial murder of Germany's honour. It is being threatened by **the sentencing of German princes, officials, officers and men by the courts of the enemy.** This brochure is being published out of concern that the movement could easily become disheartened. The situation could be underestimated and, by failing to prevent the handing over of these victims, we may not achieve our goal. Be aware that during the trial itself the battle must be fought to the bitter end and that it is for you to defend that which could still be lost: German honour, the victims, the lifebreath of future generations. **Our priority is to prevent any handing over of the victims**, but even if we only manage to demonstrate that despotism cannot be glossed over, that Truth and Justice are upheld, then we shall have won a decisive victory.

(Author's translation of fig. 20.)

APPENDIX VI

Railway Propaganda Leaflet

Make your will
before you
travel on the French trains!

Why? Just look at the people who work for the French on the railways at Ludwigshafen!
Work-shy people, criminals, prostitutes – those are the 'reliable' people to whom the French entrust the responsible task of running the railway.
To these can be added some railway officials who are **traitors** – like the notorious railway inspectors Couturier and Magnier from Speyer.
Ask how many railway accidents have occurred up till now in the Rhineland!
Those who travel on a French train do so as **traitors** with one foot in prison and with the other in the grave!

(Author's translation of fig. 28.)

NOTES

Introduction

1. Bariéty, Jacques, 'Die französische Besatzungspolitik im Rheinland nach dem Ersten Weltkrieg: Historisch-politische Mythen und geostrategische Realitäten', in Tilman Koops and Martin Vogt (eds), *Das Rheinland in zwei Nachkriegszeiten 1919–1930 und 1945–1949* (Coblenz, 1995), pp. 5–18; Köhler, Henning, *November Revolution und Frankreich: Die französische Deutschland Politik 1918–1919* (Düsseldorf, 1980), pp. 189–215; Köhler, Henning, 'Französische Besatzungspolitik 1918–1923', in Peter Hüttenberger and Hansgeorg Molitor (eds), *Franzosen und Deutsche am Rhein 1789–1918–1945* (Essen, 1989), pp. 113–26.
2. Zimmermann, Werner Gabriel, *Bayern und das Reich 1918–1923: Der bayerische Föderalismus zwischen Revolution und Reaktion* (Munich, 1953), pp. 79–133.
3. Kolb, Eberhard, *The Weimar Republic* (London, 1988), pp. 58–61; Orde, Anne, *British Policy and European Reconstruction after the First World War* (Cambridge, 1990), pp. 245–65.
4. Die Schwarze Schmach is usually translated as 'the Black Disgrace'. I argue that 'Black Humiliation' better reflects the feelings of those who coined the phrase.
5. Nelson, Keith L., 'The "Black Horror on the Rhine": race as a factor in post-World War I diplomacy', *The Journal of Modern History* 42/4 (1970), pp. 606–27.
6. Lebzelter, Gisela, 'Die Schwarze Schmach: Vorurteile – Propaganda – Mythos', *Geschichte und Gesellschaft* 11 (1985), pp. 27–58.
7. Pommerin, Reiner, *Sterilisierung der Rheinlandbastarde: Der Schicksal einer farbigen deutschen Minderheit 1918–1937* (Düsseldorf, 1979).
8. Marks, Sally, 'Black Watch on the Rhine: a study in propaganda, prejudice and prurience', *European Studies Review* 13 (1983), pp. 297–333.

9. Throughout this book I have employed the terms 'coloured', 'black' and 'negro' when referring to colonial troops. These are direct translations of *'farbige'*, *'schwarze'* and *'Neger'* – terms in common use in the Weimar period. They were frequently used interchangeably when referring to colonial troops, and without regard to the ethnicity of those concerned.
10. Koller, Christian, *Von Wilden aller Rassen niedergemetzelt: Die Diskussion um die Verwendung von Kolonialtruppen in Europa zwischen Racismus, Kolonial- und Militärpolitik (1914–1930)* (Stuttgart, 2001).
11. Poley, Jared, *Decolonization in Germany: Weimar Narratives of Colonial Loss and Foreign Occupation* (Bern, 2005).
12. Maß, Sandra, *Weiße Helden, schwarze Krieger: zur Geschichte kolonialer Männlichkeit in Deutschland 1918–1964* (Cologne, 2006).
13. Wigger, Iris, *Die 'Schwarze Schmach am Rhein': Rassistische Diskriminierung zwischen Geschlecht, Klasse, Nation und Rasse* (Münster, 2007).
14. Le Naour, Jean-Yves, *La honte noire: L'Allemagne et les troupes coloniales francaises 1914–1945* (Paris, 2003).
15. Staatskommissar für die Pfalz (ed.), *Die Pfalz unter französischer Besatzung von 1918 bis 1930: Kalendarische Darstellung der Ereignisse vom Einmarsch im November 1918 bis zur Räumung am 1. Juli 1930* (Munich, 1930), p. 34.
16. Schieder, Wolfgang and Christof Dipper, Art. VI, 'Propaganda als Methode moderner Politik', in Otto Brunner, Werner Conze and Reinhart Koselleck (eds), *Geschichtliche Grundbegriffe: Historisches Lexikon zur politisch-sozialen Sprache in Deutschland* vol. 5 (Stuttgart, 1984), p. 106.

1 The Pfalz: Focus of French Ambitions in the Weimar Crisis Years

1. *The Treaty of Peace between the Allied and Associated Powers and Germany, the Protocol annexed thereto, the Agreement respecting the military occupation of the territories of the Rhine, and the Treaty between France and Great Britain...... Signed at Versailles, June 28th 1919* (London, 1919). (Hereafter, Peace Treaty.)
2. D'Abernon, Viscount, *Ambassador for Peace: Pages from the Diary of Viscount D'Abernon (Berlin 1920–26)* vol. 1 (London, 1929–30), p. 295.
3. The borders of the Pfalz of earlier times did not correspond exactly to those of the Pfalz of 1918, but this fact is not significant in the present context.
4. Martin, Michael, 'Mélac!', *Die Zeit* 20 (6 May 2004).
5. Dumont, Franz, 'Befreiung oder Fremdherrschaft? Zur französischen Besatzungspolitik am Rhein im Zeitalter der Revolution', in Hüttenberger and Molitor (eds): *Franzosen und Deutsche*, pp. 92–3.
6. Ibid., p. 99.
7. Ibid., p. 108.
8. Baumann, Kurt, 'Probleme der pfälzischen Geschichte im 19. Jahrhundert', *Mitteilungen des Historischen Vereins der Pfalz* 51 (1953), pp. 233–7; Bayerische

Landeszentrale für politische Bildungsarbeit (ed.), *Einsichten und Perspektiven Themenheft 02/2006*, http://www.km.bayern.de/blz/eup/02_06_themenheft/3.asp#1 (see also 3.asp#2). Bavaria had considerable expansionist ambitions at this time, which she was unable to realise in the face of opposition from other European powers, and had to be content with the return of former Kurpfalz territory west of the Rhine.

9. Scherer, Karl, 'Zum Verhältnis Pfalz-Bayern in den Jahren 1816–1848', in Hans Fenske (ed.), *Die Pfalz und Bayern 1816–1956* (Speyer, 1998), pp. 9–16.
10. In 1910 the population of the Pfalz was 937,085, of whom 506,664 were registered as Protestants and 415,079 as Catholics. (Foreign Office (Great Britain), *Bavarian Palatinate: Handbooks Prepared Under the Direction of the Historical Section of the Foreign Office*, no. 32 (London, March 1919), p. 22.)
11. Ziemann, Benjamin, *War Experiences in Rural Germany 1914–1923* (Oxford and New York, 2007), p. 142.
12. Applegate, Celia, *A Nation of Provincials: The German Idea of Heimat* (Berkeley, 1990), pp. 20–8.
13. Ibid., p. 30.
14. Applegate, Celia, 'Localism and the German bourgeoisie: the Heimat movement in the Rhenish Palatinate before 1914', in David Blackbourn and Richard J. Evans (eds), *The German Bourgeoisie: Essays on the Social History of the German Middle Class from the Late Eighteenth Century to the Early Twentieth Century* (London, 1991), p. 237.
15. Fenske, Hans, 'Mehr als eine Provinz...Die Pfalz in der deutschen Geschichte des 19. und 20. Jahrhunderts', *Mitteilungen des historischen Vereins der Pfalz* 86 (1988), pp. 347–64.
16. Wünschel, Hans-Jürgen, 'Anmerkungen zum pfälzisch-bayerischen Verhältnis 1866–1914', in Fenske (ed.): *Die Pfalz und Bayern*, pp. 157–8.
17. Fenske: 'Mehr als eine Provinz', pp. 356–8.
18. Thalmann, Heinrich, *Die Pfalz im Ersten Weltkrieg* (Kaiserslautern, 1990), pp. 295–300.
19. Welch, David, *Germany, Propaganda and Total War 1914–1918* (London, 2000), pp. 12–19.
20. Verhey, Jeffrey, *The Spirit of 1914: Militarism, Myth and Mobilization in Germany* (Cambridge, 2000), p. 113.
21. Ziemann: *War Experiences*, pp. 16–19; Verhey: *Spirit*, p. 113.
22. Geinitz, Christian, *Kriegsfurcht und Kampfbereitschaft: Das Augusterlebnis in Freiburg – Eine Studie zum Kriegsbeginn 1914* (Essen, 1998), pp. 100–42.
23. Thalmann: *Die Pfalz*, p. 302.
24. Ibid., p. 263.
25. Vincent, Paul, *The Politics of Hunger: The Allied Blockade of Germany, 1915–1919* (Athens, OH, 1985), pp. 27–59.
26. Thalmann, Heinrich, 'Die Pfalz und Bayern in der Zeit des Ersten Weltkriegs', in Fenske (ed.): *Die Pfalz und Bayern*, pp. 168–9.

27. Thalmann: *Die Pfalz*, pp. 363–5.
28. Thalmann: 'Die Pfalz und Bayern', p. 175.
29. Le Naour : *La honte*, pp. 38–9.
30. Horne, John and Alan Kramer, *German Atrocities 1914: A History of Denial* (New Haven and London, 2001), pp. 9–225.
31. Thalmann: *Die Pfalz*, p. 368.
32. Ibid., p. 369.
33. Bariéty: 'Besatzungspolitik', pp. 5–18; McDougall, Walter A., *France's Rhineland Diplomacy 1914–1924: The Last Bid for a Balance of Power in Europe* (Princeton, 1978), pp. 16–67.
34. Hüttenberger, Peter, 'Methoden und Ziele der französischen Besatzungspolitik nach dem Ersten Weltkrieg in der Pfalz', *Blätter für deutsche Landesgeschichte* 108 (1972), pp. 105–21.
35. Bariéty: 'Besatzungspolitik', p. 9.
36. Nestler, Gerhard, 'Pfälzisch, rheinisch oder bayerisch? Der Kreis um den Pfälzer Volksboten und die Diskussion über die staatsrechtliche Zukunft der Pfalz in den Jahren 1918–1920', *Jahrbuch zur Geschichte von Stadt und Landkreis Kaiserslautern* 32/33 (1994), p. 362.
37. Schlegel, Dietrich, 'Der Separatismus in der Pfalz nach dem Ersten Weltkrieg', *Mitteilungen des historischen Vereins der Pfalz* 71 (1974), p. 228.
38. Süss, Martin, *Rheinhessen unter französischer Besatzung: vom Waffenstillstand im November 1918 bis zum Ende der Separatistenunruhen im Februar 1924* (Stuttgart, 1988), p. 89.
39. Jacquot, Paul, *General Gérard und die Pfalz*, Dr Ritter (ed.) (Mannheim, 1920), pp. 25–30. (Original French document by Jacquot was translated into German and republished with foreword by Dr August Ritter von Eberlein under the pseudonym Ritter.)
40. Bessel, Richard, *Germany after the First World War* (Oxford, 1993), pp. 26–48, 91–5.
41. Ibid., pp. 220–53.
42. Ibid., pp. 26–31.
43. Welch: *Propaganda*, p. 247.
44. Bessel: *Germany*, pp. 220–3.
45. Dülffer, Jost, 'Frieden schließen nach einem Weltkrieg', in Jost Dülffer and Gerd Krumeich (eds), *Der verlorene Frieden – Politik und Kriegskultur nach 1918* (Essen, 2002), p. 30.
46. Kolb: *Weimar*, pp. 34–5.
47. Allen, Henry T., *My Rhineland Journal* (Cambridge, MA, 1923), pp. 138, 142, 453, 515; Schumann, Dirk, 'Einheitssehnsucht und Gewaltakzeptanz: Politische Grundpositionen des deutschen Bürgertums nach 1918 (mit vergleichenden Überlegegungen zu den britischen *middle classes*)', in Hans Mommsen (ed.), *Der Erste Weltkrieg und die europäische Nachkriegsordnung: Sozialer Wandel und Formveränderung der Politik* (Cologne, 2000), pp. 83–105. See also in same volume: Morgan, Kenneth O., 'Die soziale und politische

Mobilisierung Großbritanniens 1918–1926', pp. 125–44, and Horne, John, 'Der Schatten des Krieges: Französische Politik in den zwanziger Jahren', pp. 145–64.
48. Vincent: *Politics*, pp. 95–117.
49. Chickering, Roger, *Imperial Germany and the Great War 1914–1918* (Cambridge, 1998), pp. 189–91.
50. Le Naour : *La honte*, p. 49.
51. Landauer, Carl, 'The Bavarian problem in the Weimar Republic, 1918–1923: Part I', *The Journal of Modern History* 16/2 (1944), p. 95.
52. Nestler: 'Pfälzisch', p. 357.
53. Translation of *Los von Berlin – Los von Preussen.*
54. Morsey, Rudolf, 'Die Rheinlande, Preußen und das Reich', *Rheinische Vierteljahrsblätter* 30 (1960), p. 184.
55. Nestler, Gerhard, 'Freie Pfalz, Rheinische Republik oder blau-weiße Bayerntreue', in Wilhelm Kreutz and Karl Scherer (eds), *Die Pfalz unter französischer Besetzung (1918/19–1930)* (Kaiserslautern, 1999), p. 106.
56. Thalmann: *Die Pfalz*, p. 369.
57. Politisches Archiv des Auswärtigen Amts (PA AA) R74550, Lerchenfeld to Auswärtiges Amt (AA) (undated document).
58. PA AA R74550, Bevollmächtiger Vertreter des AA (Hessen) to AA 27.11.1920.
59. Thalmann: *Die Pfalz*, p. 370.
60. Nestler: 'Pfälzisch', pp. 370–1.
61. Thalmann: 'Die Pfalz und Bayern', pp. 170–4.
62. Staatskommissar: *Die Pfalz*, p. 20.
63. Nestler: 'Freie Pfalz', p. 112.
64. Gembries, Helmut, 'Die Pfalz und Bayern in der Weimarer Zeit', in Fenske (ed.): *Die Pfalz und Bayern*, pp. 193–4.
65. Thalmann: *Die Pfalz*, p. 372.
66. Thalmann: 'Die Pfalz und Bayern', pp. 182–3.
67. Ibid., pp. 178–82.
68. Landauer: 'Bavarian problem I', p. 94.
69. Fenske, Hans, 'Bayern und die Pfalz', in Kreutz and Scherer (eds): *Besetzung*, pp. 31–2.
70. Thalmann: 'Die Pfalz und Bayern', p. 186.
71. Staatskommissar: *Die Pfalz*, pp. 15–18.
72. Jardin, Pierre, 'Tirard, de Metz und die Pfalz', in Kreutz and Scherer (eds): *Besetzung*, pp. 147–8.
73. Schineller, Werner, *Die Regierungspräsidenten der Pfalz: Festgabe zum 60. Geburtstag des Regierungspräsidenten Hans Keller am 6. Mai 1980* (Speyer, 1980), pp. 63–4.
74. Gembries: 'Die Pfalz und Bayern', pp. 192–3.
75. Staatskommissar: *Die Pfalz*, p. 22.
76. Nestler: 'Freie Pfalz', pp. 118–19.

77. The separatist movement Freie Pfalz later modified its aims, envisaging an autonomous state but within the Reich federation. (Bayerisches Hauptstaatsarchiv (BHStA) Ministerium des Äußeren (MA) 107715, Ritter to Staatskommissar für die Pfalz 19.11.1919.)
78. Gräber, Gerhard and Matthias Spindler, *Revolver Republik am Rhein: Die Pfalz und ihre Separatisten, Band 1 November 1918–November 1923* (Landau, 1992), pp. 39–43.
79. Staatskommissar: *Die Pfalz*, p. 28.
80. Menges, Franz, *Hans Schmelzle: Bayerischer Staatsrat im Ministerium des Äußeren und Finanzminister. Eine politische Biographie mit Quellenanhang* (Munich, 1972), p. 73.
81. Staatskommissar: *Die Pfalz*, pp. 34–6.
82. McDougall: *Diplomacy*, pp. 72–4.
83. Ibid., pp. 85–9.
84. Nelson, Keith L., *Victors Divided: America and the Allies in Germany 1918–1923* (Berkeley and London, 1975), pp. 66–96.
85. Orde: *British Policy*, p. 33.
86. Nelson: *Victors*, pp. 231–53.
87. Orde: *British Policy*, pp. 244–53.
88. Allen, Henry T., *The Rhineland Occupation* (Indianapolis, 1927), pp. 142–58.
89. McDougall: *Diplomacy*, pp. 43–4.
90. Orde: *British Policy*, p. 153.
91. Kolb: *Weimar*, pp. 34–50.
92. Zimmermann: *Bayern*, pp. 31–47.
93. Ibid., pp. 82–98.

2 The Bavarian Pfalzzentrale and the Rheinische Volkspflege: a Discordant Evolution

1. BHStA MA 107725, Eberlein to bayerischer Ministerpräsident 26.9.1919.
2. Bundesarchiv, 'Akten der Reichskanzlei, Weimarer Republik' online (Biographien – Eberlein), http://www.bundesarchiv.de/aktenreichskanzlei/1919–1933/0021/vorwort.html; Deutsche National Bibliothek (DNB), Katalog der DNB, http://d-nb.info/572948301.
3. Bundesarchiv Berlin (BArch) Reichskulturkammer (RK) (formerly BDC), B0036 2100006603, August Ritter von Eberlein (Lebenslauf).
4. Gembries, Helmut, *Verwaltung und Politik in der besetzten Pfalz zur Zeit der Weimarer Republik* (Kaiserslautern, 1992), p. 161.
5. Erdmann, Karl Dietrich and Wolfgang Mommsen (eds), *Akten der Reichskanzlei Weimarer Republik* Bd. 1–14 (Boppard am Rhein, 1968–90). Hereafter referenced as Akten Rkei. This reference: Akten Rkei Bd. 2 (Kabinett Bauer), Einleitung, pp. XLVIII–LIII; Horne and Kramer: *Atrocities*, pp. 341–3.
6. Eberlein, August Ritter von, *Die Spionin vom Rhein: Ein Spionageroman aus der Separatistenzeit in der Pfalz, sowie eine autobiographische Erzählung* (Berlin, 1930).

7. Horne and Kramer: *Atrocities*, pp. 344–6.
8. Gembries: *Verwaltung*, p. 162.
9. Horne and Kramer: *Atrocities*, pp. 348–55.
10. BArch RK B0036 2100006603, August Ritter von Eberlein (Lebenslauf); Gembries: *Verwaltung*, p. 162.
11. Bundesarchiv, 'Akten der Reichskanzlei, Weimarer Republik' online (Biographien – Eberlein), http://www.bundesarchiv.de/aktenreichskanzlei/1919–1933/0021/vorwort.html
12. Gembries: *Verwaltung*, p. 159.
13. BHStA MA 107715, Eberlein to Staatsministerium des Äusseren 26.6.1919.
14. BHStA MA 107715, Minutes of meeting 10.6.1919.
15. Akten Rkei Bd. 1 (Kabinett Scheidemann), Kabinettssitzung vom 20.5.1919, Dok. Nr. 80, p. 358 n. 9.
16. Bundesarchiv, 'Akten der Reichskanzlei, Weimarer Republik' online (Biographien – Schmidthals), http://www.bundesarchiv.de/aktenreichskanzlei/1919--1933/0021/vorwort.html
17. BHStA MA 107715, Winterstein to Staatsministerium des Äusseren 20.6.1919.
18. BHStA MA 107715, Winterstein to bay. Ministerpräsident 7.6.1919.
19. Staatskommissar: *Die Pfalz*, p. 39.
20. Welch: *Propaganda*, pp. 206–27.
21. Wippermann, Klaus, *Politische Propaganda und staatsbürgerliche Bildung: Die Reichszentrale für Heimatdienst in der Weimarer Republik* (Bonn, 1976), pp. 21–8.
22. Schivelbusch, Wolfgang, *The Culture of Defeat: On National Trauma, Mourning and Recovery* (New York, 2003), pp. 216–23.
23. Welch: *Propaganda*, p. 254.
24. Ibid., pp. 252–4.
25. Schieder and Dipper: 'Propaganda als Methode', pp. 106–8.
26. Wippermann: *Politische Propaganda*, pp. 96–109.
27. Gärtner, Margarete, *Botschafterin des Guten Willens: Aussenpolitische Arbeit 1914–1950* (Bonn, 1955), p. 54.
28. Wippermann: *Politische Propaganda*, p. 93.
29. Schöny, Otto, 'Propaganda oder Aufklärung?', *Der Heimatdienst. Mitteilungsbl. d. Reichszentrale für Heimatdienst* 30 (October 1921), p. 283, cited in Schieder and Dipper: 'Propaganda als Methode', p. 106. (Author's translation, hereafter trans.)
30. Akten Rkei Bd. 1 (Scheidemann), Kabinettssitzung vom 12.3.1919, Dok. Nr. 10a, pp. 37–8.
31. Akten Rkei Bd. 1 (Scheidemann), Kabinettssitzung vom 20.5.1919, Dok. Nr. 80, p. 358 n. 9.
32. Akten Rkei Bd. 1 (Scheidemann), Kabinettssitzung 14.5.1919, Dok. Nr. 72, p. 320 n. 2. (Trans.)
33. BHStA MA 107715, Report of meeting held 10.6.1919.
34. BHStA MA 107722, Zentrale für Heimatdienst to Amtl. Volksaufklärungsstelle, Bayern 28.7.1919.

35. Akten Rkei Bd. 1 (Scheidemann), Kabinettssitzung vom 14.5.1919, Dok. Nr. 72, p. 320 and n. 2. It was this instruction that had sparked off the dispute between the Reich Chancellery and the Reich Foreign Ministry over their respective areas of jurisdiction in matters regarding the press and propaganda.
36. BHStA MA 107715, Eberlein to Staatsministerium des Äußeren 26.6.1919.
37. BHStA MA 107722, Reichszentrale für Heimatdienst to Amtliche Volksaufklärungsstelle des Volksstaats Bayern 28.7.1919.
38. Ibid., Hoffmann's handwritten comments and signature on reverse side.
39. Akten Rkei Bd. 1 (Scheidemann), AA to Reichskanzlei 4.4.1919, Dok. Nr. 36, p. 138.
40. Hennig, Diethard, *Johannes Hoffmann, Sozialdemokrat und Bayerischer Ministerpräsident* (Munich, 1990), pp. 453–4.
41. BHStA MA 107722, Text of proposal by Amtliche Volksaufklärungsstelle 6.8.1919.
42. BHStA MA 107722, Winterstein to Ministerpräsident Hoffmann (undated report on visit by Oberhofer on 6.8.1919). (Trans.)
43. BHStA MA 107722, Winterstein to Reichskanzler Gustav Bauer 27.8.1919.
44. Gembries: *Verwaltung*, p. 165.
45. Staatskommissar: *Die Pfalz*, p. 44.
46. BHStA MA 107709, Dr Eugen Jaeger to Winterstein 9.7.1919.
47. BHStA MA 107709, Memorandum to all ministries from Hoffmann 2.8.1919.
48. Gembries: *Verwaltung*, p. 170.
49. Akten Rkei Bd. 2 (Bauer), Besprechung zwischen Reichs- und Ländervertretern über die großhessische Frage. Weimar 14.7.1919, Dok. Nr. 26, p. 120.
50. Akten Rkei Bd. 2 (Bauer), Kabinettssitzung vom 15.8.1919, Dok. Nr. 46, pp. 189–90 nn. 4, 7.
51. BHStA MA 107709, Bericht über die Sitzung zwischen Mitgliedern der Reichsregierung und Herren aus dem fr. bes. linksrheinischen Gebiet 22.8.1919. (Trans.)
52. Ibid. (Trans.)
53. Ibid.
54. Gembries: *Verwaltung*, p. 165.
55. BHStA MA 107709, Bericht über die Sitzung zw. Mitgliedern der Reichsregierung und Herren aus dem fr. besetzten Gebiet 22.8.1919.
56. Akten Rkei Bd. 2 (Bauer), Gemeinsame Sitzung des Reichskabinetts mit dem Staatsministerium 15.8.1919, Dok. Nr. 47, p. 318 n. 11.
57. Akten Rkei Bd. 2 (Bauer), Besprechung der Reichsregierung mit Abgeordneten über die Lage in den besetzten westlichen Gebieten 28.11.1919, Dok. Nr. 116, p. 434. (Trans.)
58. Ibid.
59. BHStA MA 107722, Reichsministerium des Innern to Landesregierung von Bayern, 6.2.1920.

60. Gembries: *Verwaltung*, p. 175.
61. BHStA MA 107722, Staatskommissar für die Pfalz to Reichsministerium des Innern 21.2.1920.
62. Akten Rkei Bd. 2 (Bauer), Einleitung, pp. LXXIX–LXXXII.
63. Akten Rkei Bd. 2 (Bauer), Die Preußische Gesandtschaft München to Preußische Staatsministerium, 3.12.1919, Dok. Nr. 121, p. 453.
64. Akten Rkei Bd. 3 (Müller I), Die Pr. Gesandtschaft München to AA. 6.4.1920, Dok. Nr. 18, p. 41; Landesabt. Bay. der R. f. H. to Reichswehrmin. München 10.5.1920, Dok. Nr. 90, p. 217.
65. Akten Rkei Bd. 3 (Müller I), Kabinettssitzung 25.5.1920, Dok. Nr. 115, p. 283.
66. Akten Rkei Bd. 1 (Scheidemann), Kabinettssitzung 16.5.1919, Dok. Nr. 75, p. 358 n. 9.
67. BHStA MA 107722, Report to Staatskommissar für die Pfalz from Ritter 14.4.1920.
68. BHStA MA 107722, Ritter to Staatskommissar für die Pfalz 20.5.1920.
69. BHStA MA 107722, Proposal to Staatskommissar für die Pfalz from Ritter 5.6.1920.
70. Staatskommissar: *Die Pfalz*, p. 62.
71. BHStA MA 107722, Proposal to Staatskommissar für die Pfalz from Ritter 5.6.1920.
72. Ibid.
73. Wippermann: *Politische Propaganda*, pp. 202–4.
74. BArch R1603/2169, File note (undated).
75. BArch R1603/2174, Wrochem to Deutsche Liga für Völkerbund 28.6.1921.
76. Wrochem, Alfred von, *Die Kolonisation der Rheinlande durch Frankreich* (Berlin, 1922).
77. BArch R1603/2174, Letters from Wrochem on 6.3.1922 and 9.3.1922; Letter to Wrochem 7.3.1922. (Identity of recipient of letters from Wrochem has been excised from documents.)
78. Wippermann: *Politische Propaganda*, p. 204.
79. BHStA MA 107722, Proposal to Staatskommissar für die Pfalz from Ritter 5.6.1920.
80. Gärtner: *Botschafterin*, p. 56.
81. BHStA Haupthilfsstelle für die Pfalz (HHSPf 1), Notes on discussion held at Mannheim 29.8.1920.
82. Wein, Franziska, *Deutschlands Strom – Frankreichs Grenze: Geschichte und Propaganda am Rhein 1919–1930* (Essen, 1992), pp. 105–6.
83. Akten Rkei Bd. 3 (Müller I), Zech to AA 6.4.1920, Dok. Nr. 18, pp. 41–2.
84. BHStA MA 107722, Minutes of meeting held 1.6.1920 in Reichstag. (Trans.)
85. Ibid.
86. BHStA MA 107722, Winterstein notes on a meeting held 15.6.1920 dated 25.6.1920.

87. Gärtner: *Botschafterin*, p. 75.
88. **BHStA HHSPf 1, Report on a meeting to discuss collaboration with Rheinische Volkspflege, Mannheim 23.6.1920. (Trans.)**
89. BHStA MA 107722, Report to Staatskommissar für die Pfalz from Oberleutnant Gärtner 3.7.1920.
90. BHStA MA 107722, Winterstein memorandum to Reichsministerium des Innern July 1920 (exact date unspecified).
91. BArch R1501/102881, Wrochem to Lewald 7.4.1920.
92. Gembries: *Verwaltung*, p. 179.
93. BHStA MA 107722, Winterstein to Reichsmin. des Innern, July 1920 (exact date unspecified).
94. BHStA MA 107722, Ritter to Staatskommissar für die Pfalz 25.10.1920.
95. BHStA MA 107722, Ritter to Staatskommissar für die Pfalz 6.1.1921.
96. BHStA MA 107722, Record of a meeting held in preussisches Ministerium des Innern 18.11.1920. (Trans.)
97. BHStA MA 107722, Record of a meeting held in preussisches Ministerium des Äußeren, Berlin 19.11.1920.
98. BHStA HHSPf 1, Winterstein memorandum June 1920 (exact date unspecified). (Trans.)
99. BHStA MA 107722, Handelskammer Köln to Reichskommissar für die besetzten Gebiete 21.8.1920.
100. Akten Rkei Bd. 3 (Müller I), Kabinettssitzung 25.5.1920, Dok. Nr. 115, pp. 282–3.
101. Akten Rkei Bd. 4 (Fehrenbach), Bericht des Reichsministers des Innern über seine Reise in das besetzte Gebiet 24.8.1920, Dok. Nr. 57, p. 139 n. 4.
102. BHStA HHSPf 1, Rheinische Volkspflege to Ritter 1.9.1920.
103. BHStA MA 107722, Staatskommissar für die Pfalz to Reichsministerium des Innern 14.9.1920. (Trans.)
104. BArch R1501/102823, Vorschläge für die Zusammenarbeit mit den Bundesstaaten bei der Abwehr der Abtrennungsbestrebungen 10.11.1920.
105. BArch R43 I/179, Reichsminister des Innern to Staatssekretär, Reichskanzlei 17.12.1920.
106. BArch R43 I/179, Reichsminister des Innern to AA 17.12.1920.
107. BArch R1501/102881, Staatssekretär Reichsmin. des Innern to Staatskomm. für die Pfalz Dez. 1920; Staatskomm. für die Pfalz to Staatssekretär Reichsmin. des Innern 3.1.1921.
108. BHStA MA 107722, Staatskommissar für die Pfalz to Staaatssekretär Lewald 11.2.1921.
109. BHStA MA 107710, Staatskomm. für die Pfalz: Report on meeting 14/15.2.1921 in Pr. Kultusmin.
110. BArch R1601/1630, Winterstein to Lewald 9.4.1921.
111. BHStA HHSPf 78, Wrochem to Ritter 6.5.1921.
112. BArch R1501/102883, Wrochem to Lewald 26.4.1921.

113. Staatskommissar: *Die Pfalz*, pp. 94–9.
114. BHStA MA 108025, Winterstein to Staatsministerium des Innern 15.6.1921.
115. Bundesarchiv, 'Akten der Reichskanzlei, Weimarer Republik' online, http://www.bundesarchiv.de/aktenreichskanzlei/1919--1933/0021/vorwort.html
116. BHStA MA 107711, Brugger to Reichsmin. des Innern 19.12.1921.
117. BHStA MA 108025, Winterstein to Staatsmin. des Innern 15.6.1921.
118. Gärtner: *Botschafterin*, p. 75. (Trans.)
119. BArch R1603/2174, Wrochem to Deutsche Liga für Völkerbund (et al.) 28.6.1921.
120. Schieder and Dipper: 'Propaganda als Methode', p. 107.
121. Stern-Rubarth, Edgar, *Die Propaganda als politisches Instrument* (Berlin, 1921), pp. 3–4. (Trans.)

3 The Origins of the Schwarze Schmach Campaign

1. Le Naour : *La honte*, p. 16.
2. Ibid., pp. 16–19.
3. Ibid., p. 21.
4. Koller: *Von Wilden*, p. 202 n. 7.
5. Nelson: 'Black Horror', p. 610.
6. Pommerin: *Rheinlandbastarde*, p. 12.
7. Staatskommissar: *Die Pfalz*, pp. 135, 289.
8. Allen: *Occupation*, p. 319.
9. Staatskommissar: *Die Pfalz*, p. 289.
10. BArch R1603/2182, Bericht: Dienstreise der Frauenreferentin (Pfalz, Saargebiet, Trier) 6.6.1922.
11. Marks: 'Black Watch', p. 297.
12. Koller: *Von Wilden*, p. 203.
13. Nelson: 'Black Horror', pp. 606, 612–13.
14. Le Naour : *La honte*, pp. 100–3.
15. Ibid.
16. Horne: 'Der Schatten des Krieges', pp. 148–9.
17. Koller: *Von Wilden*, p. 230.
18. BArch R1603/2210, Vierter Bericht für die Freunde und Förderer des Bundes, Der Deutsche Volksbund Rettet die Ehre, April 1922.
19. BHStA HHSPf 43, *Münchener-Augsburger Abendzeitung* 30.4.1920.
20. Nelson: 'Black Horror', p. 609.
21. Koller: *Von Wilden*, pp. 108–14.
22. Staatskommissar: *Die Pfalz*, p. 13. French troops briefly occupied parts of south-west Pfalz during 23–27 November 1918, before the date (1 December) agreed under the terms of the Armistice. The alleged offence took place during this period.

23. Staatskommissar: *Die Pfalz*, p. 16. (Trans.)
24. Marhefka, Edmund (ed.), *Der Waffenstillstand 1918. Das Dokumenten-Material der Waffenstillstands-Verhandlungen von Compiègne, Spa, Trier und Brüssel* (Berlin, 1928), pp. 46–8.
25. Akten Rkei Bd. 1 (Scheidemann), Vortrag des Generals von Hammerstein vor dem Reichskabinett über die Arbeit der Waffenstillstandskommission in Spa 4.3.1919, Dok. Nr. 5b, p. 15.
26. Akten Rkei Bd. 1 (Scheidemann), Kabinettssitzung vom 21.3.1919, Dok. Nr. 19, p. 75, also n. 4.
27. Akten Rkei Bd. 1 (Scheidemann), Richtlinien für die deutschen Friedensunterhändler, 21.4.1919, Dok. Nr. 49, p. 196. (Trans.)
28. Akten Rkei Bd. 1 (Scheidemann), Kabinettssitzung vom 21.3.1919, Dok. Nr. 19, pp. 76–7. (Trans.)
29. The National Archives (TNA): Public Record Office (PRO) FO 608/135, Foreign Office Minute 1340, 12.3.1919.
30. Edmonds, Sir James, *The Occupation of the Rhineland: 1918–1929* (London, 1987), p. 121. (Facsimile of edition published under restricted circulation (London, 1944)).
31. TNA: PRO FO 608/135, Internal memo 18.4.1919.
32. TNA: PRO FO 608/135, Foreign Office Minute 2852 8.5.1919.
33. Le Naour : *La honte*, pp. 106–7.
34. Schumann, 'Einheitssehnsucht', pp. 96–7.
35. Ibid., p. 101.
36. Schivelbusch: *Culture*, pp. 212–13.
37. Fenske, Hans, *Konservativismus und Rechtsradikalismus in Bayern nach 1918* (Bad Homburg, 1969), p. 78; Large, David Clay, 'The politics of law and order: a history of the Bavarian Einwohnerwehr 1918–1921', *Transactions of the American Philosophical Society* New Series 70/2 (1980), pp. 16–32.
38. Akten Rkei Bd. 2 (Bauer), Kabinettssitzung vom 24.10.1919, Dok. Nr. 86, p. 325.
39. Ibid., p. 326 n. 11.
40. Staatskommissar: *Die Pfalz*, p. 125.
41. Akten Rkei Bd. 4 (Fehrenbach), Bericht des Reichsministers des Innern über seine Reise in das besetzte Gebiet 24.8.1920, Dok. Nr. 57, p. 139.
42. Marks: 'Black Watch', pp. 299–300.
43. BArch R1603/2180, Ergebnisprotokoll der II. Konferenz der Rheinischen Frauenliga 10.8.1920.
44. Tirard, Paul, *La France sur le Rhin: Douze années d'occupation rhénane* (Paris, 1930), p. 302.
45. Staatskommissar: *Die Pfalz*, p. 59.
46. BArch R1603/2213, Reprint from *Frankfurter Zeitung* Nr. 846 11.11.1919. (Trans.)
47. Akten Rkei Bd. 2 (Bauer), Kabinettssitzung vom 24.10.1919, Dok. Nr. 86, p. 325 n. 11. (Trans.)

48. Tirard: *La France sur le Rhin*, p. 303. (Trans.)
49. Ibid.
50. Allen: *Occupation*, pp. 321–2.
51. Allen: *Occupation*, p. 322.
52. TNA: PRO FO 371/4799, Harmsworth to Hall 28.10.1920.
53. Nelson, 'Black Horror', pp. 619–25.
54. BArch R1603/2214, Howland Shaw to Landenberger 7.2.1921.
55. Koller: *Von Wilden*, pp. 135–73.
56. Allen: *Occupation*, p. 324.
57. TNA: PRO FO 371/5999, Note on document from Kilmarnock 27.6.1921.
58. Ibid., Parliamentary Question 27.10.1921.
59. BHStA MA 107722, Oberleutnant Gärtner to Staatskommissar für die Pfalz 3.7.1920.
60. Fenske: *Konservativismus*, pp. 100–8.
61. BHStA MA 107710, Winterstein to Staatsminister für Unterricht und Kultus 20.7.1920. (Trans.)
62. BHStA HHSPf 1, Bericht über die Zusammenkunft der Mitarbeiter der Rheinischen Volkspflege, 23.6.1920.
63. Marks: 'Black Watch', p. 310.
64. Staatskommissar: *Die Pfalz*, p. 104.
65. Koller: *Von Wilden*, p. 216.
66. Staatskommissar: *Die Pfalz*, pp. 63, 77, 114. Chlingensperg, formerly Winterstein's deputy, was appointed chairman on 1 February 1921. He, too, was expelled from the Pfalz on 23 January 1923.
67. Cited in Koller: *Von Wilden*, p. 215. (Trans.)
68. Ibid., p. 216.
69. TNA: PRO FO 371/5999, Brandt to IRHC 7.6.1921; Robertson to Curzon 21.6.1921.
70. Maréchal, G. (ed.), *La campagne contre les troupes noires* (Mayence, 1921). German translation in Eberlein, August Ritter von, *Schwarze am Rhein: Ein Weltproblem* (Heidelberg, 1921), pp. 28, 30.
71. Allen: *Occupation*, p. 321; TNA: PRO FO 371/5999, Robertson to Curzon 21.6.1921.
72. Ibid., p. 323.
73. Rheinische Frauenliga (ed.), *Farbige Franzosen am Rhein* (Berlin, 1920).
74. TNA: PRO FO 371/5999, Harmsworth to Barnes 1.7.1921.

4 Women in Rhineland Propaganda: Exploiters or the Exploited?

1. BHStA MA 107722, Winterstein Denkschrift August 1920 (exact date unspecified).
2. BArch R1603/2180, Gärtner to invited participants in Frankfurt Conference 9.6.1920.

3. BArch R1603/2169, Undated note on file; Gärtner: *Botschafterin*, pp. 7–16.
4. Gärtner: *Botschafterin*, pp. 23–4. Germany was not admitted to the League of Nations until 1926.
5. Jaeger, Hans and Gerhard Lüdtke, *Kürschners Deutscher Gelehrten-Kalender* (Berlin, 1926), section 1617; BArch R1603/2169, File note (undated).
6. Rühlmann, Paul M., *Kulturpropaganda: Grundsätzliche Darlegungen und Auslandsbeobachtungen* (Charlottenburg, 1919), pp. 11–12.
7. Gärtner: *Botschafterin*, pp. 45–6.
8. Ibid., p. 62. (Trans.)
9. Ibid.
10. Ibid., p. 63.
11. BArch R1603/2180, Ergebnisprotokoll der II. Konferenz der Rheinischen Frauenliga 10.8.1920 in Düsseldorf.
12. BArch R1603/2182, Briefing note, Gärtner to Dransfeld 9.5.1921.
13. BArch R1603/2180, Gärtner to invited participants in Frankfurt Conference 9.6.1920.
14. BArch R1603/2180, Protokoll der II. Rheinischen Konferenz (Düsseldorf) 10.8.1920.
15. The Katholischer Frauenbund was renamed Katholischer Frauenbund Deutschlands (KFD) in 1921. I have used the abbreviation KFD hereafter.
16. BArch R1603/2225, Verband hessische Frauenvereine to Gärtner 17.4.1921; Reply 17.5.1921.
17. BArch R1603/2182, Gärtner to Mende 9.5.1921.
18. Ibid.
19. Gärtner: *Botschafterin*, p. 76.
20. Akten Rkei Bd. 3 (Müller), Kabinettssitzung 25.5.1920, Dok. Nr. 115, p. 282.
21. BArch R1603/2209, Hessberger to Reichsministerium des Innern; Heilbron to Wrochem 2.11.1920.
22. BArch R1603/2213, Rheinische Frauenliga report 'Gegenwärtige Stand der Protestbewegung gegen die farbige Besatzung am Rhein', November 1920 (exact date unspecified).
23. BHStA HHSPf 43, Protest resolutions, including telegrams, sent from variety of women's organisations to Pfalzzentrale on various dates in November 1920.
24. Wigger: *Schwarze*, pp. 34–5.
25. BHStA HHSPf 4, Rheinische Frauenliga to Zentralstelle für pfälzische Angelegenheiten 8.11.1920.
26. Lebzelter: 'Schwarze Schmach', p. 38.
27. Gärtner: *Botschafterin*, p. 72. (Trans.)
28. Ibid., p. 70.
29. BHStA Bayerischer Vertreter beim Reichskommissar (BVR) 7, Winterstein to bayerischer Gesandter., Berlin 7.5.1921. (Trans.)
30. BArch R1603/2225, Ergebnisprotokoll der III. Konf. der R.F. 9.4.1921 in Homburg.

31. Kreutzer, Guido, *Die Schwarze Schmach* (Leipzig, 1921).
32. BArch R1603/2218, Gärtner to Verlag Vogel und Vogel 15.3.1921.
33. BArch R1603/2218, Börsenblatt für den Deutschen Buchhandel, Leipzig, 12.3.1921; leaflet *Die Herausforderung der Kulturwelt* (undated).
34. BArch R1603/2218, Gärtner to Kreutzer 23.3.1921.
35. BArch R1603/2218, Gärtner to Kreutzer, and Verlag Vogel und Vogel 7.4.1921.
36. BArch R1603/2218, Gärtner to Zentralstelle für pfälzische Angelegenheiten 26.3.1921.
37. BArch R1603/2218, Gärtner to Kreutzer 24.5.1921.
38. BArch R1603/2218, Gärtner to Vogel und Vogel 3.6.1921.
39. BArch R1603/2218, Gärtner to Vogel und Vogel 1.11.1921.
40. BArch R1603/2218, Engelmann to Gärtner (undated). (Trans.)
41. Frauenliga (ed.), *Farbige Franzosen am Rhein* (Berlin, 1920).
42. Ibid., p. 5.
43. TNA: PRO FO 371/4799, Gosling to Curzon 10.11.1920.
44. Evans, Richard, 'Prostitution, state and society in imperial Germany', *Past and Present* 70 (1976), p. 123.
45. Rheinische Frauenliga: *Farbige*, p. 5. (Trans.)
46. Scheck, Raffael, 'Women against Versailles: maternalism and nationalism of female bourgeois politicians in the early Weimar Republic', *German Studies Review* 22 (1999), p. 21.
47. Frauenliga: *Farbige*, p. 5.
48. BArch R1601/2180, Protokoll der II. Rheinischen Konferenz Düsseldorf 10.8.1920.
49. BArch R1603/2214, Text of speech by Gärtner to Deutsche Kolonialgesellschaft June 1921.
50. Ibid. (Trans.)
51. BArch R1603/2185, Gärtner to Frauenausschuß des deutschen Schutzbund 26.5.1921. (Trans.)
52. BArch R1603/2214, Gärtner to Schneider 11.1921 (exact date unspecified).
53. BArch R1603/2214, Gärtner to Schneider 15.12.1921 and 5.1.1922.
54. BArch R1603/2185, Gärtner to Steilberg 16.3.1921.
55. BArch R1603/2185, Steilberg to Gärtner 27.6.1921.
56. BArch R1603/2185, Gärtner to Schnell 7.6.1921.
57. BArch R1603/2185, Gärtner to Tiedje 2.5.1921.
58. BArch R1603/2185, Gärtner to Eberlein 21.5.1921.
59. BArch R1603/2214, Gärtner to Carrie Chapman Catt 22.11.1921. (Original written in English.)
60. Jaeger and Lüdtke: *Kürschners*, section 1477.
61. BArch R1603/2185, Gärtner to Poll 9.6.1921. (Trans.)
62. Pommerin: *Rheinlandbastarde*, pp. 33–84.
63. Jelavich, Peter, *Berlin Alexanderplatz: Radio, Film and the Death of Weimar Culture* (Berkeley, 2006), pp. 126–9.

64. Deutsches Filminstitut Frankfurt, Projekt Verbotene Bilder, manipulierte Filme. Zur Edition der Zensurgutachten der Film-Oberprüfstelle aus den Jahren 1920 bis 1938 (http://www.deutsches-filminstitut.de/dt2tai01.htm), Urteil der Filmprüfstelle Berlin B3452 14.6.1921; Urteil der Filmoberprüfstelle Berlin B8421 1.8.1921.
65. Ibid., p. 7. (Trans.)
66. The geneticist was the same Dr Poll to whom Gärtner had written a few days before the initial hearing. This suggests some miscalculation on her part.
67. Gärtner: *Botschafterin*, p. 69. (Trans.)
68. BArch R1603/2214, Gärtner to Carrie Chapman Catt 22.11.1921.
69. BArch R1603/2185, Gärtner to Rheinische Frauenliga 6.3.1922.
70. Heinemann, Ulrich, *Die Verdrängte Niederlage: Politische Öffentlichkeit und Kriegsschuldfrage in der Weimarer Republik* (Göttingen, 1983), pp. 120–54.
71. Watt, Donald Cameron, *Personalities and Policies: Studies in the Formulation of British Foreign Policy in the Twentieth Century* (London, 1965), pp. 117–35.
72. Ibid., p. 122.
73. Morrow, Ian F. D., 'Botschafterin des Guten Willens', *International Affairs* 32/3 (1956), p. 338.
74. Gärtner: *Botschafterin*, pp. 597–608.
75. Gärtner: *Botschafterin*, p. 76.
76. Brakelmann, Günter, *Der Kreisauer Kreis. Chronologie, Kurzbiographien und Texte aus dem Widerstand* (Münster, 2003), pp. 26–30.
77. Gärtner: *Botschafterin*, p. 500–58.
78. Berger, Stefan, 'William Harbutt Dawson: the career and politics of an historian of Germany', *The English Historical Review* 116/465 (Feb. 2001), p. 105.
79. Hertling, born 29 June 1892 at Lipik, Slovenia, succeeded Klein 22 August 1923 (BArch R1603/2162).
80. Gärtner: *Botschafterin*, p. 78.
81. BArch R1603/2185, Document: Referat II (Frauenreferat) der Rheinische Volkspflege 17.3.1922.
82. In 1922 there were several brothels in the Pfalz. In contrast to other areas in the Rhineland, there had been none in the Pfalz before the occupation. (Staatskommissar: *Die Pfalz*, p. 94; BArch R1603/2182, Bericht über den 2. Teil der Dienstreise der Frauenreferentin vom 18.5.1922–31.5.1922 (Pfalz, Saargebiet und Trier).)
83. Malnutrition was a theme exploited for example by both Ray Beveridge (this chapter) and the Deutscher Notbund (Chapter 5) from the beginning. Black troops were alleged to drink milk by the litre while starving German children had none.
84. Wigger: *Schwarze*, p. 186 n. 879.
85. BArch R1603/2182, Bericht: Dienstreise der Frauenreferentin (Pfalz, Saargebiet, Trier) 6.6.1922.
86. Ibid.
87. Maß: *Helden*, pp. 96–7.

88. Ibid., p. 97.
89. BArch R1603/2182, Bericht über die Besprechung des Frauenbeirates der RFL 29.3.1922.
90. BArch R1603/2185, Entwurf: Die Aufgaben des Referats II (Frauenreferat) der Rheinischen Volkspflege 17.3.1922.
91. Welch: *Propaganda*, pp. 149–52.
92. Scheck: 'Women', p. 24.
93. Heinemann: *Niederlage*, p. 27.
94. Lebzelter: 'Schwarze Schmach', p. 39.
95. Ibid., p. 43.
96. Scheck, Raffael, *Mothers of the Nation: Right-Wing Women in Weimar Germany* (Oxford, 2004), pp. 118–19.
97. Lange, Helene, 'Die schwerste Stunde, Juni 1919'; 'Das Versagen, Juli 1919', in Helene Lange, *Kampfzeiten: Aufsätze und Reden aus vier Jahrzehnten* (Berlin, 1928).
98. Salomon, Alice, *Character Is Destiny: The Autobiography of Alice Salomon*, Andrew Lees (ed.) (Michigan, 2004), p. 202.
99. Scheck, Raffael, 'Wahrung des Burgfriedens: Die Wirkung des Ersten Weltkrieges auf die bürgerliche Frauenbewegung der Weimarer Republik', in Dülffer and Krumeich (eds): *verlorene Frieden*, pp. 216–17.
100. Scheck: 'Women', pp. 28–9.
101. Ibid., p. 25.
102. BArch R1603/2225, Ergebnisprotokoll der III. Konf. der Rh. Frauenliga am 9.4.1921 in Homburg.
103. Lange, Helene, *Lebenserinnerungen* (Berlin, 1925), pp. 260–1. (Trans.)
104. Lüders, Marie-Elisabeth, *Fürchte Dich Nicht: Persönliches und Politisches aus mehr als 80 Jahren 1878–1962* (Cologne, 1963), p. 92.
105. Lüders: *Fürchte*, pp. 107–16.
106. Jelavich, Peter, *Berlin Cabaret* (Cambridge, MA, and London, 1993), pp. 154–8.
107. BArch R1603/2183, Bericht über den Besuch der Haremsnächtenaturalistisch exotische Pantomime, Dorothee v. Velsen 15.10.1920; Gärtner to preussisches Ministerium für Volkswohlfahrt 16.10.1920. (Trans.)
108. BArch R1603/2185, Hoppe to Gärtner 15.10.1921.
109. Scheck: 'Women', pp. 26–8.
110. BArch R1603/2182, *Der Abolitionist* XX Jahrgang, Nr. 3, 1.7.1921.
111. TNA: PRO FO 371/5999, Lesser to Macleay 12.11.1921; Netherlands Women's Association for the Improvement of Morals to Secretary-General, League of Nations 1.2.1921.
112. Süchting-Hänger, Andrea, *Das 'Gewissen der Nation'. Nationales Engagement und politisches Handeln konservativer Frauenorganisationen 1900 bis 1937* (Düsseldorf, 2002), p. 223.
113. Ibid., p. 227.
114. BArch R1603/2180, Ergebnisprotokoll der II. Konf. der Rh. Frauenliga am 10.8.1920 in Düsseldorf.

115. Lüders: *Fürchte*, p. 77. (Trans.)
116. Lüders: *Fürchte*, p. 76. (Trans.)
117. Velsen, Dorothee von, *Im Alter die Fülle: Erinnerungen* (Tübingen, 1956), p. 248. (Trans.)
118. Koller: *Von Wilden*, pp. 108–14.
119. Tynan, Katharine, *Life in the Occupied Area* (London, 1925), p. 88.
120. Ibid., p. 238.
121. Roos, Julia, 'Women's rights, nationalist anxiety, and the "moral" agenda in the early Weimar Republic: revisiting the "Black Horror" campaign against France's African occupation troops', *Central European History* 42 (2009), pp. 473–508.
122. BArch R1603/2180, Ergebnisprotokoll der II. Konferenz der Rheinischen Frauenliga 10.8.1920 in Düsseldorf.
123. Salomon: *Character*, p. 150. (Trans.)
124. Gärtner: *Botschafterin*, p. 52.
125. Salomon: *Character*, p. 157. (Trans.)
126. Maß: *Helden*, pp. 96–7.
127. BHStA HHSPf 62, Eberlein to bayerischer Vertreter beim Reichskommissar 29.9.1919.
128. BHStA HHSPf 43, 'Wer ist Miss Beveridge?' *Der Kampf* 1.3.1921.
129. Beveridge, Ray, *Mein Leben für Euch: Erinnerungen an Glanzvolle und Bewegte Jahre* (Berlin, 1937).
130. BHStA HHSPf 62, Eberlein to Beveridge 29.9.1919.
131. BHStA HHSPf 62, Eberlein to Beveridge 6.11.1919.
132. Nelson: 'Black Horror', p. 615.
133. BArch R1603/2213, Die schwarze Schmach – die weisse Schande. Vortrag von Ray Beveridge, *Fränkischer Volksfreund* Nr. 287 14.12.1920. (Trans.)
134. BArch R1603/2214, Gärtner speech to Deutsche Kolonialgesellschaft June 1921. (Trans.)
135. BArch R1603/2213, Die schwarze Schmach – die weisse Schande. Vortrag von Ray Beveridge, *Fränkischer Volksfreund* Nr. 287 14.12.1920. (Trans.)
136. Ibid. (Trans.)
137. Ibid. (Trans.)
138. Beveridge: *Mein Leben*, pp. 259–60, 269; BHStA HHSPf 41, Assmann to bayerisches Ministerium des Innern 14.2.1921; BHStA HHSPf 43, *Münchener Post* 24.2.1921; BHStA MA 107716, Ritter to Staatskommissar 23.11.1921.
139. Beveridge: *Mein Leben*, pp. 252–7.
140. BArch R1603/2185, Ellis Loring Dresel to Secretary of State, Washington, cited in Recueil de Documents Étrangers, Ministère des Affaires Étrangères, 84, 14.4.1921.
141. Beveridge: *Mein Leben*, p. 262.
142. Ibid., p. 309.
143. Ibid., p. 312.

144. BArch R1603/2214, Gärtner to Röhmer-Litzmann 26.8.1921. (Trans.)
145. BArch R1603/2214, Gärtner to Schmölder 3.11.1921.

5 Publicly Funded Propaganda and Private Initiatives: Contrasting Styles and Motivation

1. Schöny, Otto, 'Propaganda oder Aufklärung', *Der Heimatdienst* 30 (1921), p. 293, cited in Wippermann: *Politische Propaganda*, pp. 236–7. (Trans.)
2. Wippermann: *Politische Propaganda*, p. 206 n. 24.
3. Wrochem: *Kolonisation*, p. 37.
4. Poley: *Decolonization*, p. 160.
5. Ibid., p. 157.
6. This did not prevent the Heimatdienst commissioning a review of one of Eberlein's propaganda booklets for its house journal, *Heimataufbau* (BHStA HHSPf 41, Klarner to Eberlein 20.7.1921). Clearly it did not regard Eberlein's propaganda as being too extreme.
7. Wrochem: *Kolonisation*, p. 5. (Trans.)
8. Wrochem: *Kolonisation*, p. 104. (Trans.)
9. TNA: PRO FO 371/4799, Harmsworth to Hall 28.10.1920.
10. Eberlein, August Ritter von, *Schwarze am Rhein: Ein Weltproblem* (Heidelberg, 1921).
11. BArch R43 I/184, *Rheinischer Beobachter* 21.5.1922.
12. BArch R43 I/185, *Rheinischer Beobachter* 19.11.1922.
13. BArch R43 I/184, *Rheinischer Beobachter* 21.5.1922.
14. BArch R43 I/184, *Rheinischer Beobachter* 14.5.1922.
15. BHStA HHSPf 41, Constitution of the Deutscher Notbund gegen die Schwarze Schmach 15.9.1920.
16. Distler has been described in some studies as a businessman and as an engineer. The Munich police report (see n. 17 below) lists his occupations following the failure of a theatrical undertaking as medical insurance agent, director of a transcription agency and hotel bookkeeper and similar.
17. BHStA HHSPf 41, Polizeidirektion München to Staatskommissar für die Pfalz 28.9.1920; BArch R1603/2220, Polizeidirektion München to Staatsministerium des Innern 5.1.1921.
18. Distler, Heinrich, *Schwarze Schmach: Die Schändung der Deutschen Frau durch Frankreich* (Munich, 1920).
19. BHStA MA 108037, Deutscher Notbund (ed.), *Was ist Schwarze Schmach?*; Deutscher Notbund (ed.), *Farbige am Rhein – eine europäische Angelegenheit* (Munich, undated pamphlets).
20. Distler, Heinrich, *Das deutsche Leid am Rhein* (Minden in Westfalen, 1921).
21. Distler: *Schwarze Schmach*.
22. BHStA MA 108037, *Münchner Neueste Nachrichten* 19.10.1920.
23. BHStA MA 108037, Ritter to Staatskommissar, Reichsministerium des Innern 11.3.1921.

24. BHStA MA 108037, Anon. author (Dr ***), *Was droht dir, Europa?* (Munich, 1921); Deutscher Notbund (ed.): *Farbige*; Deutscher Notbund (ed.): *Was ist Schwarze Schmach?*.
25. Noma: a gangrenous inflammation of the mouth, esp. one affecting malnourished children (*Collins English Dictionary* 4th edn (Glasgow, 1998)).
26. BHStA HHSPf 41, Ritter to Staatskommissar für die Pfalz 13.9.1920.
27. Eberlein: *Schwarze*, pp. 45–9; BHStA HHSPf 42, Eberlein to Rambaud 7.9.1921.
28. BHStA HHSPf 21, Ritter to Staatskommissar für die Pfalz 13.9.1920.
29. BHStA MA 108037, Preussischer Minister des Innern to Winterstein 22.11.1920.
30. BHStA MA 108037, Winterstein to preussischer Minister des Innern 30.11.1920.
31. BHStA HHSPf 41, 'Rechtsrheinische Stimmen', *Echo du Rhin* 25.10.1920.
32. BHStA MA 108037, Reichsmin. des Innern to bayer. Staatskomm. für die Pfalz 8.11.1920.
33. BHStA MA 108037, *Münchner Neueste Nachrichten* Nr. 434, 19.10.1920.
34. BHStA HHSPf 41, Rheinische Frauenliga to Fürsorgestelle (Hessen) 22.3.1922.
35. BHStA MA 108037, Reichsministerium des Innern to Staatskommissar für die Pfalz 22.11.1921.
36. BHStA HHSPf 41, Zentralstelle für pfälzische Angelegenheiten to Gärtner 11.11.1920.
37. BHStA HHSPf 41, *Mannheimer Tageblatt* Nr. 290, 1.11.1920; *Leipziger Tageblatt* 29.4.1921; Gärtner to Ritter 8.11.1920.
38. BHStA HHSPf 41, Deutscher Notbund to Verlag Hans Robert Engelmann 28.11.1920.
39. BHStA HHSPf 41, Gärtner to Pfalzzentrale 10.12.1920.
40. BHStA MA 108037, Ritter to Staatskommissar für die Pfalz 13.1.1921.
41. BHStA HHSPf 41, *Wochenausgabe des Berliner Tageblatt für Ausland und Übersee* 9.2.1921.
42. This much is evident in the way in which Eberlein peremptorily rejected requests from a Dr Assmann in Berlin for material for a forthcoming visit to America. See correspondence in BHStA HHSPf 41, Assmann to Pfalzzentrale 2.3.1921; Assmann to bayerisches Ministerium des Innern 14.2.1921; Pfalzzentrale to Assmann 17.3.1921; Zentralfürsorgestelle (Abt. Preussen) to Min. des Innern, Berlin 15.3.1921.
43. BHStA MA 108037, Report by Polizeidirektion, München to Staatsmin. des Innern 5.1.1921.
44. BHStA MA 108037, Ritter to Staatskommissar 21.1.1921; Staatskommissar to Polizeidirektion München 15.3.1921; Statement by K H Pollog and A S Pollog 17.3.1921; Karl Heinz Pollog to Ritter (undated).
45. BHStA MA 108037, Polizeidirektion München to Staatskommissar 12.4.1921.

46. BHStA MA 108037, Polizeidirektion München report to Staatsministerium des Äußeren 30.7.1921.
47. BHStA MA 108037, Reichsministerium des Innern to Staatskommissar für die Pfalz 22.11.1921.
48. BHStA MA 108037, Authorisation document for Deutscher Notbund, Staatsministerium des Innern 6.7.1921.
49. BHStA MA 108037, Staatsministerium des Innern to Regierungspräsident, Ministerium des Äußeren 30.3.1922; Staatsministerium des Innern to Deutscher Notbund 30.3.1922.
50. BHStA MA 108037, Deutscher Notbund to Ministerpräsident 24.5.1922.
51. BHStA MA 108037, Schwelze, Staatsministerium des Innern to Ministerpräsident 30.5.1922. Prime Minister Lerchenfeld had earlier been warned by the Reich Foreign Ministry not to speak out during a visit to the Pfalz or he would risk arrest by the French authorities. The same communication expressed concern at the actions of certain officials in the Bavarian government – an issue discussed in Chapter 6 (PA AA R74557, Friedberg to Lerchenfeld 22.3.1922).
52. BHStA HHSPf 42, Klarner to Eberlein 20.7.1921.
53. BHStA HHSPf 42, Deutscher Notbund to Eberlein 28.7.1921; Notbund to Eberlein 17.8.1921.
54. BHStA HHSPf 42, Deutscher Notbund to Eberlein 20.12.1921 and reply 13.1.1922.
55. BHStA MA 108037, Betz to Staatskommissar für die Pfalz 23.7.1922. (Trans.)
56. BHStA HHSPf 42, Deutscher Notbund to August Müller (alias Eberlein) 24.5.1921.
57. BHStA MA 108037, *Münchener Zeitung* Nr. 150, 3.6.1921; Polizei-Präsident Köln to Staatskommissar für die Pfalz 25.7.1921; Staatskommissar to Schriftleitung, *Münchner Neueste Nachrichten* 1.10.1921.
58. BHStA MA 108037, French Legate in Bavaria to Kahr 1.9.1921.
59. Akten Rkei Bd. 5.1 (Wirth I), Einleitung, pp. XXXIII–XXXV.
60. BHStA MA 108037, Bayerische Gesandtschaft in Berlin to Staatsmin. des Äußeren 30.11.1921.
61. D'Abernon: *Diary* vol. I, pp. 184–204.
62. BHStA MA 108037, Staatsministerium des Innern to Staatsmin. des Äußeren 16.9.1921; Staatsministerium des Äußeren to fr. Gesandter in München (undated draft); Staatsmin. des Innern internal memorandum (undated); Staatsmin. des Äußeren to bay. Gesandtschaft in Berlin 24.9.1921.
63. BHStA MA 108037, Staatskommissar für die Regelung der Kriegswohlfahrtspflege in Preussen to Staatsmin. des Innern 12.10.1921.
64. Large: 'Einwohnerwehr', pp. 16–30.
65. Ibid., pp. 73–6.
66. Zimmermann: *Bayern*, pp. 107–12.
67. BHStA MA 108037, Staatskommissar für die Regelung der Kriegswohlfahrtspflege in Preussen to Staatsmin. des Innern 12.10.1921. (Trans.)

68. BHStA MA 108037, Staatskomm. für die Pfalz to Arbeitsausschuß Deutscher Verbände (undated).
69. See n. 57.
70. BHStA MA 108037, Staatskommissar für die Pfalz to Staatsministerium des Innern 9.1.1923.
71. BHStA MA 108037, Staatsministerium des Innern to Polizeidirektion München (undated).
72. While prostitution was regarded as fundamentally evil, there existed differences of opinion within the women's movement over the position to be taken regarding its regulation by government. Within the KFB Buchner took the minority – and feminist – view that official regulation represented an offence against human dignity, did nothing to curb prostitution and contributed to moral confusion in the wider population. See Breuer, Gisela, *Frauenbewegung im Katholizismus: Der Katholische Frauenbund 1903–1918* (Frankfurt-am-Main, 1998), pp. 122–4.
73. BArch R1603/2185, Gärtner to Staatssekretär für die besetzten Gebiete 22.12.1921.
74. TNA: PRO FO 371/5999, 'Die Schmach am Rhein', *Monatsschrift des Deutschen Notbunds* Nr. 1, 1.8.1921. (Trans.)
75. Ibid.
76. BHStA MA 108037, Deutscher Notbund (ed.), *Die Schmach am Rhein* Nr. 20, 21, 22.
77. BHStA MA 108037, Undated pamphlet.
78. BHStA MA 108037, Bayerischer Landtag to Staatsministerium des Äußeren 3.8.1922. (Trans.)
79. Deutsches Filminstitut Frankfurt, Projekt Verbotene Bilder, manipulierte Filme. Zur Edition der Zensurgutachten der Film-Oberprüfstelle aus den Jahren 1920 bis 1938 (http://www.deutsches-filminstitut.de/dt2tai01.htm), Urteil der Filmoberprüfstelle Berlin B8121 13.8.1921.
80. Landauer: 'Bavarian problem I', p. 111.
81. Landauer, Carl, 'The Bavarian problem in the Weimar Republic: Part II', *The Journal of Modern History* 16/3 (1944), pp. 207–9; Zimmermann: *Bayern*, pp. 113–16.
82. Zimmermann: *Bayern*, pp. 134–5.
83. BHStA MA 108037, Deutscher Notbund to Wappes 20.2.1924.
84. BHStA MA 108037, Deutscher Notbund to Staatskommissar für die Pfalz 23.5.1924.
85. BHStA MA 108037, Reichsministerium für die besetzten Gebiete, Staatsministerium des Äußeren to Deutscher Notbund 12.6.1924.
86. BHStA MA 108037, Deutscher Notbund (ed.), *Die Schmach am Rhein* (June and August 1924).
87. **Selig, Wolfram,** *Paul Nikolaus Cossmann und die Süddeutschen Monatshefte von 1914–1918. Ein Beitrag zur Geschichte der nationalen Publizistik im Ersten Weltkrieg* (Osnabrück, 1967), pp. 15–44; Bramsted, Ernest K., *Goebbels and National Socialist Propaganda 1925–1945* (Michigan, 1965), pp. xxiii–xxxi.

88. Selig: *Cossmann*, pp. 66–72.
89. Cossmann, Paul Nikolaus (ed.), *Süddeutsche Monatshefte* (April 1922), p. 32. (Trans.) (Official German statistics revealed that in the Pfalz in December 1924 there were 48 children of mixed race – see Pommerin: *Rheinlandbastarde*, p. 28.)
90. Deutscher Schutzbund (ed.), *Französische Mordbrenner am deutschen Rhein* (Berlin, 1923). (Introductory message to the reader.) (Trans.)
91. Hirsch, Felix E., 'Hermann Oncken and the end of an era', *The Journal of Modern History* 18/2 (1946), pp. 148–59.
92. Helmberger, Peter, 'Biographische Notiz: Hermann Oncken', Historikergalerie des Instituts für Geschichtswissenschaften, Humboldt-Universität zu Berlin 31.8.1998, http://www.geschichte.hu-berlin.de/galerie/texte/oncken.htm
93. Hirsch, 'Hermann Oncken', p. 150.
94. Oncken, Hermann, *Die historische Rheinpolitik der Franzosen* (Stuttgart, 1922), pp. 5–25.
95. Ibid., p. 53.
96. Ibid., p. 47.
97. Oncken, Hermann, *Brulez le Palatinat – Brennt die Pfalz nieder: Eine Rede zum Pfalztage* (Stuttgart, 1924), p. 19. (Trans.)
98. BHStA MA 107715, Winterstein to Hoffmann 7.6.1919.
99. Jaeger and Lüdtke: *Kürschners*, section 1132.
100. Sington, Derrick and Arthur Weidenfeld, *The Goebbels Experiment: A Study of the Nazi Propaganda Machine* (London, 1942), pp. 91–2; Zeman, Z. A. B., *Nazi Propaganda* (London, 1964), p. 73.
101. Ibid.
102. BArch R1603/2210, Zweiter Bericht für die Freunde und Förderer des Bundes, October 1920.
103. Swinemünde was ceded to Poland in the post-World War II settlement and is now known as Swinoujscie.
104. Hartwich, Otto, *Aus der Schmiede des Glücks* (Bremen, 1924), pp. 298, 315–21.
105. BArch RK B0065 2100012614, Lebenslauf des D. theol. Otto Hartwich.
106. BArch RK B0065 2100012614, Application form for membership RDS 12.12.1933. (Trans.)
107. *Gleichschaltung*, instituted by the Nazi regime, was the enforced coordination, or bringing into line, of all political, economic and cultural institutions. In 1935 it led to the creation of a Reich Ministry for Ecclesiastical Affairs.
108. Membership was mandatory for all who wished to publish and was restricted to those who could provide evidence of Aryan descent and who were supportive of Nazi ideals.
109. BArch RK B0065 2100012614, Gestapo report on Otto Hartwich 16.7.1938. (Trans.)
110. BArch RK B0065 2100012614, Report on Otto Hartwich 23.3.1939.
111. Peace Treaty, Article 228.

112. Horne and Kramer: *Atrocities*, pp. 351–5.
113. BArch R1603/2210, Vierter Bericht für die Freunde und Förderer des Bundes, April 1922.
114. BArch R1603/2210, Zweiter Bericht für die Freunde und Förderer des Bundes, October 1920.
115. BArch R1603/2210, Vierter Bericht für die Freunde und Förderer des Bundes, April 1922.
116. Hartwich, Otto, *Die große Lüge. Beitrag zur Kriegsschuld-Frage* (Bremen, 1921).
117. BArch R1603/2210, Dritter Bericht für die Freunde und Förderer des Bundes, April 1921.
118. BArch R1603/2210, Open letter from Hartwich 5.3.1921.
119. BArch R1603/2210, Vierter Bericht für die Freunde und Förderer des Bundes, April 1922. (Trans.)
120. Ibid. (Trans.)
121. Ibid. (Trans.)
122. BArch R1603/2210, Rühlmann to Volksbund 18.3.1921.
123. BArch R1603/2210, Deutscher Schutzbund to Rheinische Frauenliga 21.2.1921.
124. BArch R1603/2210, Margarete Gärtner to Volksbund 11.11.1920.
125. BArch R1603/2210, Gärtner to Volksbund 26.11.1921.
126. BArch R1603/2210, Gärtner to Volksbund 8.12.1920; Gärtner to Vereinigung Deutschen Arbeitgeberverbände 17.11.1921.
127. BArch R1603/2210, Volksbund to Gärtner 13.12.1920.
128. BArch R1603/2214, Newsletter *Rettet die Ehre* 21.10.1921.
129. Buitenhuis, Peter, *The Great War of Words: Literature as Propaganda 1914–18 and After* (London, 1989), pp. 14–15.
130. Reventlow, Ernst Graf zu, 'Foreword', in Kreutzer: *Schwarze Schmach*, p. 6. (Trans.)
131. Kreutzer: *Schwarze Schmach*, p. 16.
132. Ibid., p. 88. (Trans.)
133. Ibid., p. 30. (Trans.)
134. Ibid., p. 53. (Trans.)
135. Reventlow: 'Foreword', p. 6. (Trans.)
136. The Deutschvölkische Freiheitspartei was an extreme right-wing anti-Semitic party founded in 1922 as an offshoot from the DNVP.
137. BArch RK B0171 2100036004, Lt. *Berliner Nachtausgabe* vom 22.11.1943. (Cutting)
138. Klemperer, Klemens von, 'Towards a Fourth Reich? The history of National Bolshevism in Germany', *Review of Politics* 13 (1951), pp. 199–200; Sontheimer, Kurt, *Antidemokratisches Denken in der Weimarer Republik. Die politischen Ideen des Deutschen Nationalismus zwischen 1918 und 1933* (Munich, 1962), pp. 161–4.
139. Reventlow: 'Foreword', p. 11. (Trans.)

140. See for example the studies by Nelson, Lebzelter and Marks.
141. Voelker, Judith, 'Unerträglich, unerfüllbar und deshalb unannehmbar: Kollektiver Protest gegen Versailles im Rheinland in den Monaten Mai und Juni 1919', in Dülffer and Krumeich (eds): *verlorene Frieden*, pp. 229–41.
142. Dülffer: 'Frieden schließen', p. 33.
143. TNA: PRO FO 371/5999, Robertson to Foreign Office 21.6.1921; Brown to Curzon 2.12.1921; Foreign Office internal note 27.6.1921.
144. TNA: PRO FO 371/5999, Gannett, Lewis S., 'Those Black Troops on the Rhine – And the White', *The Nation* 112/2 (25.5.1921).
145. Apex (anon.), *The Uneasy Triangle: Four Years of the Occupation* (London, 1931), p. 24.
146. Verlag und Redaktion der Pfälzischen Rundschau (ed.), *Niemals! Dokumente aus dem Befreiungskampf der Pfalz* (Ludwigshafen, 1930).

6 The Pfalzzentrale: Metamorphosis and Dissolution

1. Allen: *Journal*, p. 270; Reynolds, Bernard Talbot, *Prelude to Hitler: A Personal Record of Ten Post-War Years in Germany* (London, 1933), p. 41; Edmonds: *Occupation*, p. 191.
2. Allen: *Journal*, pp. 21, 286, 437.
3. TNA: PRO FO 371/5999, Parliamentary Question 27.10.1921; Parliamentary Question 31.10.1921.
4. TNA: PRO FO 371/5999, Harmsworth to Barnes 1.7.1921; Parliamentary Question (Wolmer) 27.10.1921; Cooke to Harmsworth 25.11.1921; Harmsworth to Cooke 2.12.1921.
5. TNA: PRO FO 371/5999, File notes 20.8.1921 and 25.8.1921.
6. TNA: PRO FO 371/5999, Harmsworth to Barnes 1.7.1921.
7. Lentin, Anthony, 'Lloyd George, Clemenceau and the elusive Anglo-French guarantee treaty, 1919. A disastrous episode?', in Alan Sharp and Glyn Stone (eds), *Anglo-French Relations in the Twentieth Century: Rivalry and Cooperation* (London, 2000), pp. 104–19.
8. Sharp, Alan, 'Anglo-French relations from Versailles to Locarno 1919–1925: the quest for security', in Sharp and Stone (eds): *Anglo-French Relations*, pp. 120–38.
9. Butler, Rohan et al. (eds), *Documents on British Foreign Policy 1919–1939* (DBFP) (First Series), vol. XXVI, no. 369, MacDonald to Poincaré 21.2.1924, p. 551; DBFP (First Series), vol. XXVI, no. 463, MacDonald to Crewe 7.5.1924, p. 681.
10. TNA: PRO FO 371/5999, File note 25.8.1921; Waterlow to Hope 23.9.1921.
11. Allen: *Journal*, pp. 172–3.
12. Allen: *Journal*, pp. 80, 102, 109.

13. Bußmann, Walter et al. (eds), *Akten zur deutschen auswärtigen Politik 1918–1945* (ADAP), Ser. A, Bd. IV (Göttingen, 1986), Delbrueck to Friedberg 28.2.1921, Nr. 176, pp. 374–6.
14. BArch R43 I/179, Reichsminister des Innern to Staatssekretär Reichskanzlei 17.12.1920.
15. ADAP, A, IV, Delbrueck to Friedberg 28.2.1921, Nr. 176, p. 375. (Trans.) This refers to Morel, E. D., *The Horror on the Rhine* (London, 1920). Delbrueck claimed that the Reich Foreign Ministry had encouraged Morel to produce this booklet.
16. Akten Rkei Bd. 1 (Scheidemann), Kabinettssitzung 14.5.1919, Dok. Nr. 72, pp. 321–2, nn. 1, 2.
17. See n. 13 (Trans.)
18. BHStA HHSPf 43, *Münchener Post* Nr. 45 24.2.1921. (This was a reference to a recent meeting held in the Löwenbräukeller in Munich. Subsequently reported in a number of newspapers, including the *Münchener Post*, it was one of a number of occasions when Beveridge shared the platform with Eberlein.)
19. Leffler, Melvyn, *The Elusive Quest: America's Pursuit of European Stability and French Security, 1919–1933* (Chapel Hill, 1979), pp. 1–40.
20. ADAP, A, IV, Delbrueck to Friedberg 28.2.1921, Nr. 176, p. 375.
21. Ibid. (Trans.)
22. Ibid.
23. Deutsches Filminstitut Frankfurt, Projekt Verbotene Bilder, manipulierte Filme. Zur Edition der Zensurgutachten der Film-Oberprüfstelle aus den Jahren 1920 bis 1938 (http://www.deutsches-filminstitut.de/dt2tai01.htm), Urteil der Filmprüfstelle Berlin B3452 14.6.1921; Urteil der Filmoberprüfstelle Berlin B8421 11.8.1921; Urteil der Filmprüfstelle Berlin B8121 13.8.1921.
24. BHStA MA 107725, Ritter to Winterstein 4.7.1921. (Trans.)
25. BHStA MA 107725, Staatskommissar to Oberreichsanwalt in Leipzig 8.7.1921.
26. BArch R1601/1630, Report of Reichskommissar für die besetzten rheinischen Gebiete 13.7.1921.
27. As required under Articles 3 and 4 of the Rhineland Agreement. (Staatskommissar: *Die Pfalz*, p. 67.)
28. BArch R43 I/177, Bernstorff to AA 10.8.1920. (Trans.)
29. TNA: PRO FO 371/5999, Harmsworth to Barnes 1.7.1921.
30. Edmonds: *Occupation*, p. 191.
31. Allen: *Journal*, p. 138.
32. BHStA HHSPf 1, Bericht über die Zusammenkunft der Mitarbeiter der Rheinische Volkspflege 23.6.1920.
33. Allen: *Occupation*, p. 226.
34. Allen: *Occupation*, p. 148.
35. Staatskommissar: *Die Pfalz*, pp. 94–7.
36. Zimmermann: *Bayern*, pp. 90–2.

37. PA AA R74554, Reichskommissar für die besetzten Gebiete (Brandt) to Reichsministerium des Innern, AA 5.7.1921.
38. Gembries: *Verwaltung*, p. 186.
39. Staatskommissar: *Die Pfalz*, pp. 102–3.
40. PA AA R74551, Lerchenfeld to AA 27.11.1920.
41. BArch R1601/1630, Paper by Ritter, 'Vorschläge zur weiteren Ausgestaltung des mit der Heidelberger Fürsorgestelle zusammenhängenden Pressedienst, unter besondere Rücksichtigung der Saar-Pfalz', 29.7.1921.
42. BHStA HHSPf 3, Eberlein to Staatskommissar für die Pfalz 9.8.1921.
43. BArch R1601/1630, Staatssekretär für die besetzten rheinischen Gebiete – Besprechung mit Reichstagsabgeordneten Fleischer und Kraus 1.9.1921.
44. Ibid.
45. Ibid.
46. BHStA HHSPf 42, Gärtner to Eberlein 26.11.1921.
47. BHStA MA 107716, Wappes to Loehrs, Reichsministerium des Innern 9.11.1921.
48. BHStA HHSPf 78, Rheinische Volkspflege to Pfalzzentrale 13.9.1921; Margarete Gärtner to Eberlein 2.1.1922; Aug. Müller Nf. to Rheinische Volkspflege 3.2.1922.
49. BHStA MA 107725, Wappes to Oncken (undated); Wappes to Scheffelmeier, Ministerium des Innern 28.2.1922. (Trans.)
50. Gembries: *Verwaltung*, pp. 186–7.
51. Ibid., p. 189.
52. Ibid.
53. ADAP, A, IV, Delbrueck to Friedberg 28.2.1921, Nr. 176, pp. 374–6.
54. BHStA MA 107729, Staatskommissar für die Pfalz to Warburg 17.5.1922.
55. BHStA MA 107729, Notes on meeting held 11.5–12.5.1922, Ministerium des Innern, Berlin.
56. BHStA MA 108052, Eberlein to Oelhafen (cc Wappes) 13.6.1922. (Trans.)
57. BHStA MA 107729, Anon to Staatskommissar für die Pfalz 4.4.1922.
58. Gembries: *Verwaltung*, p. 192.
59. BHStA MA 107719, Thoma to Eingabe- und Beschwerdeausschuss des Bayerischen Landtags 24.6.1929.
60. BHStA MA 107725, Vormerkung (Anon.) 9.6.1925; Eberlein to Rheinische Kreditbank 16.4.1925.
61. BArch PK A0243 1000053577, Bormann to Reichsschatzmeister der NSDAP 8.10.1943.
62. BHStA MA 107726, Note by Betz and Gauleiter Bürckel 10.10.1934.
63. BHStA MA 107729, Hausmann to Wappes 12.6.1922.
64. BHStA MA 108052, Eberlein to Oelhafen and Wappes 13.6.1922. (Trans.)
65. BHStA MA 108052, Oelhafen to Wappes 7.8.1922. (Trans.)
66. BHStA HHSPf 42, Eberlein to Staatskommissar 25.3.1922.
67. Staatskommissar: *Die Pfalz*, p. 161.

68. BHStA MA 107723, Eberlein to Staatskommissar für die Pfalz 14.2.1923; Gembries: *Verwaltung*, pp. 298–301.
69. BHStA MA 107725, Staatsministerium des Äusseren to Eberlein 17.3.1923.
70. BHStA MA 108026, Text of Eberlein speech at meeting in Ebernach 17.3.1923. (Trans.)
71. Ibid. (Trans.)
72. BHStA MA 107716. An example is to be found in a letter from Wappes to Brugger (23.3.1922), requesting that increased Reich funding for Hessen be accompanied by an increase for Bavaria, whose commitments to the Pfalz were greater than those of Hessen to its Rhineland territory and where the threats from French penetration were more severe.
73. BHStA MA 107725, Eberlein to Staatskommissar für die Pfalz 8.3.1923.
74. BHStA MA 108026, Bayerischer Bevollmächtigter to Staatsministerium des Äussern, Report on discussion held in Reichsmin. des Innern 14.2.1923.
75. PA AA R74557, Friedberg to Graf von Lerchenfeld 22.3.1922.
76. BHStA MA 107725, Eberlein to Staatskommissar für die Pfalz 8.3.1923. (Trans.)
77. Ibid.
78. Betz, Otto, 'Firma August Müller Nachf. Mannheim', in Karlheinz Lintz (ed.), *Grosskampftage aus der Separatistenzeit in der Pfalz* (Edenkoben, 1930), pp. 84–9.
79. Benz, Wolfgang (ed.), 'Politik in Bayern 1919–1933: Berichte des württembergischen Gesandten Moser von Filseck', *Schriftenreihe der Vierteljahrshefte für Zeitgeschichte* 22/23 (1971), pp. 95, 96, 107, 110, 113.
80. The BMP was in essence the Bavarian wing of the DNVP. See Zimmermann: *Bayern*, p. 84.
81. BHStA MA 108025, Eberlein to Staatskommissar Wappes 25.2.1922.
82. Oberhauser, Robert, *Kampf der Westmark. Frankreich-Separatismus und Abwehrbewegung 1918–1922* (Neustadt an der Haardt, 1934), p. 119.
83. Akten Rkei Bd. 6 (Cuno), Aufzeichnung des Staatssekretärs Hamm zur Lage in den besetzten Gebieten 1.6.1923, Dok. Nr. 176, pp. 534–5. (Trans.)
84. ADAP, A, VII, Aufzeichnung des Legationsrat von Levetzow 28.5.1923, Nr. 257, pp. 635–7. (Trans.)
85. TNA: PRO FO 371/8681, Gosling to Curzon 10.5.1923. (Trans.)
86. Staatskommissar: *Die Pfalz*, p. 159.
87. Zimmermann: *Bayern*, pp. 134–7.
88. Hennig: *Johannes Hoffmann*, pp. 480–93.
89. Osmond, Jonathan, *Rural Protest in the Weimar Republic: The Free Peasantry in the Rhineland and Bavaria* (London and New York, 1993), p. 51.
90. Osmond: *Rural Protest*, pp. 37–48.
91. Staatskommissar: *Die Pfalz*, pp. 162–9.
92. DBFP (First Series), XXVI, 369, Ramsay MacDonald to Poincaré 21.2.1924, p. 551.

93. Cassels, Alan, 'Repairing the Entente Cordiale and the New Diplomacy', *The Historical Journal* 23/1 (1980), pp. 136, 137.
94. DBFP (First Series), XXVI, 315, Curzon to Crewe 4.1.1924, p. 479.
95. Staatskommissar: *Die Pfalz*, p. 184.
96. Gembries: *Verwaltung*, pp. 313–25; Gräber, Gerhard and Matthias Spindler, *Die Pfalzbefreier* (Ludwigshafen am Rhein, 2005), pp. 41–66.
97. BHStA MA 107725, Eberlein to de Metz 9.2.1924. (Trans.)
98. Ibid.
99. DBFP (First Series), XXVI, 331, Record by Mr Lampson of a conversation with the Italian Counsellor 17.1.1924, p. 500 n. 2.
100. Staatskommissar: *Die Pfalz*, p. 187.
101. DBFP (First Series), XXVI, 320, Curzon to Phipps 8.1.1924, p. 484.
102. DBFP (First Series), XXVI, 334, Kilmarnock to Curzon 19.1.1924, p. 503.
103. DBFP (First Series), XXVI, 349, MacDonald to Phipps 4.2.1924.
104. BArch R43 I/1841, Vertretung der Reichsregierung München to Reichskanzlei 14.3.1924.
105. BArch R43 I/1841, Vertretung der Reichsregierung München to AA, Reichskanzlei 14.4.1924.
106. Cassels: 'Repairing the Entente', pp. 137, 138.
107. D'Abernon: *Diary* vol. III, p. 59.
108. BArch R43 I/1841, Vertretung der Reichsregierung München to Reichskanzlei 14.4.1924. (Trans.)
109. BHStA MA 107725, Eberlein to Staatskommissar für die Pfalz 2.4.1924.
110. BArch R43 I/1841, Vertretung der Reichsregierung München to Reichskanzlei 14.4.1924.
111. PA AA R74606, AA to Köpke, Friedberg 16.6.1924.
112. BArch R43 I/1841, Internal memorandum Wienstein to Kiep 10.5.1924.
113. Benz (ed.): 'Politik' (entry for 3 March 1922), p. 92 n. 1.
114. Akten Rkei Bd. 6 (Cuno), Der Badische Staatspräs. to Reichskanzler 20.4.1923, Dok. Nr. 134, p. 416. (Trans.)
115. Akten Rkei Bd. 6 (Cuno), Der Badische Staatspräsident to Reichskanzler 23.2.1923, Dok. Nr. 81, p. 270; Akten Rkei Bd. 7 (Stresemann II), Das Badische Staatsministerium to Reichskanzler 20.11.1923, Dok. Nr. 274, p. 1154.
116. Akten Rkei Bd. 6 (Cuno), Der Badische Staatspräs. to Reichskanzler 15.6.1923, Dok. Nr. 189, p. 568.
117. BArch R43 I/1841, Vertretung der Reichsregierung München to Reichskanzlei 12.5.1924.
118. Ibid.
119. BArch R43 I/1841, Deutsche Botschaft Paris (Hoesch) to AA 12.5.1924.
120. BArch R43 I/1841, Vertretung der Reichsregierung München 13.5.1924.
121. BArch R43 I/1841, Reichskanzler Marx to Staatspräsident Köhler 15.5.1924.
122. BArch R43 I/1841, Staatspräsident to Reichskanzler 19.5.1924.
123. PA AA R74606, AA to Köpke, Friedberg 16.6.1924.
124. PA AA R74606, AA (gez. I.A. (D)) to Staatsministerium des Äußeren 28.6.1924.

125. BHStA MA 107725, Bayer. stellvertr. Bevollmächtigte to Wappes 24.7.1924.
126. Menges: *Schmelzle*, pp. 46–8.
127. Ibid., p. 46.
128. PA AA R74606, Vertreter der Reichsregierung München to AA 21.6.1924. (Trans.)
129. PA AA R74606, Vertreter der Reichsregierung München to Ministerialdirektor AA 30.6.1924.
130. PA AA R74606, Bayerisches Ministerium des Äußeren to AA 2.7.1924.
131. Staatskommissar: *Die Pfalz*, p. 246.
132. PA AA R74606, Friedberg to Staatssekretär, AA 22.7.1924.
133. PA AA R74606, Vertreter der Reichsregierung München to AA 21.6.1924.
134. BHStA MA 107726, Eberlein to Staatskommissar für die Pfalz 19.5.1931.
135. BHStA MA 107726, Eberlein to Ritter von Epp 6.5.1935.
136. BHStA MA 107726, Eberlein and Betz to bayerische Staatsregierung 26.11.1933.
137. BHStA MA 107726, Eberlein to von Epp 6.5.1935.
138. BHStA MA 107726, Pfalzkommissar to Keidel 23.5.1931.
139. PA AA R74553, Bayerischer Vertreter beim Reichskommissar to AA 10.1.1921.
140. BArch RK B0036 2100006603, August Ritter von Eberlein.
141. Krabbe, Wolfgang, 'Die Bismarckjugend der Deutschnationalen Volkspartei', *German Studies Review* 17/1 (1994), p. 10. (Trans.)
142. BArch RK B0036 2100006603, August Ritter von Eberlein.
143. Gräber and Spindler: *Pfalzbefreier*, p. 169.
144. PA AA R74554, Reichskomm. für die bes. Geb. (Brandt) to Reichsmin. des Innern 5.7.1921.
145. PA AA R74554, Vertreter des AA beim Reichskommissar to AA 10.8.1921. (Trans.)
146. PA AA R74557, Friedberg to Lerchenfeld 27.2.1922; ADAP, A, VI, Mutius to Lerchenfeld 22.3.1922, Nr. 24, pp. 50–2. (The seriousness with which the Reich Foreign Ministry regarded this matter is shown by the note from Ambassador von Mutius on 22.3.1922. This traded on the close personal connections that had existed between the two when Lerchenfeld was a diplomat. That Lerchenfeld was either unwilling or too weak to circumscribe Wappes's and Eberlein's activities is abundantly clear from subsequent terrorist incidents – and ultimately the Speyer assassinations – that took place in the Pfalz.)
147. Staatskommissar: *Die Pfalz*, p. 67.

7 Pfalzzentrale Propaganda: Anti-France, but Pro-Bavaria or Pro-Reich?

1. Thalmann: 'Die Pfalz und Bayern', pp. 186–7.
2. BHStA MA 107715, Winterstein to Staatsministerium des Äußeren, Bamberg, report of meeting of Aktionsausschuß 16.7.1919.

3. BHStA MA 107715, Ritter to Staatsministerium des Äußeren, Bamberg 22.7.1919; Staatskommisaar für die Pfalz to Reichstagsabg. Hofmann 13.8.1919; Staatskommissar: *Die Pfalz*, p. 48.
4. Gembries: 'Die Pfalz und Bayern', p. 195.
5. BHStA MA 107715, Report of meeting of Aktionsausschuß 14.7.1919.
6. BArch R43 I/1837, *Neue Badische Landeszeitung* Nr. 328 3.7.1919.
7. BHStA MA 107715, Ritter to Staatskommissar für die Pfalz 19.11.1919.
8. BArch R43 I/1837, Schmidthals to AA 5.7.1919.
9. BArch R43 I/1840, Report of meeting with Dr Wilhelm Osterheld 19.7.1919 (Anon.).
10. BArch R43 I/1837, Schmidthals to AA 5.7.1919.
11. Akten Rkei Bd. 2 (Bauer), Der Hessische Ministerpräsident to Reichspräsident 30.6.1919, Dok. Nr. 9, pp. 34–6; Besprechung zwischen Reichs- und Ländervertretern über die großhessische Frage 14.7.1919, Dok. Nr. 26, pp. 120–8.
12. BArch R43 I/1837, Schmidthals to AA 5.7.1919.
13. Ibid. (Trans.)
14. BArch R43 I/1840, Freie Pfalz leaflet: 'Die Rettung unserer Pfalz und Ihres Deutschtums' (undated).
15. BHStA MA 107715, leaflet: 'Die Pfalz, eine freie unabhängige Republik?' (undated).
16. BHStA MA 107715, Ritter to Staatsministerium des Äußeren 22.7.1919.
17. BHStA MA 107715, Report: Massnahmen in der Pfalz (undated). (Trans.)
18. Ibid.
19. BHStA MA 107715, Ritter to Staatskomm., Betr. Politische Lage in der Pfalz 19.11.1919.
20. Ibid.
21. PA AA R74550, Lagebericht 1.10.1920 (Anon.).
22. Bessel: *Germany*, pp. 125–253.
23. TNA: PRO FO 608/126, Interim report on conditions in Bavaria 31.3.1919–8.4.1919.
24. BHStA MA 107709, Bericht über die Sitzung zwischen Mitgliedern der Reichsregierung und Herren aus dem französischen besetzten Gebiet 22.8.1919; MA 107722, Oberlt. Gaertner to Staatskommissar für die Pfalz 3.7.1920; BVR 7, Staatskommissar für die Pfalz to bayerische Gesandtschaft Berlin 7.5.1921; MA 108027, Jacob to Eberlein 17.5.1923.
25. Goebel, Erwin, *Die pfälzische Presse im Abwehrkampf der Pfalz gegen Franzosen und Separatisten 1918–1924* (Ludwigshafen, 1931), pp. 43–54.
26. Jacquot, Paul, *Le Général Gérard et le Palatinat* (Strasbourg, 1919).
27. This was a strange document to have been published by a French officer in view of its political indiscretions. The account by Gräber and Spindler of the way in which the document was acquired by Eberlein is no less bizarre. No reference is given to original documentation and so their source in this instance is unknown. Confirmation of the circumstances in which

the document was originally published and the consequences that followed Eberlein's acquisition of it requires recourse to the French records of the time. These have not been accessed for this book or seemingly elsewhere. This in no way detracts from the fact that Eberlein was able to score a propaganda success from the document. (Gräber and Spindler: *Revolver Republik*, p. 80.)

28. Jacquot: *General Gérard und die Pfalz*, pp. 30–1. (Trans.)
29. Ibid., pp. 26–7, 37, 52, 90, 136–7, 155.
30. Ibid., p. 52. (Trans.)
31. Ibid., p. 136.
32. D'Abernon: *Diary* vol. II, p. 228; Allen: *Journal*, pp. 107, 109, 131, 368.
33. Staatskommissar: *Die Pfalz*, pp. 83, 85, 87, 90.
34. BArch R43 I/177, Tätigkeitsbericht des Reichs- und preussischen Staatskommissars 10.7.1920, p. 20.
35. BHStA MA 107722, Oberlt. Gärtner to Staatskommissar 3.7.1920; BHStA HHSPf 1, Winterstein Denkschrift über Abwehr und Propagandatätigkeit. (Undated, but attributable to mid-1920: it was almost certainly based on Oberlt. Gärtner's report above.)
36. Akten Rkei Bd. 2 (Bauer), Besprechung der Reichsregierung mit Abgeordneten über die Lage in den besetzten westlichen Gebieten 28.11.1919, Dok. Nr. 116, p. 434.
37. BHStA HHSPf 1, Niederschrift einer Besprechung (Ritter), Mannheim 29.8.1920. (Trans.)
38. BHStA MA 107710, Staatskommissar to Staatsministerium für Unterricht und Kultus 20.8.1920.
39. BHStA HHSPf 80, Press cuttings, *Münchener Post* 24.2.1921; *Würzburg General Anzeiger* 14.12.1920; *Kaufbeurener Zeitung* 16.3.1921.
40. Ritter, Dr, *Der Schrecken am Rhein* (Munich, 1921).
41. Eberlein: *Schwarze.*
42. BHStA HHSPf 42, Signed statement by Eberlein 25.3.1922.
43. BHStA HHSPf 42, Rondoverlag München to Ritter 6.9.1921; Ritter to Bullinger 8.9.1921.
44. Koller: *Von Wilden*, pp. 244–5.
45. Bessel: *Germany*, pp. 233–9.
46. Eberlein: *Schwarze*, p. 127.
47. Weindling, Paul Julian, *Epidemics and Genocide in Eastern Europe 1890–1945* (Oxford, 2000), pp. 111–18.
48. Hitler, Adolf, *Mein Kampf* (trans. Ralph Manheim) (London, 1992), pp. 224–34.
49. Jones, James H., *The Tuskegee Syphilis Experiment* (New York, 1981).
50. Eberlein: *Schwarze*, p. 14.
51. The Allies were in full agreement on this point. See, for example, TNA: PRO FO 371/5999, File note (Brookes) 23.6.1921; Harmsworth to Barnes 1.7.1921.

52. Eberlein: *Schwarze*, pp. 98, 100.
53. Ibid., pp. 78, 96, 118.
54. Ibid., p. 128.
55. Cited in Eberlein: *Schwarze*, p. 22. (Trans.)
56. Eberlein: *Schwarze*, p. 2.
57. Ibid., p. 45. (Trans.)
58. Ibid., p. 81.
59. Koller: *Von Wilden*, pp. 43–52, 103–14.
60. Eberlein: *Schwarze*, p. 11.
61. Allen: *Occupation*, pp. 319–22.
62. Eberlein: *Schwarze*, pp. 21, 23.
63. Ibid., pp. 25, 27.
64. Ibid., p. 31. (Trans.)
65. Ibid., p. 145.
66. Ibid., p. 15. (Trans.)
67. Noyes, Pierrepont B., *While Europe Waits for Peace* (New York, 1921), cited in Eberlein: *Schwarze*, pp. 123, 125.
68. Hitler: *Kampf*, p. 102.
69. BHStA HHSPf 42, Ritter to Staatskommissar für die Pfalz 17.8.1921.
70. BHStA HHSPf 42, Justizminister Bayern to Eberlein 5.8.1921.
71. BHStA HHSPf 42, DVP to Eberlein 20.7.1921.
72. BHStA HHSPf 42, Hessisches Kreisamt to Pfalzzentrale 30.7.1921.
73. BHStA HHSPf 42, Hessische DNVP to Pfalzzentrale 25.7.1921.
74. BHStA HHSPf 42, Eberlein to Gärtner 26.8.1921.
75. BHStA HHSPf 42, Rheinische Volkspflege to Zentralfürsorgestelle (Pfalz) 3.10.1921.
76. BHStA BVR 7, Elin Wägner to Ritter 6.4.1921.
77. PA AA R74554, Vertreter des AA beim Reichskommissar to AA 10.8.1921. (Trans.)
78. PA AA R74554, Reichskommissar für das besetzte Gebiet to AA 14.7.1921.
79. BHStA MA 108052, Hausmann to Wappes 12.6.1922.
80. BHStA MA 108052, Eberlein to Oelhafen, Wappes 13.6.1922.
81. **BHStA MA 108027, Eberlein to unknown Geheimrat in Berlin 15.4.1923. Gräber and Spindler suggest that the renaming was a consequence of a ban on** *Deutsche Nachrichten*, introduced by the French authorities in February 1923. (See Gräber and Spindler: *Revolver Republik*, p. 116.)
82. **BHStA MA 108027, Bericht über die Versammlung pfälzischer Studenten in der Universität München am 17.5.1923.**
83. **PA AA R122238, Gutensohn to Müller 27.3.1923. (Trans.)**
84. **BHStA MA 108052, Eberlein to unknown recipient 16.4.1923.**
85. **BHStA MA 108052,** *Deutsche Nachrichten* Nr. 3, Februar 1923. (Trans.)
86. **BHStA MA 108052, Eberlein to Oelhafen, Wappes 13.6.1922.**
87. **BHStA MA 108027, Eberlein to Chef der Pressestelle 15.4.1923.**
88. **BHStA MA 108027, Eberlein to Staatskommissar 28.4.1923.**

89. Fenske: 'Bayern und die Pfalz', pp. 39–40.
90. BHStA MA 108027, Knoch to Staatskommissar 27.7.1923, 22.9.1923 and 24.9.1923.
91. BHStA MA 108027, Treutler to Staatskommissar 1.9.1923 and 10.10.1923.
92. BHStA MA 108027, Treutler to unknown recipient 29.9.1923.
93. Gräber and Spindler: *Revolver Republik*, pp. 109–12.
94. PA AA R122238, Eberlein to Staatskommissar 11.10.1923.
95. PA AA R122238, Leaflet 'Der Passive Widerstand' distributed in the Pfalz 22.6.1923; Leaflet 'Pfälzische Arbeiter gebt Acht!' distributed in the Pfalz 22.6.1923. (Trans.)
96. PA AA R122238, Poster 'Pfälzer! Heidelberger! Deutsche Landesverräter' (undated).
97. Eberlein: *Spionin*.
98. Gembries: *Verwaltung*, p. 192.
99. Eberlein: *Spionin*, p. 108. (Trans.)
100. Ibid., p. 113. (Trans.)

8 German Rhineland Propaganda: The Product of a Fractured Society

1. Stern-Rubarth: *Propaganda*, p. 1.
2. Schivelbusch: *Culture*, p. 215.
3. Hitler: *Kampf*, pp. 161–2.
4. Lasswell, Harold D., *Propaganda Technique in the World War* (New York, 1927), pp. 196–9.
5. Qualter, Terence H., *Propaganda and Psychological Warfare* (New York, 1962), p. 110.
6. Welch: *Propaganda*, pp. 25–256.
7. Ibid., p. 254.
8. Lasswell: *Propaganda*, p. 4.
9. Schieder and Dipper: 'Propaganda als Methode', pp. 106–8.
10. Bruch, Rüdiger vom, *Weltpolitik und Bildungsbürgertum in Deutschland am Vorabend des Ersten Weltkrieges* (Paderborn, 1982), pp. 111–22; Kloosterhuis, Jürgen, *Friedliche Imperialisten: Deutsche Auslandsvereine und auswärtige Kulturpolitik, 1906–1918* (Frankfurt am Main, 1994), pp. 3–7, 221–32.
11. Grupp, Peter, 'Voraussetzungen und Praxis deutscher amtlicher Kulturpropaganda in den neutralen Staaten während des Ersten Weltkrieges', in Wolfgang Michalka (ed.), *Der Erste Weltkrieg. Wirkung, Wahrnehmung, Analyse. Im Auftrag des Militärgeschichtlichen Forschungsamtes* (Munich, 1994), pp. 799–823; Düwell, Kurt, *Deutschlands Auswärtige Kulturpolitik 1918–1932* (Cologne, 1976), pp. 14–21.
12. Rühlmann: *Kulturpropaganda*, p. 11. (Trans.)

13. Ibid., pp. 12–13. (Trans.)
14. Ibid., p. 15.
15. Bundesarchiv, 'Akten der Reichskanzlei, Weimarer Republik' online (Biographien), http://www.bundesarchiv.de/aktenreichskanzlei/1919--1933/0021/vorwort.html
16. Stern-Rubarth: *Propaganda*, pp. 115–16. (Trans.)
17. Stern-Rubarth: *Propaganda*, pp. 25, 114. (Trans.)
18. Jaeger and Lüdtke: *Kürschners*, section 1469.
19. Plenge, Johann, *Deutsche Propaganda. Die Lehre von der Propaganda als praktische Gesellschaftslehre* (Bremen, 1922), p. 65. (Trans.)
20. D'Abernon: *Diary* vol. I, p. 181.
21. Eberlein: *Schwarze*, p. 121. (Trans.)
22. Little, Kenneth, *Negroes in Britain*, 2nd edn (London, 1972), pp. 216–40.
23. TNA: PRO FO 371/5999, Kilmarnock to Curzon 27.6.1921 (Anon. comment on file).
24. Pommerin: *Rheinlandbastarde*, pp. 16, 20–1.
25. Peukert, Detlev, *The Weimar Republic: The Crisis of Classic Modernity* (trans. Richard Deveson) (London, 1993), pp. 66–77.
26. Eley, Geoff, *Reshaping the German Right: Radical Nationalism and Political Change after Bismarck* (London and New Haven, 1980), pp. 41–58.
27. Kolb: *Weimar*, pp. 194–5.
28. BHStA MA 108037, leaflet 'Schmach am Rhein' 24.6.1924.
29. Caplan, Jane, *Government Without Administration: State and Civil Service in Weimar and Nazi Germany* (Oxford, 1988), pp. 19–21.
30. Ibid., p. 16.
31. Ungern-Sternberg, Franziska von, *Kulturpolitik zwischen den Kontinenten: Deutschland und Amerika* (Cologne, 1994), pp. 164–5; Düwell: *Kulturpolitik*, pp. 86–7.
32. Ungern-Sternberg: *Kulturpolitik*, pp. 160–2.
33. Heinemann: *Niederlage*, pp. 37–45; Herwig, Holger, 'Clio deceived: patriotic self-censorship in Germany after the Great War', in Keith Wilson (ed.), *Forging the Collective Memory: Government and International Historians through Two World Wars* (Providence and Oxford, 1996), pp. 87–127. See also: Hahn, Erich, 'The German Foreign Ministry and the Question of War Guilt in 1918–1919', in Carole Fink, Isabel V. Hull and Macgregor Knox (eds), *German Nationalism and the European Response 1890–1945* (Norman and London, 1985), pp. 43–70. The charge of patriotic censorship, blatantly evident in the Professors' Memorandum, has also been levelled at a much larger subsequent project. This project resulted in the publication of Lepsius, Johannes, Albrecht Mendelssohn Bartholdy and Friedrich Thimme (eds), *Die Grosse Politik der Europäischen Kabinette 1871–1914. Sammlung der diplomatischen Akten des Auswärtigen Amtes. Im Auftr. d. Auswärtigen Amtes* (Berlin, 1926–7). See above reference to Herwig, pp. 95–7.
34. DBFP (First Series), IX, 609, pp. 672–5, Kilmarnock to Curzon 11.2.1920.

Appendix I: Constituent Organisations of the Rheinische Frauenliga in May 1921

1. BArch R1603/2182 Gärtner to Dransfeld 9.5.1921.

Appendix II: Presentations Made by Leading Members of the Rheinische Frauenliga in Autumn 1920

1. PA AA R74418, Rheinische Frauenliga to AA 13.11.1920.

Appendix III: Questionnaire Sent Out by the Rheinische Frauenliga, February 1922

1. BArch R1603/2182, Klein to mitarbeitenden Frauenorganisationen 15.5.1922.

BIBLIOGRAPHY

Primary Sources (Unpublished)

Bayerisches Hauptstaatsarchiv (Munich) (BHStA)

Ministerium des Äußeren (MA)

MA 107709	MA 107710	MA 107711	MA 107715
MA 107716	MA 107719	MA 107722	MA 107723
MA 107725	MA 107726	MA 107729	MA 108025
MA 108026	MA 108027	MA 108037	MA 108052

Haupthilfsstelle für die Pfalz (HHSPf)

1	3	4	21
41	42	43	62
78	80		

Bayerischer Vertreter beim Reichskommissar (BVR)

7

Bundesarchiv Berlin (Lichterfelde and Aussenstelle Dahlwitz-Hoppegarten) (BArch)

Reichskanzlei R43

R43 I/177	R43 I/179	R43 I/184	R43 I/185
R43 I/1837	R43 I/1840	R43 I/1841	

Reichsministerium des Innern

R1501/102823 R1501/102881 R1501/102883

Reichsministerium für die besetzten Gebiete R1601

R1601/1630

Rheinische Volkspflege R1603

R1603/2162 R1603/2169 R1603/2174 R1603/2180
R1603/2182 R1603/2183 R1603/2185 R1603/2209
R1603/2210 R1603/2213 R1603/2214 R1603/2218
R1603/2220 R1603/2225

Former Berlin Document Centre

Reichskulturkammer (personal files)

PK A0243 1000053577 Otto Betz
RK B0036 2100006603 August Ritter von Eberlein
RK B0065 2100012614 Otto Hartwich
RK B0171 2100036004 Graf Ernst Reventlow

Politisches Archiv des Auswärtigen Amts (Berlin) (PA AA)

Politische Angelegenheiten des bes. Rheinlandes

R74418 R74550 R74551 R74553
R74554 R74557

Politische Angelegenheiten Pfalzzentrale

R74606

Haupthilfsstelle für die Pfalz Heidelberg

R122238

The National Archives (Kew) (TNA)

Public Record Office (PRO)
Foreign Office (FO)
Political Departments: General Correspondence
FO 371/4799 FO 371/5999 FO 371/8681

Peace Conference: British Delegation, Correspondence and Papers
FO 608/126 FO 608/135

Official Documentation

Bayerischer Staatskommissar für die Pfalz (ed.), *Die Pfalz unter französischer Besatzung von 1918 bis 1930: Kalendarische Darstellung der Ereignisse vom Einmarsch bis zur Raümung am 1. Juli 1930* (Munich, 1930)

Benz, Wolfgang (ed.), 'Politik in Bayern 1919–1933: Berichte des württembergischen Gesandten Moser von Filseck', *Schriftenreihe der Vierteljahrshefte für Zeitgeschichte* 22/23 (1971)

Bußmann, Walter et al. (eds), *Akten zur deutschen auswärtigen Politik 1918–1945*, Ser. A, Bd. IV (Göttingen, 1986); Bd. VI (Göttingen, 1988); Bd. VII (Göttingen, 1989)

Butler, Rohan et al. (eds), *Documents on British Foreign Policy 1919–1939* (First Series), vols IX, XXVI (London, 1960)

Edmonds, Sir James, *The Occupation of the Rhineland: 1918–1929* (London, 1987) (facsimile of edition published under restricted circulation (London, 1944))

Erdmann, Karl Dietrich and Wolfgang Mommsen (eds), *Akten der Reichskanzlei Weimarer Republik* Bd. 1–14: 1 *Das Kabinett Scheidemann* (13. Februar–20. Juni 1919) (Boppard, 1971) 2 *Das Kabinett Bauer* (21. Juni 1919–27. März 1920) (Boppard, 1980) 3 *Das Kabinett Müller* (I & II) (27. März–21. Juni 1920) (Boppard, 1971) 4 *Das Kabinett Fehrenbach* (25. Juni 1920–4. Mai 1921) (Boppard, 1972) 5.1 *Die Kabinette Wirth*, Bd. I (10. Mai 1921–26. Oktober 1921) (Boppard, 1973) 6 *Das Kabinett Cuno* (22. November 1922–12. August 1923) (Boppard, 1968) 7 *Die Kabinette Stresemann*, Bd. II (6. Oktober–30. November 1923) (Boppard, 1978)

Foreign Office (Great Britain), *Bavarian Palatinate: Handbooks Prepared Under the Direction of the Historical Section of the Foreign Office*, no. 32 (London, March 1919)

Lepsius, Johannes, Albrecht Mendelssohn Bartholdy and Friedrich Thimme (eds), *Die Grosse Politik der Europäischen Kabinette 1871–1914. Sammlung der diplomatischen Akten des Auswärtigen Amtes. Im Auftr. d. Auswärtigen Amtes* (Berlin, 1926–7)

Marhefka, Edmund (ed.), *Der Waffenstillstand 1918. Das Dokumenten-Material der Waffenstillstands-Verhandlungen von Compiègne, Spa, Trier und Brüssel* (Berlin, 1928)

The Treaty of Peace between the Allied and Associated Powers and Germany, the Protocol annexed thereto, the Agreement respecting the military occupation of the territories of the Rhine, and the Treaty between France and Great Britain... Signed at Versailles, June 28th 1919 (London, 1919)

Deutsches Filminstitut Archive

Deutsches Filminstitut Frankfurt, Projekt Verbotene Bilder, manipulierte Filme. Zur Edition der Zensurgutachten der Film-Oberprüfstelle aus den Jahren 1920 bis 1938 (http://www.deutsches-filminstitut.de/dt2tai01.htm), Urteil der Filmprüfstelle Berlin B3452 14.6.1921; Urteil der Filmoberprüfstelle Berlin B8421 11.8.1921; Urteil der Filmprüfstelle Berlin B8121 13.8.1921.

Memoirs, Diaries and Contemporary Propaganda Material

Allen, Henry T., *My Rhineland Journal* (Cambridge, MA, 1923)
——, *The Rhineland Occupation* (Indianapolis, 1927)
Amrhein, Dr, *Spielen wir unser Spiel am Rhein* (Munich-Pasing, 1922)
Apex (anon.), *The Uneasy Triangle: Four Years of the Occupation* (London, 1931)
Beveridge, Ray, *Mein Leben für Euch: Erinnerungen an Glanzvolle und Bewegte Jahre* (Berlin, 1937)
Cossmann, Paul Nikolaus (ed.), *Süddeutsche Monatshefte* (April 1922)
D'Abernon, Viscount, *Ambassador for Peace: Pages from the Diary of Viscount D'Abernon (Berlin 1920–1926)* vols I–III (London, 1929–30)
Denk, Peter, *Ehre verloren, Alles verloren. Ein Aufruf an alle echten Deutschen im Januar 1920* (Bremen, 1920)
Deutscher Schutzbund (ed.), *Französische Mordbrenner am deutschen Rhein* (Berlin, 1923)
Distler, Heinrich, *Schwarze Schmach: Die Schändung der Deutschen Frau durch Frankreich* (Munich, 1920)
——, *Das deutsche Leid am Rhein* (Minden in Westfalen, 1921)
Eberlein, August Ritter von, *Schwarze am Rhein: Ein Weltproblem* (Heidelberg, 1921)
——, *Die Spionin vom Rhein: Ein Spionageroman aus der Separatistenzeit in der Pfalz, sowie eine autobiographische Erzählung* (Berlin, 1930)
Gärtner, Margarete, *Botschafterin des Guten Willens: Aussenpolitische Arbeit 1914–1950* (Bonn, 1955)
Goebel, Erwin, *Die pfälzische Presse im Abwehrkampf der Pfalz gegen Franzosen und Separatisten 1918–1924* (Ludwigshafen, 1931)
Hartwich, Otto, *Die große Lüge. Beitrag zur Kriegsschuld-Frage* (Bremen, 1921)
——, *Aus der Schmiede des Glücks*, 2nd edn (Bremen, 1924)
Hitler, Adolf, *Mein Kampf* (trans. Ralph Manheim) (London, 1992)
Jacquot, Paul, *Le Général Gérard et le Palatinat* (Strasbourg, 1919); republished as *General Gérard und die Pfalz*, Dr Ritter (ed.) (Mannheim, 1920)
Jaeger, Hans and Gerhard Lüdtke, *Kürschners Deutscher Gelehrten-Kalender* (Berlin, 1926)
Kreutzer, Guido, *Die Schwarze Schmach* (Leipzig, 1921)
Lange, Helene, *Kampfzeiten: Aufsätze und Reden aus vier Jahrzehnten* (Berlin, 1928)
——, *Lebenserinnerungen* (Berlin, 1925)
Lasswell, Harold D., *Propaganda Technique in the World War* (New York, 1927)
Lintz, Karlheinz (ed.), *Grosskampftage aus der Separatistenzeit in der Pfalz* (Edenkoben, 1930)
Lüders, Marie-Elisabeth, *Fürchte Dich Nicht: Persönliches und Politisches aus mehr als 80 Jahren 1878–1962* (Cologne, 1963)
Maréchal, G. (ed.), *La campagne contre les troupes noires* (Mayence, 1921)
Noyes, Pierrepont B., *While Europe Waits for Peace* (New York, 1921)
Oberhauser, Robert, *Kampf der Westmark. Frankreich-Separatismus und Abwehrbewegung 1918–1922* (Neustadt an der Haardt, 1934)
Oncken, Hermann, *Die historische Rheinpolitik der Franzosen* (Stuttgart, 1922)
——, *Brulez le Palatinat – Brennt die Pfalz nieder: Eine Rede zum Pfalztage* (Stuttgart, 1924)

Plenge, Johann, *Deutsche Propaganda. Die Lehre von der Propaganda als praktische Gesellschaftslehre* (Bremen, 1922)
Reynolds, Bernard Talbot, *Prelude to Hitler: A Personal Record of Ten Post-War Years in Germany* (London, 1933)
Rheinische Frauenliga (ed.), *Farbige Franzosen am Rhein* (Berlin, 1920)
Ritter, Dr, *Der Schrecken am Rhein* (Munich, 1921)
Rühlmann, Paul M., *Kulturpropaganda: Grundsätzliche Darlegungen und Auslandsbeobachtungen* (Charlottenburg, 1919)
Salomon, Alice, *Character Is Destiny: The Autobiography of Alice Salomon*, Andrew Lees (ed.) (Michigan, 2004)
Stern-Rubarth, Edgar, *Die Propaganda als politisches Instrument* (Berlin, 1921)
Tirard, Paul, *La France sur le Rhin: Douze années d'occupation rhénane* (Paris, 1930)
Tynan, Katharine, *Life in the Occupied Area* (London, 1925)
Velsen, Dorothee von, *Im Alter die Fülle: Erinnerungen* (Tübingen, 1956)
Verlag und Redaktion der Pfälzischen Rundschau (ed.), *Niemals! Dokumente aus dem Befreiungskampf der Pfalz* (Ludwigshafen, 1930)
Wrochem, Alfred von, *Die Kolonisation der Rheinlande durch Frankreich* (Berlin, 1922)

Secondary Sources

Applegate, Celia, *A Nation of Provincials: The German Idea of Heimat* (Berkeley, 1990)
——, 'Localism and the German bourgeoisie: the Heimat movement in the Rhenish Palatinate before 1914', in David Blackbourn and Richard J. Evans (eds), *The German Bourgeoisie: Essays on the Social History of the German Middle Class from the Late Eighteenth Century to the Early Twentieth Century* (London, 1991), pp. 224–54
Bariéty, Jacques, 'Die französische Besatzungspolitik im Rheinland nach dem Ersten Weltkrieg: Historisch-politische Mythen und geostrategische Realitäten', in Tilman Koops and Martin Vogt (eds), *Das Rheinland in zwei Nachkriegszeiten 1919–1930 und 1945–1949* (Coblenz, 1995), pp. 5–18
Baumann, Kurt, 'Probleme der pfälzischen Geschichte im 19. Jahrhundert', *Mitteilungen des Historischen Vereins der Pfalz* 51 (1953), pp. 231–72
Berger, Stefan, 'William Harbutt Dawson: the career and politics of an historian of Germany', *The English Historical Review* 116/465 (Feb. 2001), pp. 76–113
Bessel, Richard, *Germany after the First World War* (Oxford, 1993)
Blackbourn, David and Richard J. Evans (eds), *The German Bourgeoisie: Essays on the Social History of the German Middle Class from the Late Eighteenth Century to the Early Twentieth Century* (London, 1991)
Brakelmann, Günter, *Der Kreisauer Kreis. Chronologie, Kurzbiographien und Texte aus dem Widerstand* (Münster, 2003)
Bramsted, Ernest K., *Goebbels and National Socialist Propaganda 1925–1945* (Michigan, 1965)
Breuer, Gisela, *Frauenbewegung im Katholizismus: Der Katholische Frauenbund 1903–1918* (Frankfurt-am-Main, 1998)

Bruch, Rüdiger vom, *Weltpolitik und Bildungsbürgertum in Deutschland am Vorabend des Ersten Weltkrieges* (Paderborn, 1982)

Brunner, Otto, Werner Conze and Reinhart Koselleck (eds), *Geschichtliche Grundbegriffe: Historisches Lexikon zur politisch-sozialen Sprache in Deutschland* vol. 5 (Stuttgart, 1984)

Buitenhuis, Peter, *The Great War of Words: Literature as Propaganda 1914–18 and After* (London, 1989)

Caplan, Jane, *Government Without Administration: State and Civil Service in Weimar and Nazi Germany* (Oxford, 1988)

Cassels, Alan, 'Repairing the Entente Cordiale and the New Diplomacy', *The Historical Journal* 23/1 (1980), pp. 135–53

Chickering, Roger, *Imperial Germany and the Great War 1914–1918* (Cambridge, 1998)

Dülffer, Jost, 'Frieden schließen nach einem Weltkrieg', in Jost Dülffer and Gerd Krumeich (eds), *Der verlorene Frieden – Politik und Kriegskultur nach 1918* (Essen, 2002), pp. 19–38

—— and Gerd Krumeich (eds), *Der verlorene Frieden – Politik und Kriegskultur nach 1918* (Essen, 2002)

Dumont, Franz, 'Befreiung oder Fremdherrschaft? Zur französischen Besatzungspolitik am Rhein im Zeitalter der Revolution', in Peter Hüttenberger and Hansgeorg Molitor (eds), *Franzosen und Deutsche am Rhein 1789–1918–1945* (Essen, 1989), pp. 91–112

Düwell, Kurt, *Deutschlands Auswärtige Kulturpolitik 1918–1932* (Cologne, 1976)

Eley, Geoff, *Reshaping the German Right: Radical Nationalism and Political Change after Bismarck* (London and New Haven, 1980)

Evans, Richard, 'Prostitution, state and society in imperial Germany', *Past and Present* 70 (1976), pp. 106–29

Fenske, Hans, *Konservativismus und Rechtsradikalismus in Bayern nach 1918* (Bad Homburg, 1969)

——, 'Mehr als eine Provinz...Die Pfalz in der deutschen Geschichte des 19. und 20. Jahrhunderts', *Mitteilungen des historischen Vereins der Pfalz* 86 (1988), pp. 347–64

——, 'Bayern und die Pfalz', in Wilhelm Kreutz and Karl Scherer (eds), *Die Pfalz unter französischer Besetzung (1918/19–1930)* (Kaiserslautern, 1999), pp. 31–48

——(ed.), *Die Pfalz und Bayern 1816–1956* (Speyer, 1998)

Fink, Carole, Isabel V. Hull and Macgregor Knox (eds), *German Nationalism and the European Response 1890–1945* (Norman and London, 1985)

Geinitz, Christian, *Kriegsfurcht und Kampfbereitschaft: Das Augusterlebnis in Freiburg – Eine Studie zum Kriegsbeginn 1914* (Essen, 1998)

Gembries, Helmut, *Verwaltung und Politik in der besetzten Pfalz zur Zeit der Weimarer Republik* (Kaiserslautern, 1992)

——, 'Die Pfalz und Bayern in der Weimarer Zeit', in Hans Fenske (ed.), *Die Pfalz und Bayern 1816–1956* (Speyer, 1998), pp. 189–212

Gräber, Gerhard and Matthias Spindler, *Revolver Republik am Rhein: Die Pfalz und ihre Separatisten, Band 1 November 1918–November 1923* (Landau, 1992)

——, *Die Pfalzbefreier* (Ludwigshafen am Rhein, 2005)

Grupp, Peter, 'Voraussetzungen und Praxis deutscher amtlicher Kulturpropaganda in den neutralen Staaten während des Ersten Weltkrieges', in Wolfgang Michalka (ed.), *Der Erste Weltkrieg. Wirkung, Wahrnehmung, Analyse. Im Auftrag des Militärgeschichtlichen Forschungsamts* (Munich, 1994), pp. 799–823

Heinemann, Ulrich, *Die Verdrängte Niederlage: Politische Öffentlichkeit und Kriegsschuldfrage in der Weimarer Republik* (Göttingen, 1983)

Hennig, Diethard, *Johannes Hoffmann, Sozialdemokrat und Bayerischer Ministerpräsident* (Munich, 1990)

Herwig, Holger, 'Clio deceived: patriotic self-censorship in Germany after the Great War', in Keith Wilson (ed.), *Forging the Collective Memory: Government and International Historians through Two World Wars* (Providence and Oxford, 1996), pp. 87–127

Hirsch, Felix E., 'Hermann Oncken and the end of an era', *The Journal of Modern History* 18/2 (1946), pp. 148–59

Horne, John, 'Der Schatten des Krieges: Französische Politik in den zwanziger Jahren', in Hans Mommsen (ed.), *Der Erste Weltkrieg und die europäische Nachkriegsordnung: Sozialer Wandel und Formveränderung der Politik* (Cologne, 2000), pp. 145–64

—— and Alan Kramer, *German Atrocities 1914: A History of Denial* (New Haven and London, 2001)

Hüttenberger, Peter, 'Methoden und Ziele der französischen Besatzungspolitik nach dem Ersten Weltkrieg in der Pfalz', *Blätter für deutsche Landesgeschichte* 108 (1972), pp. 105–21

—— and Hansgeorg Molitor (eds), *Franzosen und Deutsche am Rhein 1789–1918–1945* (Essen, 1989)

Jardin, Pierre, 'Tirard, de Metz und die Pfalz', in Wilhelm Kreutz and Karl Scherer (eds), *Die Pfalz unter französischer Besetzung (1918/19–1930)* (Kaiserslautern, 1999), pp. 145–68

Jelavich, Peter, *Berlin Alexanderplatz: Radio, Film and the Death of Weimar Culture* (Berkeley, 2006)

——, *Berlin Cabaret* (Cambridge, MA, and London, 1993)

Jones, James H., *The Tuskegee Syphilis Experiment* (New York, 1981)

Klemperer, Klemens von, 'Towards a Fourth Reich? The history of National Bolshevism in Germany', *Review of Politics* 13 (1951), pp. 191–210

Kloosterhuis, Jürgen, *Friedliche Imperialisten: Deutsche Auslandsvereine und auswärtige Kulturpolitik, 1906–1918* (Frankfurt am Main, 1994)

Köhler, Henning, *November Revolution und Frankreich: Die französische Deutschland Politik 1918–1919* (Düsseldorf, 1980)

——, 'Französische Besatzungspolitik 1918–1923', in Peter Hüttenberger and Hansgeorg Molitor (eds), *Franzosen und Deutsche am Rhein 1789–1918–1945* (Essen, 1989), pp. 113–26

Kolb, Eberhard, *The Weimar Republic* (London, 1988)

Koller, Christian, *Von Wilden aller Rassen niedergemetzelt: Die Diskussion um die Verwendung von Kolonialtruppen in Europa zwischen Rassismus, Kolonial- und Militärpolitik (1914–1930)* (Stuttgart, 2001)

Koops, Tilman and Martin Vogt (eds), *Das Rheinland in zwei Nachkriegszeiten 1919–1930 und 1945–1949* (Coblenz, 1995)
Krabbe, Wolfgang, 'Die Bismarckjugend der Deutschnationalen Volkspartei', *German Studies Review* 17/1 (1994), pp. 9–32
Kreutz, Wilhelm and Karl Scherer (eds), *Die Pfalz unter französischer Besetzung (1918/19–1930)* (Kaiserslautern, 1999)
Landauer, Carl, 'The Bavarian problem in the Weimar Republic, 1918–1923: Part I', *The Journal of Modern History* 16/2 (1944), pp. 93–115
——, 'The Bavarian problem in the Weimar Republic: Part II', *The Journal of Modern History* 16/3 (1944), pp. 205–23
Large, David Clay, 'The politics of law and order: a history of the Bavarian Einwohnerwehr 1918–1921', *Transactions of the American Philosophical Society* New Series 70/2 (1980)
Lebzelter, Gisela, 'Die Schwarze Schmach: Vorurteile – Propaganda – Mythos', *Geschichte und Gesellschaft* 11 (1985), pp. 27–58
Leffler, Melvyn, *The Elusive Quest: America's Pursuit of European Stability and French Security, 1919–1933* (Chapel Hill, 1979)
Lentin, Anthony, 'Lloyd George, Clemenceau and the elusive Anglo-French guarantee treaty, 1919. A disastrous episode?', in Alan Sharp and Glyn Stone (eds), *Anglo-French Relations in the Twentieth Century: Rivalry and Cooperation* (London, 2000), pp. 104–19
Little, Kenneth, *Negroes in Britain*, 2nd edn (London, 1972)
McDougall, Walter A., *France's Rhineland Diplomacy 1914–1924: The Last Bid for a Balance of Power in Europe* (Princeton, 1978)
Marks, Sally, 'Black Watch on the Rhine: a study in propaganda, prejudice and prurience', *European Studies Review* 13 (1983), pp. 297–333
Martin, Michael, 'Mélac!', *Die Zeit* 20 (6 May 2004)
Maß, Sandra, *Weiße Helden, schwarze Krieger: zur Geschichte kolonialer Männlichkeit in Deutschland 1918–1964* (Cologne, 2006)
Menges, Franz, *Hans Schmelzle: Bayerischer Staatsrat im Ministerium des Äußeren und Finanzminister. Eine politische Biographie mit Quellenanhang* (Munich, 1972)
Michalka, Wolfgang (ed.), *Der Erste Weltkrieg. Wirkung, Wahrnehmung, Analyse. Im Auftrag des Militärgeschichtlichen Forschungsamtes* (Munich, 1994)
Mommsen, Hans (ed.), *Der Erste Weltkrieg und die europäische Nachkriegsordnung: Sozialer Wandel und Formveränderung der Politik* (Cologne, 2000)
Morgan, Kenneth O., 'Die soziale und politische Mobilisierung Großbritanniens 1918–1926', in Hans Mommsen (ed.), *Der Erste Weltkrieg und die europäische Nachkriegsordnung: Sozialer Wandel und Formveränderung der Politik* (Cologne, 2000), pp. 125–44
Morrow, Ian F. D., 'Botschafterin des Guten Willens', *International Affairs* 32/3 (1956), p. 338
Morsey, Rudolf, 'Die Rheinlande, Preußen und das Reich', *Rheinische Vierteljahrsblätter* 30 (1960), pp. 176–220
Le Naour, Jean-Yves, *La honte noire: L'Allemagne et les troupes coloniales francaises 1914–1945* (Paris, 2003)

Nelson, Keith L., 'The "Black Horror on the Rhine": race as a factor in post-World War I diplomacy', *The Journal of Modern History* 42/4 (1970), pp. 606–27

——, *Victors Divided: America and the Allies in Germany 1918–1923* (Berkeley and London, 1975)

Nestler, Gerhard, 'Pfälzisch, rheinisch oder bayerisch? Der Kreis um den Pfälzer Volksboten und die Diskussion über die staatsrechtliche Zukunft der Pfalz in den Jahren 1918–1920', *Jahrbuch zur Geschichte von Stadt und Landkreis Kaiserslautern* 32/33 (1994), pp. 355–75

——, 'Freie Pfalz, Rheinische Republik oder blau-weiße Bayerntreue', in Wilhelm Kreutz and Karl Scherer (eds), *Die Pfalz unter französischer Besetzung (1918/19–1930)* (Kaiserslautern, 1999), pp. 105–22

Orde, Anne, *British Policy and European Reconstruction after the First World War* (Cambridge, 1990)

Osmond, Jonathan, *Rural Protest in the Weimar Republic: The Free Peasantry in the Rhineland and Bavaria* (London and New York, 1993)

Peukert, Detlev, *The Weimar Republic: The Crisis of Classic Modernity* (trans. Richard Deveson) (London, 1993)

Poley, Jared, *Decolonization in Germany: Weimar Narratives of Colonial Loss and Foreign Occupation* (Bern, 2005)

Pommerin, Reiner, *Sterilisierung der Rheinlandbastarde: Der Schicksal einer farbigen deutschen Minderheit 1918–1937* (Düsseldorf, 1979)

Qualter, Terence H., *Propaganda and Psychological Warfare* (New York, 1962)

Roos, Julia, 'Women's rights, nationalist anxiety, and the "moral" agenda in the early Weimar Republic: revisiting the "Black Horror" campaign against France's African occupation troops', *Central European History* 42 (2009), pp. 473–508

Scheck, Raffael, 'Women against Versailles: maternalism and nationalism of female bourgeois politicians in the early Weimar Republic', *German Studies Review* 22 (1999), pp. 21–42

——, 'Wahrung des Burgfriedens: Die Wirkung des Ersten Weltkrieges auf die bürgerliche Frauenbewegung der Weimarer Republik', in Jost Dülffer and Gerd Krumeich (eds), *Der verlorene Frieden – Politik und Kriegskultur nach 1918* (Essen, 2002), pp. 215–28

——, *Mothers of the Nation: Right-Wing Women in Weimar Germany* (Oxford, 2004)

Scherer, Karl, 'Zum Verhältnis Pfalz-Bayern in den Jahren 1816–1848', in Hans Fenske (ed.), *Die Pfalz und Bayern 1816–1956* (Speyer, 1998), pp. 9–40

Schieder, Wolfgang and Christof Dipper, Art. VI, 'Propaganda als Methode moderner Politik', in Otto Brunner, Werner Conze and Reinhart Koselleck (eds), *Geschichtliche Grundbegriffe: Historisches Lexikon zur politisch-sozialen Sprache in Deutschland* vol. 5 (Stuttgart, 1984), pp. 104–12

Schineller, Werner, *Die Regierungspräsidenten der Pfalz: Festgabe zum 60. Geburtstag des Regierungspräsidenten Hans Keller am 6. Mai 1980* (Speyer, 1980)

Schivelbusch, Wolfgang, *The Culture of Defeat: On National Trauma, Mourning and Recovery* (New York, 2003)

Schlegel, Dietrich, 'Der Separatismus in der Pfalz nach dem Ersten Weltkrieg', *Mitteilungen des historischen Vereins der Pfalz* 71 (1974), pp. 217–46

Schumann, Dirk, 'Einheitssehnsucht und Gewaltakzeptanz: Politische Grundpositionen des deutschen Bürgertums nach 1918 (mit vergleichenden Überlegegungen zu den britischen *middle classes*)', in Hans Mommsen (ed.), *Der Erste Weltkrieg und die europäische Nachkriegsordnung: Sozialer Wandel und Formveränderung der Politik* (Cologne, 2000)

Selig, Wolfram, *Paul Nikolaus Cossmann und die Süddeutschen Monatshefte von 1914–1918. Ein Beitrag zur Geschichte der nationalen Publizistik im Ersten Weltkrieg* (Osnabrück, 1967)

Sharp, Alan, 'Anglo-French relations from Versailles to Locarno 1919–1925: the quest for security', in Alan Sharp and Glyn Stone (eds), *Anglo-French Relations in the Twentieth Century: Rivalry and Cooperation* (London, 2000), pp. 120–38

—— and Glyn Stone (eds), *Anglo-French Relations in the Twentieth Century: Rivalry and Cooperation* (London, 2000)

Sington, Derrick and Arthur Weidenfeld, *The Goebbels Experiment: A Study of the Nazi Propaganda Machine* (London, 1942)

Sontheimer, Kurt, *Antidemokratisches Denken in der Weimarer Republik. Die politischen Ideen des deutschen Nationalismus zwischen 1918 und 1933* (Munich, 1962)

Süchting-Hänger, Andrea, *Das 'Gewissen der Nation'. Nationales Engagement und politisches Handeln konservativer Frauenorganisationen 1900 bis 1937* (Düsseldorf, 2002)

Süss, Martin, *Rheinhessen unter französischer Besatzung: vom Waffenstillstand im November 1918 bis zum Ende der Separatistenunruhen im Februar 1924* (Stuttgart, 1988)

Thalmann, Heinrich, *Die Pfalz im Ersten Weltkrieg* (Kaiserslautern, 1990)

——, 'Die Pfalz und Bayern in der Zeit des Ersten Weltkriegs', in Hans Fenske (ed.), *Die Pfalz und Bayern 1816–1956* (Speyer, 1998), pp. 163–88

Ungern-Sternberg, Franziska von, *Kulturpolitik zwischen den Kontinenten: Deutschland und Amerika* (Cologne, 1994)

Verhey, Jeffrey, *The Spirit of 1914: Militarism, Myth and Mobilization in Germany* (Cambridge, 2000)

Vincent, Paul, *The Politics of Hunger: The Allied Blockade of Germany, 1915–1919* (Athens, OH, 1985)

Voelker, Judith, 'Unerträglich, unerfüllbar und deshalb unannehmbar: –Kollektiver Protest gegen Versailles im Rheinland in den Monaten Mai und Juni 1919', in Jost Dülffer and Gerd Krumeich (eds), *Der verlorene Frieden – Politik und Kriegskultur nach 1918* (Essen, 2002)

Watt, Donald Cameron, *Personalities and Policies: Studies in the Formulation of British Foreign Policy in the Twentieth Century* (London, 1965)

Wein, Franziska, *Deutschlands Strom – Frankreichs Grenze: Geschichte und Propaganda am Rhein 1919–1930* (Essen, 1992)

Weindling, Paul Julian, *Epidemics and Genocide in Eastern Europe 1890–1945* (Oxford, 2000)

Welch, David, *Germany, Propaganda and Total War 1914–1918* (London, 2000)

Wigger, Iris, *Die 'Schwarze Schmach am Rhein': Rassistische Diskriminierung zwischen Geschlecht, Klasse, Nation und Rasse* (Münster, 2007)

Wilson, Keith (ed.), *Forging the Collective Memory: Government and International Historians through Two World Wars* (Providence and Oxford, 1996)

Wippermann, Klaus, *Politische Propaganda und staatsbürgerliche Bildung: Die Reichszentrale für Heimatdienst in der Weimarer Republik* (Bonn, 1976)

Wünschel, Hans-Jürgen, 'Anmerkungen zum pfälzisch-bayerischen Verhältnis 1866–1914', in Hans Fenske (ed.), *Die Pfalz und Bayern 1816–1956* (Speyer, 1998), pp. 131–61

Zeman, Z. A. B., *Nazi Propaganda* (London, 1964)

Ziemann, Benjamin, *War Experiences in Rural Germany 1914–1923* (Oxford and New York, 2007)

Zimmermann, Werner Gabriel, *Bayern und das Reich 1918–1923: Der bayerische Föderalismus zwischen Revolution und Reaktion* (Munich, 1953)

Internet-Based Sources

Bayerische Landeszentrale für politische Bildungsarbeit (ed.), *Einsichten und Perspektiven Themenheft 02/2006*, (http://www.km.bayern.de/blz/eup/02_06_themenheft/3.asp#1

Bundesarchiv, 'Akten der Reichskanzlei, Weimarer Republik' online (Biographien), http://www.bundesarchiv.de/aktenreichskanzlei/1919–1933/0021/vorwort.html

Deutsche National Bibliothek (DNB), Katalog der DNB, http://d-nb.info/572948301

Helmberger, Peter, 'Biographische Notiz: Hermann Oncken', Historikergalerie des Instituts für Geschichtswissenschaften, Humboldt-Universität zu Berlin 31.8.1998, http://www.geschichte.hu-berlin.de/galerie/texte/oncken.htm

IEG Maps, University of Mainz, http://www.ieg-maps.uni-mainz.de

INDEX

C

D

E

W